Fodor's

PUERTO RICO

Welcome to Puerto Rico

It's easy to have a Caribbean vacation in Puerto Rico, but this island offers much more than sun and sand. In vibrant San Juan, you're sure to find your scene—at art museums, posh boutiques, or trendy bars. Nearby El Yunque rain forest provides a lush, peaceful retreat. Colonial towns such as Ponce and San Germán bring history to life in centuries-old plazas.

Note that this book was produced in the middle of the COVID-19 pandemic. As you plan your travels, please confirm that places are still open, and let us know when we need to make updates by writing to us at: editors@fodors.com.

TOP REASONS TO GO

★ **Dining:** From Nuevo Latino restaurants to simple spots serving *comida criolla*.

★ **Old San Juan:** Cobblestone streets, cafés, and boutique hotels in a charming neighborhood.

★ **Beaches:** From lively resort-fronted strands to remote coves with calm waters.

★ **El Yunque:** The only tropical rain forest managed by the U.S. Forest Service.

★ **History:** Sixteenth-century fortifications such as El Morro and La Muralla still stand.

★ **Vieques and Culebra:** Laid-back islands with unspoiled beauty and quiet towns.

Contents

MAPS

Fodor's Features

Chapter 1

EXPERIENCE PUERTO RICO

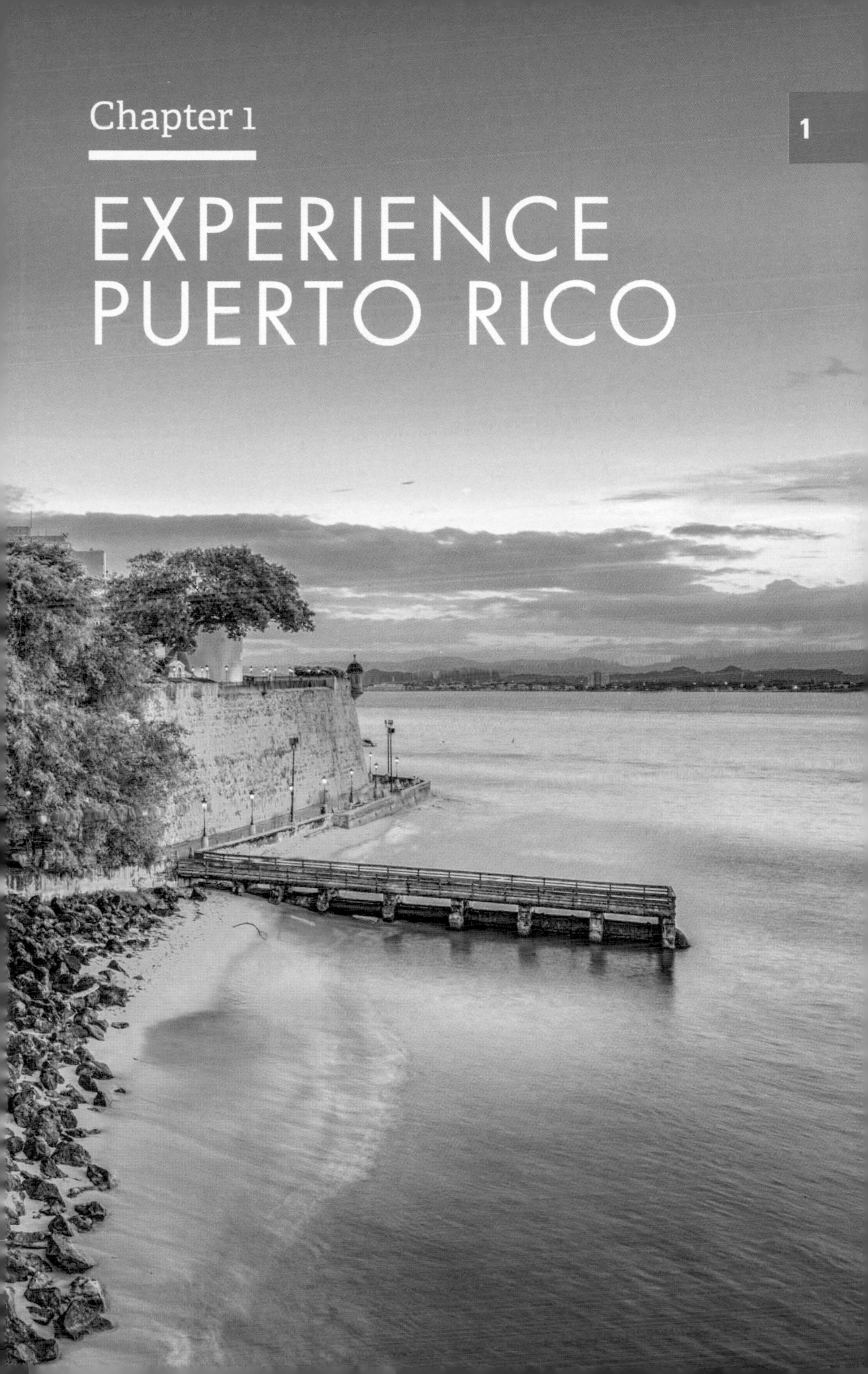

20 ULTIMATE EXPERIENCES

Puerto Rico offers terrific experiences that should be on every traveler's list. Here are Fodor's top picks for a memorable trip.

1 A Day Trip to Culebra and Playa Flamenco

Culebra, a one-hour ferry ride from Ceiba, is home to Playa Flamenco, the famous beach known for its white sand and turquoise water. Kiosks serve a small selection of drinks and fritters but you may want to bring snacks. The UV rays are strong, so bring sunscreen. *(Ch. 5)*

2 Surfing in Rincón

Domes Beach is popular for morning surf sessions; Tres Palmas serves up big waves. For beginners, María's is great when waves are smaller. *(Ch. 7)*

3 Taking in the Views from El Morro

El Castillo de San Felipe del Morro was built in the 1500s to protect San Juan from pirates and other sea-based attacks. *(Ch. 3)*

4 Parque de las Cavernas del Río Camuy

This hidden gem is the third-largest underground cave system in the world, filled with waterfalls and rushing water. *(Ch. 6)*

5 Desecheo Island

Desecheo Island is an uninhabited island off the west coast of Puerto Rico, a former bombing range that offers beautiful dive sites teeming with marine life. *(Ch. 7)*

6 Relaxing on Seven Seas Beach

Seven Seas Beach in Fajardo is ideal for mellow beach days thanks to its calm, reef-protected waters and mangrove-shaded, semiprivate feel. *(Ch. 4)*

7 Eating Fresh Fish in Boquerón

This Cabo Rojo beach town is filled with food stands, bars, and restaurants, making it the perfect place to go out with friends for some beers and fresh seafood. *(Ch. 7)*

8 Spend a Night Out in La Placita de Santurce

Start or end your night in this hub of San Juan nightlife, which has ever-present music and a festive, block-party vibe that encourages barhopping. *(Ch. 3)*

9 Strolling Through Old San Juan

The colorful buildings and narrow streets of Old San Juan are iconic. Swarmed with tourists in high season, its many bars and restaurants are also popular with locals. *(Ch. 3)*

10 Salsa Dancing

Puerto Ricans grow up dancing salsa, so if you want to keep up with the locals, you'll need to pick up a few steps. Take a crash course, or practice at a salsa bar. *(Ch. 3)*

11 Ron del Barrilito Distillery

Not often seen outside the island, Ron del Barrilito has been around since 1880 and is a favorite in Puerto Rico. Visit the distillery for a tour that includes history and mixology lessons. *(Ch. 3)*

12 Visiting the Kioskos

Luquillo's kioskos (food stalls) are lined up in a row, making them the perfect place to sample all of Puerto Rico's favorite frituras (fried foods) and grab a cold drink. *(Ch. 4)*

13 Luquillo's Beaches

While surfers flock to Playa la Pared, families often prefer the more full-service Balneario La Monserrate, and swimmers are drawn to the swaying palm trees and calm waters of Playa Costa Azul. *(Ch. 4)*

14 Hike El Yunque National Forest

The only U.S. tropical rain forest is laced with hiking trails and full of flowing waterfalls, cool rivers, and beautiful mountain views. *(Ch. 4)*

15 Barhopping in Esperanza, Vieques

Vieques is a great spot if you like to relax in a simple local bar with a stiff cocktail or cheap beer. Calle Flamboyan in Esperanza has several places to choose from, including the famous Duffy's. *(Ch. 5)*

16 Visiting a Local Coffee Farm

Hacienda Buena Vista, in the southern town of Ponce, has played an important role in Puerto Rico's coffee industry and still plants, harvests, and processes its coffee and cacao crops. *(Ch. 8)*

17 Refugio Nacional de Vida Silvestre de Culebra

The bird-watcher's paradise, managed by the U.S. Fish and Wildlife Service, is home to over 50,000 birds and 13 different species, as well as leatherback sea turtles. *(Ch. 5)*

18 Kayaking in Puerto Mosquito

The blue-glowing waters of Vieques's most notable bioluminescent bay (there are three here) are a truly incredible sight as long as you visit on a dark night, ideally during a new moon phase. *(Ch. 5)*

19 Driving the Island

Do it in a day, or do it slowly over several days, but circumnavigate the island to see beautiful beaches, green mountains, expansive valleys, and much more. *(Ch. 4, 6, 7, 8)*

20 Bosque Estatal de Toro Negro

In the state park with the island's tallest mountain, hike to Lago Guineo, the island's highest lake, or the impressive Salto de Doña Juana, a 200-foot cascade. *(Ch. 6)*

WHAT'S WHERE

1 San Juan. The capital has tremendous museums, a vivacious bar scene, restaurants from the earthy to the trendy, plus fabulous boutiques and galleries. Old San Juan is a visual delight of forts, churches, convents, and cobbled streets dating back centuries. Hotels concentrate in the beach-lined Condado and Isla Verde districts, where the nightlife sizzles.

2 El Yunque and the Northeast. El Yunque is the most popular day trip from San Juan: hiking trails snake through this tropical rain forest, leading to hidden pools and mountaintop *miradores* (lookouts). Luquillo has one of the island's best-known beaches, the Balneario La Monserrate. Westward, Reserva Natural Las Cabezas de San Juan teems with wildlife in several distinct ecosystems, including mangroves. Fajardo is a base for exploring exquisite offshore cays, including Palomino and Icacos islands.

3 Vieques and Culebra. Once used by U.S. armed forces for military exercises, this pair of sand-fringed isles is now famous for jaw-dropping beaches. Boutique hotels and trendy eateries have popped up alongside beachy bars on Vieques; Culebra remains less developed and sleepier. Ecotourism is big, with

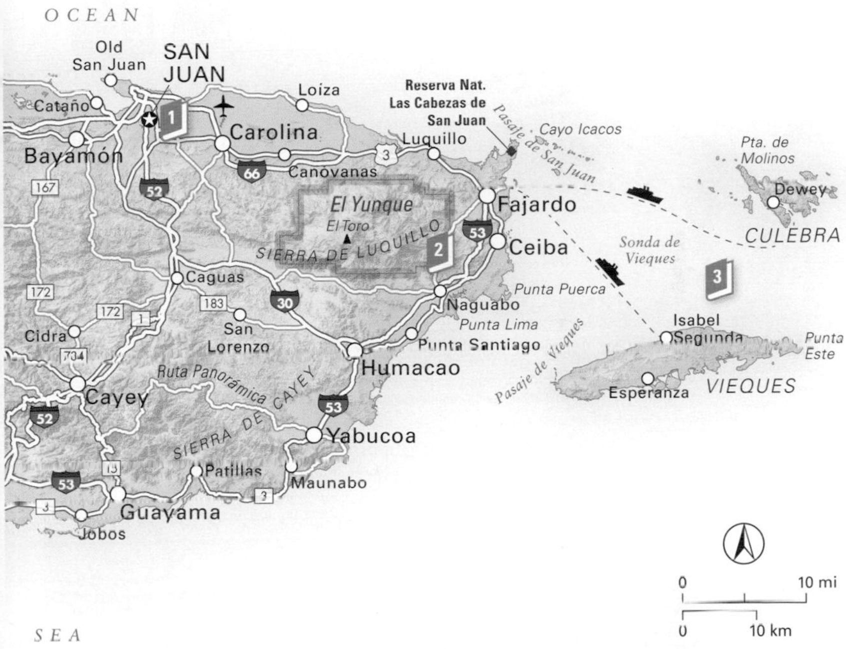

popular activities including snorkeling, diving, kayaking, and visits to the stunning bioluminescent bay in Vieques.

4 The North Coast and the Cordillera Central. Puerto Rico's north coast is an easy drive from San Juan, convenient for day trips, while the rugged mountain spine that runs the length of the island is festooned with forest.

5 Rincón and the Porta del Sol. The jagged coastline of the west is renowned for world-class surfing, centered on Rincón, where dozens of beaches beckon those who like to hang 10. Cabo Rojo offers great birding. Architecture buffs appreciate the grandeur of downtown Mayagüez.

6 Ponce and the Porta Caribe. The southern coast is studded with tropical dry forests, such as Bosque Estatal de Guánica, a destination for hikers and birders. The colonial center of Ponce has one of the finest art museums in the Caribbean, and the hilltop town of San Germán charms visitors.

What to Eat and Drink in Puerto Rico

FLAN

Flan might be a favorite throughout Latin America, but in Puerto Rico, it's iconic. This creamy custard-based dessert comes in a number of flavors, including caramel, cheese (made with cream cheese), and coconut (made with coconut milk).

MOFONGO

The national dish of Puerto Rico is officially *arroz con gandules* (rice with pigeon peas), but most locals will tell you mofongo is the standout dish of the Island of Enchantment. Fried plantains are mashed together with garlic, oil, and salt and then stuffed, usually with chicken or shrimp.

MALTA

As its name suggests, Malta is a malt beverage, a lightly carbonated soft drink (nonalcoholic) made from hops, barley, and water. High in vitamin B, malt-based beverages are said to metabolize carbs and fat into energy while helping to regulate appetite. There might still be hope for our fried food–filled bellies!

QUESITO

Quesitos, or "little cheeses," are long sticks of puff pastry filled with sweetened cream cheese and are a breakfast favorite. They are usually topped with a dusting of powdered sugar, or with a thin, sweet glaze. A popular variation of the quesito includes guava along with the cream-cheese filling.

EMPANADILLAS
Empanadas, or *empanadillas*, are another go-to snack in Puerto Rico. These half-moon-shape flaky pastries are stuffed and then fried. The filling is traditionally chicken or ground beef, but you'll also find them stuffed with shrimp, crab, or lobster in beach towns.

PASTELES
Similar to tamales, *pasteles* are made by enclosing adobo pork in green banana masa, and then wrapping that in banana leaves. While tamales are traditionally steamed, Puerto Rican pasteles are boiled.

AREPAS
Typically, arepas are made of corn flour and are toasted or grilled on a stove top. Puerto Rican arepas, however, are made with wheat flour and are fried. They are a specialty of the Fajardo coastal region and are stuffed with seafood like shrimp or octopus.

Tripleta

COFFEE
Coffee was Puerto Rico's largest export once upon a time, and while that's no longer the case, the island's coffee retains its top-notch quality: rich, bold, and flavorful. It's typically served in one of three ways: *pocillo*, the local term for an espresso; *cortadito*, an espresso with steamed milk; or *café con leche*, a large cup of coffee and milk similar to a latte.

TRIPLETA
The *tripleta* is sometimes referred to as the Puerto Rican version of a Cubano sandwich. Each tripleta will vary from the next, but they are generally made with a combination of three grilled meats served on a slightly sweet bread and topped with *papitas*, small and thin crispy fries.

MAVÍ
Maví is a drink made from the fermented bark of the Mauby tree. The tree bark is boiled together with ginger and cinnamon, mixed with sugar, and then left to ferment for several hours. Maví is often compared to root beer and is a specialty of Puerto Rico's southern region.

What to Buy in Puerto Rico

ARTESANÍA

Artesanías are handmade works, also known as *artistas del patio.* Examples include art carved out of coconuts, *santos* (the figures of saints used in home altars), or even furniture. Some popular elements often displayed on these crafts are the Puerto Rican flag, the Taíno sun, and coquí frog.

HAMMOCK

The Taíno people, the original natives of the island, are rumored to have invented the hammock (*hamaca* in Taíno). Hammocks are incredibly easy to come by here, and you can find several canvas varieties. Alternatively, you can get a handwoven cotton hammock in artisan or craft shops.

PIQUE

Pique is made by combining chili peppers, herbs, and seasonings that have been steeped in vinegar. There's no standard set of ingredients; each version is unique, and it can be added to any type of food to give it a little zing. Homemade pique is often served in restaurants and food stands, but you can also buy it in supermarkets.

PILÓN

This type of wooden mortar and pestle is used to grind together different ingredients. As with many typical "Puerto Rican" objects, the *pilón* was originally used by the Taíno and is a culinary staple on the island.
Once the coffee bean was introduced to the island, the pilón was even used to process beans.

PANDERETA

The *pandereta* is a handheld percussion instrument similar to a tambourine, except that it doesn't have cymbals. Panderetas, also known as *panderos*, are the key instrument in *plena*, a genre of music created by agricultural workers in Puerto Rico's southernmost region, and they come in three different sizes.

CIGARS

Puerto Rico was once one of the world's top exporters of tobacco, and cigar making remains a tradition despite the industry's decline in the last 60 to 70 years. There are three types of tobacco native to the island, the most famous of which is Hoja Prieta. Don Collins is the best-known brand.

GÜIRO

A popular instrument in Puerto Rico, güiros are made from hollowed-out gourds with parallel ridges carved into one side. The music is made by running a "scraper," a stick or metal tine, up and down the ridges. They are believed to have originated with the Taíno or Arawak people.

Coffee

RUM

While many of Puerto Rico's export industries have faded out, one remains steadfast: rum. Rum continues to be Puerto Rico's main export. Don Q is a local favorite, said to be the best rum on the island. Palo Viejo, Caliche, Ron del Barrilito, and Ron Llave are popular brands, as is Bacardí.

COFFEE

More than a century ago, Puerto Rico was actually one of the worlds largest coffee producers. While less than 5% of the island's coffee is exported today, Puerto Rico's rich, bold, dark coffee is often rated as some of the best in the world. The mountain city of Yauco is one of the island's more famous coffee producers.

ADOBO

In 1966, Goya Foods released a seasoning called adobo, which is now a Puerto Rican kitchen staple. There are several varieties, each meant to be used with a different type of food such as beef, chicken, fish, etc. If you're looking for a food souvenir, adobo can be found at any grocery store.

Beaches of Puerto Rico

PUNTA TUNA BEACH
Although currents in the waters off this southeastern beach make swimming here unsafe, it's a beautiful place to relax with a book or walk along the shore. It's also home to the Punta Tuna Reserve, where turtles nest from March to July. *(Ch. 8)*

CAYO ICACOS
Cayo Icacos is one of about 10 small islands that make up the Cordillera Nature Reserve just off the northeastern coast of Puerto Rico. Icacos can only be reached via a 15- to 20-minute boat ride, and it has no facilities, so bring along whatever you might need for the day. *(Ch. 4)*

DOMES BEACH
Rincón is a west coast tourist hot spot, and Domes is one of its most popular beaches. Its name comes from the dome-shape building there, which used to be a nuclear plant. Domes Beach is also a well-known surfing destination, and it's a good place for whale-watching in winter. *(Ch. 7)*

BORÍNQUEN BEACH
On the west coast, this big, beautiful stretch of white sand leads to large rocks and a cliff that juts into the sea. The water can be too rough and choppy for swimming in the winter. Summer months are great for swimming and snorkeling, though. Just beware of sea urchins along the rocky walls. During low tide, you'll find a small cave at the far end as well as the ruins of a lighthouse. *(Ch. 7)*

FLAMENCO BEACH
Flamenco Beach's claim to fame is a No. 2 rating on the Discovery Channel's list of best beaches in the world, making it a source of pride for Puerto Ricans. And rightfully so. This crescent-shape, white-sand Culebra beach with crystal clear turquoise waters is a swoon-worthy spot made for social media. It's a popular weekend day trip for both locals and visitors. *(Ch. 5)*

ISLA VERDE BEACH
San Juan's best beach is technically not in San Juan but rather in Carolina, where the airport located. It's made up of three different stretches, each with its own unique vibe. The first, El Alambique, is the most lively, with hotels, restaurants, and water sports. Pine Grove Beach sits between two large hotels and is a popular surf spot. Balneario de Carolina is the third. *(Ch. 3)*

POZA DE LAS MUJRES
Poza de las Mujeres is another natural swimming hole protected by rock

Flamenco Beach

formations, and this beach is almost split in two. On the left-hand side, the water is shallow, calm, and protected from the rougher waters outside the natural barricade. On the right-hand side, however, the rocks do not form a protective barrier, and the water is much rougher. *(Ch. 6)*

PLAYA SUCIA

Playa Sucia, in the southwest, actually means "dirty beach." While it can be "dirty" from seaweed on occasion, the water is usually a beautiful turquoise, and this beach is known as one of the most beautiful on the island. Playa Sucia is also home to a lighthouse, Faro de los Morrillos, as well as limestone cliffs and caves. The only downside is the access via a rutted dirt road. *(Ch. 7)*

PLAYA PEÑA BLANCA

Swimming in the crystal clear waters of Peña Blanca is best in the summer months during low tide. In winter, the waters reach the rocks around the beach, eliminating the already fairly small shoreline. *(Ch. 7)*

MAR CHIQUITA

The north coast beaches are unique in that many of them are formed from natural pools surrounded by limestone walls that protect these swimming holes from the rough waters of the Atlantic Ocean. This is one of them. Food trucks selling all of the local favorite fried goodies are always set up here, and arts vendors come out on the weekends when the beach is busier. The water gets rough in the winter months, and swimming may not always be a good idea. *(Ch. 6)*

Puerto Rico Today

If you've heard there's trouble in paradise, it's true: Puerto Rico has been reeling from an economic crisis that's been years in the making. The problems became more acute in 2015, when the island's government began defaulting on debt payments. The impact on citizens has been profound—with cost-of-living increases that aren't matched by increases in salaries, a poor electric system that causes countless outages, and cuts in many services, especially those provided or subsidized by the government.

Hurricane Maria, which battered the island in 2017, deepened the crisis, impacting tourism, the island's most important industry, profoundly. Many hotels and attractions were closed for months, and island infrastructure was severely affected. Then, in January 2020, a 6.4-magnitude earthquake and a series of aftershocks rocked the southern coast, causing still more damage.

Together, these events, along with a global pandemic, have presented major challenges to privately and publicly owned sites; you may still notice some lingering effects, especially beyond San Juan. Always call ahead to confirm that the key points of interest are open.

THE STATUS ISSUE

Puerto Rico is a commonwealth of the United States, a complicated status that extends U.S. citizenship to Puerto Ricans but without all of its benefits. The island's government holds a "status" referendum periodically to assess Puerto Ricans' current preferences: do they want to remain a commonwealth, pursue independence, or seek statehood? Results are in no way binding, and the U.S. Congress would be required to enact legislation to allow a change in status. The most recent referendum was held in November 2020 (with the question presented to voters whether they were in favor of or opposed to statehood); 52% of voters supported statehood.

SOME CARIBBEAN COMPETITION

The "opening" of Cuba to American citizens has long been an issue of concern for the Puerto Rican tourism industry, which feared that its Caribbean neighbor would not only draw travelers away from the island because of its former forbidden status, but also because of its geographical proximity: Cuba is closer to the United States than Puerto Rico is.

The fact remains, however, that for travelers who don't want to worry about passports, visas, and currency exchange, Puerto Rico remains the easiest option.

AN ENTREPRENEURIAL, ARTISANAL MOMENT

Despite doom-and-gloom news about the economy, a growing number of younger Puerto Ricans understand that the current crisis brings enormous opportunity. Exciting entrepreneurial ventures touch every sector of the economy, from tech to tourism, and from agricultural to artisan-powered design.

For visitors, this means new-to-Puerto-Rico options like tree-house "glamping," pet-friendly accommodations and businesses, and cutting-edge bars and restaurants.

Kids and Family

Puerto Rico is a family-friendly island with no end of fun things for kids to see and do, including cave exploration, snorkeling with marine turtles, and nighttime excursions to bioluminescent lagoons. Many resort hotels arrange children's activities or have kids' clubs, freeing parents for romantic beach strolls and candlelit dinners.

CHOOSING A PLACE TO STAY

Resort hotels make a point of catering to family needs. Most offer free rooms to children under 12 and can provide cribs. Here are a few questions to help you gauge the level of family-friendliness: Are there discounted meals and activities? Do restaurants have kids' menus? Are there children's programs, and is there an age range? A children's pool?

El Conquistador, a Waldorf Astoria Resort, near Fajardo, has a long list of facilities for children, including the sensational Coquí Water Park. On the south coast, **Copamarina Beach Resort and Spa** has a children's pool and playground, plus kayaks, pedal boats, tennis, and heaps of other activities.

Condos and vacation rentals offer an inexpensive option, especially for larger families. They typically have multiple bedrooms, and you can cook for yourselves.

THINGS TO DO

Vacationing in the Caribbean is all about the outdoors. Kids may even forget video games when they see the options: snorkeling, whale-watching, body boarding, and cave exploring. And the list of great beaches is nearly endless. The wave action around Rincón can get a little rough for youngsters, but Vieques and Culebra have the most fantastic, reef-protected sands, which are good for snorkeling, and kids can also go kayaking and fishing. Of course, many beaches have riptides, so do play it safe and heed posted warnings, such as red flags.

Parque de las Cavernas del Río Camuy. This huge cavern will leave kids wide-eyed. They'll have fun trying to discern imaginary figures in the surreal dripstone formations. And they'll also enjoy a number of not-so-imaginary figures, like the tiny coquí frogs hopping around the cavern entrance, crabs and blind fish in the underground river, and bats flitting about overhead. The tram ride to reach the caverns is icing on the cake.

Arecibo Lighthouse and Historical Park. Local families flock to this small theme park built around Los Morrillos lighthouse. It has a museum on seafaring and that includes pirates. In winter, kids can look for whales from the lighthouse observation platform. The playground has a pirate cave and replica galleon, as well as a Taíno village.

Toro Verde. This adventure park is known for its adrenaline-filled ziplining. The mountain views of the town of Orocovis are spectacular.

History You Can See

PRE-COLONIAL PUERTO RICO

The Taínos were the indigenous group that populated the island prior to its "discovery" by Christopher Columbus on his second trip to the New World in 1493. The Taínos' name for the island was Borinquen, and even today, Puerto Ricans honor their Taíno heritage by referring to themselves as *boricuas*.

What to See: The island's two main ceremonial centers—Tibes and Caguana—have preserved the limited artifacts of Taíno culture that have been discovered over the years. At **Tibes,** just north of Ponce, visitors can see reproductions of the *bohíos* in which Taínos lived, as well as fields believed to have served as ritual sites.

Closer to San Juan, those curious to get a window into the Taíno world can visit La Cueva de María de la Cruz, a cave in Loíza where archaeologists discovered Taíno artifacts in the mid-20th century. A guided tour of the cave can be arranged through the local group, Parque Histórico Cueva María de la Cruz.

COLONIAL PUERTO RICO

Columbus arrived in 1493, and the Spanish crown controlled the island—though with a determinedly laissez-faire approach—until the Spanish-American War of 1898 ended with the concession of Puerto Rico to the United States. The first Spanish governor of the island was Juan Ponce de León, the explorer famous for his legendary pursuit of the elusive Fountain of Youth. Spain's Queen Isabela charged Ponce de León with the task of "compel[ling] and forc[ing] the Indians to work for the Christian inhabitants." According to the late historian and archaeologist Ricardo Alegría, the Taínos were decimated, refusing to resist the Spanish conquistadores because they believed that Spaniards were immortal; thus, taking up arms against them was futile.

By the 1530s, Africans had been brought to the island for slave labor; they built San Juan's two biggest fortresses, Castillo San Felipe del Morro and Castillo San Cristóbal, massive construction projects that took more than 250 years of intense, arduous labor. Slavery in Puerto Rico was finally abolished in 1873.

What to See: Built in 1521, **Casa Blanca** was the intended home of Juan Ponce de León, who never actually lived here. His descendants, however, called the Old San Juan property home for 250 years.

Castillo San Felipe del Morro and **Castillo San Cristóbal** aren't San Juan's only forts—there's also Fortín San Gerónimo del Boquerón, just behind the Caribe Hilton, and the Fortín El Cañuelo on Goat Island, visible across San Juan Bay—but they're certainly the largest and most impressive. Both offer commanding views of the Atlantic from their upper levels.

Built between 1533 and 1540, **La Fortaleza** was intended to serve as a perch from which the Bay of San Juan could be monitored and protected. Its strategic limitations were soon discovered, though, and the UNESCO-recognized structure is home to Puerto Rico's governor, as it has been since the late 16th century. Guided tours allow the public to glimpse how the governor lives.

A predominantly Afro–Puerto Rican town, Loíza was founded in 1719 and was populated by escaped slaves. Separated from the mainland by the Río Grande, the town remained geographically and socially isolated until the mid-1970s, allowing many Afro–Puerto Rican traditions to be preserved. Called the "capital of tradition," Loíza is home to popular *bomba* and *plena* music and dance, and is famous for *vejigantes* (coconut masks), used during annual festivals (see also the "Masks of Puerto Rico" feature in Chapter 8). Although it's most lively in early July, when the Santiago Apóstol festival is underway, a visit at any other time of year should include a stop at **San Patricio,** one of the island's oldest churches and home to what may be the only black St. Patrick statue in the world.

THE TRANSITION TO THE COMMONWEALTH

Puerto Rico became a U.S. territory in 1898. Although few would argue that life was better under the Spanish, many have had misgivings about the transfer. As Puerto Rican historians Kal Wagenheim and Olga Jiménez de Wagenheim remarked, "The invasion of Puerto Rico [by the United States] ended four centuries of oppressive Spanish colonial rule, only to replace it with a more subtle brand of colonialism."

Although the island was now part of the United States, Puerto Ricans were without formal citizenship for more than a decade. The educational system underwent frequent upheavals during this time, as did the structure of island government, in accordance with U.S.-imposed policies that reflected evolving defense and economic interests. Even when U.S. citizenship was granted with the Jones–Shafroth Act (1917), this development did little to resolve the ambiguous relationship between Puerto Rico and the United States; citizenship for Puerto Ricans was not, after all, conferred with all the rights and privileges enjoyed by state citizens. Puerto Ricans don't, for example, have a voting representative in Congress, nor can they vote for president. The island became a commonwealth (or a "free associated state") in 1952, but this made little difference in the day-to-day lives of the islanders.

Fierce debates continue among Puerto Ricans about the status of the island. Of the three major political parties, one is in favor of statehood, one prefers being a commonwealth, and the third advocates independence.

What to See: Built between 1919 and 1929, Puerto Rico's beaux arts–style **Capitolio** building is an often-overlooked site that shouldn't be missed. Its rotunda is inlaid with colorful mosaic tiles depicting the major periods of Puerto Rican history, and the Puerto Rican Constitution is displayed in glass cases. Busts of important Puerto Rican politicians are also on display. Visitors will often encounter protesters on the Capitolio steps; citizens gather here frequently in peaceful protest against government policies.

Built in 1911, the neoclassical masterpiece known as the Casa Wiechers-Villaronga today houses the **Museo de la Arquitectura Ponceña,** where exhibits provide insight into the city's designers and their buildings during this period. At the time of this writing, Casa Wiechers remains closed due to earthquake damage.

■ TIP→ Every town has its own culture trolley (often free), offering a historic guided tour of the area's highlights. Stops generally can be found in the town's plaza, in front of the city hall.

What to Read and Watch

Puerto Rico is often used as a stand-in location to film movies set in different, harder-to-access places, like Vietnam or Cuba—which doesn't do justice to a land so beautiful in its own right. Works that do focus on Puerto Rico show a vibrant, diverse island full of rebellion and resilience.

AMISTAD

This Steven Spielberg film is based on the true story of an 1839 slave uprising aboard a ship on its way from Cuba to the United States. Amid some debate of its historical accuracy, the movie frames the legal battle following the uprising as of great importance to United States history and the mounting tensions around slavery. The scenes set in Africa—at a slave fortress and beyond—were all filmed around San Juan.

THE RUM DIARY BY HUNTER S. THOMPSON

Hunter S. Thompson's lost novel, found after his death by friend Johnny Depp (who went on to produce and star in the movie), is loosely based on the chunk of time Thompson spent living in San Juan, in the late 1950s and '60s, among journalists and businessmen.

MALA MALA

This 2014 documentary is comprised of several stories from within the Puerto Rican LGBTQ+ community, including those of drag queens, transgender individuals, and others across a spectrum of gender identities. Among the film's stars is April Carrión, who later became a contestant on *RuPaul's Drag Race*.

RUNNER RUNNER

While this feature film's named setting is Costa Rica, all scenes were shot in Puerto Rico. In the plot, Justin Timberlake gets caught up in a high-stakes cheating scheme at an online poker site and travels to Costa Rica to find the owner, Ben Affleck. Instead, Timberlake is drawn further into the scheme until he finds it virtually impossible to get out. It's mostly your run-of-the-mill thriller, with an expensive cast and plenty of plot holes, but the scenes of Puerto Rican coasts and cities are lovely.

MUNDO CRUEL: STORIES BY LUIS NEGRÓN

Negrón's collection of stories describe growing up gay in Puerto Rico, an experience often tangled up in religion, secrecy, and violence. Negrón, born in Guayama, sets his stories in the Santurce district of San Juan. Originally published in Spanish, the 2010 collection won the Lambda Literary Award for Gay Fiction.

WAR AGAINST ALL PUERTO RICANS: REVOLUTION AND TERROR IN AMERICA'S COLONY BY NELSON A. DENIS

Author and attorney Nelson A. Denis pieces together interviews, testimonies, and personal accounts to explain the unsuccessful 1950 political uprising against the United States—a violent event central to Puerto Rican political history, yet rarely covered in textbooks.

WHEN I WAS A PUERTO RICAN BY ESMERALDA SANTIAGO

Santiago's 1993 autobiography about growing up both in San Juan and in rural Macun, is the first book of a series (followed by *Almost a Woman* and *The Turkish Lover*) about her life. Much of the book deals with her mother's decision (and the subsequent transition) to move the family to New York City.

THE MAN WITH MY FACE

In perhaps the only film noir ever set in Puerto Rico, a man returns home from a trip to find that an eerie double of himself has taken his place. It's a fun black-and-white thriller, and the scenes of San Juan are some of the film's best characteristics.

SILENT DANCING BY JUDITH ORTIZ COFER

Judith Ortiz Cofer's lyrical work explores her life spent back and forth between Puerto Rico and United States and the mixed cultural identity it has produced for her. *Silent Dancing* is a mixed-genre ode to Puerto Rico and the author's memories of her childhood spent there.

SONG OF THE SIMPLE TRUTH: THE COMPLETE POEMS OF JULIA DE BURGOS BY JULIA DE BURGOS

Burgos (1914–1953) was born in Carolina, Puerto Rico, attended the University of Puerto Rico, and later lived in Cuba and New York City. Also a key early feminist and political activist, Burgos is considered one of Puerto Rico's greatest poets.

MARUJA

This 1959 film became a Puerto Rican classic, telling the story of the obsession around a beautiful woman in a small town. It was filmed in the northern valley of Bayamón. While the plot is somewhat corny, it's a beautiful depiction of rural mid-century Puerto Rican life. It's also the first feature film known to use an all-local Puerto Rican cast, and many of the actors in it went on to become stars.

Weddings and Honeymoons

Puerto Rico is making a big splash as a wedding destination. It has all the ingredients of a spectacular place to wed and/or honeymoon. Gorgeous beaches dissolving into warm turquoise waters and a sensual tropical climate induce romance, and many an enamored couple has tied the knot here on the spur of the moment.

CHOOSING THE PERFECT PLACE

You can be as stylish or as informal as you wish. Although Puerto Rico has fewer ritzy beach resorts than many other islands, there's no shortage of exquisite boutique hotels with just the right ambience to inspire "I do." In Old San Juan, El Convento has just the right romantic style. The Hix Island House on Vieques will suit honeymooners seeking a reclusive escape. The Ritz Carlton Reserve in Dorado is the ultimate luxury resort. In Guánica, along the island's southeast coast, consider the Copamarina Beach Resort, which has spa- and diving-themed packages for honeymooners. Siesta Alegre at the foothills of El Yunque rain forest is a popular hacienda for those wanting a mountain feel.

Many larger hotels have their own wedding planners to take care of all arrangements, although you can easily hire a private planner to do all the research and planning for you.

GETTING YOUR LICENSES

You must get an application from the Demographic Registry Office, which is in the Plaza Las Américas Mall in the Hato Rey neighborhood of San Juan. There are no special residency requirements, but U.S. citizens must produce a birth certificate, as well as a driver's license or other state-issued photo identification. Non-U.S. citizens must produce a valid passport for identification purposes. Medical certificates that conform to the requirements for marriage in your state of residence are required; these can be completed by your own doctor, but must be valid for 10 days beyond their issue date. Finally, you must produce a letter from an attorney or a Puerto Rican affidavit affirming that you are not a resident of Puerto Rico and that you intend to marry in Puerto Rico. Again, this document is also only considered valid for 10 days after issuance.

Both you and your intended must appear together at the office to purchase a marriage license. A judge or any member of the clergy may then perform your ceremony. The fee is usually between $150 and $350. Most large hotels on the island have marriage coordinators who can explain the necessary paperwork and help you complete it on time for your marriage ceremony.

Chapter 2

TRAVEL SMART

Updated by
Paulina Salach Antonetti

★ CAPITAL:
San Juan

POPULATION:
2.86 million

LANGUAGE:
Spanish and English

$ CURRENCY:
U.S. dollar

AREA CODE:
787, 939

EMERGENCIES:
911

DRIVING:
On the right

ELECTRICITY:
120–220 v/60 cycles; plugs have two or three rectangular prongs

TIME:
One hour later than New York (the same as New York during daylight saving time)

WEB RESOURCES:
www.discoverpuertorico.com
www.prtourism.com

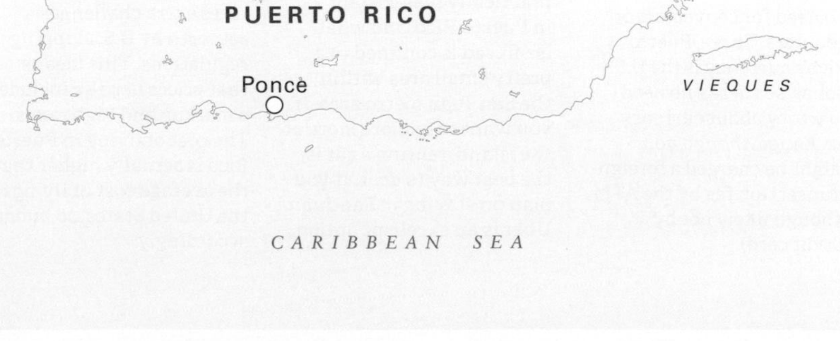

Know Before You Go

There are many reasons why Puerto Rico is a fantastic Caribbean getaway: no matter where you stay, you're never far from a dreamy beach, and U.S. citizens needn't worry about currency exchange or a passport. There are, however, some things you should know before visiting the Island of Enchantment.

IT'S HEAVILY INFLUENCED BY THE UNITED STATES
It's surprising that many people still think Puerto Rico is an independent nation, but it's actually a U.S. commonwealth. This also means that it's heavily influenced by all things American, including fast-food chains, department stores, tech, and more. This also means that, if you're a U.S. citizen, three things will simplify your trip: One, you don't need a passport, so if your government-issued ID is sufficient to allow you to fly, that's all you need (you do undergo an agricultural inspection on your return trip, but no customs or immigration in either direction). Two, Puerto Rico uses the same electrical outlets as the United States, so there's no need for convertors or adapters. Three, Puerto Rico's currency is the U.S. dollar, so there's no need to worry about currency exchange, though you might be charged a foreign-transaction fee by the ATM (though likely not by a credit card).

LEARN A BIT OF SPANISH
Despite Puerto Rico's official relationship with the United States, Spanish remains the most commonly used language on the island. While most people do speak English in the more touristy areas, you can expect to find many areas of the island where this isn't quite the case. Additionally, it's important to be aware that the English language often conjures insecurity and feelings of inferiority for some people who don't know English as well or at all. Learning some basic Spanish before a trip to Puerto Rico will not only simplify things for you, but it can also serve as a sign of respect for the local people.

RENT A CAR
Public transportation is practically nonexistent in Puerto Rico, and what is offered is confined to a pretty small area within the San Juan metro area. If you want to explore more of the island, renting a car is the best way to do it. If you plan on staying in San Juan, Uber is an excellent option. As you plan your travel to different parts of the island, be aware that the center of the island is full of mountains (and that many roads were damaged during Hurricane Maria), making it difficult and time-consuming to cut across. If you plan to drive from east to west, you will need to do so via the north or south highways. Also, be sure to carry a bit of cash on you; many areas require you to pay for parking, and often cash is the only way to do so.

SOMETIMES YOU JUST NEED A BOAT
While a car grants you the flexibility and freedom to see much more of the island, many of Puerto Rico's most iconic beach attractions can only be accessed by boat. In some cases, you can take a ferry, but in other cases you will need to either rent a boat or book a boat excursion. Either way, some of the best spots simply aren't reachable without a boat.

IT'S NOT CHEAP
The slow-paced rest and relaxation of island life doesn't come without a price. Many islands face economic issues due to the need to import most products, and Puerto Rico faces extra challenges set forth by U.S. shipping regulations. This means that prices usually include a markup and high taxes. The cost of living in Puerto Rico is actually higher than the average cost of living in the United States, so budget accordingly.

KIOSKOS ARE A WALLET'S BEST FRIEND

Street food stalls and vendors, known as *kioskos*, are the best place to get the most local and most affordable food. These are set up all over the island and are easy to spot. Many areas, including Luquillo, Loíza, and Ponce, have a kiosko area where they are set up one after another, each serving either local Puerto Rican food or a mix of more "American" food, like pizza and hamburgers.

FRIED EVERYTHING

The local diet of Puerto Rico doesn't offer many options for health-conscious travelers. Nearly every dish or snack contains some kind of meat, and the majority of food is served fried. This isn't the most food-friendly destination for vegetarians or vegans, either. While you will still be able to find things to eat, you may miss out on most of the local flavors if you're unable to eat meat or if you have a strong aversion to all things fried.

TEMPERATURES MAY VARY

Although Puerto Rico is located in the Caribbean, it can get quite breezy and chilly, particularly in the mountainous areas where many of the rivers and waterfalls are found. High season, from December to April, brings the coolest temperatures of the year. It doesn't necessarily get cold, especially during the day, but temperatures do drop at night, and the breeze coming in from the ocean can also create a bit of a wind chill. Be sure to pack something a bit warmer that you can easily throw on when needed.

DON'T GET YOUR METRICS TWISTED

One thing that may strike you as confusing in Puerto Rico is the fact that the island uses a mix of both the metric and U.S. customary measurement systems. For example, distances are marked in kilometers, while speed limits are marked in miles per hour. Additionally, gas is sold in liters rather than gallons. This can be confusing, especially if you only have familiarity with one of these systems. Consider downloading a unit converter to your phone.

IT RAINS IN THE RAIN FOREST

It kind of seems self-explanatory that it rains in the rain forest, but a common observation from people working in tourism is that tourists always complain about the rain in El Yunque, which is Puerto Rico's rain forest. On a visit to this national forest, expect the weather to be wetter than elsewhere on the island; wear closed-toe shoes suitable for trekking in muddy conditions; and have a rain jacket, poncho, or some other form of protective gear.

PUERTO RICO, POST-HURRICANE MARIA

Although it's been several years since Hurricane Maria devastated the island, Puerto Rico is still struggling to recover, particularly outside of San Juan. Subsequent natural disasters, including earthquakes, have further impacted key tourist sites. Be especially cautions while driving—many stoplights are still broken, some of the signage that blew away has not yet been replaced, the roads continue to be blighted by massive potholes, and the lighting is still poor in places. In addition, many one-way streets won't come up as such in your GPS. Business has resumed as usual for many tourist attractions and activities, but some information you find online may be outdated (and a few major attractions and hotels are still closed), so do look for sources that were either written or updated post-Maria, or call for current information.

Getting Here and Around

Air

Nonstop flights to San Juan are approximately 3¾ hours from New York; 2½ hours from Miami; 3½ hours from Atlanta; 3¾ hours from Boston; 4½ hours from Chicago; and 4½ hours from Dallas.

There are dozens of daily flights to Puerto Rico from the United States, and connections are particularly good from the East Coast, although there are a few nonstop flights from the Midwest as well. San Juan's international airport is a major regional hub, so many travelers headed elsewhere in the Caribbean make connections here. Because of the number of flights, fares to San Juan are among the region's most reasonably priced.

AIRPORTS

The island's main airport is Aeropuerto Internacional Luis Muñoz Marín (SJU), 20 minutes east of Old San Juan in the neighborhood of Isla Verde. San Juan's secondary airport is the small Fernando L. Ribas-Dominicci Airport (SIG), also called Isla Grande, near the city's Miramar section. From either airport you can catch flights to Culebra and Vieques, and from SJU you can also connect to other destinations in Puerto Rico and throughout the Caribbean.

Other Puerto Rican airports include Aeropuerto Internacional Rafael Hernández (BQN) in the northwestern town of Aguadilla; Aeropuerto Eugenio María de Hostos (MAZ) in the west-coast community of Mayagüez; Mercedita (PSE) in the south-coast town of Ponce; José Aponte de la Torre (RVR) in the east-coast town of Ceiba; Antonio Rivera Rodríguez (VQS) on Vieques; and Aeropuerto Benjamin Rivera Noriega (CPX) on Culebra.

GROUND TRANSPORTATION

Before arriving, check with your hotel about transfers: except in San Juan, where it's not allowed, some hotels and resorts offer transport from the airport (fee or no fee) to their guests; some larger resorts run shuttles regularly. Otherwise, your best bets are *taxis turísticos* (tourist taxis). Uniformed officials at the airport can help you make arrangements. They will give you a slip with your exact fare to hand to the driver. Rates are based on your destination: the base rate for a taxi turístico is $12 to Isla Verde, $17 to Condado, and $21 to Old San Juan. There's a $1 charge for each bag handled by the driver. Other costs include a fuel surcharge (currently at $2 per ride), an "airport fee" ($3 per ride to or from the airport), and fees for rides with more than five passengers ($2 for each additional passenger up to seven passengers), as well as a nighttime surcharge ($1 per ride, 10 pm–6 am).

Uber is now able to pick up at the airport.

FLIGHTS TO PUERTO RICO

San Juan's busy Aeropuerto Internacional Luis Muñoz Marín receives flights from all major American carriers. American Airlines flies nonstop from Charlotte, Chicago, Dallas/Fort Worth, Miami, and Philadelphia. Delta flies nonstop from Atlanta and New York–JFK. JetBlue flies nonstop from Boston, Fort Lauderdale, Hartford, Newark, New York–JFK, Orlando, Tampa, and Washington National. Southwest flies nonstop from Baltimore/Washington, Chicago–Midway, Fort Lauderdale, Houston–Hobby, Newark, Orlando, and Tampa. Spirit Air flies nonstop from Fort Lauderdale and Orlando. United flies nonstop from Chicago, Cleveland, Houston, Newark, and Washington, D.C.–Reagan National.

It used to be that travelers arriving at San Juan's international airport had to transfer to nearby Aeropuerto Fernando L. Ribas-Dominicci (known as Isla Grande Airport) to take a flight to Vieques or Culebra. These days, all carriers servicing the islands run flights from the international airport as well. (That said, if you don't mind changing airports, flights to Vieques and Culebra are much cheaper from Isla Grande than they are from SJU—and even cheaper, by as much as half, from Ceiba, about a 90-minute drive from San Juan.) Air Flamenco and Vieques Air Link offer daily flights from both airports in San Juan, as well as from Ceiba, to Vieques and Culebra. Cape Air flies between the international airport and Culebra, Mayagüez, and Vieques.

San Juan is not the only gateway into Puerto Rico. If you're headed to the western part of the island, you can fly directly into Aguadilla. United flies here from Newark; JetBlue flies here from Fort Lauderdale, New York–JFK, and Orlando, and Spirit Air flies nonstop from Fort Lauderdale. If the southern coast is your goal, JetBlue flies to Ponce from New York–JFK and Orlando.

FLIGHTS TO THE CARIBBEAN

Puerto Rico is also a good spot from which to hop to other Caribbean islands. Cape Air connects San Juan to St. Thomas, St. Croix, Nevis, Tortola, and Virgin Gorda. Seaborne Airlines departs from San Juan International to Anguilla, Antigua, Dominica, Martinique, Nevis, St. Croix, St. Kitts, St. Maarten, St. Thomas, Tortola, and Virgin Gorda. JetBlue offers direct flights from SJU to St. Thomas, St. Croix, Punta Cana, Santo Domingo, and Santiago.

Bus

Autoridad Metropolitana de Autobuses (AMA) thread through San Juan, running in exclusive lanes on major thoroughfares and stopping at signs marked "Parada." Destinations are indicated above the windshield. Bus B-21 will take you from Condado to Old San Juan, and Bus A-5 runs from San Juan through Santurce and the beach area of Isla Verde. Note that bus service has been reduced significantly due to the island's financial crisis. Service starts at around 5:30 am and generally continues until 8 pm, but buses are not viewed by visitors as an efficient or easy way of getting around San Juan. Fares are 75¢ and are paid in exact change upon entering the bus. Most buses are air-conditioned and have wheelchair lifts and lockdowns.

There's no bus system covering the rest of the island. If you do not have a rental car, your best bet is to travel by *públicos,* which are usually shared, 17-passenger vans. They have license plates ending in "P" or "PD," and they scoot around the island, stopping at a terminal in each town's main plaza. They operate primarily during the day; routes and fares are fixed by the public service commission, but schedules aren't set, so you have to call ahead. The público system is centered around San Juan, so if you aren't beginning or ending your trip there, it may not be much use to you and renting a car is a better option.

Getting Here and Around

Car

Several well-marked, multilane highways link Puerto Rico's major population centers. Route 26 is the main artery through San Juan, connecting Condado and Old San Juan to Isla Verde and the airport. Route 22, which runs east–west between San Juan and Camuy, and Route 52, which runs north–south between San Juan and Ponce, are toll roads. Route 2, a smaller highway, travels west from San Juan toward Rincón, and Route 3 heads east toward Fajardo. The latter can be mind-numbingly slow, so consider taking Route 66, a toll road that bypasses the worst of the traffic. Note that most toll plazas are cashless, so the EZ-Pass option is a worthwhile convenience—some companies, including Payless, even offer unlimited toll use for a flat daily rate.

Five highways are particularly noteworthy for their scenery and vistas. The island's tourism authorities have even given them special names. The Ruta Panorámica (Panoramic Route) runs east–west through the Cordillera Central. The Ruta Cotorra (Puerto Rican Parrot Route) travels along the north coast. The Ruta Paso Fino (Paso Fino Horse Route, after a horse breed) takes you north–south and west along the south coast. The Ruta Coquí, named for the famous Puerto Rican tree frog, runs along the east coast. And the Ruta Flamboyán, named after the island tree, goes from San Juan through the mountains to the east coast. Note, however, that signposting for all of these highways tends to be poor and inconsistent.

From:	To:	Rte./ Distance:
San Juan	Aguadilla	Rte. 22/130 km (81 miles)
San Juan	El Yunque	Rte. 3/55 km (35 miles)
San Juan	Fajardo	Rte. 3/59 km (36 miles)
San Juan	Mayagüez	Rte. 22/160 km (98 miles)
San Juan	Ponce	Rte. 52/117 km (73 miles)

GASOLINE

All types of fuel—regular, super premium, and diesel—are available by the liter. Most stations are self-service. Hours vary, but stations generally operate daily from early in the morning until 10 or 11 pm; in metro areas, many are open 24 hours. In the Cordillera Central and other rural areas stations are few and far between, so plan accordingly. In cities, you can pay with cash and bank or credit cards; in more remote areas, cash is occasionally your only option. Note, too, that you cannot pay at the pump, even with a debit or credit card; you'll need to go inside the station to pay before pumping.

ROAD CONDITIONS

Puerto Rico has some of the Caribbean's best roads, but potholes, sharp turns, speed bumps, sudden gradient changes, and poor lighting can sometimes make driving difficult, especially outside of the metropolitan area. Be particularly cautious when driving after heavy rains; roads and bridges might be washed out or damaged. Many mountain roads are very narrow and steep, with unmarked curves and cliffs. Locals are familiar with such roads and often drive at high speeds, which can give you quite a scare. When traveling on a narrow, curving road, it's best to honk your horn before you take any sharp turn. Roads—even major ones—are often poorly marked, if at all.

Traffic around cities—particularly San Juan, Ponce, and Mayagüez—is heavy during rush hours (weekdays 7–10 am and 3–7 pm).

ROADSIDE EMERGENCIES

In an emergency, dial ☎ *911*. If your car breaks down, call the rental company for a replacement. Before renting, investigate the company's policy regarding replacement vehicles and repairs out on the island, and ask about surcharges that might be incurred if you break down in a rural area and need a new car.

RULES OF THE ROAD

U.S. driving laws apply in Puerto Rico. Street and highway signs are most often in Spanish. They also use international symbols, but brushing up on a few key Spanish terms before your trip will help. The following words and phrases are especially useful: *calle sin salida* (dead-end street), *carril* (lane), *cruce de peatones* (pedestrian crossing), *cuidado* (caution), *desvio* (detour), *estación de peaje* (tollbooth), *no entre* (do not enter), *no estacione* (no parking), *salida* (exit), *tránsito* (one-way), *zona escolar* (school zone).

Distances are posted in kilometers (1 mile = 1.6 km), but speed limits are posted in miles per hour. Speeding and drunk-driving penalties are much the same as on the U.S. mainland. Police cars often travel with their lights flashing, so it's difficult to know when they're trying to pull you over. If the siren is on, move to the right lane to get out of the way. If the lights are on, it's best to pull over—but make sure that the vehicle is a *marked* police car before doing so.

Ferry

The Autoridad de Transporte Marítimo (Maritime Transportation Authority) runs passenger ferries from the terminal in Ceiba, about a 90-minute drive from San Juan, to Culebra and Vieques. Trips take 90 minutes, and there are multiple departures daily. Food kiosks on Vieques start the day early to accommodate morning arrivals and departures. Culebra has casual eateries within a short walking distance of the ferry.

Tickets ($2 each way for Vieques, $2.25 for Culebra) must be purchased in advance at *www.puertoricoferry.com*, which also has current schedules. Note that ferries have a limited number of seats, and priority is given to island residents, so plan in advance. Also, schedules and service can sometimes be disrupted due to weather and other circumstances.

Essentials

Addresses

Addresses in Puerto Rico (especially in and around San Juan) can be confusing, because Spanish terms like *avenida* and *calle* are used interchangeably with English terms like *avenue* and *street.* This means that the shopping strip in Old San Juan may be called Calle Cristo or Cristo Street (and it might just be called "Cristo," as it is on many maps). A highway is often called an *expreso,* and an alley or pedestrian-only street is labeled a *paseo.*

Outside a metropolitan area, addresses are most often given by the kilometer mark along the road. That means that the address for Parque de las Cavernas del Río Camuy, south of Arecibo, is given as Route 129, Kilometer 18.9.

Dining

Throughout the island you can find everything from French haute cuisine to sushi bars, as well as superb local eateries serving *comida criolla,* or traditional Puerto Rican food. Note that the *mesón gastronómico* label is used by the government to recognize restaurants that preserve culinary traditions. By law, every menu has a written warning about the dangers of consuming raw foods; therefore, if you want something medium rare, you need to be specific about how you'd like it cooked.

⇨ *For information on food-related health issues, see Health, below.*

The restaurants we list are the cream of the crop in each price category.

⇨ *Restaurant reviews have been shortened. For full information, visit Fodors.com.*

MEALS AND MEALTIMES

Puerto Ricans' eating habits mirror those of their counterparts on the mainland United States. They eat breakfast, lunch, and dinner, although they don't tend to drink as much coffee throughout the day. Instead, islanders like a steaming, high-test *café con leche* in the morning and another between 2 and 4 pm, perhaps alongside a local pastry or other sweet treat. They may finish a meal with coffee, but they never drink coffee *during* a meal.

People tend to eat dinner late in Puerto Rico. Many restaurants don't open until 6 pm, and you may find yourself alone in the restaurant before 7; from 8 onward, it may be quite busy.

Unless otherwise noted, restaurants listed in this guide are open daily for lunch and dinner.

RESERVATIONS AND DRESS

Regardless of where you are, make a reservation if you can. In some places, it's expected. We mention reservations specifically only when they're essential (there's no other way you'll get a table) or when they are not accepted. For popular restaurants, book as far ahead as you can (often 30 days), and reconfirm as soon as you arrive. (Large parties should always call ahead to check the reservations policy.)

Puerto Ricans generally dress up to go out, particularly in the evening. And always remember: beach attire is only for the beach. We mention dress only when men are required to wear a jacket or a jacket and tie.

WINES, BEER, AND SPIRITS

Puerto Rico isn't a notable producer of wine, although many upscale and trendy restaurants will have a great wine list. The island does however, make several well-crafted local beers and, of course, lots of rum. Legends trace the birthplace of the piña colada to several San Juan establishments. Puerto Rican rum is popular mixed with cola (known as a Cuba libre), soda, tonic, fruit juice, or water—or served on the rocks or even straight. Look for Don Q, Palo Viejo, Caliche, Ron Pepón, Barrilito, and Bacardí. The drinking age in Puerto Rico is 18.

What It Costs in U.S. Dollars

$	$$	$$$	$$$$
AT DINNER			
Under $12	$12–$20	$21–$30	Over $30

Lodging

San Juan's high-rise hotels on the Condado and Isla Verde beach strips cater primarily to the cruise-ship and casino crowds, although some also target business travelers and families. Outside San Juan, particularly on the east coast, you'll find self-contained luxury resorts that cover hundreds of acres. In the west, southwest, and south—as well as on the islands of Vieques and Culebra—smaller inns, villas, condominiums, and government-sponsored *paradores* are the norm.

Most hotels and other lodgings require you to give your credit-card details before they will confirm your reservation. If you don't feel comfortable emailing this information, ask if you can call it in. However you book, get confirmation in writing, and have a copy of it handy when you check in.

Be sure you understand the hotel's cancellation policy. Some places allow you to cancel without any kind of penalty—even if you prepaid to secure a discounted rate—if you cancel at least 24 hours in advance. Others require you to cancel a week in advance or penalize you the cost of one night. Small inns and B&Bs are most likely to require you to cancel far in advance. Note that hotels in Puerto Rico add a hotel tax to your bill; the tax varies by hotel type, so ask at the time of booking if the amount is not clear. Many hotels, even if they do not market themselves as all-inclusive resorts, also add a resort fee, typically charged as a daily rate. Most hotels allow children under a certain age to stay in their parents' room at no extra charge, but others do charge for them as extra adults; inquire about the cutoff age for discounts.

HOTELS

In the most expensive hotels, rooms are large enough for two to move around comfortably, with two double beds or one queen- or king-size bed, air-conditioning, a phone, Wi-Fi or other Internet access, a private bath, an in-room safe, cable TV, a hair dryer, iron and ironing board, room service, shampoo and toiletries, and possibly a view of the water. There is a concierge and at least one hotel restaurant and lounge, a pool, a shop, and an exercise room or spa. In Puerto Rico's smaller inns, rooms have private baths, air-conditioning or fans, a double- to king-size bed, possibly room service, and breakfast (continental or full) included in the rate. Most also have Wi-Fi or other Internet access in guest rooms, although some have Wi-Fi in public areas only. In some smaller hotels, several rooms share baths—it's a good idea to ask before booking. Throughout the island, smoking is prohibited in public places, including restaurants, bars, cafés, casinos, and hotel common areas.

All hotels listed in this guide have private baths unless otherwise noted. *Hotel reviews have been shortened. For more information, visit Fodors.com.*

Essentials

PARADORES

Some paradores are rural inns offering no-frills apartments, and others are large hotels; all must meet certain standards, such as proximity to an attraction or beach. Most have a small restaurant that serves local cuisine. They're often good bargains (usually $85–$125 per night for a double room).

What It Costs in U.S. Dollars			
$	$$	$$$	$$$$
LODGING FOR TWO			
Under $150	$150–$250	$251–$350	Over $350

Health and Safety

The most common types of illness are caused by contaminated food and water. Make sure food has been thoroughly cooked and is served to you fresh and hot; avoid vegetables and fruits that you haven't washed (in bottled or purified water) or peeled yourself. If you have problems, mild cases of traveler's diarrhea may respond to Imodium (known generically as loperamide) or Pepto-Bismol. Be sure to drink plenty of fluids; if you can't keep fluids down, seek medical help immediately.

Infectious diseases can be airborne or passed via mosquitoes and ticks and through direct or indirect physical contact with animals or people. Some, including Norwalk-like viruses that affect your digestive tract, can be passed along through contaminated food. Condoms can help prevent most sexually transmitted diseases, but they aren't absolutely reliable, and their quality varies from country to country. Speak with your physician and/or check the Centers for Disease Control and Prevention (CDC) or World Health Organization (WHO) websites for health alerts, particularly if you're pregnant, traveling with children, or have a chronic illness.

SPECIFIC HEALTH ISSUES IN PUERTO RICO

Dengue fever, a mosquito-borne disease, is a reality in the Caribbean. Puerto Rico has experienced several recent epidemics, most recently in 2010 and 2012. Virulent forms of the virus can cause high fever, joint pain, nausea, rashes, and occasionally death, but the most common strain is relatively mild, causing mostly flu-like symptoms. Most cases were reported in urban areas far from the usual tourist destinations.

In 2015, the island also reported its first cases of another mosquito-borne virus, **Zika,** which poses serious risks to pregnant women and children in particular. The CDC issued travel warnings for Puerto Rico and other countries where Zika has been reported, but those warnings have since expired (and the number of new cases is down dramatically); check the CDC website for current warnings.

To prevent against mosquito-borne diseases, the U.S. Centers for Disease Control and Prevention (CDC) advises the use of an insect repellent with DEET and clothing that covers the arms and legs. While it's especially important to do this at dusk, when mosquitoes are most active, some mosquitoes are also active during daytime hours.

Health care in Puerto Rico is among the best in the Caribbean, but expect long waits and often a less-than-pleasant bedside manner. If you require treatment, it is likely you will be charged in cash, even if you have active health insurance. Be sure to obtain a receipt for services that you can submit to your insurer. At all hospitals and medical centers you can find English-speaking medical staff, and many large hotels have an English-speaking doctor on call.

Tap water on the island is generally fine for drinking, but avoid drinking it after storms (when the water supply can become mixed with sewage). Thoroughly wash or peel produce you buy in markets before eating it.

Do not fly within 24 hours of scuba diving.

OVER-THE-COUNTER REMEDIES

All the U.S. brands of sunscreen and over-the-counter medicines (for example, Tylenol, Advil, Robitussin, and NyQuil) are available in pharmacies, supermarkets, and convenience stores.

SAFETY

As in any big city, guard your wallet or purse in markets, on buses, and in other crowded areas. Avoid beaches at night, when muggings have been known to occur, even in Condado and Isla Verde. Don't leave anything unattended on the beach. If you must keep valuables in your vehicle, put them in the trunk. Always lock your car. The exception is at the beaches of Vieques, where rental-car agencies advise you to leave the car unlocked so thieves don't break the windows to search for valuables. (This happens extremely rarely, but it does happen.)

We recommend that women carry only a handbag that closes completely and wear it bandolier-style (over one shoulder and across your chest). Open-style bags and those allowed to dangle from one shoulder are prime targets for pickpockets and purse snatchers. Avoid walking anywhere alone at night.

Money

Puerto Rico, which is a commonwealth of the United States, uses the U.S. dollar as its official currency. Prices for most items are a bit higher than those in the States, and that includes restaurants and hotel rates. As in many places, city prices tend to be higher than those in rural areas, but you're not going to go broke staying in the city: a soft drink or a cup of coffee runs about $1–$2; a local beer in a bar, $3–$6; museum admission, $5–$15. Prices listed here are for adults. ATMs are prevalent in San Juan but may be scarce in rural areas. Substantially reduced fees are almost always available for children, students, and senior citizens.

Taxes

You must pay a tax on your hotel room rate: 11% for hotels with casinos, 9% for other hotels, and 7% for government-approved paradores. Ask your hotel before booking. The tax, in addition to each hotel's discretionary service charge (5%–16%), can add a hefty 12%–27% to your bill. The island's sales tax is 11.5% (the highest in the United States).

Tipping

Some hotels (usually those classified as resorts) automatically add a 5%–16% service charge to your bill. Check ahead to confirm whether this charge is built into the room rate or will be tacked on at checkout. Tips are expected—and appreciated—by restaurant waitstaff (15%–20%), hotel porters ($1 per bag), maids ($1–$2 per day), and taxi drivers (10%–15%).

Essentials

Tipping Guides for Puerto Rico

Bartender	15%
Hotel Staff	15%
Hotel Room Service Waiter	15%
Housekeeping	15%
Spa Personnel	15%
Tour Guide	15–20%
Taxi Drivers	10%
Porter at Airport	10%
Waiter	18–25%

Passport

All visitors to the United States require a passport that is valid for six months beyond your expected period of stay. U.S. citizens do not need a passport to visit Puerto Rico, which is considered part of the United States for immigration purposes.

Visa

Except for citizens of Canada and Bermuda, most visitors to the United States must have a visa. If you are from one of the 39 designated members of the Visa Waiver Program, then you only require an ESTA (Electronic System for Travel Authorization) as long as you are staying for 90 days or less. However, some changes were made in the Visa Waiver Program in 2015, and nationals of Visa Waiver nations who have traveled to Democratic People's Republic of Korea, Iran, Iraq, Libya, Somalia, Sudan, Syria, or Yemen no longer qualify for ESTA. Also, if you have been denied a visa to visit the United States, your application for the ESTA program most likely will be denied.

Immunizations

There are no immunization requirements for visitors traveling to Puerto Rico for tourism.

U.S. Embassy/Consulate

There are no foreign embassies in Puerto Rico, but several countries have consulates.

Visitor Information

In addition to the Puerto Rico Tourism Company's *¡Qué Pasa!* magazine, an excellent resource is *www.DiscoverPuertoRico.com*.

When to Go

Low Season: From August to late October, temperatures can climb to oppressive heights, and the weather grows muggy, with a high risk of tropical storms. Many upscale hotels offer deep discounts.

Shoulder Season: From late April to July and November to mid-December, hotel prices drop 20%–50% from high season. There's a chance of scattered showers, but expect sun-kissed days and fewer crowds.

High Season: From mid-December through mid-April, the weather is typically sunny and warm. Good hotels are often booked far in advance, everything is open, and prices are highest.

On the Calendar

January

Fiestas de la Calle San Sebastián (*San Sebastián Street Festival*). The January festival in Old San Juan features four nights of live music as well as food festivals and *cabezudos* parades, where folk legends are caricatured in oversize masks. 🌐 *www.discoverpuertorico.com/en/experiences/culture.*

February–March

Carnival. In the days preceding Lent, Ponce celebrates Carnival with flamboyant costumes, parades, and music. 🌐 *www.visitponce.com.*

Casals Festival. Every year, San Juan honors world-renowned cellist Pablo Casals, who lived in Puerto Rico for nearly three decades until his death. Classical music performances feature the Puerto Rico Symphony Orchestra, as well as local and international soloists, trios, and quartets. ☎ *787/723–5005.*

Jayuya Fiesta del Café. One of several coffee festivals held annually around the island, Jayuya's Fiesta del Café features all the usual activities at these types of events, but is notable for *la colada del café,* which organizers contend is the largest coffeepot on the island, brewing up to 100 pounds of coffee at once. 🎫 *Free*

Saborea Puerto Rico. Puerto Rico's largest culinary event is a two-day extravaganza held at Vivo Beach Club in San Juan. It includes presentations by island and international chefs, as well as food from local restaurants, featuring beer, wine, and rum tastings. 🌐 *saboreapuertorico.com.*

June–July

Aibonito Flower Festival. This popular festival displays incredible tropical foliage, including countless varieties of colorful orchids and ginger plants. There's also plenty of food and music.

Puerto Rico Restaurant Week (*PRRW*). This one-week islandwide dining celebration, held every June, is the perfect opportunity to visit top restaurants and enjoy specially priced prix-fixe menus at top restaurants. 🌐 *www.prrestaurantweek.com.*

September

Puerto Rico Symphony Orchestra. The annual season of the Puerto Rico Symphony Orchestra begins in San Juan with classical and pop performances by the island's finest orchestra. ☎ *787/723–5005.*

November

Festival de Café (*Coffee Harvest Festival*). The mountain towns of Maricao and Yauco host the annual Festival de Café. Performers play music, and artisans and home cooks sell their crafts and regional foods.

December

Festival de las Máscaras. The annual Festival de las Máscaras honors the mask-making traditions of Hatillo, where colorful masks used in religious processions have been crafted for centuries.

Great Itineraries

Colonial Treasures

More than almost any other Caribbean island, Puerto Rico has a trove of well-preserved colonial cities. Old San Juan is the best known—and it's a must-see for anyone interested in the region's rich history—but the southern coast also has some gems, from the graceful square in Coamo to the churches of San Germán to the heady mix of neoclassical and art deco masterpieces in Ponce.

DAY 1: OLD SAN JUAN

To fully experience Old San Juan, stay within the city walls. **El Convento,** once a Carmelite convent, is one of Old San Juan's most luxurious lodgings. **The Gallery Inn** has the most personality, while the **CasaBlanca Hotel** is charming yet affordable. After dropping off your suitcases, hit the cobblestone streets. Stroll along the city walls, and visit one of the forts—most people pick **Castillo San Felipe del Morro,** but the nearby **Castillo San Cristóbal** is equally impressive. Old San Juan isn't just for sightseeing: when the sun goes down, the streets light up, turning this historic neighborhood into a nightlife center. For dinner, head to Calle Fortaleza, where you'll find great dining options; then while away the night at one of the happening bars.

Logistics: Believe us when we tell you that you don't want the headache of parking in Old San Juan. At San Juan's Aeropuerto Internacional Luis Muñoz Marín, take a taxi turístico (tourist taxi) or Uber to your hotel. The streets here were made for walking, and that's just what you'll do. Wait to pick up a car when you're ready to leave the city for the countryside.

DAY 2: COAMO

Head south from San Juan, and if you get an early enough start, take a short detour to Guayama, where you'll find the gorgeous **Casa Cautiño.** This 19th-century manor house, transformed into a museum, is one of Puerto Rico's most beautifully restored colonial-era structures. Continue west to Coamo, known for its thermal springs. On Coamo's lovely main square is the gleaming white **Iglesia Católica San Blas,** one of the island's oldest churches. In terms of distance, Coamo isn't so far from San Juan—only about 96 km (60 miles)—so you don't have to leave at the crack of dawn to have most of a day to explore the town.

Logistics: Head south from San Juan toward Ponce on Route 52 (toll road). For a detour, pick up Route 15 near Cayey, and follow it south to Guayama. From there, you can take Route 3 (which runs into Route 1 at Salinas) west to Santa Isabel; then turn north on Route 153 to reach Coamo.

DAY 3: PONCE

Your destination on your third day is Ponce, the "Pearl of the South." You'll know you've arrived when you drive through the massive letters spelling the name of the city. The main square, the Plaza de las Delicias, is a delight: here you'll find the **Catedral de Nuestra Señora de Guadalupe,** a church dating from 1835, and **Parque de Bombas,** a firehouse from 1882, painted in bold red and black stripes. Of the city's several museums, the most interesting is the **Museo de la Arquitectura Ponceña,** set in a small house built in 1911. In a city filled with neoclassical confections, this is one of the most elaborate. Strolling the downtown streets, you'll also marvel at other examples of neoclassical architecture, as well as some art deco gems. Don't miss

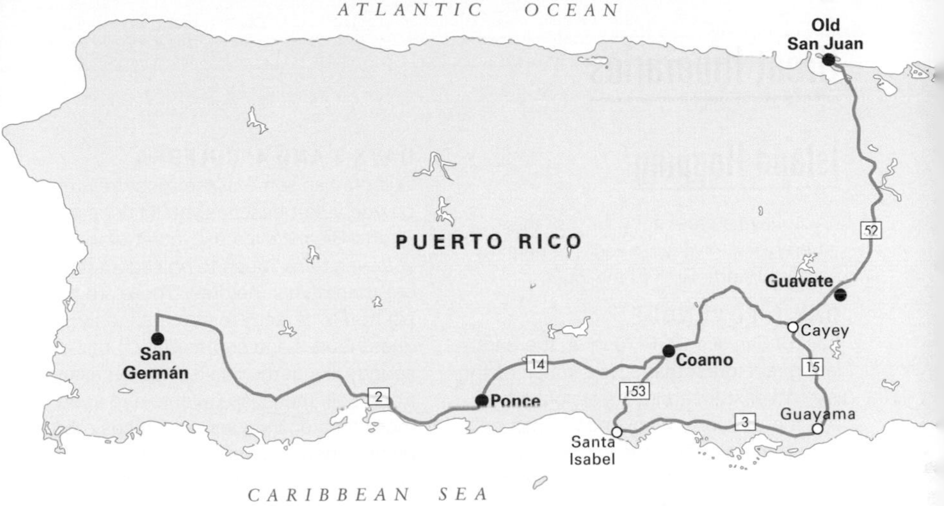

the **Museo de Arte de Ponce,** one of the Caribbean's best art museums.

Logistics: From Coamo, follow Route 14 to Ponce; to continue downtown, take Route 12.

DAY 4: SAN GERMÁN

Less than an hour west of Ponce is San Germán, a must-see for anyone interested in the colonial era. The best place to start a tour is Plazuela Santo Domingo, the small park in the center of the historic district, which itself is listed on the National Register of Historic Places. At the park's eastern edge is the **Capilla de Porta Coeli.** This chapel, at the top of some steep stone steps, is now a museum of religious art. Stroll west past the delightful assemblage of buildings of every architectural style from mission to Victorian. Make sure to see the other gorgeous church, the **Iglesia San Germán de Auxerre,** a few blocks north.

Logistics: San Germán is easy to reach—simply take Route 2 west from Ponce. When you reach Route 122, head south into town.

DAY 5: GUAVATE

If you have time on your way back to San Juan, stop for lunch at one of the open-air eateries near Guavate, off Route 52. You can try the famous *lechón,* a whole pig roasted on a spit.

Logistics: From San Germán take Route 2 until you reach Ponce. Exit onto Route 52; a toll road takes you all the way to San Juan.

Tips

- If you're staying in Old San Juan, pick up your rental car at one of the hotel desks. You'll avoid an expensive taxi ride back to the airport.
- Pack comfortable shoes for exploring these colonial-era cities. You'll be glad you brought sneakers after a few hours traipsing around on cobblestones.
- Old San Juan is hillier than it first appears, and, in Ponce, avoid walking to Castillo Serrallés—a steep hike through an unsavory area. Take advantage of the free trolleys that depart from main plazas and will take you to the most popular tourist sites in both cities.

Great Itineraries

Island Hopping

If you have a week for your trip, this itinerary will give you a taste of each of eastern Puerto Rico's highlights.

DAY 1: EL YUNQUE

East of San Juan is El Yunque, the undulating rain forest that covers much of the island's eastern edge. It's a highlight of any trip to Puerto Rico, and you can still have a memorable time with only one day to spend there. Several of the trails can be hiked in an hour or less. Spend the night in Río Grande; a good bet along this stretch of shoreline is the luxurious **St. Regis Bahia Beach Resort,** known for its Robert Trent Jones golf course, beautiful private beach, and first-rate service.

Logistics: Take Route 3 east from San Juan; then head south on Route 191, which leads through El Yunque.

DAY 2: RESERVA NATURAL LAS CABEZAS DE SAN JUAN

Next stop: Fajardo, on the island's northeastern tip. Drop your stuff off at your hotel—the best ones are smaller accommodations like the **Fajardo Inn**—then head out on a tour (reserve ahead) of the mangrove forests in the **Reserva Natural Las Cabezas de San Juan.** Exploring this area isn't just a daytime experience, however. You may want to return at night, when you can kayak through its bioluminescent bay. Companies offer trips nightly, although the experience is more dramatic under a moonless sky. In the afternoon, take a boat excursion from Fajardo to **Isla Palomino.**

Logistics: Continue on Route 3 to Fajardo, where Route 987 leads to Las Cabezas de San Juan.

DAYS 3 AND 4: CULEBRA

Culebra has some of the most beautiful, powdery soft beaches you'll find in all of Puerto Rico. It's a small, quiet island, so you won't find much to do except relax—but then, that's the draw. There are no big hotels or fancy restaurants, only small guesthouses and some villas. If this sounds like getting a little too far away from it all, then skip Culebra and spend more time on Vieques, which has more resorts, better restaurants, and plenty of eco-centric activities. If you want to visit both islands, you can fly between Culebra and Vieques, but note that there's no ferry link.

Logistics: Drop off your rental car in Ceiba—you'll want to rent a sturdier four-wheel-drive vehicle once you get to Culebra. Take the 90-minute ferry trip—or a 10-minute puddle-jumper flight—to the island from Ceiba. (If possible, take the plane; the views are spectacular.)

DAYS 5 AND 6: VIEQUES

Close to the U.S. Virgin Islands—in terms of both atmosphere and geography—Vieques has an entirely different feel from the rest of Puerto Rico. If you've never been, try to spend at least one night there. The beaches are seemingly endless, the snorkeling is remarkable, and the **Puerto Mosquito Bioluminescent Bay** is one of nature's best shows. One great way to explore the island is on a bicycle tour arranged by a local operator.

Logistics: You'll want to fly between Culebra and Vieques—there are scheduled direct flights between the islands. For ferry service, you'll need to return to Ceiba first; there are no ferries between the islands.

DAY 7: SAN JUAN

From Vieques, take a puddle-jumper flight back to San Juan (or to Ceiba's airport to pick up your rental car). If you want to spend a day in Old San Juan, fly into Aeropuerto Fernando L. Ribas-Dominicci; it's a short taxi ride from the airport's Isla Grande location to Old San Juan's colonial heart.

Logistics: If you are connecting to a flight back home, make sure your flight to San Juan is headed to Aeropuerto Internacional Luis Muñoz Marín. If you're flying to San Juan's regional airport, Aeropuerto Fernando L. Ribas-Dominicci, instead, you'll have to take a taxi between the airports.

Tips

- Don't plan on taking your rental car to Vieques or Culebra—it's not allowed.
- Check to see if you have to reserve in advance for certain tours, such as the daily trip to Fajardo's Reserva Natural Las Cabezas de San Juan.
- Vieques and Culebra are both popular weekend destinations for Puerto Ricans. Ferries can get very crowded, and tickets are prioritized for residents. If possible, plan your travel for a weekday and book ahead via *PuertoRicoFerry.com*.

Helpful Phrases in Spanish

BASICS

Hello	Hola	**oh**-lah
Yes/no	Sí/no	see/no
Please	Por favor	pore fah-**vore**
May I?	¿Me permite?	may pair-**mee**-tay
Thank you	Gracias	**Grah**-see-as
You're welcome	De nada	day **nah**-dah
I'm sorry	Lo siento	lo see-**en**-toh
Good morning!	¡Buenos días!	**bway**-nohs **dee**-ahs
Good evening!	¡Buenas noches!	**bway**-nahs **no**-chess
Good-bye!	¡Adiós!/¡Hasta luego!	ah-dee-**ohss/ah** -stah **lwe**-go
Mr./Mrs.	Señor/Señora	sen-**yor**/ sen-**yohr**-ah
Miss	Señorita	sen-yo-**ree**-tah
Pleased to meet you	Mucho gusto	**moo**-cho **goose**-toh
How are you?	¿Cómo está usted?	**ko**-mo es-**tah** oo-**sted**

NUMBERS

one	un, uno	oon, **oo**-no
two	dos	dos
three	tres	tress
four	cuatro	**kwah**-tro
five	cinco	**sink**-oh
six	seis	saice
seven	siete	see-**et**-eh
eight	ocho	**o**-cho
nine	nueve	new-**eh**-vey
ten	diez	dee-**es**
eleven	once	**ohn**-seh
twelve	doce	**doh**-seh
thirteen	trece	**treh**-seh
fourteen	catorce	ka-**tohr**-seh
fifteen	quince	**keen**-seh
sixteen	dieciséis	dee-**es**-ee-**saice**
seventeen	diecisiete	dee-**es**-ee-see-**et**-eh
eighteen	dieciocho	dee-**es**-ee-**o**-cho
nineteen	diecinueve	dee-**es**-ee-new-**ev**-eh
twenty	veinte	**vain**-teh
twenty-one	veinte y uno/ veintiuno	**vain**-te-**oo**-noh
thirty	treinta	**train**-tah
forty	cuarenta	kwah-**ren**-tah
fifty	cincuenta	seen-**kwen**-tah
sixty	sesenta	sess-**en**-tah
seventy	setenta	set-**en**-tah
eighty	ochenta	oh-**chen**-tah
ninety	noventa	no-**ven**-tah
one hundred	cien	see-**en**
one thousand	mil	meel
one million	un millón	oon meel-**yohn**

COLORS

black	negro	**neh**-groh
blue	azul	ah-**sool**
brown	café	kah-**feh**
green	verde	**ver**-deh
orange	naranja	na-**rahn**-hah
red	rojo	**roh**-hoh
white	blanco	**blahn**-koh
yellow	amarillo	ah-mah-**ree**-yoh

DAYS OF THE WEEK

Sunday	domingo	doe-**meen**-goh
Monday	lunes	**loo**-ness
Tuesday	martes	**mahr**-tess
Wednesday	miércoles	me-**air**-koh-less
Thursday	jueves	hoo-**ev**-ess
Friday	viernes	vee-**air**-ness
Saturday	sábado	**sah**-bah-doh

MONTHS

January	enero	eh-**neh**-roh
February	febrero	feh-**breh**-roh
March	marzo	**mahr**-soh
April	abril	ah-**breel**
May	mayo	**my**-oh
June	junio	**hoo**-nee-oh
July	julio	**hoo**-lee-yoh
August	agosto	ah-**ghost**-toh
September	septiembre	sep-tee-**em**-breh
October	octubre	oak-**too**-breh
November	noviembre	no-vee-**em**-breh
December	diciembre	dee-see-**em**-breh

USEFUL WORDS AND PHRASES

Do you speak English?	¿Habla usted inglés?	**ah**-blah oos-**ted** in-**glehs**
I don't speak Spanish.	No hablo español	no **ah**-bloh es-pahn-**yol**
I don't understand.	No entiendo	no en-tee-**en**-doh
I understand.	Entiendo	en-tee-**en**-doh
I don't know.	No sé	no **seh**
I'm American.	Soy americano (americana)	soy ah-meh-ree-**kah**-no (ah-meh-ree-**kah**-nah)
What's your name?	¿Cómo se llama usted?	koh-mo seh **yah**-mah oos-**ted**
My name is . . .	Me llamo . . .	may **yah**-moh
What time is it?	¿Qué hora es?	keh **o**-rah es
How?	¿Cómo?	**koh**-mo
When?	¿Cuándo?	**kwahn**-doh
Yesterday	Ayer	ah-**yehr**
Today	hoy	oy
Tomorrow	mañana	mahn-**yah**-nah

Tonight	Esta noche	**es**-tah **no**-cheh
What?	¿Qué?	keh
What is it?	¿Qué es esto?	keh es **es**-toh
Why?	¿Por qué?	pore **keh**
Who?	¿Quién?	kee-**yen**
Where is . . .	¿Dónde está . . .	**dohn**-deh es-**tah**
. . . the train station?	la estación del tren?	la es-tah-see-**on** del trehn
. . . the subway station?	la estación del tren subterráneo?	la es-ta-see-**on** del trehn la es-ta-see-**on** soob-teh-**rrahn**-eh-oh
. . . the bus stop?	la parada del autobus?	la pah-**rah**-dah del ow-toh-**boos**
. . . the terminal? (airport)	el aeropuerto	el air-oh-**pwar**-toh
. . . the post office?	la oficina de correos?	la oh-fee-**see**- nah deh koh-**rreh**-os
. . . the bank?	el banco?	el **bahn**-koh
. . . the hotel?	el hotel?	el oh-**tel**
. . . the museum?	el museo?	el moo-**seh**-oh
. . . the hospital?	el hospital?	el ohss-pee-**tal**
. . . the elevator?	el ascensor?	el ah-sen-**sohr**
Where are the restrooms?	el baño?	el **bahn**-yoh
Here/there	Aquí/allá	ah-**key**/ah-**yah**
Open/closed	Abierto/cerrado	ah-bee-**er**-toh/ ser-**ah**-doh
Left/right	Izquierda/derecha	iss-key-**eh**-dah/ dare-**eh**-chah
Is it near?	¿Está cerca?	es-**tah** **sehr**-kah
Is it far?	¿Está lejos?	es-**tah** **leh**-hoss
I'd like . . .	Quisiera . . .	kee-see-**ehr**-ah
. . . a room	un cuarto/una habitación	oon **kwahr**-toh/**oo**-nah ah-bee-tah-see-**on**
. . . the key	la llave	lah **yah**-veh
. . . a newspaper	un periódico	oon pehr-ee-**oh**-dee-koh
. . . a stamp	un sello de correo	oon **seh**-yo deh korr-**eh**-oh
I'd like to buy . . .	Quisiera comprar . . .	kee-see-**ehr**-ah kohm-**prahr**
. . . soap	jabón	hah-**bohn**
. . . suntan lotion	Loción bronceadora	loh-see-**ohn** brohn-seh-ah-**do**-rah
. . . envelopes	sobres	**so**-brehs
. . . writing paper	papel	pah-**pel**
. . . a postcard	una tarjeta postal	**oon**-ah tar-**het**-ah post-**ahl**
. . . a ticket		
How much is it?	¿Cuánto cuesta?	**kwahn**-toh **kwes**-tah
It's expensive/ cheap	Está caro/barato	es-**tah** **kah**-roh/ bah-**rah**-toh
A little/a lot	Un poquito/mucho	oon poh-**kee**-toh/ **moo**-choh
More/less	Más/menos	mahss/**men**-ohss
Enough/too (much)	Suficiente/	soo-fee-see-**en**-teh/

I am ill/sick	Estoy enfermo(a)	es-**toy** en-**fehr**-moh(mah)
Call a doctor	Llame a un medico	**ya**-meh ah oon **med**-ee-koh
Help!	Socorro	soh-**koh**-roh
Stop!	Pare	**pah**-reh

DINING OUT

I'd like to reserve a table . . .	Quisiera reservar una mesa . . .	kee-**syeh**-rah rreh-sehr-**bahr** **oo**-nah **meh**-sah . . .
. . . for two people.	para dos personas.	**pah**-rah dohs pehr-**soh**-nahs
. . . for this evening.	para esta noche.	**pah**-rah **ehs**-tah **noh**-cheh
. . . for 8 PM	para las ocho de la noche.	**pah**-rah lahs **oh**-choh deh lah **noh**-cheh
A bottle of . . .	Una botella de . . .	**oo**-nah bo-**teh**-yah deh
A cup of . . .	Una taza de . . .	**oo**-nah **tah**-sah deh
A glass of . . .	Un vaso de . . .	oon **vah**-so deh
Bill/check	La cuenta	lah **kwen**-tah
Bread	El pan	el pahn
Breakfast	El desayuno	el deh-sah-**yoon**-oh
Butter	La mantequilla	lah man-teh-**kee**-yah
Coffee	Café	kah-**feh**
Dinner	La cena	lah **seh**-nah
Fork	El tenedor	el ten-eh-**dor**
I don't eat meat	No como carne	noh koh-moh **kahr** neh
I cannot eat . . .	No puedo comer . . .	noh **pweh**-doh koh-**mehr**
I'd like to order . . .	Quiero ordenar . . .	**kee**-yehr-oh **ohr**-deh-nahr
I'd like . . .	Me gustaría . . .	Meh goo-stah-**ee**-ah
I'm hungry/thirsty	Tengo hambre.	**Tehn**-goh **hahm**-breh
Is service/the tip included?	¿Está incluida la propina?	es-**tah** in-cloo-**ee**-dah lah pro-**pee**-nah
Knife	El cuchillo	el koo-**chee**-yo
Lunch	La comida	lah koh-**mee**-dah
Menu	La carta, el menú	lah **cart**-ah, el meh-**noo**
Napkin	La servilleta	lah sehr-vee-**yet**-ah
Pepper	La pimienta	lah pee-mee-**en**-tah
Plate	plato	
Please give me . . .	Por favor déme . . .	pore fah-**vor** **deh**-meh
Salt	La sal	lah sahl
Spoon	Una cuchara	**oo**-nah koo-**chah**-rah
Sugar	El ázucar	el ah-**su**-kar
Tea	té	teh
Water	agua	**ah**-gwah
Wine	vino	**vee**-noh

Contacts

Air

U.S. AIRLINE CONTACTS **American Airlines.** ✉ *Luiz Muñoz Marin Airport* ☎ *800/433–7300* 🌐 *www.aa.com*. **Delta Airlines.** ✉ *Luiz Muñoz Marin Airport* ☎ *800/221–1212 U.S. reservations, 800/241–4141 international reservations* 🌐 *www.delta.com*. **JetBlue.** ✉ *Luiz Muñoz Marin Airport* ☎ *800/538–2583* 🌐 *www.jetblue.com*. **Southwest Airlines.** ☎ *800/435–9792* 🌐 *www.southwest.com*. **Spirit Airlines.** ✉ *Luiz Muñoz Marin Airport* ☎ *800/401–2222* 🌐 *www.spirit.com*. **United Airlines.** ✉ *Luiz Muñoz Marin Airport* ☎ *800/864–8331* 🌐 *www.united.com*.

REGIONAL AIRLINE CONTACTS **Air Flamenco.** ✉ *Isla Grande Airport, Calle Lindbergh 7* ☎ *787/724–1818* 🌐 *www.flyairflamenco.com*. **Cape Air.** ✉ *Luiz Muñoz Marin Airport* ☎ *800/227–3247* 🌐 *www.capeair.com*. **Seaborne Airlines.** ☎ *787/946–7800 in San Juan* 🌐 *www.seaborneairlines.com*. **Vieques Air Link.** ✉ *Luiz Muñoz Marin Airport* ☎ *787/741–8331, 888/901–9247* 🌐 *www.viequesairlink.com*.

AIRPORT CONTACTS **Aeropuerto Antonio Rivera Rodríguez.** ☎ *787/741–0515*. **Aeropuerto Benjamin Rivera Noriega.** ☎ *787/742–0022*. **Aeropuerto Eugenio María de Hostos.** ✉ *Mayagüez* ☎ *787/833–0148* 🌐 *www.prpa.pr.gov*. **Aeropuerto Fernando L. Ribas-Dominicci.** (*Isla Grande*). ✉ *Calle Lindburgh, Isla Grande* ☎ *787/741–3809*. **Aeropuerto Internacional Luis Muñoz Marín.** ✉ *San Juan* ☎ *787/289–7240* 🌐 *www.aeropuertosju.com*. **Aeropuerto José Aponte de la Torre.** ✉ *Ceiba* ☎ *787/729–8462*. **Aeropuerto Mercedita.** ✉ *Ponce* ☎ *787/842–6292* 🌐 *www.prpa.pr.gov*. **Aeropuerto Rafael Hernández.** ✉ *Aguadilla* ☎ *787/840–3151*.

Bus

Autoridad Metropolitana de Autobuses. ☎ *787/294–0500*.

Lodging

RENTAL CONTACTS **Rainbow Realty.** ☎ *787/741–4312, 787/435–2063* 🌐 *www.viequesrainbowrealty.com*.

PARADOR CONTACTS **Puerto Rico Tourism Company.** ☎ *787/721–2400, 800/866–7827* 🌐 *www.discoverpuertorico.com*.

Visitor Information

Discover Puerto Rico. ☎ *787/522–5960* 🌐 *www.discoverpuertorico.com*.

Chapter 3

SAN JUAN

Updated by
Paulina Salach Antonetti

Sights	Restaurants	Hotels	Shopping	Nightlife
★★★★☆	★★★★★	★★★★☆	★★☆☆☆	★★★★☆

WELCOME TO SAN JUAN

TOP REASONS TO GO

★ **Take a stroll:** Wander the cobblestone streets of Old San Juan. The fortifications and governor's mansion are UNESCO World Heritage sites.

★ **Climb a battlement:** Explore Castillo San Felipe del Morro, the 16th-century fortress that dominates the waterfront; rangers provide fascinating insight.

★ **See the art:** Head to Santurce, San Juan's art district. Visit the Contemporary Museum of Art and stroll down Calle Cerra to view spectacular street art.

★ **Catch some rays:** Take it easy at San Juan's best beach, Balneario de Carolina, at the eastern tip of Isla Verde. Book a surfing lesson.

★ **Explore the culinary scene:** Try island classics like mofongo (deep-fried, mashed plantains), *pernil* (roast pork), and *chillo frito* (fried red snapper). Throughout San Juan, stellar restaurants do modern takes on traditional dishes made using local ingredients.

San Juan's metro area stretches 19 km (12 miles) along Puerto Rico's north coast. Mapping the city is rather like working a jigsaw puzzle; neighborhoods are irregular in shape and sometimes overlap. The areas most visited by tourists run along the coast.

1 Old San Juan. Enclosed by its original fortified walls, this superbly preserved enclave of cobblestone streets has more than 800 structures of historic importance, many from the 16th century. Laid out in an easy-to-navigate grid, Old San Juan has enough sights, bars, restaurants, and boutiques to enthrall for days.

2 Puerta de Tierra. Just east of the Old City, Puerta de Tierra has a few notable hotels, several parks, and a nice public beach.

3 Condado. The most vibrant pedestrian area outside Old San Juan is home to hotels, restaurants, shops, and residences of the moneyed elite. Its main street is Avenida Ashford.

4 Miramar and Isla Grande. Bordering Santurce and across the bay from Condado is Miramar, a residential district with great dining options. Isla Grande has the city's municipal airport, the convention center, and the District Live entertainment complex.

5 Santurce and Hato Rey. South of Condado and Ocean Park, Santurce—home of the city's main art museums and galleries—melds into Hato Rey, the city's business district.

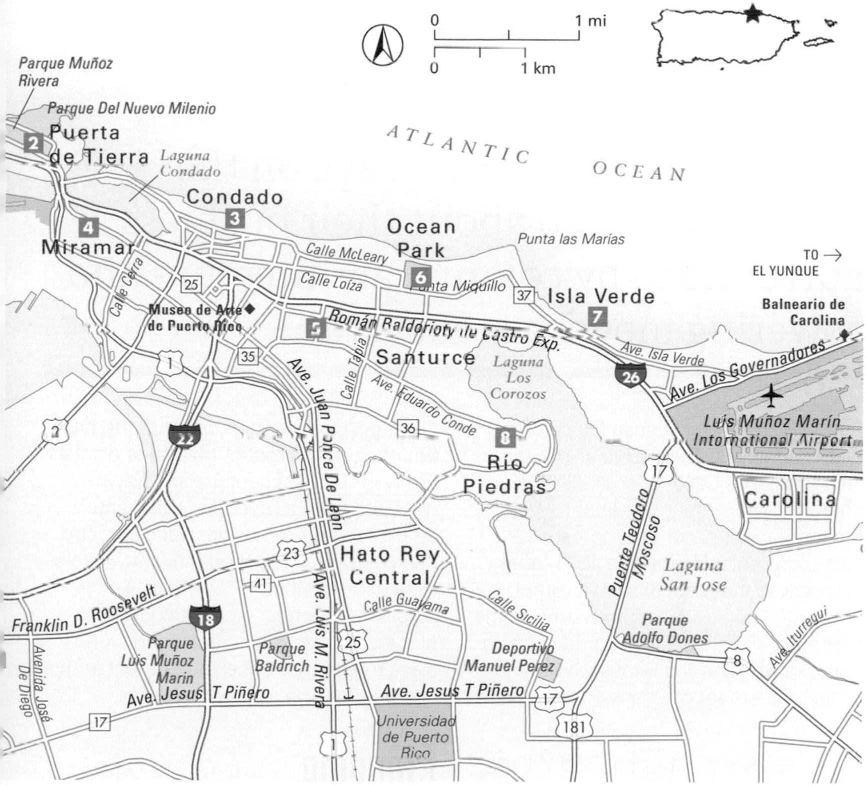

6 Ocean Park. Partially gated and steps from the beach, this primarily residential area east of Condado nevertheless has a few small hotels, lots of short-term rentals, and popular restaurants.

7 Isla Verde and Carolina. East of Ocean Park, Isla Verde, home to the international airport, and Carolina have many large hotels and the city's best beach.

8 Río Piedras. The Universidad de Puerto Rico and Jardín Botánico are in this residential area.

9 Cataño. Primarily industrial, Cataño is best known as the site of the Bacardí rum distillery. The town center has a boardwalk and a recent addition of dining on the bay.

10 Guaynabo. A mix of residential and industrial areas, this neighborhood is worth visiting for its historical sights, including the island's first settlement.

11 Bayamón. The distillery that produces the island's distinctive Ron del Barrilito rum is in this suburb.

Puerto Rico's capital, which radiates out from a bay on the Atlantic, is most commonly associated with the colorful colonial streets and forts of Old San Juan, but that's only part of the picture. This major metropolis may be rooted in the past, but it has its eye on the future. Locals go about their business surrounded by colonial architecture and towering modern structures.

By 1508, the explorer Juan Ponce de León had established a colony in an area now known as Caparra, southeast of present-day San Juan. He later moved the settlement north to a more hospitable peninsular location. In 1521, after he became the first colonial governor, Ponce de León switched the name of the island—then called San Juan Bautista, in honor of St. John the Baptist—with that of the settlement of Puerto Rico, or "rich port."

Defended by the imposing Castillo San Felipe del Morro (El Morro) and Castillo San Cristóbal, Puerto Rico's administrative and population center remained firmly in Spain's hands until 1898, when it came under U.S. control after the Spanish-American War. Centuries of Spanish rule left an indelible imprint on the city, particularly in the walled area now known as Old San Juan, an area filled with cobblestone streets, brightly painted colonial-era structures, and fortifications that have been designated UNESCO World Heritage sites.

Old San Juan is a monument to the past, but most of the rest of the city is planted firmly in the 21st century and draws migrants from all over the island and beyond to jobs in business and industry. The city captivates residents and visitors alike with its vibrant lifestyle as well as its balmy beaches, creative cocktail bars, globe-spanning restaurants, and world-class museums. Once you set foot in this city, you may never want to leave.

Planning

When to Go

During high season (mid-December–mid-April) hotels tend to fill up, and rates are a bit higher than in the off-season. Fall and spring are less expensive, plus the weather's still fantastic and the tourist crush less intense. However, a winter visit may allow you to participate in many of San Juan's annual events—in particular, the lively Christmas celebrations, which extend through mid-January. The

Fiestas de la Calle San Sebastián, held in Old San Juan every January, consist of several nights of live music, food festivals, and *cabezudos* (giant heads on daily parade).

San Juan's weather is moderate and tropical year-round, with an average temperature of about 82°F (26°C). And although it's true that much of summer and fall is considered hurricane season, San Juan is still an attractive destination during those months: room rates are at their lowest, restaurant reservations are easier to come by, and fewer tourists roam the streets.

Getting Here and Around

AIR

American, Delta, Frontier, JetBlue, Southwest, Spirit, and United fly to San Juan from the United States. International carriers include United from Toronto, Virgin Atlantic from Paris, Air France (operated by Delta) from London, Iberia and Air Europa from Madrid, and Avianca from Colombia.

Vieques Air Link offers daily flights from San Juan's Aeropuerto Internacional Luis Muñoz Marin (SJU) and Aeropuerto Fernando L. Ribas Dominicci, also known as Isla Grande Airport (SIG), to Vieques and Culebra. Air Flamenco flies to both islands from Isla Grande; Cape Air flies between SJU and Vieques.

AIRPORTS Aeropuerto Fernando L. Ribas Dominicci. (*SIG*) ✉ *Calle Lindbergh, San Juan* ☎ *787/729–8715.* **Aeropuerto Internacional Luis Muñoz Marín.** (*SJU*) ✉ *Carolina* ☎ *787/253–2329* 🌐 *www.aeropuertosju.com.*

AIRPORT TRANSFERS

Before you leave for Puerto Rico, check with your hotel about transfers; many larger hotels offer transport from the airport (sometimes free) to their guests. Otherwise, take a *taxi turístico* (tourist taxi) or an Uber. Uniformed officials at the airport can help you make arrangements; they will give you a slip with your exact fare written on it to hand to the driver. Rates are based on your destination: a taxi turístico costs $10 to Isla Verde, $15 to Condado, and $19 to Old San Juan and the cruise-ship piers. There's a $1 charge for each bag handled by the driver.

The Baldorioty de Castro Expressway (Route 26) runs from the airport into the city. Exits are clearly marked, although you should check with your hotel to determine which one is best for you to take. Plan on 25–30 minutes for the drive from the airport all the way west to Old San Juan.

BUS AND TROLLEY

The Municipio de San Juan operates free trolleys throughout Old San Juan. They follow three routes beginning at Pier 4, on Calle Gilberto Concepción de Gracia, and running to the two forts plus Plaza de Armas.

The Autoridad Metroplitana de Autobuses (AMA) maintains a network of bus routes throughout San Juan, running in exclusive lanes on major thoroughfares and stopping at signs marked "Parada."

Destinations are displayed above their windshields. Bus B-21 runs through Condado all the way to Plaza Las Américas in Hato Rey. Bus A-5 runs from San Juan through Santurce and the beach area of Isla Verde. Fares are 75¢ and must be paid in exact change upon entering the bus. Most buses are air-conditioned and have wheelchair lifts and lock-downs. However, they are slow and inefficient and not suitable for most vacationers.

CONTACTS AMA. (*Autoridad Metropolitana de Autobuses*) ✉ *San Juan* ☎ *787/294–0500* 🌐 *act.dtop.pr.gov.*

CAR

Although car rentals are inexpensive (as little as $20 per day if booked in advance), we don't recommend that you rent a car if confining your stay to

San Juan. (At most, you might want to rent a car for a day trip elsewhere on the island.) Parking is difficult—particularly in Old San Juan (watch out for resident-only parking on some streets—you will get a ticket if you park in the wrong spot)—and most hotels charge hefty rates (at least $20 per day); also, traffic can be very heavy. With relatively reasonable taxi and Uber rates, it simply doesn't pay to rent a car unless you are leaving the city.

The main highways into San Juan are Route 26 from the east (it becomes the Baldorioty de Castro Expressway after passing the airport), Route 22 (José de Diego Expressway) from the west, and Route 52 (Luis A. Ferré Expressway) from the south.

MAJOR CAR-RENTAL CONTACTS Avis. ✉ *San Juan International Airport, Terminal Bldg., Carolina* ☎ *787/253–5926* 🌐 *www.avis.com.* **Hertz.** ✉ *Luis Muñoz Marín International Airport, Salvador Caro Ave., Carolina* ☎ *787/791–0840* 🌐 *www.hertz.com.* **National.** ✉ *Luis Muñoz Marín International Airport, Salvador Caro Ave., Carolina* ☎ *787/791–1805* 🌐 *www.nationalcar.com.* **Thrifty.** ✉ *10030 Marginal Los Angeles, Carolina* ☎ *787/253–2525* 🌐 *www.thrifty.com.*

LOCAL AGENCIES Charlie Car Rental. ✉ *6050 Isla Verde Ave., Carolina* ☎ *787/728–2418* 🌐 *www.charliecars.com.* **Vias.** ✉ *Hotel Villa del Sol, 4 Rosa St., Isla Verde* ☎ *787/791–4120* 🌐 *www.viascarrental.com.*

TAXI

Taxis turísticos—painted white, with the *garita* (sentry box) logo—run from the airport and cruise-ship piers to Isla Verde, Condado, Ocean Park, and Old San Juan. They charge set rates based on zones (usually $10–$20); make sure to agree on a price before you get inside. City tours start at $36 per hour.

Although you can hail cabs on the street, virtually every San Juan hotel has taxis waiting outside to transport guests; if none are available, have one called. (Once called, taxis may charge an extra $1 for the pickup.)

Uber, the popular ride-sharing company, operates in major cities throughout Puerto Rico. Fares are generally lower than those of traditional taxis, and cars are readily available. Uber is also authorized to pick up at the airport.

You'll find electric scooters parked on sidewalks throughout San Juan. Download the Skootel app, to activate your scooter, but keep in mind you must have a valid driver's license. You can zoom through San Juan for about 30 cents a minute.

CONTACTS Go Puerto Rico Shuttle. ✉ *Calle Sirio, Urb Los Angeles #80, Isla Verde* ☎ *787/400–2100* 🌐 *www.puertoricoshuttle.com.* **Metro Taxi.** ✉ *959 Calle Suau, Miramar* ☎ *787/945–5555.*

TRAIN

The Tren Urbano, an elevated light-rail system, travels throughout the metropolitan area, with stops at the University of Puerto Rico and Bayamón. It doesn't stop near the main tourist areas or at the airport, though, so you're unlikely to ride it on a typical visit. The fare is 75¢, which includes transfers to city buses. The system runs 5:30 am–11 pm and is operated by the Alternativa de Transporte Integrado (ATI).

Beaches

Just because you're staying in the city doesn't mean you'll have to forgo time on *la playa*. Indeed, San Juan's beaches are among the island's best. With 365 different beaches in Puerto Rico, choosing where to spread out your towel might seem like a daunting task, but that decision is easier now that seven have been designated with a Blue Flag. Chosen by the Foundation for Environmental Education, a nonprofit agency, Blue Flag beaches have to meet more than 30 criteria, focusing on water quality, the presence of a trained staff, and the availability of facilities such as water fountains and restrooms.

Two beaches on the east side of the island, Seven Seas in Fajardo and Luquillo Beach, made the cut. More surprisingly, two of the beaches are in San Juan: Balneario El Escambrón in Puerta de Tierra and Balneario de Carolina in Isla Verde. A fifth is Punta Salinas in nearby Toa Baja. This means that five of Puerto Rico's finest beaches are within an hour's drive of the capital. The other two Blue Flag beaches are in the west and south: Boquerón in Cabo Rojo and Pelicano Beach in Ponce.

Hotels

San Juan prides itself on its plentiful clean and comfortable accommodations, and hoteliers, by and large, aim to please. Big hotels and resorts, several with casinos, and a few smaller establishments line the sandy strands along Condado and Isla Verde. If you want to do little but relax on the beach, enjoy ample resort amenities, and partake in lively nightlife, either area is a good option. Between them, the Ocean Park neighborhood has homey inns, as do Miramar and Santurce, although the latter two areas aren't directly on the beach. They're likely to be more popular with independent travelers, artistic types, and anyone who wants to stay a little bit off the beaten tourist track.

What It Costs in U.S. Dollars

$	$$	$$$	$$$$
LODGING FOR TWO			
under $150	$150–$250	$251–$350	over $350

Old San Juan has fewer lodging options, only one of which has a casino, but many of the city's best boutique hotels are here. If you're a history or architecture buff or looking for a unique romantic experience, definitely stay in one of these colonial inns; many of their structures date back several hundred years, and you'll feel as if you've been transported to another era (even though most have flat-screen televisions and Wi-Fi). Keep in mind, though, that these buildings are old, and Puerto Rico's climate is tropical, so minor inconveniences like room mustiness or ongoing repairs are possible. Also consider Old San Juan if you're in town for a cruise, since the main cruise piers are within walking distance. Wherever you stay, keep in mind that all guest rooms are now no-smoking.

Staying in a self-catering apartment or condo has advantages over a resort, especially for families, mainly due to the considerable autonomy of more residential lodging. For example, the option to cook for yourself means you can eat when and what you want. Several companies represent such properties in San Juan. When booking, be sure to ask about maid service, swimming pools, and any other amenities that are important to you.

Airbnb rentals are abundant in San Juan (and throughout Puerto Rico) and have become very popular. You can rent everything from from low-budget apartments to mansions near the beach to colonial homes in Old San Juan. If you decide to rent through Airbnb or any other online service, ensure that you complete your rental through the company; you run greater risks and do not receive any buyer protection by making side deals with home or apartment owners.

PRICES

Room rates generally aren't inexpensive: for a high-end beach-resort room, expect to pay $250–$350 for a double in high season (roughly mid-November–mid-April); for smaller inns and hotels, doubles start at $100–$150. As a rule, if your room is less than $50 in high season, then the quality of the hotel might be questionable. Some hotels include breakfast in their basic rates, but most hotels offer no other meal plans. There are no all-inclusive resorts in San Juan.

⇨ *Hotel reviews have been shortened. For full information, visit Fodors.com.*

APARTMENT RENTALS

Dreamer's Welcome

$$ | **APARTMENT** | The owners of The Dreamcatcher have expanded their portfolio to include stunning properties throughout San Juan as well as the rain forest. *Rooms from: $150* ✉ *San Juan* 🌐 *www.dreamerswelcome.com.*

Restaurants

In cosmopolitan San Juan, European, Asian, Middle Eastern, and chic fusion eateries vie for your attention, with family-owned restaurants specializing in seafood or *comida criolla* (Puerto Rican food). U.S. chains such as McDonald's and Subway compete with chains like Pollo Tropical and El Mesón, which specialize in local cuisine. Many celebrity chefs have restaurants in the city's large hotels, but don't be shy about venturing into stand-alone establishments—a lot of them are concentrated in Condado, Old San Juan, and Santurce.

Locals prefer to dine in Santurce, an off-the-beaten-path area known for its art galleries and an emerging culinary scene spearheaded by the island's young chefs. Here you'll find artisanal-style cuisine—crop-to-cup coffee, rustic homemade pizzas, creative vegetarian food, and farm-to-table restaurants. There's a radiant pride in what the local land can provide, and these enthusiastic restaurateurs are redefining what Puerto Rican food is, bite by tasty bite.

The dress code varies greatly from place to place, although a restaurant's price category can be taken as a good indication. For less expensive places anything but beachwear is fine; ritzier spots will expect collared shirts and long pants for men ("jacket and tie" requirements are rare) and chic attire for women. When in doubt, do as the Puerto Ricans often do: dress up.

For breakfast outside of your hotel, cafés or *panaderías* (local bakeries) are your best bets. It's rare for such establishments to close between breakfast and lunch; it's slightly more common for restaurants to close between lunch and dinner. Although some places don't accept reservations, it's always a good idea to make them for dinner whenever possible. This is especially true during the busy season from November through April and on weekends at any time of the year.

⇨ *Restaurant reviews have been shortened. For full information, visit Fodors.com.*

What It Costs in U.S. Dollars

$	$$	$$$	$$$$
AT DINNER			
under $12	$12–$20	$21–$30	over $30

Nightlife

From Thursday through Sunday it's as if there's a celebration going on nearly everywhere in San Juan. Be sure you dress to party, particularly on Friday and Saturday nights. Puerto Ricans have flair, and both men and women love dressing up to go out. Bars are usually casual, but if you're wearing jeans, sneakers, and a T-shirt, you may be refused entry at nightclubs and discos.

Well-dressed visitors and locals often mingle in the lobby bars of large hotels,

If You Like

Architecture

San Juan has been under construction for nearly 500 years, as evinced by the city's wide range of architectural styles. The Old City's Spanish colonial row houses—brick construction with plaster facades painted in pastel blues, oranges, and yellows—line narrow streets and alleys paved with *adoquines* (blue-gray stones originally used as ballast in Spanish ships). Several churches, including the Catedral de San Juan Bautista and Iglesia de San José, were built in the 16th century, the latter in the ornate Gothic style. The massive, white marble Capitolio, home of Puerto Rico's legislature, was completed in 1929. Firmly rooted in the 21st century are the gleaming high-rise resorts along the beaches in Condado and Isla Verde and the glistening steel-and-glass towers in the business and financial district of Hato Rey.

Music

Music is a source of Puerto Rican pride and an inescapable part of nearly every festival, holiday, party, and even political protest. The brash Latin sound is best characterized in the music and dance of *salsa*, which shares not only its name with the word "sauce" but also its zesty, hot flavor. A fusion of West African percussion, jazz (especially swing and big band), and other Latin beats (mambo, merengue, flamenco, cha-cha, rumba), salsa music is sexy and primal. Dancers are expected to let go of all inhibitions. Most nightspots, including restaurants, offer live music several nights a week, especially Friday and Saturday.

Nightlife

As befits a metropolitan capital city, San Juan has a wide variety of restaurants and bars for people with all sorts of palates and party habits. Old San Juan, Condado, and the up-and-coming arts district of Santurce are big nighttime destinations. Many establishments have set their tables on terraces, the beach, indoor patios, or streetside to take advantage of the late-night atmosphere. Clubs and bars stay open into the wee hours of morning, closing only when the last patron leaves.

many of which feature bands in the evening. Some hotels also have clubs with shows and/or dancing; the cover generally starts at $10. Casino rules have been relaxed, injecting life into what was once a conservative hotel-gaming scene, but you still won't be allowed in wearing a tank top or shorts. There are more games, plus such gambling perks as free drinks and live music.

In Old San Juan, Calle San Sebastián is lined with bars and restaurants. Salsa music blaring from jukeboxes in cut-rate pool halls competes with mellow Latin jazz in top-flight nightspots. Mid-January sees the Fiestas de la Calle San Sebastián, one of the Caribbean's best street parties.

Young professionals as well as a slightly older bohemian crowd fill Santurce, San Juan's historical downtown area, until the wee hours. The revitalized Plaza del Mercado (Calle Dos Hermanos at Calle Capital) has structures—many painted in bright colors—dating from the 1930s or earlier. On weekend nights, the area's streets are closed to vehicular traffic. You can wander from dive bars to trendy nightspots and sway to music that pours

Did You Know?

Old San Juan is over 500 years old, making it the oldest city under the United States jurisdiction.

from countless open-air establishments and the marketplace's front plaza.

For Spanish-speaking visitors, the weekend section of Spanish-language newspaper *El Nuevo Día* lists activities; the paper also gives a weekly rundown of events on its website (🌐 *endi.com*). Discover Puerto Rico is a great resource in English (🌐 *discoverpuertorico.com*).

Performing Arts

San Juan is arguably one of the most important cultural centers of the Caribbean, known both for its homegrown arts and the healthy influx of visiting artists that the local population supports. The city hosts the Puerto Rico Symphony Orchestra, the world-renowned Pablo Casals classical music festival in winter, and an annual series of opera concerts. Many hit plays in New York and other large markets are produced locally, and there are often three or four other local theatrical productions taking place on any given weekend, many of them downright adventurous.

MAJOR EVENTS

The Casals Festival

FESTIVALS | The Casals Festival has been bringing some of the most important figures in classical music to San Juan ever since Pablo Casals, the famous cellist, conductor, and composer, started the festival in 1957. Casals went on to direct it until his death in 1973, and it has continued to serve as a vibrant stage for top-notch classical performers since then. Most of the shows are held at the Centro de Bellas Artes Luis A. Ferré, but performances are also at the University of Puerto Rico and other venues. The festival takes place from mid-February through mid-March. Tickets are available at the box office of the Centro de Bellas Artes Luis A. Ferré. ✉ *Luis A. Ferré Performing Arts Center, 22 Av. Ponce de León, Santurce* ☎ *787/918–1106*.

Saborea Puerto Rico

CULTURAL FESTIVALS | If you love all things gastronomy, you'll thoroughly enjoy the Saborea Puerto Rico food festival held every spring. This highly anticipated, two-day, culinary extravaganza draws chefs from across the island and abroad. Watch them prepare dishes at the demo kitchen, sample an array of foods at the tasting pavilion, and listen to live music—all while enjoying the unbeatable beachfront setting. ✉ *Vivo Beach Club, Calle Av. Boca de Cangrejos, 7000 Carr. 187 RR2, Isla Verde* 🌐 *www.saboreapuertorico.com*.

TICKETS

Two major outlets sell tickets for events throughout Puerto Rico.

Ticket Center

With ticket counters available in many of the malls on the island, Ticket Center is a convenient way to score seats to most large-scale events. ☎ *787/792–5000* 🌐 *tcpr.com*.

Ticketpop

This outfit makes it fast and easy to purchase tickets online for major concerts, sporting events, and other shows. ☎ *866/994–0001, 787/294–0001* 🌐 *ticketpop.com*.

Shopping

In Old San Juan, Calle Fortaleza and Calle San Francisco have everything from T-shirt emporiums to jewelry stores to shops that specialize in made-to-order Panama hats. Running perpendicular to those streets is Calle Cristo, with factory-outlet stores, including Coach and Tommy Hilfiger. On weekends, artisans sell their wares at stalls around Paseo de la Princesa.

Just as in most other American cities, however, the real shopping occurs in the mall, and Plaza Las Américas—the largest in the Caribbean—is not to be missed. Known to locals simply as

"Plaza," it's often host to crafts fairs, art exhibitions, antiques shows, live Latin music, and pageants, depending on the time of year. For high-end shopping at stores like Louis Vuitton, Gucci, Hugo Boss, Carolina Herrera, and Jimmy Choo head to the newer Mall of San Juan.

Thanks to Puerto Rico's vibrant arts scene, numerous galleries and studios are opening, and many are doing so in Santurce, Puerta de Tierra, and other neighborhoods outside the walls of Old San Juan.

Activities

Many of San Juan's most enjoyable outdoor activities take place in and around the water. With miles of beach stretching across Isla Verde, Ocean Park, and Condado, there's a full range of water sports, including sailing, kayaking, windsurfing, paddleboarding, kiteboarding, Jet Skiing, deep-sea fishing, scuba diving, and snorkeling.

Land-based activities include biking, tennis, and walking or jogging at local parks. With a bit of effort—meaning a short drive out of the city—you'll discover a world of championship golf courses and rain-forest trails perfect for hiking. Baseball is big in Puerto Rico, and the players are world-class; many are recruited from local teams to play in the U.S. major leagues. The season runs October through February, and games are played in venues all over the island.

BIKING

Automobile traffic makes bike travel somewhat risky, mostly because most streets lack dedicated bike lanes—plus, all those fumes can be hard to take. That said, recreational cyclists are increasingly donning their helmets and wheeling through the streets, albeit with great care.

Your best bet for a safe and enjoyable experience is to book a bike tour through an outfitter. One popular 45-minute journey takes riders from the cobblestone streets of Old San Juan to Condado. It passes El Capitolio and runs through either Parque del Tercer Milenio (oceanside) or Parque Luis Muñoz Rivera, by way of the Caribe Hilton Hotel and over Puente Dos Hermanos (Dos Hermanos Bridge) onto Avenida Ashford. The truly ambitious can continue east to Ocean Park, Isla Verde, and right on out of town to the eastern community of Piñones and its beachside bike path.

Rent the Bicycle
BIKING | For about $40 per day, this friendly operation offers bicycle rental with free delivery to all major San Juan hotels. They also offer guided tours of Old San Juan and greater San Juan beaches and parks. The bilingual guides are authorized by the National Park Service to give tours of the forts. ✉ *Capitolio Plaza, 100 Calle del Muelle, Suite 205, Old San Juan* ☎ *787/661–2728* 🌐 *www.rentthebicycle.com.*

FISHING

Puerto Rico's waters are home to large game fish such as snook, wahoo, dorado, tuna, and barracuda; as many as 30 world records for catches have been set off the island's shores. Prices for fishing expeditions vary, but they tend to include all your bait and tackle, as well as refreshments, and start at $600 (for a boat with as many as six people) for a half-day trip to around $1,000 for a full day, or around $200 per person for a full day on a split charter.

GOLF

Puerto Rico is the birthplace of golf legend and raconteur Chi Chi Rodriguez, and he had to hone his craft somewhere. The island has more than a dozen courses, including some of championship caliber; several make good day trips from San Juan. Be sure to call ahead for details on reserving a tee time; hours vary, and several hotel courses allow only guests to play or give preference to them. Greens fees start at $25 and go as high as $190.

Three golf clubs are within fairly easy striking distance of San Juan. The two 18-hole golf courses at TPC Dorado Beach are just west of San Juan. More options lie east of the city. The Palmas del Mar Golf Club at the Wyndham Candelero Beach Resort and the spectacular Wyndham Grand Río Mar Golf & Beach Resort both have two 18-hole courses.

HIKING

El Yunque is the only tropical rain forest within the U.S. National Forest system. The park is officially known as the Bosque Nacional del Caribe (Caribbean National Forest) and is a great day trip from San Juan, about an hour's drive east.

SURFING

Although the west-coast beaches around Isabela and Rincón are considered *the* places to surf in Puerto Rico, San Juan was actually the place where the sport got its start on the island. In 1958, legendary surfers Gary Hoyt and José Rodríguez Reyes began surfing at the beach in front of Bus Stop 2½, facing El Capitolio. This spot is known for big waves, but the conditions must be nearly perfect to surf it. Today, many surfers head to Puerta de Tierra and a spot known as La Ocho (in front of Bus Stop 8). Another, called the Pressure Point, is behind the Caribe Hilton Hotel.

In Condado you can surf or body board La Punta, a reef break behind the Presbyterian Hospital. In Isla Verde, white water on the horizon means that the waves are good at Pine Grove, the beach break near the Ritz-Carlton. East of the city, in Piñones, the Caballo has deep-to-shallow-water shelf waves that require a big-wave board known as a "gun." Surf culture frowns upon aficionados who divulge the best spots to outsiders; if you're lucky, though, maybe you'll make a few friends who'll let you in on where to find the best waves.

Tours

Old San Juan Walk and Taste Tour
FOOD AND DRINK TOURS | Let history and culinary experts take you on a 3½ hour walking tour of Old San Juan. You'll stop at many of the best restaurants, bars, and dessert shops while learning about Puerto Rican culture and food. ✉ *501 C. Norzagaray, Old San Juan* ☎ *787/598–6008* 🌐 *thespoonexperience.com* 🎫 *$129.*

PR Historic Building Society
SPECIAL-INTEREST TOURS | Architect Andy Rivera gives fascinating architecture tours in San Juan. ✉ *Old San Juan* 🌐 *www.prhbds.org.*

Visitor Information

You'll find Puerto Rico Tourism Company information officers (identified by their caps and shirts with a company patch) near the baggage-claim areas at Luis Muñoz Marín International Airport. Information officers are also posted around Old San Juan (near the cruise-ship piers and at the Catedral de San Juan Bautista) during the day. Discover Puerto Rico, the island's destination marketing organization (DMO) whose mission is to promote Puerto Rico as a premier destination, also has up-to-date travel information on its website.

In Old San Juan, the tourism headquarters is at the old city jail, La Princesa, and its main information bureau is opposite Pier 1 on Calle Tanca at Calle Gilberto Concepción de Gracia. Pick up a free copy of *¡Qué Pasa!*, the official visitor guide. In addition, La Oficina de Turismo del Municipio de San Juan, run by the city, has information bureaus in Old San Juan and in Condado.

CONTACTS Discover Puerto Rico DMO. ✉ *Ochoa Bldg., Calle Tanca and Calle Comercio, across from Pier 1, Old San Juan* ☎ *787/721–2400* 🌐 *www.discoverpuertorico.com.* **Oficina de Turismo del Municipio de San Juan.** ✉ *Alcaldía, Plaza de Armas, 153 Calle San Francisco, Old San Juan* ☎ *787/480–2548.*

Old San Juan

Old San Juan's 16th-century cobblestone streets, ornate Spanish town houses with wrought-iron balconies, ancient plazas, and eclectic museums together form a repository of the island's colorful history. Founded in 1521 by the Spanish explorer Juan Ponce de León, Old San Juan sits on an islet separated from the "new" parts of the city by a couple of miles and a few centuries. Today, however, it is culturally youthful and vibrant, reflecting the sensibilities of the stylish professionals, bohemian art crowd, and university students who people its streets. You'll find more street-front cafés and innovative restaurants, more contemporary art galleries, and more musicians playing in plazas than anywhere else in San Juan.

Old San Juan slopes north, uphill, to Calle Norzagaray, which runs along the Atlantic shoreline and connects the twin fortifications of Castillo San Cristóbal and El Morro. On the north side of Calle Norzagaray you'll find a small neighborhood wedged between the city walls and the ocean—this is La Perla, a rough area you'd be wise to avoid. The west end of Old San Juan overlooks the bay, and it's here that the rugged, towering walls of the original city are most evident. On the south side, along Calle Gilberto Concepción de Gracia (also called Calle la Marina), you'll find cruise ships and commercial piers jutting into San Juan Harbor.

GETTING AROUND

If you try to explore Old San Juan by car, you'll likely find yourself sitting in traffic much of the day—especially on weekends, when police change traffic patterns. Old San Juan is a walking neighborhood, with narrow one-way streets, narrower alleys, little parking, and sights and shops packed together in an area hardly larger than one square mile. Some of the streets are steep and many are paved with cobblestones, so wear comfortable shoes as well as a hat and sunscreen—and drink plenty of water.

In Old San Juan, free trolleys can take you around, and the tourist board can provide you with a copy of *¡Qué Pasa!* as well as a map that contains a self-guided walking tour.

Ferry: The ferry between Old San Juan and Cataño is operated by the Autoridad de Transporte Marítimo. It costs a mere 50¢ one-way and runs every 30 minutes daily 6 am–10 pm. The ferry, which departs Pier 2, is the one to take if you wish to visit the Bacardí rum factory.

Parking: If you can't avoid taking a car into Old San Juan, park at La Puntilla, at the head of Paseo de la Princesa. It's an outdoor lot with the cheapest rates, at less than $5 for all-day parking. You could also try the Felisa Rincón de Gautier lot on Calle Gilberto Concepción de Gracia or the Frank Santaella (known as "Doña Fela" to locals) lot between Paseo de Covadonga and Calle Gilberto Concepción de Gracia. Parking starts at around $2 or so for the first hour. Many lots open early and close late; some, like Doña Fela, are even open 24 hours.

Trolleys: Free trolleys swing through Old San Juan all day, every day; they depart the main bus terminal area across from Pier 4 and take one of three routes. One route heads north to Calle Norzagaray, then west to El Morro, dropping you off at the long footpath leading to the fort.

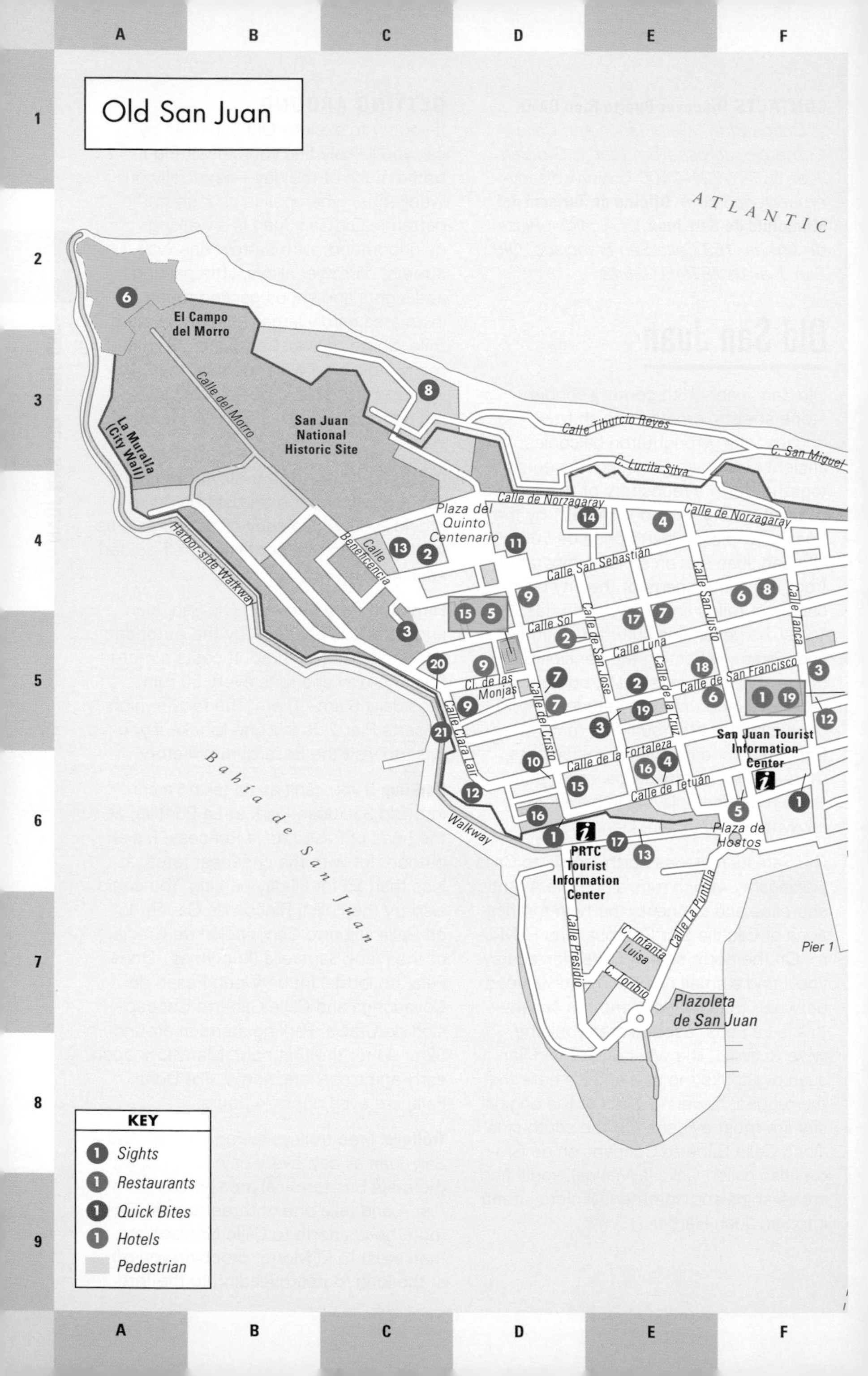
Old San Juan
A
B
C
D
E
F
1
2
3
4
5
6
7
8
9
ATLANTIC
El Campo del Morro
Calle del Morro
La Muralla (City Wall)
San Juan National Historic Site
Harbor-side Walkway
Calle Tiburcio Reyes
C. Lucila Silva
C. San Miguel
Calle de Norzagaray
Plaza del Quinto Centenario
Calle Beneficencia
Calle San Sebastián
Calle Sol
Calle de San José
Calle San Justo
Calle Tanca
Calle Luna
Calle de San Francisco
Calle de la Cruz
Cl. de las Monjas
Calle del Cristo
Calle Clara Lair
Calle de la Fortaleza
Calle de Tetuán
San Juan Tourist Information Center
Plaza de Hostos
Walkway
PRTC Tourist Information Center
Bahía de San Juan
Calle Presidio
C. Intanta Luisa
C. Toribio
Calle La Puntilla
Pier 1
Plazoleta de San Juan
KEY
Sights
Restaurants
Quick Bites
Hotels
Pedestrian

Sights

1 Capilla del Cristo........ D6
2 Casa Alcadía de San Juan................ E5
3 Casa Blanca.............. C5
4 Casa de Ramón Power y Giralt........... E6
5 Castillo San Cristóbal..... I4
6 Castillo San Felipe del Morro A2
7 Catedral de San Juan Bautista...... D5
8 Cementerio Santa María Magdalena de Pazzis ... C3
9 Fundación Felisa Rincón de Gautier D5
10 Fundación Nacional Para la Cultura Popular.................. D6
11 Iglesia de San José D4
12 La Fortaleza D6
13 Museo de las Américas C4
14 Museo de San Juan..... E4
15 Museo La Casa del Libro.................. D6
16 Parque de las Palomas D6
17 Paseo de la Princesa.... E6
18 Plaza Colón.............. G5
19 Plaza de Armas E5
20 Plazuela La Rogativa C5
21 Puerta de San Juan C5

Restaurants

1 Bodega Chic.............. F5
2 Café Berlin............... G5
3 Cafeteria Mallorca F5
4 Caficultura............... G5
5 Carli's Fine Bistro & Piano........... F6
6 Casa Cortés ChocoBar................ E5
7 Deaverdura............... E4
8 El Jibarito F4
9 El Patio de Sam D4
10 La Madre G5
11 Marmalade............... G5
12 Pirilo Pizza Rustica F5
13 Princesa Cocina Creativa......... E6
14 Raíces.................... G5
15 Santísimo D5
16 Señor Paleta E6
17 St. Germain Bistro & Café............ E5
18 Stuffed Avocado......... E5
19 Trois Cent Onze F5

Quick Bites

1 Café Cuatro Sombras ... F6
2 Café Don Ruiz C4
3 Café 4 Estaciones........ E5

Hotels

1 CasaBlanca Hotel G5
2 Decanter Hotel........... E5
3 El Colonial Hotel......... G5
4 The Gallery Inn........... E4
5 Hotel El Convento....... D5
6 La Terraza de San Juan............. F4
7 Palacio Provincial D5
8 Sheraton Old San Juan Hotel.......... G6
9 Villa Herencia Hotel D5

Then it retraces its route past Castillo San Cristóbal, west to Plaza de Armas, east on Fortaleza, west on Recinto Sur, and then back along Calle Gilberto Concepción de Gracia to the piers. A second route takes you east to the Puerta de Tierra district, then via Castillo San Cristóbal to El Morro, then via Calle Norzagaray and Plaza Colón and back to the piers. The third route follows a figure eight from Pier 4 north on Tanca, then west along San Francisco and east on Fortaleza, returning via Plaza Colón. The trolleys make regular stops (at 24 signs marked "Parada") along the way. When you're finished touring, taxis can be found in several spots: in front of Pier 2, near the Catedral de San Juan Bautista, on the Plaza de Armas, or in Plaza Colón. A map of trolley routes is available from the Puerto Rico Tourism Company information offices.

CONTACTS Autoridad de Transporte Marítimo. ☎ *787/497–7740.*

SAFETY

Old San Juan is generally safe, but keep in mind that pickpockets visit the same places as tourists. Keep money and credit cards out of back pockets, and avoid carrying open handbags. Avoid the Perla district and, if walking, stick to well-policed areas and well-lighted streets by night.

TIMING

Old San Juan is a small neighborhood, approximately seven city blocks north to south and eight east to west. In strictly geographical terms, it's easily traversed in a day. But to truly appreciate the numerous plazas, museums, boutiques, galleries, and cafés you need two or three days.

⇨ *For a great half-day itinerary, see "Walking Old San Juan."*

Sights

Capilla del Cristo

RELIGIOUS BUILDING | According to legend, in 1753 a young horseman named Baltazar Montañez got carried away during festivities in honor of San Juan Bautista (St. John the Baptist), raced down Calle Cristo, and plunged over its steep precipice. Historical records maintain the man died, but legend contends that he lived. (Another version of the story has it that the horse miraculously stopped before plunging over the cliff.) Regardless, this chapel was built partly to prevent further calamities. Inside is a small silver altar dedicated to the Christ of Miracles. Above the altar hang two religious paintings by Puerto Rico's famous painter José Campeche. You can peer in through the wrought-iron gates, which are usually closed. ✉ *Calle Cristo, at the end, Old San Juan* 🎫 *Free.*

Casa Alcaldía de San Juan (*San Juan City Hall*)

GOVERNMENT BUILDING | San Juan's city hall was built between 1602 and 1789. In 1841, extensive alterations made it resemble Madrid's city hall, with arcades, towers, balconies, and an inner courtyard. Renovations have refreshed the facade and some interior rooms, but the architecture remains true to its colonial style. Only the patios are open to public viewings. A municipal tourist information center and an art gallery with rotating exhibits are in the lobby. Call ahead to schedule a free tour. ✉ *153 Calle San Francisco, Plaza de Armas, Old San Juan* ☎ *787/480–2910* 🎫 *Free* ⏲ *Closed weekends.*

Casa Blanca

HISTORIC HOME | The original structure here was a wooden house built in 1521 as a home for Ponce de León; he died in Cuba without ever living here. His descendants occupied the house's sturdier replacement, a lovely colonial mansion with tile floors and beamed ceilings, for more

It's easy to see why San Cristóbal fortress was once called "the Gibraltar of the West Indies."

than 250 years. It was the home of the U.S. Army commander in Puerto Rico from the end of the Spanish-American War in 1898 to 1966. Several rooms decorated with colonial-era furnishings are open to the public. The lush garden, complete with watchtower, is a quiet place to unwind. ✉ *1 Calle San Sebastián, Old San Juan* ☎ *787/725–1454* 🎫 *$3* ⏲ *Closed Mon. and Tues.*

Casa de Ramón Power y Giralt

HISTORIC HOME | FAMILY | The restored home of 18th-century naval hero Don Ramón Power y Giralt is now the headquarters of the Conservation Trust of Puerto Rico. On-site are several displays highlighting the physical, cultural, and historical importance of land and properties on the island under the trust's aegis. The goal of the trust is to increase the amount of protected lands in Puerto Rico from (currently) 8% to 33% by the year 2033. Displays are in Spanish, but there are note cards in English for the changing exhibitions. A gift shop sells toys, Puerto Rican candies, and eco-friendly souvenirs. ✉ *155 Calle Tetuán, Old San Juan* ☎ *787/722–5882* 🌐 *paralanaturaleza.org* 🎫 *Free* ⏲ *Closed Sun. and Mon.*

★ Castillo San Cristóbal

MILITARY SIGHT | FAMILY | This huge stone fortress, built between 1634 and 1783, guarded the city from land attacks from the east. The largest Spanish fortification in the New World, San Cristóbal was known in the 17th and 18th centuries as "the Gibraltar of the West Indies." Five freestanding structures divided by dry moats are connected by tunnels. You're free to explore the gun turrets (with cannon in situ), officers' quarters, re-created 18th-century barracks, and gloomy passageways. Along with El Morro, San Cristóbal is a National Historic Site administered by the U.S. National Park Service; it's a UNESCO World Heritage site as well. Rangers conduct tours in Spanish and English. ✉ *Calle Norzagaray at Av. Muñoz Rivera, Old San Juan* ☎ *787/729–6777* 🌐 *www.nps.gov/saju* 🎫 *$10, includes Castillo San Felipe del Morro.*

Old San Juan's Cementerio Santa María Magdelena de Pazzis is one of the city's best-kept secrets and offers a peaceful respite from the bustle of the busy streets.

★ **Castillo San Felipe del Morro** (*El Morro*)
MILITARY SIGHT | **FAMILY** | At the northwestern tip of Old San Juan, El Morro (the promontory) was built by the Spaniards between 1539 and 1790. Rising 140 feet above the sea, the massive six-level fortress was built to protect the port and has a commanding view of the harbor. It is a labyrinth of cannon batteries, ramps, barracks, turrets, towers, and tunnels, through which you're free to wander. The cannon emplacement walls and the dank secret passageways are a wonder of engineering. A small but enlightening museum displays ancient Spanish guns and other armaments, military uniforms, and blueprints for Spanish forts in the Americas, although Castillo San Cristóbal has more extensive and impressive exhibits. There's also a gift shop. The fort is a National Historic Site administered by the U.S. National Park Service, and a UNESCO World Heritage site as well. Various tours and a video are available in English. ✉ *Calle del Morro, Old San Juan* ☎ *787/729–6960* 🌐 *www.nps.gov/saju* 🎫 *$10, includes Castillo San Cristóbal.*

Catedral de San Juan Bautista
CHURCH | The Catholic shrine of Puerto Rico had humble beginnings in the early 1520s as a thatch-roofed wooden structure. After a hurricane destroyed the church, it was rebuilt in 1540, when it was given a graceful circular staircase and vaulted Gothic ceilings. Most of the work on the present cathedral, however, was done in the 19th century. The remains of Ponce de León are behind a marble tomb in the wall near the transept, on the north side. The trompe-l'oeil work on the inside of the dome is breathtaking. Unfortunately, many of the other frescoes have suffered water damage. ✉ *151 Calle Cristo, Old San Juan* ☎ *787/722–0861* 🎫 *$1 suggested donation.*

Cementerio Santa María Magdalena de Pazzis
CEMETERY | One of Old San Juan's best-kept secrets, this remarkable cemetery provides a peaceful respite from the bustle of the city. Sandwiched between El Morro and La Perla, it offers a panoramic

view of the Atlantic Ocean and an enviable resting place for the many notable figures fortunate enough to be buried here. Dating from the early 1800s, the cemetery was originally administered by Carmelite nuns. Today you can stop by the ornate tombs (many of which are topped with graceful marble sculptures) to pay your respects to an illustrious group of Puerto Rican political figures, intellectuals, artists, and revolutionaries, including José Celso Barbosa, José Ferrer, Pedro Albizu Campos, Rafael Hernández, and Ricardo Alegría.

⚠ **While a robust police presence has made this area bordering La Perla safer than it once was, it's still best to avoid coming after hours or at night.** ✉ *West end of Calle Norzagaray, Old San Juan* 🎫 *Free.*

Fundación Felisa Rincón de Gautier
OTHER MUSEUM | This tiny but fascinating museum honors Felisa Rincón de Gautier, who served as San Juan's mayor from 1946 to 1968. Throughout her life, "Doña Felisa" worked tirelessly on various public causes, including women's voting rights and health care for the poor. Her preschools, known as Escuelas Maternas, were used as the model for the United States' Head Start program. Extremely well connected politically, both on the island and abroad, she was an egalitarian figure who rose to power at a time when women and politics were not mentioned in the same breath. Even if you have no interest in her story, stop by for a peek inside one of Old San Juan's historic houses. Guided tours in English or Spanish are available. ✉ *51 Caleta de San Juan, Old San Juan* ☎ *787/724–7239* 🌐 *www.museofelisarincon.com* 🎫 *Free* 🕓 *Closed Sun. and Mon.*

Fundación Nacional Para la Cultura Popular
PERFORMANCE VENUE | This nonprofit foundation serves many functions: museum; performance space; dance and music school; and archive preserving Puerto Rican contributions to music, dance, television, theater, film, and other aspects of culture. In a 300-year-old building once used by the Spanish as a meteorological lookout, you can view rotating exhibitions, hear live Latin music in the evenings, or take a *bomba* or *plena* dance class. A small store sells music by Puerto Ricans in every genre, from classical to salsa. Signed posters from El Gran Combo, Tito Puente, and Willie Colón—as well as Ricky Martin's platinum record—line the walls. Check the website or call ahead for the performance schedule. ✉ *56 Calle Fortaleza, Old San Juan* ☎ *787/724–7165* 🌐 *www.prpop.org* 🎫 *Free* 🕓 *Closed Sun. and Mon.*

Iglesia de San José
RELIGIOUS BUILDING | With its vaulted ceilings, this little church is a splendid example of 16th-century Spanish Gothic architecture. It was built under the supervision of Dominican friars in 1532, making it the second-oldest church in the western hemisphere. The body of Ponce de León, the Spanish explorer who came to the New World seeking the Fountain of Youth, was buried here for almost three centuries before being moved to the Catedral de San Juan Bautista in 1909. ✉ *Calle San Sebastián, Plaza de San José, Old San Juan* ☎ *787/918–3800* 🌐 *www.iglesiasanjosepr.org.*

La Fortaleza
GOVERNMENT BUILDING | Sitting atop the fortified city walls overlooking the harbor, La Fortaleza was built between 1533 and 1540 as a fortress, but it proved insufficient, mainly because it was built inside the bay. It was attacked numerous times and occupied twice, by the British in 1598 and the Dutch in 1625. When the city's other fortifications were finished, this became the governor's palace. Changes made over the past four centuries have resulted in the current eclectic yet eye-pleasing collection of marble and mahogany, medieval towers, and stained-glass galleries. It is still the official residence of the island's governor, making it the western hemisphere's

oldest executive mansion in continuous use. Guided tours of the gardens and exterior are conducted several times a day in English and Spanish; call ahead, as the schedule changes daily. Proper attire is required: no sleeveless shirts or very short shorts. Tours begin near the main gate in a yellow building called the Real Audiencia, housing the Oficina Estatal de Conservación Histórica (State Historic Preservation Office). ✉ *West end of Calle Fortaleza, Old San Juan* ☎ *787/721–7000* 🌐 *www.fortaleza.pr.gov* 🎫 *Free* 🕒 *Closed weekends.*

Museo de las Américas

ART MUSEUM | On the second floor of the imposing former military barracks, Cuartel de Ballajá, this museum houses four permanent exhibits covering folk art, African and Native American heritage, and colonization. You'll also find temporary exhibitions of works by regional and international artists. A wide range of handicrafts is available in the gift shop. Before visiting, it's best to check the website for current hours. ✉ *Calle Norzagaray and Calle del Morro, Old San Juan* ☎ *787/724–5052* 🌐 *www.museolasamericas.org* 🎫 *$6* 🕒 *Closed Mon. and Tues.*

Museo de San Juan

ART MUSEUM | A bustling marketplace in 1857, this handsome building now houses the small San Juan Museum. You'll find rotating exhibits of Puerto Rican art, plus tableaux and audiovisual shows that present the island's history. Concerts and other cultural events take place in the huge interior courtyard. ✉ *150 Calle Norzagaray, at Calle MacArthur, Old San Juan* ☎ *787/480–3530* 🎫 *Free* 🕒 *Closed Mon. and Tues.*

Museo La Casa del Libro

HISTORY MUSEUM | Dedicated to the artistry of the printed word, this museum counts among its holdings approximately 400 books printed before the 15th century—one of the larger such collections in the western hemisphere. It also owns two royal decrees from King Ferdinand and Queen Isabella that date from 1493, the year Columbus first reached Puerto Rico. Because the museum is in a temporary location while long-term restorations to the permanent building are underway, only a small portion of the 6,000-piece collection is on display. Highlights include a page from the Gutenberg Bible and a 12th-century lunar-cycle calendar. The gift shop has a terrific collection of posters that draws customers from all over the world. ✉ *255 Calle Cristo, Old San Juan* ☎ *787/723–0354* 🌐 *www.lacasadellibro.org* 🎫 *$4.50* 🕒 *Closed Sun. and Mon.*

Parque de las Palomas

CITY PARK | **FAMILY** | Thanks to a large stone wall with holes cut into it, hundreds of *palomas* (pigeons) roost in this small park, which is also often full of cooing local children chasing the well-fed birds. Bordering Old San Juan's Capilla del Cristo, the park also affords broad views over Paseo de la Princesa and the San Juan bay. ✉ *End of Calle Cristo, Old San Juan.*

Paseo de la Princesa

PROMENADE | Built in the mid-19th century to honor the Spanish princess of Asturias, this street has a broad pedestrian walkway and is spruced up with flowers, trees, benches, and streetlamps. Unfurling westward from Plaza del Inmigrante along the base of the fortified city walls, it leads to the Fuente Raíces, a striking fountain depicting the various ethnic groups of Puerto Rico. Take a seat, and watch boats zip across the water. Beyond the fountain is the beginning of Paseo del Morro, a well-paved shoreline path that hugs Old San Juan's walls, leading past the city gate at Calle San Juan and continuing to the tip of the headland, beneath El Morro. ✉ *Paseo de la Princesa, Old San Juan.*

Continued on page 76

WALKING OLD SAN JUAN

Old San Juan is Puerto Rico's quintessential colonial neighborhood. Narrow streets and plazas are still enclosed by thick fortress walls, and bougainvillea bowers spill over exquisite facades. A walk along streets paved with slate-blue cobblestones leads past colonial mansions, ancient churches, and intriguing museums and galleries. Vivacious restaurants and bars that teem with life young and old are always nearby, making it easy to refuel and reinvigorate anytime during your stroll.

by Christopher P. Baker

left, Old San Juan; top right, a view from El Morro; bottom right, dancers in front of Castillo San Cristóbal

A STROLL THROUGH OLD SAN JUAN

La Fortaleza

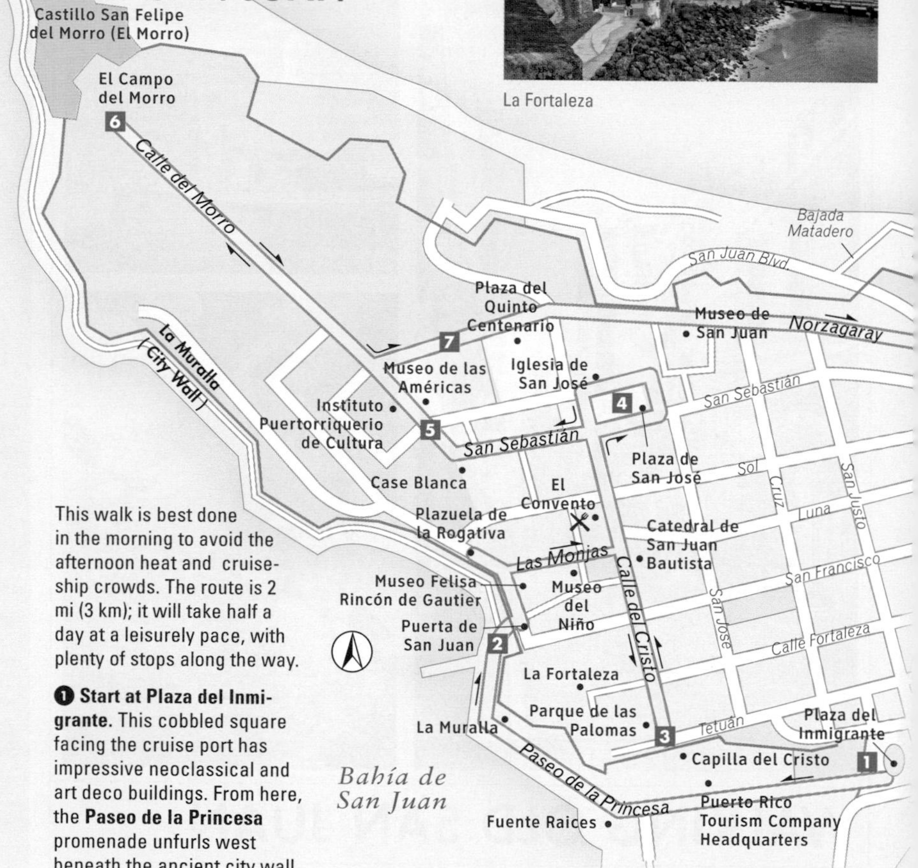

This walk is best done in the morning to avoid the afternoon heat and cruise-ship crowds. The route is 2 mi (3 km); it will take half a day at a leisurely pace, with plenty of stops along the way.

❶ **Start at Plaza del Inmigrante.** This cobbled square facing the cruise port has impressive neoclassical and art deco buildings. From here, the **Paseo de la Princesa** promenade unfurls west beneath the ancient city wall, **La Muralla**. Artisans set up stalls under the palms on weekends. Midway along the brick-paved walkway, stop to admire the **Fuente Raíces** monument and fountain: dolphins cavort at the feet of figures representing Puerto Rico's indigenous, Spanish, and African peoples.

Puerta de San Juan

❷ **Pass through the Puerta de San Juan.** This fortified entrance in La Muralla was built in 1520 and still retains its massive wooden gates, creaky on their ancient hinges. Immediately beyond, turn left and ascend to **Plazuela de la Rogativa**, a tiny plaza where a contemporary statue recalls the torch-lit procession that thwarted an English invasion in 1797. The harbor views are fantastic. Then, walk east one block to reach the **Catedral de San Juan Bautista**, the neoclassical 19th-century cathedral containing the mausoleum of Ponce de León.

❸ **Head south on Calle del Cristo.** Sloping gradually, this lovely street is lined with beautifully restored colonial mansions housing cafés, galleries, and boutiques. Passing Calle Fortaleza, note **La Fortaleza**, the official residence of the Puerto Rican Governor

Castillo San Cristóbal

Plazuela de la Rogativa

Catedral de San Juan Bautista

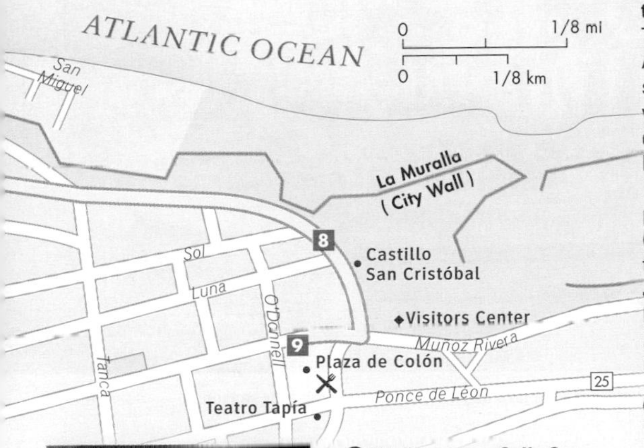

Castillo San Felipe del Morro

at the end of the street. Calle del Cristo ends at **Capilla del Cristo**, a chapel adorned within by silver *milagros* (token requests).

❹ **Return via Calle del Cristo and continue to Plaza de San José.** Catercorner to the cathedral you'll find **El Convento**, a former convent turned hotel, with an excellent tapas bar. At **Plaza de San José** visit the **Iglesia de San José**, a simple church dating from 1532 that is one of the oldest churches in the Western Hemisphere.

❺ **Walk west on Calle San Sebastián.** This narrow street with colonial mansions painted in vibrant pastels ends at the gleaming white **Casa Blanca**. The oldest continually occupied residence in the Americas was originally the home of Ponce de León. Today it's a delightful museum furnished with period pieces. The garden is a tranquil spot for contemplation.

❻ **Follow Calle del Morro north.** One block from Casa Blanca you'll emerge upon a broad grassy headland—the Campo del Morro—popular with kite-flying families. It's skewered by an arrow-straight gravel path that aims at the imposing **Castillo San Felipe del Morro (El Morro)**, guarding the harbor entrance. Allow one-hour to roam the small museum, turrets, labyrinthine tunnels, and six levels of ramparts soaring 140 feet above the ocean.

❼ **Retrace your steps and turn left on Calle Norzagaray.** This street runs atop the Atlantic shoreline, offering sweeping ocean vistas. On your right you'll pass the **Plaza del Quinto Centenario**, pinned by an impressive statue: the *Tótem Telúrico*. Beyond, stroll past the Galería Nacional (Convento de los Domínicos) to reach the **Museo de San Juan**. Housed in a former market, it traces the city's history and displays works by Puerto Rico's master painters.

❽ **Continue east to Castillo San Cristóbal.** Spanning 27 acres, this multitiered fortress was completed in 1771 with mighty bulwarks that protected the city from eastern attack by land. It features superb historical exhibits and reenactments by soldiers in period costumes.

❾ **Exit the castle, turn south and walk one block to Plaza de Colón**, This leafy square is lined with excellent cafés and restaurants where you can rest your feet and enjoy a great meal.

The statues of the 19th-century fountain in the Plaza de Armas represent the four seasons.

Plaza Colón

PLAZA/SQUARE | A statue of Christopher Columbus stands atop a soaring column and fountain in this bustling Old San Juan square, catercorner to Castillo San Cristóbal. Once called St. James Square, it was renamed in 1893 to honor the 400th anniversary of Columbus's arrival in Puerto Rico; bronze plaques on the statue's base relate episodes in his life. Local artisans often line the plaza, so it's a good place to hunt for souvenirs. Cool off with a fresh fruit frappé or smoothie at the kiosk. ✉ *Old San Juan.*

Plaza de Armas

PLAZA/SQUARE | The Old City's original main square was once used as military drilling grounds. Bordered by Calles San Francisco, Rafael Cordero, San José, and Cruz, it has a fountain with 19th-century statues representing the four seasons as well as a bandstand, a small café, and a kiosk selling snacks and fruit frappés. The Alcaldía commands the north side. This is a popular, bustling meeting place, often filled with artists sketching caricatures, pedestrians in line at the food stands, and hundreds of pigeons waiting for handouts. ✉ *Calle San José, Old San Juan.*

Plazuela La Rogativa

PLAZA/SQUARE | According to legend, the British, while laying siege to the city in 1797, mistook the flaming torches of a *rogativa* (religious procession) for Spanish reinforcements and beat a hasty retreat. In this little plaza, a monument of a bishop and three women commemorates the legend. The striking contemporary statue was created in 1971 by the artist Lindsay Daen to mark the Old City's 450th anniversary. The fine view of La Fortaleza and the harbor is a bonus. ✉ *Caleta de las Monjas, Old San Juan.*

Puerta de San Juan

RUINS | Dating from 1520, this was one of the five original entrances to the city and is the only one still in its original state. The massive gate, painted a brilliant shade of red, gave access from the port and welcomed diplomats into the city. It resembles a tunnel because it passes through La Muralla, the 20-foot-thick city walls. ✉ *Paseo de la Princesa, Old San Juan.*

Restaurants

Bodega Chic

$$ | **FRENCH** | Chef and owner Brahim runs this French bistro in Old San Juan that's loved by locals. Crab cakes, duck à l'orange, steamed mussels, and veal shank can be found on the small but tasty menu. **Known for:** French cuisine; Sunday brunch; relaxed, neighborhood feel. *Average main: $18 ✉ 313 Fortaleza St., Old San Juan ☎ 787/721–6083 ⏲ Closed Mon. and Tues.*

Café Berlin

$$ | **INTERNATIONAL** | **FAMILY** | A handful of tables spill onto a sidewalk deck adorned with tiny lights at this romantic, bohemian restaurant overlooking Plaza Colón. There's something on the international menu for everyone, including a good selection of vegan and vegetarian dishes. **Known for:** breakfast; variety of vegan and vegetarian choices; street-side dining. *Average main: $19 ✉ 407 Calle San Francisco, Old San Juan ☎ 787/722–5205 🌐 www.cafeberlinpr.com.*

Cafetería Mallorca

$ | **CAFÉ** | **FAMILY** | The specialty at this old-fashioned, 1950s-style diner is the *mallorca,* a sweet pastry that's buttered, grilled, and then sprinkled with powdered sugar. Wash one down with a cup of *café con leche.* For something more substantial, try the breakfast mallorca with ham and cheese. **Known for:** old-school diner feel; mallorcas; café con leche. *Average main: $10 ✉ 300 Calle San Francisco, Old San Juan ☎ 787/724–4607 ⏲ No dinner.*

Caficultura

$$ | **CAFÉ** | Caficultura prides itself on its full coffee bar, its mimosas made with fresh juice, and its all-day breakfast and brunch menu (try the coconut-milk French toast with pineapple jam and coconut shavings). Numerous vegetarian options are available, especially at lunch, when you'll also find many delicious gourmet sandwiches and heartier dishes. **Known for:** all-day breakfast; beautifully presented lattes; outside seating. *Average main: $15 ✉ 401 Calle San Francisco, Old San Juan ☎ 787/723–7731 ⏲ No dinner.*

Carli's Fine Bistro & Piano

$$$ | **INTERNATIONAL** | As you might guess from the name, the music is as much of a draw as the food at Carli's. The genial owner and host, Carli Muñoz, toured for a number of years with the Beach Boys (note the gold album on the wall) and plays nightly with his jazz trio, often accompanied by singers and musicians who happen to drop in. **Known for:** live jazz; Caribbean-style tapas; classy ambience. *Average main: $25 ✉ Plazoleta Rafael Carrión, Calle Recinto Sur at Calle San Justo, Old San Juan ☎ 787/725–4927 🌐 www.carlisworld.com ⏲ Closed Sun. No lunch.*

★ Casa Cortés ChocoBar

$$ | **CONTEMPORARY** | **FAMILY** | The Cortés family has been making bean-to-bar chocolate for more than 90 years, and, in 2013, they opened Puerto Rico's first "chocobar" to share their passion. The walls in this vivid, modern space are decorated with ads from the 1950s, original chocolate-bar molds, a timeline of chocolate, and two flat screens showing the chocolate-making process. **Known for:** chocolate incorporated into many dishes; breakfast specialties and pastries; locally made chocolates. *Average main: $12 ✉ 210 Calle San Francisco, Old San Juan ☎ 787/722–0499 🌐 www.casacortespr.com ⏲ No dinner weekdays.*

Deaverdura

$ | **PUERTO RICAN** | This casual, no-frills restaurant in the residential section of Old San Juan serves some of the best comida criolla in town. The short menu is packed with flavor, featuring favorites like roasted pork, rice and beans (which pair

Great Itineraries

If You Have 1 Day

Many people find themselves with a single day (or even less) to explore the city, and there should be no question about your destination: Old San Juan. Spend the entire day rambling around the cobblestone streets and ducking into the many shops, and leave plenty of time for exploring the turrets, towers, and dungeons of **Castillo San Felipe del Morro,** the original fortress on a rocky northwestern promontory.

If You Have 3 Days

It's only fitting that you spend the first day on a walking tour of Old San Juan. What to see? **Castillo San Felipe del Morro** should be at the top of your list, but you may want to explore the equally enthralling **Castillo San Cristóbal,** which has underground tunnels and hidden passages, plus cannons and a more impressive museum than El Morro's. **La Fortaleza,** the city's original fortress, wasn't much protection from marauding pirates, but it does a great job sheltering the governor and can be toured. And **Casa Blanca,** a home built for Juan Ponce de León, is a wonderful place to explore how the Spanish lived in colonial days. Reserve Day 2 for lounging on a *playa* (beach). Choose from the city's finest at Condado, Ocean Park, or Isla Verde, then park yourself in a rented chair with a good book, a cold drink, and plenty of sunscreen. In the evening, make sure you enjoy the warm weather by dining alfresco. On Day 3, hop the ferry across the bay to Cataño for a tour of the **Casa Bacardí Visitor Center.** Return in time for some shopping in the shops and delightful arts-and-crafts galleries along Calles San Francisco and Fortaleza, followed by dinner—there are lots of great restaurants to choose from.

If You Have 5 Days

Follow the itinerary above for your first three days in San Juan. On Day 4, head for the Santurce district. You can immerse yourself in island art at the **Museo de Arte de Puerto Rico** and, nearby, the **Museo de Arte Contemporáneo de Puerto Rico.** Afterward, wander through the produce stalls at the Plaza del Mercado in Santurce, with a fresh papaya or soursop shake in hand. Note the giant bronze sculptures of avocados by artist Annex Burgos. If hunger strikes, head to Santaella or El Pescador, both favorites among locals. Don't miss Calle Cerra, a street filled with striking murals. On the morning of Day 5, hit the beach once more in Piñones, a rustic beachfront neighborhood past Isla Verde. The area has dozens of food stalls selling local fritters cooked over a wood fire. Wash them down with an ice cold Medalla beer or *coco frío* (coconut water).

perfectly with the homemade hot sauces), empanadas, tostones, and homemade sausage. **Known for:** comida criolla; roasted pork with rice and beans; sample platter big enough for two. *Average main: $10 ✉ 200 Calle Sol, Old San Juan ☎ 787/463–1038 ⊙ Closed Sun.*

El Jibarito

$$ | PUERTO RICAN | FAMILY | The menus are handwritten, and the tables wobble, but locals in the know have favored this no-frills, family-run restaurant—tucked away on a quiet cobblestone street—for years. The *bistec encebollado,* goat fricassee, and shredded beef stew stand out on the comida criolla menu. **Known for:** traditional Puerto Rican comfort food; casual atmosphere; gentle prices. *Average main: $14 280 Calle Sol, Old San Juan 787/725–8375.*

El Patio de Sam

$$ | **PUERTO RICAN** | The airy courtyard and the comida criolla are among the draws at this local, come-as-you-are restaurant—the perfect spot to end a workweek or a long day of sightseeing. The menu consists mostly of American and Puerto Rican fare. **Known for:** typical Puerto Rican specialties; homemade flan; casual atmosphere. *Average main: $16 102 Calle San Sebastián, Old San Juan 787/723–1149.*

La Madre

$$ | **MEXICAN** | La Madre is a hip Mexican restaurant, with a stylish, young clientele to match. Yes, it covers the standards, including some very tasty tacos, enchiladas, and chilaquiles, but you'll also find innovative, modern, international interpretations of Mexican cuisine. **Known for:** popular weekend brunch; outdoor seating; large variety of margaritas. *Average main: $17 351 Calle San Francisco, Old San Juan 787/647–5392.*

★ Marmalade

$$$$ | **ECLECTIC** | Peter Schintler, the U.S.-born owner-chef of Old San Juan's hippest—and finest—restaurant, apprenticed with Raymond Blanc and Gordon Ramsay. His dishes incorporate local and organic ingredients, and his cuisine is influenced by both California and French styles of cooking, resulting in complex flavors and strong aromas. **Known for:** varying prix-fixe menus; exceptional service; excellent wine list. *Average main: $32 317 Calle Fortaleza, Old San Juan 787/724–3969 www.marmaladepr.com Closed Sun.*

Pirilo Pizza Rustica

$$ | **PIZZA** | Day and night, locals flock to Pirilo to indulge in San Juan's finest pizza. Owner Eduardo Rubio makes everything from scratch, most notably the crust, which uses a 300-year-old starter as its base. **Known for:** pizza, both traditional and not; late-night eats; 50 craft beers. *Average main: $14 207 Calle Tanca, Old San Juan 787/721–3322.*

Princesa Cocina Creativa

$$ | **PUERTO RICAN** | Set in a gorgeous setting along the fortified wall, Princesa Cocina Creativa serves dishes inspired by recipes from the 19th and 20th centuries. Surrounded by trees and the sound of coquí frogs, its a memorable dining experience. *Average main: $20 Paseo de la Princesa, Old San Juan www.princesapr.com.*

Raíces

$$$ | **PUERTO RICAN** | **FAMILY** | You can't miss this lively restaurant, thanks to its waitresses in all-white *campesina* (peasant) dresses. Themed as a country venue, with artsy re-creations of rustic life, it feels a bit Disneyfied, but that doesn't stop the locals and tourists—who may have seen it featured on various TV shows and who are willing to wait more than an hour for a table—from packing in for comida criolla. **Known for:** kan kan pork chop and churrasco; themed ambience; long waits. *Average main: $21 315 Calle Recinto Sur, Old San Juan 787/289–2121.*

Santísimo

$$$ | **CONTEMPORARY** | Tucked away on the second floor of the historic El Convento Hotel, Santísmo is a dreamy and romantic dining destination. A stone oven is used to cook many of the dishes, including the catch of the day. All dining is alfresco on two terraces overlooking the hotel's striking arches. **Known for:** alfresco dining; creative menu; charming bar. *Average main: $30 Hotel el Convento, 100 Calle Cristo, Old San Juan 787/723–9020 www.elconvento.com/dining.*

★ Señor Paleta
$ | **CAFÉ** | **FAMILY** | There's nothing more refreshing on a hot day than an ice pop from Señor Paleta. All the ingredients used to make these artisanal *paletas* are fresh, and many use local fruits. **Known for:** fruity ice pops on a stick; long waits on weekends; ice cream. *Average main: $4* *153 Calle Tetuan, Old San Juan* *787/724–2337.*

St. Germain Bistro & Café
$ | **INTERNATIONAL** | The service at this charming, French-inspired café-restaurant on a quiet cobblestone corner is friendly, and the interior is inviting, with rustic, white wooden tables and benches. The sandwiches, entrée salads, quiches, pita pizzas, and other menu items are made with fresh ingredients. **Known for:** vegetarian and vegan options; aguas frescas; weekend brunch. *Average main: $10* *156 Calle Sol, Old San Juan* *787/725–5830* *www.stgermainpr.com* *Closed Mon.*

Stuffed Avocado
$ | **FAST FOOD** | The stuffed avocado bowls served at this small eatery, run by brothers Joel and Javier Pierluisi, make it a great spot for a quick, healthy bite. Build your own, or choose from signature options like chipotle chicken with cilantro cream, spicy salmon with masago and seaweed salad, or pulled pork with *mamposteao* rice. **Known for:** stuffed avocado bowls; quick and healthy lunch; vegetarian and vegan options. *Average main: $11* *209 Calle San Francisco, Old San Juan* *787/303–1111* *www.stuffedavocadoshop.com.*

Trois Cent Onze (*311*)
$$$ | **FRENCH** | The perfectly lighted dining room—with crystal chandeliers, colonial arches, Moorish tiles, long drapes, and checkered marble floors—is a true example of Old San Juan charm. The menu is a mix of classic French with nouveau interpretations. **Known for:** romantic atmosphere; French-inspired cuisine; small but well-chosen wine list. *Average main: $30* *311 Calle Fortaleza, Old San Juan* *787/725–7959* *www.311restaurantpr.com* *Closed Sun. and Mon. No lunch.*

Coffee and Quick Bites

★ Café Cuatro Sombras
$ | **CAFÉ** | **FAMILY** | If you want to try local, single-origin, shade-grown coffee, this micro-roastery and café is the place to do it. Owners Pablo Muñoz and Mariana Suárez grow their beans in the mountains of Yauco on a hacienda that has been in the Muñoz family since 1846. **Known for:** locally grown coffee; pastries and sandwiches; coffee tastings. *Average main: $7* *259 Calle Recinto Sur, Old San Juan* *787/724–9955* *www.cuatrosombras.com* *No dinner.*

Café Don Ruiz
$ | **CAFÉ** | **FAMILY** | Tucked away in the corner of the old Spanish military barracks, Café Don Ruiz serves some of the finest coffee in town. It's sourced from a family-run hacienda in Yauco that's known for its handpicked coffee, grown more than 3,000 feet above sea level. **Known for:** locally grown coffee; light bites; historic location. *Average main: $5* *Cuartel de Ballajá, Calle Norzagaray at Calle Beneficiencia, Old San Juan* *787/723–1462* *www.cafedonruiz.com* *No dinner.*

Café 4 Estaciones
$ | **CAFÉ** | At this tiny kiosk, the tables and chairs under a canvas canopy that's surrounded by potted plants invite you to put down your shopping bags and rest your tired feet. Grab a café con leche (coffee with hot milk), an espresso, or cold drink, and watch the children chase the pigeons. **Known for:** café con leche; mallorcas; quesitos. *Average main: $2* *Plaza de Armas, Old San Juan* *No credit cards.*

Plucky pontiff: the bronze bishop of Plazuela de la Rogativa is a monument to the religious procession that, according to legend, repelled a British invasion.

Hotels

CasaBlanca Hotel

$ | **HOTEL** | Mere steps from some of the best dining in town, this boutique hotel not only adds Moroccan-themed panache to Old San Juan but also offers real value. **Pros:** exotic decor; close to restaurants and nightclubs; elevator. **Cons:** some rooms are dark; noise from street can be an issue; smallish rooms. *Rooms from: $139 ✉ 316 Calle Fortaleza, Old San Juan ☎ 787/316–2698 🌐 www.hotelcasablancapr.com 32 rooms No Meals.*

Decanter Hotel

$$$ | **HOTEL** | Tucked behind the cathedral, this restored 19th-century colonial mansion houses one of Old San Juan's newest hotels, where many of the charming, spacious, modern guest rooms have terraces and balconies. **Pros:** excellent location; rooftop terrace; good restaurant. **Cons:** some street noise; no pool; unassuming lobby. *Rooms from: $280 ✉ 106 Calle San José, Old San Juan ☎ 787/305–3320 🌐 www.decanterhotel.com 20 rooms No Meals.*

El Colonial Hotel

$$$ | **B&B/INN** | Formerly the Da House Hotel, El Colonial is a 33-room adults-only boutique hotel that mixes modern with historic charm. **Pros:** pet friendly; friendly staff; rooftop terrace. **Cons:** noise from nearby bars; no elevator. *Rooms from: $280 ✉ 312 Calle San Francisco, Old San Juan ☎ 787/610–5182 🌐 elcolonialhotel.com 33 rooms No Meals.*

The Gallery Inn

$$ | **B&B/INN** | No two rooms in this 200-year-old mansion are alike, but all have four-poster beds, handwoven tapestries, and quirky antiques; indeed, every nook and cranny here is adorned with owner Jan D'Esopo's paintings, bronze sculptures, ceramic busts, and plaques. **Pros:** one-of-a-kind lodging; ocean views; wonderful classical music concerts. **Cons:** several narrow, winding staircases; an uphill walk from the rest of Old San Juan; sometimes-raucous pet macaws

and cockatoos. 💲 *Rooms from: $150* ✉ *204–206 Calle Norzagaray, Old San Juan* ☎ *787/722–1808* 🌐 *www.thegallery-inn.com* 25 rooms 🍽 *Free Breakfast.*

★ Hotel El Convento

$$$$ | **HOTEL** | There's no longer anything austere about this 350-year-old former convent: all the guest rooms are lavish and inviting, with wrought-iron and hand-hewn wood furniture, shuttered windows, and mahogany-beamed ceilings joining high-tech amenities like Wi-Fi and flat-screen TVs. **Pros:** lovely historic building; atmosphere to spare; plenty of nearby dining options. **Cons:** near some noisy bars; small pool; small bathrooms. 💲 *Rooms from: $400* ✉ *100 Calle Cristo, Old San Juan* ☎ *787/723–9020* 🌐 *www.elconvento.com* 58 rooms 🍽 *No Meals.*

La Terraza de San Juan

$$ | **HOTEL** | A stay in this charming, colonial-era boutique hotel on a quiet, residential street is the perfect way to experience Old San Juan like a local. **Pros:** rooftop pool and bar; elevator; 24-hour concierge. **Cons:** noise from rooftop terrace; some rooms have no windows; far from the beach. 💲 *Rooms from: $222* ✉ *262 Calle Sol, Old San Juan* ☎ *787/722–2014* 🌐 *www.laterrazahotel-sanjuan.com* 24 rooms 🍽 *No Meals.*

Palacio Provincial

$$ | **HOTEL** | Modern design meets colonial charm at this hotel, which opened in 2021 in a beautifully restored, 19th-century building with high ceilings, striking arches, courtyards, and a rooftop pool. **Pros:** brand-new; rooftop pool and dining; centrally located. **Cons:** no spa; smallish pool; breakfast is pricey. 💲 *Rooms from: $230* ✉ *103 Calle San Francisco, Old San Juan* ☎ *787/425–0164* 🌐 *www.palacioprovincial.com* 43 rooms 🍽 *No Meals.*

Sheraton Old San Juan Hotel

$$$ | **HOTEL** | **FAMILY** | Rooms facing the water at this triangular hotel have spectacular views of the mammoth cruise ships that sail in and out of the nearby harbor. **Pros:** harbor views; near many dining options; great precruise option. **Cons:** chain-hotel feel to guest rooms; uphill walk to the rest of Old San Juan; casino has closed. 💲 *Rooms from: $259* ✉ *100 Calle Brumbaugh, Old San Juan* ☎ *787/289–1914* 🌐 *www.sheratonoldsan-juan.com* 240 rooms 🍽 *No Meals.*

Villa Herencia Hotel

$$ | **B&B/INN** | You'll be transported back to the 19th century in this exquisitely restored former mansion with timeworn bare walls, original floral-tile floors, and beamed ceilings. **Pros:** delightful furnishings; close to shops and cafés; rooftop terraces with baths. **Cons:** no in-room phone; no elevator; smallish rooms. 💲 *Rooms from: $250* ✉ *23 Caleta de las Monjas, Old San Juan* ☎ *787/722–0989* 🌐 *www.villaherencia.com* 8 rooms 🍽 *No Meals.*

Nightlife

BARS

Antiguo 26

BARS | Set in a former Soda Factory, Antiguo 26 serves homemade sodas, craft cocktails, and creative tapas in a setting reminiscent of *The Great Gatsby*. ✉ *261 Tetuan St., Old San Juan* 🌐 *www.antiguo26.com.*

Birra y Empanadas

BARS | As the name suggests, this small bar is known for its beers and its small but tasty selection of baked empanadas. Ask for the homemade sauces. ✉ *150 Calle Cruz, Old San Juan* ☎ *787/721–6073.*

El Batey

BARS | This legendary dive bar won't win any prizes for decor, but it has an irresistibly artsy and welcoming vibe. Add your own message to the graffiti-covered walls—they have a "B.Y.O.S." policy (Bring Your Own Sharpie)—or hang your business card alongside the hundreds that cover the light fixtures. The jukebox has the best selection of oldies in town, and locals crowd the back room for billiards. ✉ *101 Calle Cristo, Old San Juan* 🌐 *www.elbateytavernpr.com.*

El Vino Crudo

BARS | Tucked away in an alleyway off Calle Fortaleza, Old San Juan's newest bar pays tribute to a world selection of natural wines. The lovely owners, an expat husband-and-wife team from New York, passionately serve their carefully curated wines that are farmed organically or biodynamically. It's a great place to start your night or end with a nightcap in a romantic setting. Pop-ups by local chefs are hosted monthly. ✉ *320 Fortaleza St., Old San Juan* 🌐 *www.elvinocrudo.com.*

★ La Factoría

BARS | La Factoría, the former Hijos de Borinquen, is hands down the best cocktail bar in San Juan. Here, artisanal drinks are crafted with the highest-quality ingredients. Many bitters are homemade, as is the ginger beer, which is used in the popular Lavender Mule. Whether it's sweet, spicy, bitter, or something completely out of the box, these drinks will blow your mind. Behind the bar, there is a secret wooden door that leads to Vino Wine Bar, which has a great speakeasy feel. Tasty tapas are available and can be enjoyed in the adjacent room. These bars stay open till sunup, and a DJ spins in the back room on weekends. Salsa is played on Sunday and Monday. There's no sign on the door, so just look for the terra-cotta building at the corner of San Sebastián and San José. ✉ *148 Calle San Sebastián, Old San Juan* ☎ *787/594–5698.*

La Taberna Lúpulo

BARS | If you love beer, don't leave Puerto Rico without visiting Lúpulo. At the island's largest craft beer bar you'll find over 25 varieties on tap and more than 100 bottles of the finest European and American brews. This casual hipster bar is open late and a great option for night bites. ✉ *151 Calle San Sebastián, Old San Juan* ☎ *787/721–3772.*

La Verguenza

BARS | This lively, three-story bar has spectacular views of La Perla and the Atlantic. On weekends, it's popular with locals (be prepared to wait in line) who come to sip flavored mojitos, local beer, or rum with fresh juice. In addition to limited seating on the second and third floors, there are some outdoor tables across the street. On Sunday, there's live music in the adjacent alleyway (Callejón de la Tanca). The bar has a second San Juan location, across the street from La Concha hotel. ✉ *280 Calle Norzagaray, Old San Juan* ☎ *939/415–4367.*

The Mezzanine

BARS | Set in the former headquarters of the Nationalist Party, this contemporary take on a 1920s speakeasy is a chic space that's conducive to sipping a creative cocktail. Tapas are served all day, making this an even more refreshing stop after walking the hills of Old San Juan. Although the Mezzanine is typically closed on Monday, from Tuesday to Friday it hosts one of the best happy hours in town, with half-price select tapas and cocktails. You can't beat that in San Juan! Weekend brunch is also very popular. ✉ *St. Germain Bistro & Café, 156 Calle Sol, 2nd fl., Old San Juan* ☎ *787/724–4657.*

Scryer Rum

COCKTAIL LOUNGES | Scryer Rum is a small-batch, premium spirit that's distilled in Barbados and aged on-site in Old San Juan. The first floor is home to the finishing casks and a beautiful bar that evokes the Roaring '20s. The second floor has a small lounge, and the spacious rooftop overlooks the street. Tours are available by reservation. ✉ *259 Calle Tetuan, Old San Juan* ☎ *954/815–6182* 🌐 *www.scryerrum.com.*

The Piña Colada Wars

This mixture of pineapple juice, coconut cream, and liberal amounts of rum, always garnished with a wedge of pineapple and a maraschino cherry, was, depending on who you talk to, invented either by Ramón "Monchito" Marrero at the Caribe Hilton back in 1954 or by Ramón Portas Mingot at the bar in Old San Juan's Barrachina restaurant in 1963. Was it Marrero, a young bartender who is said to have spent three months on a concoction that would appeal to patrons at the Beachcomber's Bar? (His secret? Using only fresh pineapple juice.) Or was it Mingot, an elderly bartender meeting the whims of his Old San Juan patrons? (He said his were so frothy because he froze the pineapple juice and coconut cream mixture instead of simply adding crushed ice.)

The two venues have fought over bragging rights for decades. The Caribe Hilton issues press release after press release reminding people that the drink was born in its seaside bar. (If what its public relations department says is true, the drink celebrated its 65th anniversary in 2019.) The Barrachina Bar put up a plaque that tells passersby that it is the true birthplace of the beverage. It seems the Caribe Hilton has a slight edge: local bartenders insist Marrero was the one who invented the famous drink. And Coco López, the company that makes the coconut cream most often used in the drink, honored him in 1978. In gratitude for his contribution to the "bartending arts," they presented him with a color TV. But the origins of the piña colada—which means "strained pineapple"—remain as cloudy as the cocktail itself. You may have to sample several before making up your own mind.

Señor Frog's

BARS | Latin America's answer to the Hard Rock Cafe, Señor Frog's attracts both hard-partying tourists and the cruise-ship crowd—no surprise, as it's located directly in front of the dock. (Look for the giant inflatable frog.) The just-okay menu is a nod to Mexico, with south-of-the-border favorites like nachos and quesadillas. When it comes to drinks, expect quantity over quality; their signature is the Yard, a tall plastic cup filled with your favorite adult beverage. There's often live music, a ladies' night, or other special events. ✉ *102 Calle Marina, corner of Brumbaugh, Old San Juan* ☎ *787/977-4142* 🌐 *www.senorfrogs.com.*

Performing Arts

MAJOR VENUES

Fundación Nacional Para la Cultura Popular

ARTS CENTERS | This multifaceted foundation hosts a variety of events, including Latin music and dance performances and classes. Check the schedule online or call ahead. ✉ *56 Calle Fortaleza, Old San Juan* ☎ *787/724-7165* 🌐 *www.prpop.org.*

Teatro Tapia

THEATER | Named for Puerto Rican playwright Alejandro Tapia y Rivera, the island's oldest theater hosts traveling and locally produced theatrical and musical productions. Matinees for families are also held, especially around the holidays. ✉ *Plaza Colón, Calle Fortaleza, Old San Juan* ☎ *787/480-5004.*

Shopping

ART GALLERIES

Galería Botello

ART GALLERIES | This influential gallery displays art by the late Angel Botello, who was hailed as the Caribbean Gauguin as far back as 1943. (His works also hang in the Museo de Arte de Puerto Rico.) His paintings often feature the bright colors of the tropics and usually depict island scenes. Also on display here are works by other prominent local artists, Puerto Rican santos, and sculptures by Botello. ✉ *208 Calle Cristo, Old San Juan* ☎ *787/723–9987* 🌐 *www.botello.com.*

Haitian Gallery

CRAFTS | This shop carries Haitian masks, statues, paintings, and wooden works of art. The second floor houses a large selection of paintings from the Caribbean. ✉ *367 Calle Fortaleza, Old San Juan* ☎ *787/725–0986* 🌐 *facebook.com/haitian.gallery.puertorico/.*

CIGARS

Cigar House

TOBACCO | The Cigar House has an eclectic selection of local and imported cigars from Nicaragua, Honduras, and the Dominican Republic. At the lounge and bar, you can enjoy your purchase with a glass of your favorite spirit. ✉ *257 Calle Fortaleza, Old San Juan* ☎ *787/723–5223* 🌐 *www.facebook.com/thecigarhouse.*

CLOTHING

Cappalli

WOMEN'S CLOTHING | Noted local designer Lisa Cappalli sells her feminine, sensuous designs in this elegant boutique, which specializes in ready-to-wear and custom fashions including a small collection of whimsical, lacy wedding gowns. ✉ *206 Calle O'Donnell, Old San Juan* ☎ *787/289–6565* 🌐 *www.lisacappalli.com.*

Collective Request

MIXED CLOTHING | Set in a restored colonial building, this gorgeous boutique caters to stylish young women and men. Owners Joel and Ashley are frequently on-site to help with any shopping needs. ✉ *159 Calle Luna, Old San Juan* ☎ *787/977–7707.*

Concalma

JEWELRY & WATCHES | Here designer Matilsha Marxuach, who is keen on sustainable fashion, sells her hip line of fair-trade messenger and handbags, as well as bathing suits, vintage clothing, and items made by other local designers. ✉ *207 Calle San Francisco, Old San Juan* ☎ *787/421–4212* 🌐 *shopconcalma.com.*

El Galpón

CRAFTS | At El Galpón, knowledgeable owners Betsy and Gustavo will fit you with a Panama hat ($65–$900), and you'll learn that the genuine article is actually made in Ecuador. They also carry a large selection of Puerto Rican santos, hand-carved wooden saints. ✉ *154 Calle Cristo, Old San Juan* ☎ *787/725–3945* 🌐 *www.elgalpon.net.*

MUNS

JEWELRY & WATCHES | Sisters Bianca and Paola Muns sell sustainable clothing and jewelry under their own label at this pretty boutique. They also carry a curated selection of clothing, swimwear, and accessories by other Puerto Rican designers. ✉ *201 Calle Luna, Old San Juan* ☎ *939/245–5962* 🌐 *www.munsthebrand.com.*

Olé

CRAFTS | Aficionados of the famous Panama hat, made from delicately handwoven straw, should stop at Olé. The shop sells top-of-the-line toppers for as much as $1,000, as well as more affordable options that can be custom-fit. Take a few moments to browse the other goods for sale like decades-old santos and used books. ✉ *105 Calle Fortaleza, Old San Juan* ☎ *787/724–2445* 🌐 *www.olepuertorico.com.*

Pure Soul

JEWELRY & WATCHES | Sylma Cabrera sells chic resort wear made of natural fabrics by local artists and under her own label, Pure Soul. You'll also find stunning handmade jewelry with semiprecious stones like quartz and lapis lazuli. ✉ *258 Calle San Justo, corner Tetuán, Old San Juan* ☎ *787/723–2800.*

CRAFTS

Mi Pequeño San Juan

CRAFTS | You might find a reproduction of your hotel at this shop, which specializes in tiny ceramic versions of San Juan doorways. The works are created by hand in the shop, which also carries fine art prints. ✉ *152 Calle Fortaleza, Old San Juan* ☎ *787/721–5040.*

Mundo Taíno

CRAFTS | This is a good place to shop for high-quality folk art from around the island. You can also pick up local coffee and other food specialty items like hot sauce. ✉ *200 Calle Fortaleza, Old San Juan* ☎ *787/724–2005.*

Puerto Rican Arts & Crafts

CRAFTS | For one-of-a-kind santos, art, ceramics, and festival masks, head to Puerto Rican Arts & Crafts. All items are made by local artists. ✉ *204 Calle Fortaleza, Old San Juan* ☎ *787/725–5596* 🌐 *www.puertoricanart-crafts.com.*

GIFTS

Eclectika

SOUVENIRS | Here the inventory, most of it Indonesian, ranges from bedspreads and furnishings to beaded jewelry and hand fans. ✉ *204 Calle O'Donnell, Plaza Colón, Old San Juan* ☎ *787/721–7236.*

Spicy Caribbee

SOUVENIRS | Kitchen items, cookbooks, jams, spices, and sauces from around the Caribbean are on offer. ✉ *154 Calle Cristo, Old San Juan* ☎ *888/725–7259* 🌐 *www.spicycaribbee.com.*

JEWELRY

Catalá Joyeros

JEWELRY & WATCHES | Family-run since the 1930s, this store is known for its large selection of pearls and precious stones, as well as for its jewelry design. ✉ *Plaza de Armas, 152 Calle Rafael Cordero, Old San Juan* ☎ *787/722–3231* 🌐 *www.catalajoyeros.com.*

Club Jibarito

JEWELRY & WATCHES | Club Jibarito has a fantastic collection of high-end watches by Audemars Piguet, Chopard, H.Stern, Harry Winston, Panerai, and other designers. ✉ *202 Calle Cristo, Old San Juan* ☎ *787/724–7797* 🌐 *www.clubjibarito.com.*

Coquí el Original

JEWELRY & WATCHES | This Old San Juan establishment has been in the Barquet family for four generations, and items from their Coquí el Original line—depicting the local tree frog—have become popular souvenirs. Choose from 14K-gold or sterling-silver coquí pendants, rings, bracelets, and more. If you're looking for unique and high-end jewels, ask to browse the private back room. ✉ *201 Calle Fortaleza, Old San Juan* ☎ *787/721–3366* 🌐 *coquieloriginal.com.*

Portofino

JEWELRY & WATCHES | Portofino has an especially good selection of watches. ✉ *250 Calle San Francisco, Old San Juan* ☎ *787/723–5113.*

OUTLETS

Old San Juan has turned into an open-air, duty-free marketplace for people pouring off the cruise ships. Although fewer outlets remain, they are still popular with visitors. The prices aren't particularly good, but nobody seems to mind.

Coach

OUTLET | Stylish, upscale handbags for men and women can be purchased at Coach for a discounted price. ✉ *158 Calle Cristo, Old San Juan* ☎ *787/722–6830.*

Ralph Lauren
OUTLET | Ralph Lauren's shop in front of the piers has some of the best deals around. Stop here toward the end of your trip, as there are plenty of items (e.g., peacoats and scarves) that you won't be wearing until you get home. ✉ *105 Paseo Gilberto Concepcinó de Gracia, Harbor Plaza Bldg., Old San Juan* ☎ *787/724–1020.*

Puerta de Tierra

Just east of the Old City, Puerta de Tierra is home to a few notable hotels, a nice public beach, several parks, and some high-end furniture stores.

Sights

El Capitolio
GOVERNMENT BUILDING | The white-marble Capitol, a fine example of Italian Renaissance style, dates from 1929. The grand rotunda, which can be seen from all over San Juan, was completed in the late 1990s. Fronted by eight Corinthian columns, it's a dignified home for the Commonwealth's constitution. Although the Senate and House of Representatives have offices in the more modern buildings on either side, the Capitol is where the legislators meet. Guided tours, which last about an hour and include the rotunda, are by appointment only. ✉ *Av. Constitución, Puerta de Tierra* ☎ *787/724–2030, 787/721–5200 for guided tours* *Free* *Closed weekends.*

Fortín San Gerónimo del Boquerón
MILITARY SIGHT | At the eastern tip of Puerta de Tierra, this tiny, 16th-century fort is perched on a hilltop like an afterthought. It was, however, an essential part of San Juan's defense, as it guarded the entrance to the city. ✉ *Calle Rosales, Puerta de Tierra* *$5* *Closed weekends.*

Beaches

Balneario El Escambrón
BEACH | **FAMILY** | This government-run beach has a patch of honey-color sand shaded by coconut palms. An offshore reef generally makes surf gentle, so it's favored by families. **Amenities**: lifeguards; parking (fee); showers; toilets. **Best for**: swimming; walking; snorkeling. ✉ *Av. Muñoz Rivera, Puerta de Tierra* *Parking $5.*

Restaurants

Celeste
$$$ | **WINE BAR** | Celeste is Puerta de Tierra's first upscale restaurant. Chef and proprietor, Sebastian Sarda, alongside his wildly talented team, serve some of Puerto Rico's most creative dishes with quality ingredients. **Known for:** funky wines; locally caught fish; creative cuisine with seasonal menu. *Average main: $22* ✉ *200 Calle Pelayo, Puerta de Tierra* *Closed Tues.–Thurs.*

El Hamburguer
$ | **BURGER** | After a day at Playa Escambron, grab a bite and a beer at this hole-in-the-wall joint, where a tiny kitchen rapidly custom-charbroils burgers. You might want to order two, as they're small, like sliders; regardless, you can top them with Roquefort, cheddar, or American cheese. **Known for:** cheap burgers; local favorite; sweet-potato fries. *Average main: $6* ✉ *402 Av. Muñoz Rivera, Puerta de Tierra* ☎ *787/721–4269.*

Hotels

Caribe Hilton San Juan
$$$ | **RESORT** | **FAMILY** | Not many hotels can boast about having their own fort, but Fortín San Gerónimo del Boquerón, which once guarded the entrance to San Juan Bay, is on the grounds of this 17-acre sprawling resort. **Pros:** family-friendly atmosphere; private beach; lovely pool area. **Cons:** noisy lobby area;

Did You Know?

East of Old San Juan, a more contemporary city unfolds. Looks can be deceiving, though: Puerta de Tierra is home to a 16th-century fort and early-20th-century El Capitolio, whose stately rotunda houses the commonwealth's constitution. The vistas here are classic, too.

somewhat isolated, with few attractions or restaurants within walking distance; daily resort fee. *Rooms from: $350* ✉ *1 San Gerónimo Grounds, Puerta de Tierra* ☎ *787/721–0303, 800/468–8585* 🌐 *www.caribehilton.com* *652 rooms* *No Meals.*

Shopping

ART GALLERIES

Walter Otero Contemporary Art

ART GALLERIES | This gorgeous, 5,000-square-foot gallery (open by appointment only) showcases contemporary works by local and international artists. ✉ *402 Hwy. 25, Puerta de Tierra* ☎ *787/998–9622* 🌐 *www.walterotero.com.*

Condado

For multiple dining options within walking distance of one another, look to Condado. Home to many of the city's moneyed elite, it's the most vibrant pedestrian neighborhood outside of Old San Juan. Here you'll find old Spanish-style homes next to sleek, modern apartment buildings and beachfront hotels (although the beach isn't as big or alluring as those in Isla Verde). The main street, Avenida Ashford, is fun to stroll, but quieter residential areas are also very attractive.

Beaches

Condado Beach

BEACH | **FAMILY** | East of Old San Juan and west of Ocean Park, this long, wide beach is overshadowed by an unbroken string of hotels and apartment buildings. Beach bars, water-sports outfitters, and chair-rental places abound. You can access the beach from several roads off Avenida Ashford, including Calles Cervantes, Vendig, Condado, and Candina. The protected water at the small stretch of beach west of the Condado Plaza Hilton hotel is particularly calm and popular with families; surf elsewhere in Condado can be a bit strong. The stretch of sand near Calle Vendig (behind the Atlantic Beach Hotel) is especially popular with the gay community. If you're driving, street parking is your only option. **Amenities:** none. **Best for:** partiers. ✉ *Av. Ashford, Condado.*

Restaurants

Ali Baba Turkish Restaurant

$$ | **MIDDLE EASTERN** | Standing discreetly just off Avenida Ashford, Ali Baba turns out delicious, meticulously prepared Middle Eastern and Mediterranean food, thanks to its Turkish chef-owner. Given how unpretentious this small place is, the presentation is surprisingly elegant. **Known for:** tangy, smooth hummus; iskender kebab; no reservations. *Average main: $15* ✉ *1214 Av. Ashford, Condado* ☎ *787/722–1176* *Closed Sun.*

Bebo's Café

$$ | **PUERTO RICAN** | **FAMILY** | Huge platters of delicious comida criolla are constantly streaming out of the kitchen here. Low prices and a family atmosphere ensure that this longtime local favorite—located near the DoubleTree on the border of Condado and Santurce—is always packed. **Known for:** large portions; family-friendly atmosphere; breakfast. *Average main: $12* ✉ *1600 Calle Loíza, Condado* ☎ *787/726–5700.*

Cocina Abierta

$$$$ | **ECLECTIC** | Modern light fixtures, exposed walls, and repurposed decorative accents give Cocina Abierta one of the coolest decors in Condado. Chef Martin Louzao prepares eclectic, multicourse omnivore, pescatarian, and vegetarian menus. **Known for:** tasting menus; octopus terrine and mofongo with duck confit; great wine list. *Average main: $45* ✉ *58 Calle Caribe, Condado* ☎ *787/946–1333* 🌐 *cocinaabierta.net* *No credit cards.*

San Juan's well-equipped balnearios (public beaches) are among the best on the island.

Jose Enrique

$$$ | **PUERTO RICAN** | Although it recently moved from Santurce to Condado, the restaurant of chef Jose Enrique—who's been nominated for the prestigious James Beard Award multiple times—remains popular with locals and visitors for its elevated Puerto Rican cuisine. The setting is casual, and the menu is ever-changing, though it always includes *carne guisada* (a local beef stew), fritters, and a catch of the day. **Known for:** focus on locally grown produce and other ingredients; ever-changing menu; celebrity chef. *Average main: $30* *1021 Av. Ashford, Condado* *787/705–8130* *Closed Sun. and Mon.*

Kabanas

$$ | **MEXICAN** | **FAMILY** | Parmesan-crusted tacos are the draw here, with favorites including the fish, pulled pork, or vegetarian-friendly falafel versions. Pair yours with a margarita or mojito, and sit outside on the small terrace. **Known for:** fish tacos and margaritas; prime people-watching from the terrace; breakfast and weekend brunch. *Average main: $12* *1104 Av. Magdalena, Condado* *787/519–1016.*

Mario Pagan

$$$$ | **CARIBBEAN** | Celebrity-chef Mario Pagan dazzles diners—among them businesspeople trying to impress their counterparts—with his creative, modern Puerto Rican fare and a setting that's reminiscent of a sleek, midtown-Manhattan restaurant. An attentive, professional waitstaff serves dishes like Gouda *croquetas* with sweet papaya, Chilean sea bass with yuca-truffled mousse, and lamb-shoulder confit. **Known for:** trendy patrons; sophisticated dining; well-known chef. *Average main: $40* *1110 Av. Magdalena, Condado* *787/522–6444* *www.mariopaganrest.com* *Closed Sun. and Mon.*

★ 1919 Restaurant

$$$$ | **ECLECTIC** | Michelin-starred, Puerto Rico–born chef Juan José Cuevas operates this successful fine-dining restaurant in San Juan's most striking hotel, built in 1919 by the Vanderbilt family. The international dishes—served prix fixe or à

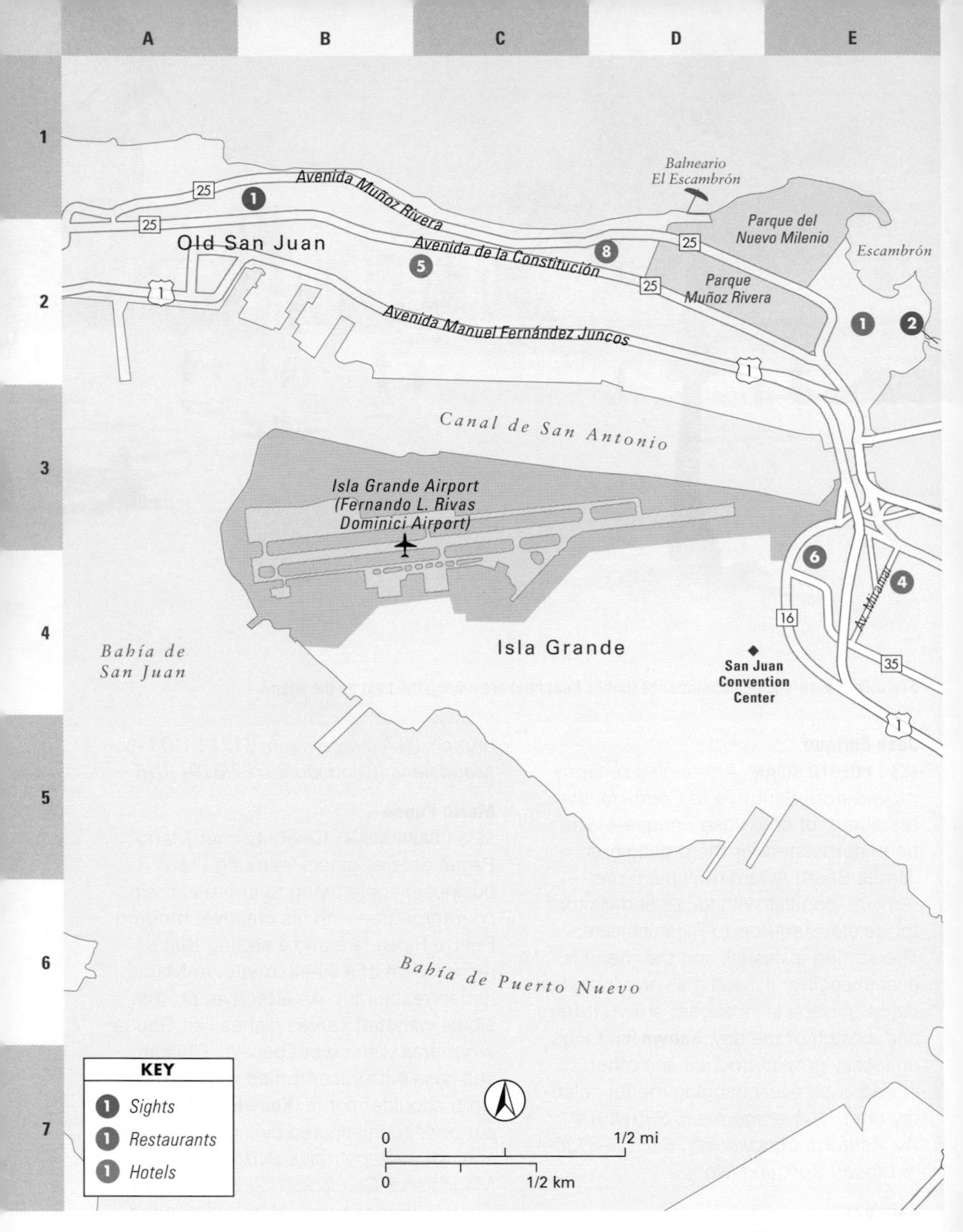

Sights

1 El Capitolio............... **B1**
2 Fortín San Gerónimo del Boquerón............ **E2**
3 MADMI (Museum of Art & Design Miramar)..... **F4**
4 Museo de Arte Contemporáneo de Puerto Rico **G5**
5 Museo de Arte de Puerto Rico **I5**
6 Plaza del Mercado **H5**

Restaurants

1 Ali Baba Turkish Restaurant.............. **H4**
2 Ariel **F4**
3 Bebo's Café.............. **I5**
4 Casita Miramar **E4**
5 Celeste.................... **C2**
6 Cocina Abierta **H4**
7 Cocina al Fondo......... **G5**
8 El Hamburguer **D2**
9 Gustos Café **F4**
10 Jose Enrique **F3**
11 Kabanas **G4**
12 La Santurcina **G5**
13 Mai Pen Rai **H5**
14 Mario Pagan **G4**
15 Miramar Food Truck Park **F4**
16 1919 Restaurant......... **G3**
17 Paulina Escanes......... **I4**
18 Rosa & Elena **F4**

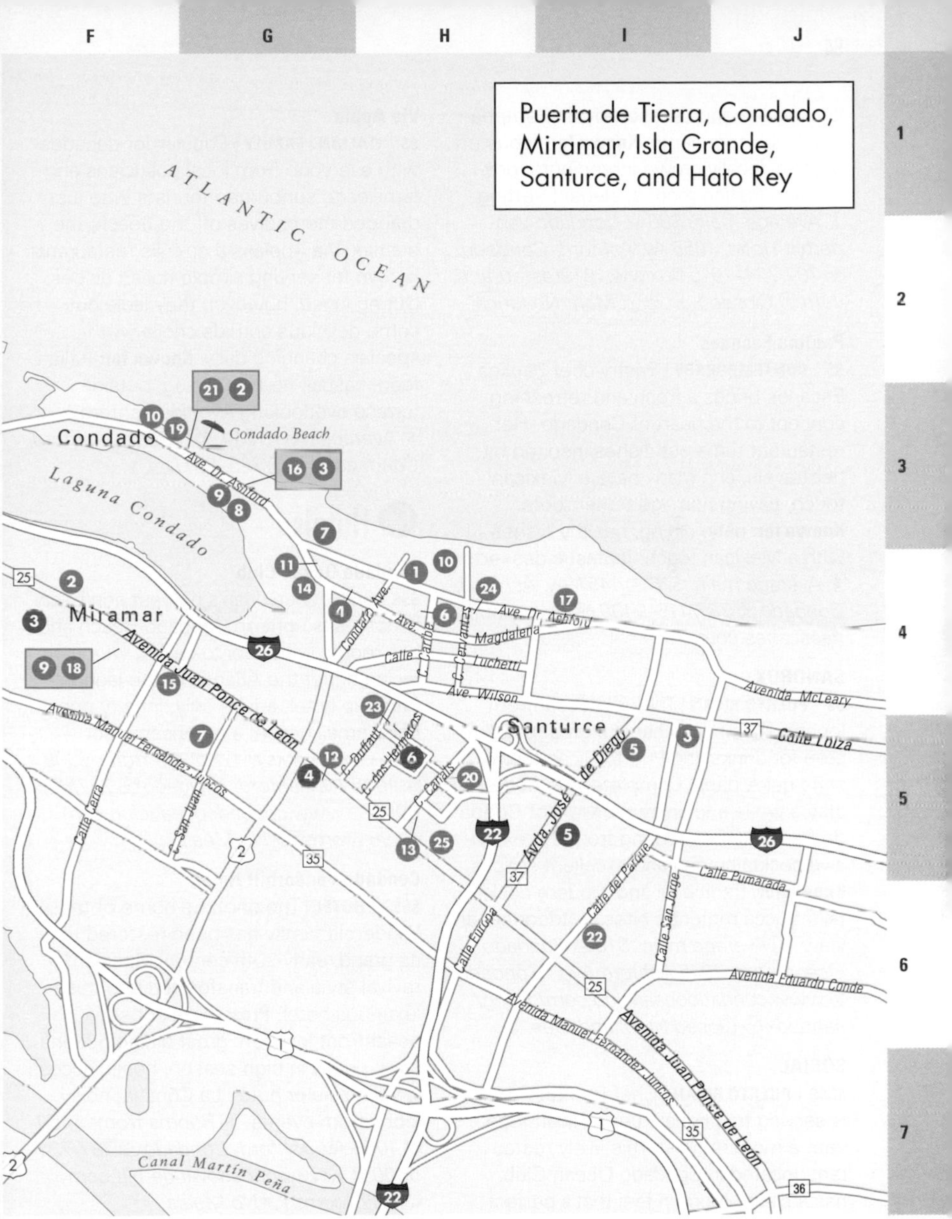

19 SANDBOX F3
20 Santaella H5
21 SOCIAL G3
22 SUR Barra Nikkei I6
23 Tasca El Pescador H5
24 Via Appia H4
25 Vianda H5

Hotels ▼

1 Caribe Hilton San Juan E2
2 Condado Ocean Club G3
3 Condado Vanderbilt Hotel G3
4 Coral Princess Hotel G4
5 DoubleTree by Hilton San Juan at Gallery Plaza I5
6 Hyatt House San Juan E4
7 La Concha— A Renaissance Resort G3
8 O:live Boutique Hotel G3
9 O:LV Fifty Five G3
10 San Juan Marriott Resort & Stellaris Casino H4

la carte—change seasonally and emphasize local ingredients. **Known for:** focus on organic, locally grown ingredients; prix-fixe and tasting menus; elegant setting. *Average main: $36 ✉ Condado Vanderbilt Hotel, 1055 Av. Ashford, Condado ☎ 787/724–1919 ⊕ www.1919restaurant.com ⊙ Closed Sun. and Mon. No lunch.*

Paulina Escanes

$$ | **CONTEMPORARY** | Pastry chef Paulina Escanes brings a fresh and refreshing concept to the heart of Condado. Her restaurant turns out dishes inspired by her travels, and many have a Mexican touch, paying homage to her roots. **Known for:** patio dining; healthy dishes with a Mexican touch; fantastic desserts. *Average main: $16 ✉ 1451 Av. Ashford, Condado ☎ 787/415–9400 ⊕ www.paulinaescanes.com.*

SANDBOX

$$ | **PUERTO RICAN** | The new oceanfront lounge-style beach bar is a great place to stop for drinks and Puerto Rican tapas-style quick bites. Completely outdoors, stay a while and enjoy the view of Condado Beach while ordering from the extensive cocktail menu and excellent snacks. **Known for:** traditional and modern cocktails; yucca mofongo bites; outdoor ocean view. *Average main: $16 ✉ Condado Ocean Club, 1045 Ashford Ave., Condado ⊕ www.condadooceanclub.com/dining/sandbox ⊙ Closed Mon. and Tues.*

SOCIAL

$$$$ | **PUERTO RICAN** | Chef Ramon Cruz is serving traditional Puerto Rican food with a modern twist. This lively restaurant, located in Condado Ocean Club, has a clean, modern feel that's perfect for date nights, girls' night out, or any special occasion calling for a lively place to socialize over wine and an extensive menu. **Known for:** ocean views; extensive wine list; lively atmosphere. *Average main: $35 ✉ Condado Ocean Club, 1045 Ashford Ave., Condado ☎ 787/625–5900 ⊕ www.condadooceanclub.com/dining/social.*

Via Appia

$$ | **ITALIAN** | **FAMILY** | Popular for decades with everyone from local politicians and families to sunburned tourists who just dragged themselves off the beach, the bustling Via Appia is a no-frills restaurant known for serving simple Italian dishes. During lunch, however, they ladle out some delicious comida criolla, with specials changing daily. **Known for:** Italian food; casual, no-frills dining; outside terrace overlooking Avenida Ashford. *Average main: $14 ✉ 1350 Av. Ashford, Condado ☎ 787/725–8711.*

Hotels

Condado Ocean Club

$$$ | **HOTEL** | San Juan's newest adults-only hotel sits right on Condado Beach and has rooms with floor-to-ceiling windows facing either the Atlantic or the lagoon. **Pros:** hip hotel; adults only; infinity pool. **Cons:** small beach; a bit pricey; pool area can be noisy. *Rooms from: $309 ✉ 1045 Av. Ashford, Condado ☎ 787/625–6000 ⊕ www.condadooceanclub.com 96 rooms No Meals.*

Condado Vanderbilt Hotel

$$$$ | **HOTEL** | The onetime home of the Vanderbilt family has been restored to its grand, early-20th-century, Spanish revival style and transformed into this luxurious hotel. **Pros:** excellent service; oceanfront location; great dining options. **Cons:** pricey in high season; beach access is via its sister hotel, La Concha; noisy lobby from events. *Rooms from: $450 ✉ 1055 Av. Ashford, Condado ☎ 787/721–5500 ⊕ www.condadovanderbilt.com 317 rooms No Meals.*

Coral Princess Hotel

$$ | **HOTEL** | This affordable boutique hotel is a good choice for a quiet, romantic getaway: the hotel is only a block from the neighborhood's main drag, and the beach is a three-minute walk away. **Pros:** comfortable common areas; Wi-Fi in rooms; friendly staff. **Cons:** not directly

on the beach; small pool; limited parking. $ *Rooms from: $165* ✉ *1159 Av. Magdalena, Condado* ☎ *787/977–7700* 🌐 *www.coralpr.com* *25 rooms* *No Meals.*

DoubleTree by Hilton San Juan at Gallery Plaza

$$$ | **HOTEL** | Slightly geared to business travelers, the DoubleTree offers attractive rooms and an excellent value for anyone who doesn't need to be in central Condado or on the beach. **Pros:** excellent value for the neighborhood; good on-site dining options; free shuttle to beach. **Cons:** a bit of a walk to the beach and the main drag in Condado; chain-hotel feel; random location. $ *Rooms from: $275* ✉ *105 Av. de Diego, Condado* ☎ *787/721–1200* 🌐 *www.sanjuandoubletree.com* *184 rooms* *No Meals.*

★ **La Concha—A Renaissance Resort**

$$$ | **RESORT** | Not only does this property epitomize the chic Caribbean resort, but it's also an icon of tropical modernist architecture—from the undulating ceiling in the sprawling lobby to Perla, the shell-shape event space. **Pros:** numerous on-site social activities; beautiful guest rooms; beachfront location. **Cons:** noisy bar/lobby, particularly when there's live music; beach can be narrow at high tide; pricey bar. $ *Rooms from: $350* ✉ *1077 Av. Ashford, Condado* ☎ *787/721–7500* 🌐 *www.laconcharesort.com* *483 rooms* *No Meals.*

★ **O:live Boutique Hotel**

$$ | **HOTEL** | Tucked away on a quiet street overlooking the lagoon, this luxurious, all-suites boutique hotel recalls the south of France, with artwork from Italy, Spain, Morocco, and France. **Pros:** beautiful decor; close to shops and restaurants; rooftop terrace. **Cons:** small pool; see-through bathrooms not for everyone; no parking lot. $ *Rooms from: $350* ✉ *55 Calle Aguadilla, Condado* ☎ *787/705–9994* 🌐 *www.oliveboutiquehotel.com* *15 suites* *Free Breakfast.*

O:LV Fifty Five

$$$$ | **HOTEL** | Opulent and luxurious, this adults-only Condado hotel has 26 lavish guest suites. **Pros:** adults-only hotel; over-the-top, luxurious decor; rooftop pool and bar. **Cons:** service can be brash; not on the beach; some noise from the rooftop. $ *Rooms from: $500* ✉ *55 Barranquitas St., Condado* 🌐 *www.olvhotel.com* *26 rooms* *No Meals.*

San Juan Marriott Resort & Stellaris Casino

$$$$ | **RESORT** | **FAMILY** | The shape and color of a cardboard box, this lively, popular hotel doesn't add much to the skyline of Condado, but step inside the impressive lobby—with its stunning coral sculpture carved from wood, chic spots for lounging, and welcoming bar—and you'll feel you've arrived in the Caribbean. **Pros:** on one of the area's best beaches; near dozens of dining options; lots of amenities. **Cons:** uninspired architecture; lots of conventions; noise from lobby. $ *Rooms from: $500* ✉ *1309 Av. Ashford, Condado* ☎ *787/722–7000, 787/631–0595* 🌐 *www.marriottsanjuan.com* *527 rooms* *No Meals.*

Nightlife

CASINOS

By law, all casinos are in hotels, and the government keeps a close eye on them. They're allowed to operate 24 hours a day, but individual casinos set their own hours. That said, an easing of gaming regulations has set a more relaxed tone and made such perks as free drinks and live music more common. The range of available games has also greatly expanded. Typical offerings include blackjack, roulette, craps, Caribbean stud poker (a five-card stud game), and *pai gow* poker (a combination of American poker and the ancient Chinese game of pai gow, which employs cards and dice), in addition to the usual slot machines. The minimum age is 18. Dress for the larger casinos in San Juan tends to be on the formal side, and the atmosphere is

Design Lions

Puerto Rico's young fashion designers have opened many a boutique and atelier in metropolitan San Juan over the past few years. Their styles may differ, but these young lions all share an island heritage—complete with a tradition of true craftsmanship—and a level of sophistication acquired after studying and traveling abroad. The result is a fascinating assortment of original, exclusive, high-quality designs.

With all the warmth and sun, it goes without saying that Puerto Rico's designers are most inspired when it comes to attire for the spring and summer seasons. Lacy, flowing creations and lightweight, if not sheer, fabrics dominate designs for women. For men, the trend is toward updated linen classics in tropical whites and creams. Whatever you find will be one of a kind, with stylish—if not playful or downright sexy—lines. Some of these designers have their own shops in San Juan.

Which designers should you check out? Lisa Cappalli, a graduate of New York City's Parsons School of Design, favors lace, as lace making is a tradition in her family. David Antonio uses upbeat colors—bold reds and vibrant oranges—in his updated classics. Harry Robles is a bit more established than his peers; he specializes in gowns for women, and his draping designs are often dramatic and always elegant. Jean Cintrón is Puerto Rico's rising star. Not yet 30 years old, he has taken the fashion world by storm with his resort and ready-to-wear collections.

—Isabel Abislaimán

refined; tank tops and shorts are usually not acceptable attire.

Stellaris Casino

CASINO | The crowd is casual and the decor tropical and bubbly at this spacious gaming room. Right outside, there's a huge bar where Latin musicians perform on weekends, and an adjacent café. ✉ *San Juan Marriott Resort, 1309 Av. Ashford, Condado* ☎ *787/722–7000.*

Shopping

CLOTHING

Monsieur

MEN'S CLOTHING | The quality clothing at Monsieur is very sleek and stylish—everything for the well-dressed man. ✉ *1126 Av. Ashford, Condado* ☎ *787/722–0918* 🌐 *www.monsieurpuertorico.com.*

Nativa

WOMEN'S CLOTHING | The window displays are almost as daring as the clothes at this shop, which caters to trendy young ladies looking for party dresses, jumpers, accessories, and shoes. ✉ *55 Calle Cervantes, Condado* ☎ *787/724–1396* 🌐 *www.nativabtq.com.*

Olivia Boutique

JEWELRY & WATCHES | Here you'll find luxury designer clothing, shoes, and accessories for women. The curated collections are beautiful. ✉ *1400 Av. Magdalena, Condado* ☎ *787/722–6317* 🌐 *shop-olivia.com.*

Otto

MEN'S CLOTHING | Otto Bauzá stocks international lines of casual and formal wear for younger men. ✉ *69 Av. Condado, Condado* ☎ *787/722–4609.*

Suola

SHOES | Fittingly for a shop named after the Italian word for "sole," the boot-shape country is the origin of many of the mile-high heels that it sells. Look for designs by Christian Louboutin, YSL, Roberto Cavalli, and John Galliano. ✉ *1124 Av. Ashford, Condado* ☎ *787/723–6653.*

Activities

KAYAKING AND PADDLEBOARDING

The Laguna del Condado is popular for kayaking and paddleboarding, especially on weekends. You can simply paddle around it or head out under the Puente Dos Hermanos to the San Gerónimo fort right behind the Caribe Hilton and across from the Conrad San Juan Condado Plaza. Kayak rentals cost $25–$35 per hour.

VIP Adventures Puerto Rico

KAYAKING | **FAMILY** | This company rents paddleboards and kayaks ($30 per hour) in the Condado Lagoon. The friendly, attentive staff will give you a basic lesson, ensuring you're comfortable and relaxed before you head out on your own. If you're lucky, you'll see the family of manatees that live in the lagoon. ✉ *860 Av. Ashford, Condado* ☎ *787/466–0131* 🌐 *www.adventurespuertorico.com.*

SPAS

Zen Spa

HEALTH CLUB | This family-run spa focuses on wellness—with staff trained in Western, Chinese, and Ayurvedic techniques—but all kinds of treatments are available. One facial uses silk fibers to firm and tone skin. You can also get a green tea clay wrap or a lymphatic drainage massage. An attached shop sells Kiehl's and Eminence Organics products, as well the house line, Zendera. ✉ *1054 Av. Ashford, Condado* ☎ *787/722–8433, 866/936–7720* 🌐 *www.zen-spa.com.*

Miramar and Isla Grande

Across the bay from Condado is **Miramar,** a quiet, mostly residential neighborhood. Recently, many young professionals have moved to the area, resulting in a wave of great bars and restaurants. It's also where you'll find the Convention District and the Puerto Rico Conservatory of Music. Home to the Puerto Rico Convention Center, the San Juan Marina, and Isla Grande airport, the once-industrial area of **Isla Grande** is rapidly developing along the waterfront. The District Live complex brings a mix of shopping, dining, and entertainment to the area.

Sights

MADMI (Museum of Art & Design Miramar)

ART MUSEUM | Housed in a gorgeous, pastel-pink, 20th-century structure that was once the home of famous Puerto Rican artists, MADMI opened its doors in 2018. It's an interactive museum that hosts rotating exhibits, workshops, and pop-ups. The on-site shop sells items made by local artists. Grab a coffee next door at La Hacienda, which has a shady outdoor terrace. ✉ *607 Calle Cuevillas, Miramar* ☎ *787/995–7063* 🌐 *www.madmi.org* 🎟 *$5 donation.*

Restaurants

Ariel

$$$$ | **EUROPEAN** | Under the direction of noted chef Ariel Rodríguez, one of the city's more celebrated restaurants is popular with the local elite for its old-school, fine-dining atmosphere and its international cuisine with strong French influences. A prix-fixe menu is available with or without wine pairings. **Known for:** well-executed European cuisine; Sunday brunch; superb and extensive wine list. 💲 *Average main: $35* ✉ *Courtyard Marriott Miramar, 801 Av. Ponce de León, Miramar* ☎ *787/725–7700* 🕑 *Closed Mon. No dinner Sun.*

★ **Casita Miramar**
$$ | **PUERTO RICAN** | **FAMILY** | This family-run restaurant in the heart of residential Miramar is known for its traditional comida criolla. It feels more like a home than a restaurant, so it's a great place to just sit back, relax, and enjoy your meal. **Known for:** excellent, friendly service; old-fashioned dishes like crab-stuffed avocado; great drinks and sangria. *Average main: $20* ✉ *605 Av. Miramar, Miramar* ☎ *787/200–8227* ⏲ *Closed Mon. and Tues.*

Gustos Café
$ | **CAFÉ** | In addition to serving its signature Gustos coffee, grown in the mountains of Yauco, this café has simple sandwiches and pastries. You'll be lucky to get a seat, as it's wildly popular. **Known for:** great coffee; popular with locals; artisanal products for sale. *Average main: $4* ✉ *Miramar Plaza, Suite 105, Miramar* ☎ *787/300–2580* 🌐 *www.gustoscoffee-co.com* ⏲ *Closed Sun.*

Miramar Food Truck Park
$$ | **ECLECTIC** | **FAMILY** | Proprietor Yareli Manning runs this food-truck park in the heart of Miramar, where seating is at communal picnic tables. Though the roster of vehicles changes, regulars include Meatball Company, Yummy Dumplings, and Pa'l Pita. **Known for:** variety of quick-bite options; outdoor dining; family-friendly atmosphere. *Average main: $12* ✉ *1006 Av. Ponce de Leon, Miramar* ☎ *787/398–3305* ⏲ *Closed Mon.*

Rosa & Elena
$$ | **AMERICAN** | At breakfast, this Instagram-friendly restaurant serves dishes like avocado toast on grilled sourdough with a poached egg or bagels with smoked salmon and lemon-dill cream cheese. Lunch options include pasta carbonara, shaved Brussels sprouts Caesar salad, or a turkey club with basil mayo. **Known for:** breakfast and brunch; Instagram-friendly decor; sourdough breads. *Average main: $13* ✉ *Miramar Plaza, 954 Av. Ponce de Leon, Miramar* ☎ *787/705–2890* 🌐 *www.rosaandelena.com.*

Hotels

Hyatt House San Juan
$$ | **HOTEL** | Close to the convention center and popular with business travelers, this all-suites hotel is also a great option for families. **Pros:** great complimentary breakfast; rooms have full kitchens; friendly staff. **Cons:** long walk to restaurants and bars; chain-hotel feel; not on or near a beach. *Rooms from: $250* ✉ *615 Av. Fernandez Juncos, Isla Grande* ☎ *787/977–5000* 🌐 *sanjuan.house.hyatt.com* *126 suites* *Free Breakfast.*

Nightlife

BARS

Bar La Unidad
BARS | Dark, sexy, and romantic, this hidden speakeasy is a lovely spot for a cocktail. There's a cigar lounge in the back room, and the sliders are delicious. There's no sign, so look for the three red rings on the door. ✉ *562 Calle Cuevillas, Miramar* ☎ *787/985–9292* 🌐 *www.launidadpr.com.*

Shopping

ART GALLERIES

Galería Petrus
ART GALLERIES | Among those who have displayed their works at Galería Petrus are Dafne Elvira, whose surreal oils and acrylics tease and seduce (witness a woman emerging from a banana peel); Marta Pérez, another surrealist, whose bewitching paintings examine such themes as how life on a coffee plantation might have been; and Elizam Escobar, a former political prisoner whose oils depict typically dark subjects. Exhibitions change frequently and focus on local artists like Bobby Cruz and Carlos Dávila.

Artistic history unfolds at the Museo de Arte de Puerto Rico. Highlights include colonial-era ecclesiastical works and later secular paintings by Francisco Oller.

✉ *Galeria Petrus, 726 Calle Hoare, Miramar* ☎ *787/289–0505* 🌐 *www.petrusgallery.com.*

Santurce and Hato Rey

Venture into **Santurce** to explore a mixed commercial and residential district with a growing artistic community, thanks to the Museo de Arte de Puerto Rico, the Museo de Arte Contemporáneo, and sprouting art galleries. You'll also find a thriving nightlife scene on weekends. Nearby, **Hato Rey** is a busy financial district that's home to the large Plaza Las Américas Mall.

Sights

Museo de Arte Contemporáneo de Puerto Rico

ART MUSEUM | This Georgian-style structure, once a public school, displays a dynamic range of works by established and up-and-coming Latin American artists. Many works have strong political messages, including pointed commentaries on Puerto Rico's status as a commonwealth. Only part of the permanent collection's more than 900 works is on display at a time, but it might be anything from ceramics to videos. ✉ *1220 Av. Ponce de León, at Av. R. H. Todd, Santurce* ☎ *787/977–4030* 🌐 *www.museomac.org* 🎟 *$5* ⏲ *Closed Sun. and Mon.*

★ Museo de Arte de Puerto Rico

ART MUSEUM | One of the Caribbean's biggest museums, this beautiful neoclassical building was once the San Juan Municipal Hospital. The collection of Puerto Rican art starts with the colonial era, when most art was commissioned for churches. Works by José Campeche, the island's first great painter, include his masterpiece, *Immaculate Conception,* finished in 1794. Also well represented is Francisco Oller, who was the first to move beyond religious subjects to paint local scenes; another room has the works of artists who were inspired by him. The original building, built in the

1920s, proved too small to house the collection. A newer east wing is dominated by a five-story, stained-glass window by local artist Eric Tabales. The museum also has a beautiful garden with native flora and a 400-seat theater with a remarkable hand-crocheted lace curtain. ✉ *299 Av. José de Diego, Santurce* ☎ *787/977–6277* 🌐 *www.mapr.org* 🎟 *$6* 🕓 *Closed Mon. and Tues.*

Plaza del Mercado (*La Placita*)
MARKET | Though often overlooked by tourists, charming La Placita (as it's known by locals) is one of San Juan's liveliest spots. At its center is a market hall (circa 1910) where you—perhaps alongside chefs from the city's top restaurants—can shop for fruits and vegetables, including exotic options like *guanábana* and *caimito*. The many restaurants and bars facing the central square are quiet during the day but busy in the evening, especially on weekends. Nearby are Santaella, a stellar restaurant by renowned chef Jose Santaella, and Junglebird, known for its craft and tiki cocktails. The area also has many *botánicas*—small shops that sell herbs, candles, and religious items. The square is between the Museo de Arte de Puerto Rico and the Museo de Arte Contemporáneo de Puerto Rico, making it a good place to stop for dinner and drinks after a day of museum-hopping. ✉ *Calle Dos Hermanos, at Calle Capital, Santurce.*

Restaurants

★ Cocina al Fondo
$$$ | **PUERTO RICAN** | Dining at chef Natalia Vallejo's restaurant in the heart of Santurce is a magical experience. The restored home is simply yet tastefully decorated and leads to a large outdoor patio in a lush and vibrant setting. **Known for:** charming outdoor patio; creative Puerto Rican cuisine; award-winning chef. 💲 *Average main: $25* ✉ *658 Calle San Juan, Santurce* 🌐 *www.cocinaalfondo.com* 🕓 *Closed Mon. and Tues.*

La Santurcina
$$ | **PIZZA** | **FAMILY** | It's an exciting time for pizza in San Juan and one of the newest and most delicious additions to the scene is La Santurcina. Brought to you by the owners of the upscale restaurant Vianda, this full-service pizza joint is a pizza-churning, bustling machine that's always packed. **Known for:** family-friendly vibe; vegetable-forward menu; creative pizzas. 💲 *Average main: $20* ✉ *1250 Ponce de Leon Ave, Santurce.*

Mai Pen Rai
$$ | **THAI** | Chef Kelly Piro perfectly executes such Thai dishes as *som tam* (papaya salad), drunken noodles with barbecue pork, and green curry with shrimp. The bar serves excellent cocktails, although it's best known for its large gin selection. **Known for:** reservations are recommended; gin cocktails; drunken noodles and green curry. 💲 *Average main: $16* ✉ *303 Calle Canals, Santurce* ☎ *787/998–6338* 🌐 *www.maipenraisanturce.com* 🕓 *Closed Tues. No lunch Mon., Wed., and Thurs.*

★ Santaella
$$$ | **PUERTO RICAN** | A career working with top chefs and a successful catering business prefaced chef José Santaella's namesake restaurant in La Placita marketplace. The menu is dominated by tapas, and favorites include the ahi tuna skewers, goat-cheese quesadilla, and *morcilla* (blood sausage) fritters. **Known for:** small plates of nouveau Puerto Rican specialties; trendy ambience; great cocktails. 💲 *Average main: $29* ✉ *La Placita de Santurce, 219 Calle Canals, Santurce* ☎ *787/725–1611* 🌐 *www.santaellapr.com* 🕓 *Closed Sun. and Mon. No lunch Sat.*

SUR Barra Nikkei
$$ | **PERUVIAN** | Chef Rafael Ubior's time in Lima working under Peru's esteemed Gastón Acurio led him to open his restaurant fusing Peruvian and Japanese cuisines. Start with the *tiradito* (raw fish) Nikkei or any of the ceviches; then order anything that's on special that day, as well as a pisco sour. **Known for:** variety

of ceviches; pisco sours and creative cocktails; outdoor terrace. *Average main: $20* *411 Calle del Parque, Santurce* *939/775–0365* *Closed Sun. and Mon.*

Tasca El Pescador

$$ | SEAFOOD | If you want Spanish-style seafood dishes, head to this restaurant, one of a dozen that surround the Plaza del Mercado. The *chillo entero frito* (fried whole red snapper) and *camarones al ajillo* (shrimp with garlic) are tasty, but the standout is the *arroz con calamari*: this dramatic, inky-black rice dish will elicit "oohs" and "aahs" from nearby diners when it arrives at your table. **Known for:** local popularity; squid-ink rice; outdoor dining. *Average main: $19* *178 Calle Dos Hermanos, Santurce* *787/721–0995* *Closed Mon. and Tues.*

★ Vianda

$$$ | ECLECTIC | Driven by local ingredients and seasonality, chef Francis Guzman's dishes are culinary delights (think: California cuisine with Puerto Rican and Caribbean influences). The service is fantastic, and the wine list and cocktail menu are strong—anything with mezcal is a particularly good choice. **Known for:** farm-to-table-focused menu; fantastic crudos; excellent service. *Average main: $24* *1413 Av. Ponce de León, Santurce* *939/475–1578* *www.viandapr.com* *Closed Mon. and Tues. No lunch.*

Nightlife

BARS

Esquina el Watusi

BARS | For a non-touristy experience, head to this lively dive bar in the heart of Santurce, and order a Medalla or a rum drink with fresh juice. There's often live music being played on the street to a packed house. Be sure to take in the incredible street art on a stroll through the area. *801 Calle Elisa Cerra, Santurce* *787/388–7434.*

Junglebird

BARS | Run by the same guys as La Factoría in Old San Juan, this tropical tiki bar is steps from La Placita. Although it has a charming patio, its dark, cozy interior is a pleasant respite from the busy marketplace, and the bar food is excellent, with a rotating, seasonal menu. *254 Calle Canals, Santurce* *787/995–9706* *www.junglebirdbar.com.*

La Penúltima

PUBS | After a night of drinking at La Placita, head to hipster favorite, La Penúltima, for a nightcap (perhaps a carbonated Negroni) and fantastic late-night bites! *1359 Av. Ponce de León, Santurce* *787/523–6538.*

GAY AND LESBIAN BARS AND CLUBS

With its sophisticated nightlife, San Juan has become a popular destination for gay tourists. Each June, the annual pride march, full of music and dancing, rivals those in similar cities around the world. Condado Beach has a strong gay following, while Santurce, just south of Condado, is known for nightlife.

Oasis

BARS | This gay-friendly bar is just steps from Condado beach. *6 Av. Condado, San Juan* *917/570–4787.*

Performing Arts

MAJOR VENUES

Centro de Bellas Artes Luis A. Ferré (*Luis A. Ferré Center for the Performing Arts*)

ARTS CENTERS | With four different theaters, the largest of which holds up to 1,900 people, this is the largest venue of its kind in the Caribbean. There's something going on nearly every night, from pop or jazz concerts to plays, operas, and ballets. It's also the home of the Puerto Rico Symphony Orchestra. *22 Av. Ponce de León, Santurce* *787/724–4747, 787/620–4444* *www.cba.gobierno.pr.*

Coliseo de Puerto Rico José Miguel Agrelot
CONCERTS | Seating up to 18,000 people, this relatively new arena, affectionately known as "El Choliseo," is the top venue for international musical events on the island. Past performers have included Ozzy Osbourne, Paul McCartney, Shakira, Beyoncé, and, of course, hometown favorites Ricky Martin and Bad Bunny. ✉ *50 Calle Arterial B, Hato Rey* ☎ *787/777–0800* 🌐 *www.coliseodepuertorico.com.*

Coliseo Roberto Clemente
ARTS CENTERS | Named after the baseball hall-of-famer, this arena has become an important island venue for concerts and fairs in addition to its status as a sports facility. Rap, reggae, salsa, jazz, and pop musicians play to crowds of up to 8,000 people. ✉ *500 Av. Roosevelt, across from Plaza Las Américas, Hato Rey* ☎ *787/781–2586.*

Estadio Hiram Bithorn (*Hiram Bithorn Stadium*)
ARTS CENTERS | Particularly big acts often use this outdoor stadium (adjacent to the Coliseo Roberto Clemente), which hosts baseball games as well as large concerts. There's seating capacity for at least 18,000, more when the infield is used to accommodate fans. ✉ *Av. Roosevelt at Plaza Las Américas, Hato Rey* ☎ *787/725–2110.*

CLASSICAL MUSIC

Orquesta Sinfónica de Puerto Rico (*Puerto Rico Symphony Orchestra*)
MUSIC | Under the direction of conductor Maximiano Valdés, this 80-member orchestra performs a 52-week season that includes classical music, operas, ballets, and popular music. The orchestra mainly plays at the Centro de Bellas Artes Luis A. Ferré, but they also do outdoor concerts at museums, universities, and landmarks around the island, in addition to educational outreach in island schools. Pablo Casals helped create the group in 1956. ✉ *San Juan* ☎ *787/918–1107* 🌐 *www.cba.pr.gov.*

Shopping

CLOTHING

Jean Cintrón
OTHER SPECIALTY STORE | Up-and-coming young designer Jean Cintrón has his appointment-only shop on Calle Cerra. Visit the website to schedule a visit. ✉ *615 Calle Cerra, Santurce* ☎ *787/400–5775* 🌐 *www.jeancintron.com.*

Stella Nolasco
WOMEN'S CLOTHING | Celebrated local designer Stella Nolasco has showcased her creations in both New York and Paris. You'll find bold colors, lace, and intricate beading in her luxurious pieces. Stella also designs one-of-a-kind wedding gowns. ✉ *Condominio Plaza de Diego, 305 Av. de Diego, Santurce* ☎ *787/723–2897* 🌐 *stellanolasco.shop.*

JEWELRY

Reinhold Jewelers
JEWELRY & WATCHES | Reinhold Jewelers sells designs by Stephen Dweck, David Yurman, Tiffany & Co., and others. ✉ *Plaza Las Américas, 525 Av. Franklin Delano Roosevelt, Hato Rey* ☎ *787/754–0528* 🌐 *www.reinholdjewelers.com.*

MARKETS AND MALLS

Plaza Las Américas
MALL | For a complete shopping experience, head to the massive Plaza Las Américas, which has more than 300 retailers, including Zara, Gap, Macy's, Sephora, and Kiehl's, as well as multiple restaurants and movie theaters. ✉ *525 Av. Franklin Delano Roosevelt, Hato Rey* ☎ *787/767–1525* 🌐 *www.plazalasamericas.com.*

Activities

BASEBALL

Does the name Roberto Clemente ring a bell? The late, great Pittsburgh Pirate, who died in a 1972 plane crash en route to deliver supplies to Nicaraguan earthquake victims, was born near San Juan and got his start in the Puerto

Rican professional league. Many other Puerto Rican stars have gone on to play for Major League Baseball, including the brothers Roberto Alomar and Sandy Alomar Jr. and their father, Sandy Alomar. Three players have been inducted into the National Baseball Hall of Fame: Clemente, Orlando Cepeda, and Roberto Alomar.

Estadio Hiram Bithorn

BASEBALL & SOFTBALL | Baseball games in the San Juan area are played at Estadio Hiram Bithorn, named for the first Puerto Rican to play in the major leagues. It's the home of the Cangrejeros de Santurce. ✉ *Hato Rey* ☎ *787/725–2110.*

TENNIS

Parque Central Municipio de San Juan

TENNIS | The Parque Central Municipio de San Juan has several lighted courts. Fees are minimal for one hour of tennis. You can also bike, walk, or run throughout the park's trails, or exercise on the popular racetrack. There is a $2 fee to access the park by car; it's free for pedestrians. ✉ *Calle Cerra, exit on Rte. 2, Santurce* ☎ *787/480–2980.*

Ocean Park

Ocean Park is a partially gated residential community with a laid-back feel. If you dream of staying in a quiet guesthouse on a more secluded beach—away from the crowds—this might be the spot for you.

Beaches

Playa de Ocean Park

BEACH | The residential neighborhood east of Condado and west of Isla Verde is home to this 1½-km-long (1-mile-long) stretch of golden sand. The waters are often choppy but still swimmable—take care, however, as there are no lifeguards on duty. Windsurfers say the conditions here are nearly perfect. The tranquil beach is popular with young people as well as gay men—particularly on weekends. Parking is a bit difficult, as many of the streets are gated and restricted to residents. **Amenities:** none. **Best for:** partiers; windsurfing. ✉ *Calle Santa Ana, Ocean Park.*

Restaurants

Acapulco Taquería Mexicana

$ | MEXICAN | Located behind a pawn shop, Acapulco doesn't have the most inspiring location, but you should seek out this tiny restaurant for some of the best Mexican food in Puerto Rico. The tacos and guacamole are always made from scratch, and the owners pride themselves on authenticity: you won't find iceberg lettuce or a chimichanga slathered in cheddar here. **Known for:** delicious tacos and guacamole; friendly service; excellent margaritas made with fresh juices. *Average main: $8* ✉ *2021 Calle Loíza, Ocean Park* ☎ *787/727–5568* *Closed Mon.*

Bocca Osteria Romana

$$ | ITALIAN | FAMILY | Located at the end of Calle Loíza, this family-run restaurant specializes in Roman dishes. The open kitchen turns out dishes like spaghetti carbonara, penne puttanesca, and bucatini all'amatriciana. **Known for:** Roman-style dishes; Italian comfort food; carbonara. *Average main: $18* ✉ *1059 Calle Loíza, Ocean Park* ☎ *787/727–8017* *www.boccapr.com.*

Egg Joint

$ | BURGER | Tasty sandwiches and burgers are available all day long at this small joint. The onion smasher comes with two beef patties, finely shredded onions, and cheese on a warm brioche bun, and specials may include a perfectly crisp, chicken-tender sandwich or a decadent pork belly with fried egg and sweet-and-sour chipotle sauce. **Known for:** burgers; tater tots; excellent sandwiches. *Average*

The color of the beach chairs stylishly matches that of the sea on this palm-lined stretch, one of San Juan's many beautiful beaches.

main: $9 ✉ *1802 Calle Loíza, Ocean Park* ☎ *787/625–1547* 🌐 *www.eggjoint.com.*

Kasalta

$$ | **CAFÉ** | **FAMILY** | This local bakery is always buzzing with locals and tourists. Display cases are full of luscious pastries, including the *quesito* (cream cheese–filled puff pastry), and sandwiches include the *medianoche,* made famous when President Obama ordered one while campaigning. **Known for:** great baked goods, including cream cheese–filled quesitos; medianoche sandwiches; sometimes curt service. $ *Average main: $16* ✉ *1966 Calle McLeary, Ocean Park* ☎ *787/727–7340* 🌐 *www.kasalta.com.*

La Cueva del Mar

$$ | **SEAFOOD** | **FAMILY** | Families with kids, beachgoers in flip-flops, and businesspeople all flock to this casual, marine-themed restaurant, renowned for its seafood dishes. Grouper tacos, lightly fried and topped with a spicy slaw, are a best seller—don't leave without trying at least one. **Known for:** house-made hot sauce; fish tacos; conch in season. $ *Average main: $15* ✉ *1857 Calle Loíza, Ocean Park* ☎ *787/726–8700* 🌐 *www.lacuevatogo.com.*

Nonna

$$ | **ITALIAN** | This cozy spot does a wonderful job with traditional Italian dishes of the kind that your *nonna* (grandmother) might have made. The ravioli *di anatra,* filled with braised duck and pear in a port-wine reduction and topped with truffle butter, is great. **Known for:** all house-made pastas and mozzarella di buffala; cozy ambience; creative cocktails. $ *Average main: $19* ✉ *103 Calle San Jorge, Ocean Park* ☎ *787/998–6555* 🌐 *www.nonnapr.com.*

Pinky's

$ | **CAFÉ** | **FAMILY** | People pack this playful café—where bustling servers wear cheeky "Eat Me!" T-shirts—to enjoy fresh wraps, sandwiches, salads, *batidas* (fruit smoothies), and coffee. You might not need another meal for the rest of the day if you finish the Drunken Pilot, a breakfast dish with four eggs, spinach, tomato, onion, mushroom, and goat cheese. **Known for:** a variety of batidas; the Surfer sandwich with turkey, mozzarella, basil, tomato, and pesto mayo; all-day breakfast. *Average main: $8 1902 Calle Loíza, Ocean Park 787/222–5222 No dinner.*

Sabrina

$$ | **BISTRO** | Named after the classic film starring Audrey Hepburn, this lively, tropical-chic bistro serves creative Caribbean dishes such as poached lobster in clarified butter or mussels in coconut broth. Sunday brunch is a draw, too, with options like eggs Benedict with *mangú*. Fashionable locals also come to sip cocktails and enjoy the live music that's often being played. **Known for:** seasonal menu; fashionable crowd; live music and cocktails. *Average main: $19 1801 Calle Loíza, Ocean Park 787/302–5419 Closed Mon.*

Tia Dora

$$ | **ISRAELI** | **FAMILY** | Chef Raúl Correa's newest venture pays tribute to Israeli and Mediterranean cuisines. Dishes are meant to be shared at this casual neighborhood restaurant that's walking distance from the beach. **Known for:** popular chef; vegan-friendly dishes; Mediterranean cuisine. *Average main: $13 51 Maria Mosco St., Ocean Park.*

Tresbé

$ | **CARIBBEAN** | The three "B's" in this bright-yellow restaurant's name stand for *bueno, bonito, y barato,* a common saying that means "good, pretty, and affordable." Tasty and inexpensive—no wonder it's such a hit with everyone from beachgoers to artists to young professionals. Order at the window, and sit at one of the picnic-style tables on the wooden deck. **Known for:** alfresco dining; grouper ceviche and beef sliders; drinks. *Average main: $8 1765 Calle Loíza, Ocean Park 787/294–9604.*

YOKO

$$$ | **JAPANESE** | The decor is minimalist yet inviting, a nod to Japan's tradition of elegant simplicity, and the culinary experience is spectacular. Start with the pork *gyozas* (dumplings) or *tomorokoshi* (grilled corn), before moving on to the sushi rolls. **Known for:** izakaya; sushi; toro flown in from Japan. *Average main: $23 1762 Calle Loíza, Ocean Park 787/624–6120 Closed Sun.*

Hotels

Andalucía Guest House

$$ | **B&B/INN** | In a Spanish-style house, this friendly little inn evokes its namesake region with such details as hand-painted tiles and ceramic pots filled with greenery. **Pros:** terrific value; helpful hosts; gorgeous courtyard. **Cons:** not right on the beach; some rooms smaller than others; could use an update. *Rooms from: $165 2011 Calle McLeary, Ocean Park 787/309–3373 11 rooms No Meals.*

★ **The Dreamcatcher**

$$ | **B&B/INN** | Each room of this guest house—a relaxing oasis in the heart of Ocean Park and just steps from the beach—is uniquely decorated with vintage furniture and works of art that the owner has collected over the years. **Pros:** house chef on-site; yoga offered daily; two blocks from beach. **Cons:** no pool; some rooms share bathrooms; no in-room TVs. *Rooms from: $220 2009 Calle España, Ocean Park 787/455–8259 www.dreamerspuertorico.com 18 rooms No Meals.*

Numero Uno Beach House

$$$$ | **HOTEL** | This relaxing inn is so close to the beach that you can hear the crashing waves. **Pros:** friendly atmosphere; on-site, beachfront dining; on the beach. **Cons:** in a residential neighborhood far from other tourist areas; small pool; rooms are fairly basic. *Rooms from: $380 1 Calle Santa Ana, Ocean Park 787/726–5010, 866/726–5010 www.numerounobeachhouse.com 11 rooms No Meals.*

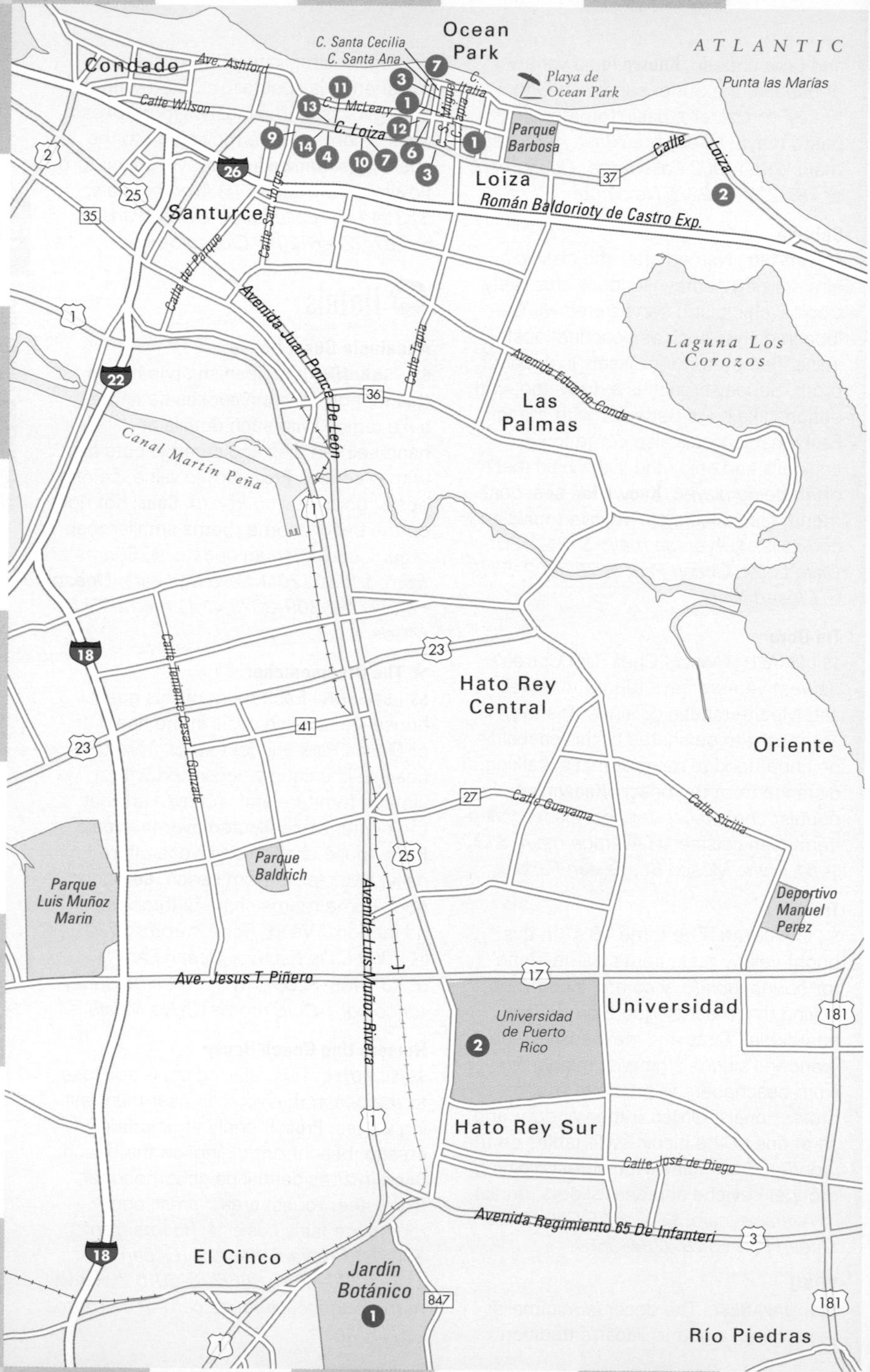

A
B
C
D
E
F
1
2
3
4
5
6
7
8
9
Ocean Park
ATLANTIC
C. Santa Cecilia
C. Santa Ana
Condado
Ave. Ashford
C. Italia
Playa de Ocean Park
Punta las Marías
Calle Wilson
C. McLeary
C. Loiza
Parque Barbosa
Calle Loiza
Loiza
Santurce
Román Baldorioty de Castro Exp.
Calle San Jorge
Calle del Parque
Avenida Juan Ponce De León
Calle Tapia
Laguna Los Corozos
Avenida Eduardo Conde
Las Palmas
Canal Martín Peña
Calle Teniente Cesar Gonzale
Hato Rey Central
Oriente
Calle Guayama
Calle Sicilia
Parque Baldrich
Parque Luis Muñoz Marin
Avenida Luis Muñoz Rivera
Deportivo Manuel Perez
Ave. Jesus T. Piñero
Universidad
Universidad de Puerto Rico
Hato Rey Sur
Calle José de Diego
Avenida Regimiento 65 De Infanteri
El Cinco
Jardín Botánico
Río Piedras

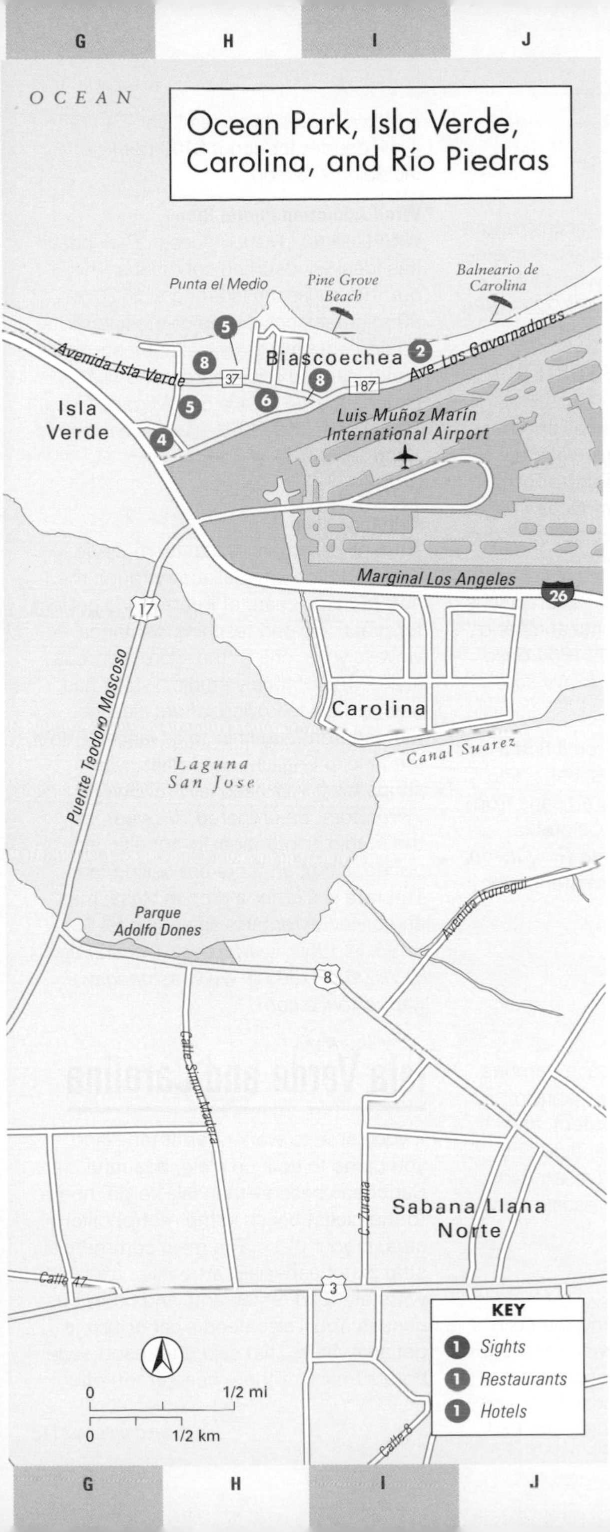

Sights

1 Jardín Botánico....................C9

2 Museo de Historia, Antropología y Arte.............. D7

Restaurants

1 Acapulco Taquería Mexicana.... D1

2 Bistro Café..........................E2

3 Bocca Osteria Romana C1

4 Egg Joint.............................C1

5 Entrevinos H3

6 Kasalta...............................C1

7 La Cueva del Mar...................C1

8 Metropol Restaurant and Bar..... I3

9 Nonna.............................. B1

10 Pinky's..............................C1

11 Sabrina..............................C1

12 Tia Dora C1

13 Tresbé...............................C1

14 YOKO C1

Hotels

1 Andalucía Guest House............C1

2 Courtyard by Marriott Isla Verde Beach Resort........................ I2

3 The Dreamcatcher C1

4 Embassy Suites by Hilton San Juan Hotel & Casino I3

5 Fairmont El San Juan Hotel....... H2

6 Hampton Inn and Suites San Juan H3

7 Numero Uno Beach House........C1

8 Royal Sonesta San Juan.......... H2

Shopping

CLOTHING

Harry Robles

WOMEN'S CLOTHING | Puerto Rican couture designer Harry Robles specializes in elegant evening and bridal gowns. ✉ *1752 Calle Loíza, Ocean Park* ☎ *787/727–3885* 🌐 *www.harryrobles.com.*

JEWELRY AND ACCESSORIES

Luca

JEWELRY & WATCHES | This small shop sells modern clothing and jewelry by independent artists from Puerto Rico and abroad. ✉ *59 Calle Taft, Ocean Park* ☎ *787/398–3468* 🌐 *www.shop-luca.com.*

T Playa

JEWELRY & WATCHES | Owner Tanamá sells an array of vintage straw hats and handbags in her tiny boutique. ✉ *1804 Calle Loíza, Ocean Park* 🌐 *www.tplaya.com.*

UNBOX

JEWELRY & WATCHES | Here you'll find a selection of handmade hats, bags, and other accessories made by artisans from Latin America, particularly Colombia. ✉ *110 Calle del Parque, Suite GB, Ocean Park* ☎ *787/948–7985* 🌐 *www.unboxpr.com.*

Activities

SURFING

Tres Palmas Surf Shop

SURFING | At Ocean Park Beach, famous surfer and proprietor Carlos Cabrero rents boards, repairs equipment, and sells all sorts of hip beach and surfing gear. ✉ *1911 Av. McLeary, Ocean Park* ☎ *787/728–3377* 🌐 *www.trespalmaspr.com.*

WINDSURFING AND PADDLEBOARDING

The waves can be strong and the surf choppy, but the constant wind makes for good sailing, windsurfing, or paddleboarding, particularly in Ocean Park and Punta Las Marías (between Ocean Park and Isla Verde). In general, you can rent a windsurfer for about $100 per hour, including a lesson.

Wind Addiction Puerto Rico

WINDSURFING | **FAMILY** | Ocean Park beach has ideal windsurfing conditions. This outfitter's classes (starting at $120 for 90 minutes) include top-of-the-line rental equipment, and the excellent instructors make learning a fun, adrenaline-filled experience. ✉ *1 Calle San Miguel, Ocean Park* ☎ *787/599–4976* 🌐 *www.windaddictionpr.com.*

YOGA

Ashtanga Yoga

YOGA | Husband-and-wife team David Kyle and Elizabeth Sallaberry found the hot, humid climate of Puerto Rico perfect for practicing and teaching Ashtanga vinyasa yoga, one of the more vigorous styles. Their friendly studio, which has a large local following, offers classes ranging from beginner to advanced (most are held in English), as well as workshops from internationally renowned instructors. Be prepared to sweat, as the studio is intentionally not air-conditioned, although there are ceiling fans. The rate is $21 for a drop-in class; mat and/or towel rental is an additional $3 to $5. ✉ *1950 Av. McLeary, Ocean Park* ☎ *787/677–7585* 🌐 *www.ashtangayogapuertorico.com.*

Isla Verde and Carolina

If you came to work on your tan—and you came to do it on a big, beautiful Caribbean beach—then Isla Verde, home to the nicest beach in the metropolitan area, is your place. The main commercial strip is not especially attractive: it's filled with fast-food restaurants and other businesses. You'll also need a car or taxi to get anywhere. That said, the resort-style hotels (many of them beachfront) offer

Continued on page 113

Salsa

A Guide to Puerto Rico's Favorite Music and Dance

Salsa: its hip-shaking rhythms and sensual moves embody the spirit of the Caribbean and Latin America. The songs and the steps create a language all their own—one that's spoken by passionate dancers and musicians the world over. But it's the Puerto Ricans who are the most fluent. Welcome to the home of salsa! Are you ready to dance?

by Julie Schwietert Collazo

As the first notes of the song sound, dancers come alive, eager to take their place on the floor with a partner whose skill matches their own. These are the most daring salsa devotees who are found in every corner of the island, dancers who won't quit moving until the music stops. Even as a bystander, it's impossible to stand still.

Salsa isn't a passive rhythm: it's animated, hot, and sensual, a metaphor for the Caribbean itself. In general, the themes of the songs mirror the moves of the dance, with choruses alluding to love, both forbidden and open. In the music and the movement, there's occasional improvisation among those who know the genre. Hips shake to the clave, which marks the basic rhythm, and shoulders shake from one side to the other, fanning the air. It's a democratic form, where experimentation is encouraged . . . you just have to be willing to get out there.

SALSA HISTORY

Timbale master Tito Puente

Though salsa has its roots outside Puerto Rico, the island is directly responsible for the rhythm known by this name. As a musical form, the components of salsa can be traced back to Europe and Africa. During the colonial period, Spanish conquistadores arriving from the West Indies brought island rhythms along with them. They also brought the complex, multi-rhythmic riffs of Arabic music, an artifact of the Muslim conquest of the Iberian Peninsula that had become embedded in the music of Spain and Portugal. In Puerto Rico, all of these musical strands came together to create a new rhythm known as bomba.

The emergence of salsa was deeply influenced by musical forms from Cuba and other parts of the Caribbean, as well as musical experimentation by diaspora Puerto Ricans living in New York. Among the most important of these mainland musicians was the late percussionist and band leader Tito Puente.

The history of salsa is the history of the new world. In salsa, there's evidence of rhythms from past ages, as well as the musical history of our own time. Salsa isn't a "pure" musical form, but represents—like Puerto Rico itself—a mixture of rhythmic elements, adapted by the inhabitants of the new world.

DID YOU KNOW?

- The first use of the word "salsa" related to music was in 1937 by Cuban composer Igancio Pineiro in his popular song, "Echale Salsita." It continues to be a frequently recorded song today by artists in and outside Cuba.
- The song "Oye Como Va" was originally composed by Tito Puente in 1963 and later recorded by Carlos Santana, who made it a number-one hit.
- The contribution of salsa to jazz music dates from 1940, when Dizzie Gillespie and Stan Kenton incorporated salsa in their tunes, giving birth to "Latin jazz."
- More than 30 countries celebrate salsa with annual festivals, among them, Poland, Israel, France, Serbia, and Japan.

SALSA SPEAK

ABRAZO: The *abrazo* is the positioning of the partners' hands and arms. The woman's left hand rests lightly on her partner's shoulder, while his right hand is placed on the small of her back to guide her. The abrazo establishes the space each partner maintains during turns.

Abrazo

Vueltas

VUELTAS: *Vueltas*, turns, are an important component of salsa. There are numerous styles, and they can occur in both directions, but all are determined and initiated by the male partner. Turns are spontaneous; their complexity depends upon the skill and experience of the dancers.

Solos

SOLOS: Solos—a favorite move of experienced dancers—are moments when the partners separate to move independently though still in response to each other. These are often synchronized with the solos of percussion musicians. Solos are also used as a means of rest after a series of complex turns before the pair comes together again for even more intricate turns.

SALSA STYLE

Two elements define salsa fashion: comfort and sensuality. Men and women both draw from the best of their wardrobes, with men often dressed in guayabera shirts, linen pants, and two-toned dance shoes. Suede shoes permit optimal movement for men and add a touch of elegance. Women typically wear dresses—often knee length or shorter—and open-toed, medium-heeled dance shoes with ankle support. For both men and women, freedom of movement and maximum ventilation are important elements of a salsa wardrobe.

The dance is an opportunity to show off your elegance and your sensuality, but your clothing should also honor the significance of the event and venue. Many dance organizers impose dress policies, prohibiting running shoes, sleeveless shirts, and overly informal or provocative clothing. Dress to impress.

Salsa dance shoes

NEXT STEPS

If you're ready to take to the dance floor, here are some of the best places to learn—and then show off—your moves.

LESSONS

The Academia de Baile Julie Mayoral. On the Plaza de las Delicias in Ponce, Mayoral's second floor studio is steaming hot, and her young, enthusiastic instructors will have you doing proper vueltas in no time. For a bit more than $5 for an hour lesson, Mayoral probably offers the best deal in Puerto Rico. Mayoral also has studios in Coamo and Yauco. Call her Ponce studio (☎ 787/843–2830) for information about lessons at any of the three studios.

In San Juan, dancer Paulette Beauchamp offers salsa classes for children and adults on Tuesday. Her studio, **DanzActiva** (☎ 787/775–9438 🌐 www.danzactiva.com), is in the historic Cuartel de Ballaja building in Old San Juan.

HOTELS

Locals and tourists alike take to the dance floor at the **San Juan Marriott Resort** and **Stellaris Casino** on weekends, when homegrown musicians provide a soundtrack for the salsa experience. Entry is free, but you'll need to purchase drinks if you decide to rest at one of the tables circling the dance floor.

CLUBS

Old San Juan's **Nuyorican Café** looks like a dive—and it is—but it's the heart of Puerto Rico's salsa scene. Though the café also hosts jazz and rock groups as well as poetry readings and experimental theatre, its reputation for world-class salsa has expanded far beyond the island. Call ahead for the current schedule (☎ 787/977–1276).

FESTIVALS

As the home of salsa, Puerto Rico hosts an annual **International Salsa Congress.** It's held in San Juan each July, though the site changes each year. The congress attracts thousands of aficionados from the island and from surprisingly far-flung places, including Japan, Korea, and Norway.

so many restaurants and other on-site amenities, you may not need—or want—to leave very often.

Beaches

Balneario de Carolina

BEACH | FAMILY | When people talk about a "beautiful Isla Verde beach," this Blue Flag beach is the one—even though it's so close to the airport that leaves rustle when planes take off. Thanks to an offshore reef, the surf here is not as strong as at other nearby beaches, so it's good for families. There's plenty of room to spread out underneath the palm and almond trees, and there are picnic tables and grills. Although there's a charge for parking, there's not always someone to take the money. On weekends, the beach is crowded; get here early to nab parking. The Vivo Beach Club offers lounge chairs and beautiful facilities for food and drink, including a brewery. **Amenities:** food and drink; lifeguards; parking (fee); showers; toilets. **Best for:** swimming; walking. ✉ *Av. Los Gobernadores, Carolina* *Parking $4.*

Pine Grove Beach

BEACH | This beach at the end of the Isla Verde strip is a great spot to take a surfing lesson. The sandy bottom and waves are perfect for beginners. **Amenities**: food and drink; water sports. **Best For**: surfing; swimming. ✉ *Pine Grove Beach, Isla Verde.*

Restaurants

Bistro Café

$$ | CAFÉ | FAMILY | This café is wildly popular and doesn't take reservations, but the offerings are worth the wait. Order the pancakes with Nutella, and the mocha coffee with whipped cream and a rim of Oreos. **Known for:** all-day breakfast; large portions; creative coffee drinks. [$] *Average main: $13* ✉ *29 Calle Júpiter, Isla Verde* ☎ *787/603–5757.*

Entrevinos

$$$$ | WINE BAR | Here, the wines are reasonably priced, and the menu is varied, with favorites like osso bucco, beef carpaccio, grilled octopus, lobster risotto, and Wagyu-and-foie-gras dumplings. Portions are large, service is excellent, and brunch is served on weekends. **Known for:** affordable and varied wine list; large portions; weekend brunch. [$] *Average main: $35* ✉ *6150 Av. Isla Verde, #187, Isla Verde* ☎ *787/705–7600* 🌐 *www.entrevinospr.com.*

Metropol Restaurant and Bar

$$ | CARIBBEAN | FAMILY | Across the street from a string of major hotels, this casual restaurant doesn't look like much from the outside, but inside it's decorated in warm, tropical colors. The kitchen turns out delicious versions of Cuban and Puerto Rican favorites at reasonable prices. **Known for:** local vibe; large portions of typical dishes like churrasco and ropa vieja; family-friendly atmosphere. [$] *Average main: $18* ✉ *Av. Isla Verde, Anexo Club Gallistico, Isla Verde* ☎ *787/791–5585* 🌐 *www.metropolrestaurant.com.*

Hotels

Courtyard by Marriott Isla Verde Beach Resort

$$$ | RESORT | FAMILY | This 12-story resort tries to be all things to all people—and succeeds to a great degree. **Pros:** on a great beach; family-friendly environment; good value. **Cons:** you can hear airport noise from some rooms; lobby is busy and noisy; far from Condado and Old San Juan. [$] *Rooms from: $339* ✉ *7012 Av. Boca de Cangrejos, Isla Verde* ☎ *787/791–0404, 787/999–6300* 🌐 *www.sjcourtyard.com* *281 rooms* *No Meals.*

Embassy Suites by Hilton San Juan Hotel & Casino

$$$ | HOTEL | Minutes from the airport, this hotel is known for its friendly staff, its perks, and its glass elevators that rise amid a plant-filled atrium with a pond and waterfall. **Pros:** family-friendly place; pretty pool; free cocktail receptions. **Cons:** not on beach; chain-hotel feel; far from Condado and Old San Juan. *Rooms from: $295* ✉ *8000 Calle Tartak, Isla Verde* ☎ *787/791–0505, 888/791–0505* 🌐 *www.embassysuitessanjuan.com* *299 suites* *Free Breakfast.*

★ Fairmont El San Juan Hotel
$$$$ | RESORT | FAMILY | Post-hurricane renovations gave the rooms a more modern look (with shades of blue, white, and cream), but elsewhere, this hotel's classic appeal remains, including in the lobby, which has intricately carved mahogany walls. **Pros:** beautiful pool; fantastic beach; large guest rooms. **Cons:** noise in lobby from bars; parking lot a long walk from hotel entrance; small bathrooms. *Rooms from: $395* ✉ *6063 Av. Isla Verde, Isla Verde* ☎ *787/791–1000* 🌐 *www.elsanjuanhotel.com* *388 rooms* *No Meals.*

Hampton Inn and Suites San Juan
$$$$ | HOTEL | If you don't mind a short walk to the beach, you can get a room at this friendly hotel for much less than its competitors across the road. **Pros:** helpful staff; close to airport; good value. **Cons:** 5–10-minute walk from the beach; bit pricey for a chain-hotel feel; some highway noise in pool area. *Rooms from: $380* ✉ *6530 Av. Isla Verde, Isla Verde* ☎ *787/791–8777* 🌐 *www.hamptoninn.com* *200 rooms* *Free Breakfast.*

Royal Sonesta San Juan
$$$ | RESORT | FAMILY | Although it's somewhat dowdy on the outside, the Royal Sonesta's remodeled guest rooms are spacious and contemporary, done in soothing shades of white, cream, and brown. **Pros:** lovely pool; on one of the city's best beaches; recently renovated rooms. **Cons:** unattractive facade; cramped lobby; no longer has a casino. *Rooms from: $350* ✉ *5961 Av. Isla Verde, Isla Verde* ☎ *787/791–6100, 800/443–2009* 🌐 *www.sonesta.com* *398 rooms* *No Meals.*

A Golf Great

Juan "Chi Chi" Rodriguez, who was born in Río Piedras in 1935, was the first Puerto Rican golfer to be inducted into the World Golf Hall of Fame. During his career, he won eight PGA Tour events and 37 tournaments overall. He continued playing on the Senior PGA Tour, winning 22 additional victories between 1986 and 1993. He founded the Chi Chi Rodriguez Youth Foundation in 1979 to help at-risk youth. He has designed two Puerto Rico golf courses: El Legado golf Resort in Guayama and the course at the Embassy Suites Dorado del Mar Beach & Golf Resort.

Nightlife

BARS

KUMO
BARS | On the roof of Aire de O:live, this sexy, bohemian spot offers some of Isla Verde's best ocean views. The Japanese-inspired menu offers creative sushi rolls, charcoal-grilled skewers, *sakanas* (Japanese snacks served with sake), and a selection of excellent cocktails. ✉ *San Juan Water Beach Club Hotel, 2 Calle Tartak, Isla Verde* ☎ *787/725–4664* 🌐 *www.airedeolive.com.*

CASINOS

DANCE CLUBS

Brava
DANCE CLUBS | Dress to impress at this chic hotel dance club, where a long line of young people (21-plus) wait to get in Thursday through Saturday. Each of the two levels has its own DJ and dance floor. ✉ *El San Juan Hotel, 6063 Av. Isla*

Verde, Isla Verde ☎ *787/791–2781* 🌐 *bravamanagementgroup.com.*

Shopping

MARKETS AND MALLS

Plaza Carolina

MALL | About 15 minutes east of San Juan, you'll find Plaza Carolina, with locals shops, as well as chain stores like Clarks, Forever 21, and T.J. Maxx. Get there via Route 26. ✉ *Av. Jesús M. Fragoso, Carolina* ☎ *787/768–0514* 🌐 *www.simon.com/mall/plaza-carolina.*

OUTLETS

The Outlet 66 Mall

OUTLET | This complex in Canóvanas, about 25 minutes east of San Juan, has more than 50 factory outlet stores, including Adidas, Nautica, Guess, Tommy Hilfiger, and Calvin Klein. Those who aren't into shopping can head to the entertainment center, where offerings include kart racing, virtual reality experiences, bowling, and an arcade. ✉ *18400 Rte. 3, Km 18.4, Canóvanas* ☎ *787/256–7040* 🌐 *www.theoutletmall66.com.*

Activities

DIVING AND SNORKELING

The waters off San Juan aren't the best places to scuba dive, but several outfitters conduct short excursions to where tropical fish, coral, and seahorses are visible at depths of 30–60 feet. Escorted half-day dives start around $70 for one or two tanks, including all equipment; in general, double those prices for night dives. Packages that include lunch and other extras start at $100; others that include accommodations are also available.

Snorkeling excursions, which include transportation, equipment rental, and sometimes lunch, start at $55–$60. Equipment rental runs about $10 at beaches. Avoid unsupervised areas, as rough waters and strong undertows make some places dangerous.

Ocean Sports

SCUBA DIVING | Ocean Sports offers certified scuba courses; snorkeling excursions; specialty courses in nitrox diving; diving trips; air-tank fill-ups; and equipment repairs, sales, and rentals. ✉ *3086 Av. Isla Verde, Isla Verde* ☎ *787/723–8513* 🌐 *www.osdivers.com.*

SURFING

Pine Grove Surf Club

SURFING | **FAMILY** | It's likely you'll be standing up and riding a wave soon after your surfing class ($75 an hour for individual lessons) with these patient, encouraging instructors. Surfboards are also available for rent ($25 for two hours). Look for the kiosk at Pine Grove Beach. ✉ *Pine Grove Beach, Isla Verde* ☎ *787/361–5531* 🌐 *www.pinegrovesurfclub.com.*

TENNIS

If you'd like to use the tennis courts at a property where you aren't a guest, call in advance for information about reservations and fees.

Club Tennis de Isla Verde

TENNIS | These four lighted courts are open to nonmembers at $20 per hour for up to four people (daily 8 am–10 pm). Reservations are required. ✉ *Isla Verde Park, Calles Emma at Delta Rodriguez, Isla Verde* ☎ *787/727–6490, 787/642–3208* 🌐 *islaverdetennis.com.*

Río Piedras

The mostly residential Río Piedras area is home to the University of Puerto Rico, on whose campus you'll find the Botanical Garden and an interesting museum.

Sights

Jardín Botánico (*Botanical Garden*)

GARDEN | This 75-acre forest of more than 200 species of tropical and subtropical

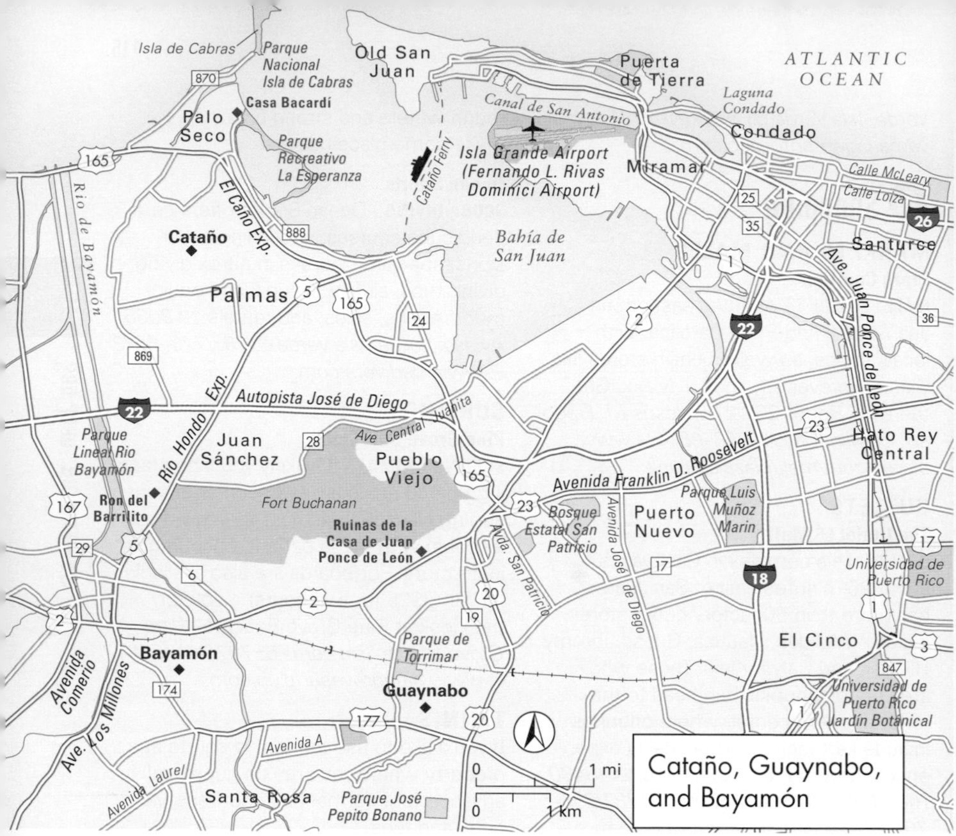

Cataño, Guaynabo, and Bayamón

vegetation is the Universidad de Puerto Rico's main attraction. Gravel footpaths lead to a graceful lotus lagoon and a bamboo promenade, as well as orchid and palm gardens. Not all plants and trees are labeled, so the garden is more of a tranquil retreat than an opportunity to learn about the vegetation. Trail maps are available at the entrance gate; the $5 tour is well worth it. ✉ *Universidad de Puerto Rico, Rte. 1 at Rte. 847, at entrance to Barrio Venezuela, Río Piedras* ☎ *787/758–9957* 🌐 *www.upr.edu* 🎟 *Free.*

Museo de Historia, Antropología y Arte

ART MUSEUM | The Universidad de Puerto Rico's small Museum of History, Anthropology and Art offers rotating exhibitions in three areas. Its archaeological and historical collection covers the Native American influence on the island and the Caribbean, the colonial era, and the history of slavery. There's also a small collection of Egyptian antiquities. Art holdings include a range of Puerto Rican popular, graphic, folk, and fine art; the museum's prize exhibit is the painting *El Velorio* (*The Wake*), by the 19th-century artist Francisco Oller. If you're looking to see something in particular, call before you go, as only a small portion of the collection is on display at a time. Guided tours in English are available; call for reservations. ✉ *Universidad de Puerto Rico, Av. Ponce de León, Río Piedras* ☎ *787/763–3939* 🌐 *museo.uprrp.edu* 🎟 *Free* ⏲ *Closed weekends.*

Shopping

MARKETS AND MALLS

The Mall of San Juan

MALL | This upscale mall is the most luxurious in the Caribbean. Shops include

Ron del Barrilito, distilling since 1880, produces just 14,000 cases of its local-favorite rum each year.

Hugo Boss, Bulgari, Jimmy Choo, Williams-Sonoma, Louis Vuitton, and more. The top floor houses Il Nuovo Mercato, an Italian food court where you can sample fresh pastas and brick-oven pizzas—don't miss the gelato stand. ✉ *1000 Mall of San Juan Blvd., Ramon Antonini, Río Piedras* ☎ *787/759–6310* 🌐 *themallofsanjuan.com.*

Cataño

Catano, bordered by the Bahía de San Juan in the north, is an industrial suburb, perhaps most noted for its distillery belonging to Bacardí. Bayamón can be reached in 15–30 minutes from central San Juan; if you come by car, stop by the attractive central park, bordered by historic buildings. The waterfront is in development with restaurants and bars sprouting up. Many have fantastic views of Old San Juan.

Sights

Casa Bacardi

DISTILLERY | The Bacardí family built a small rum distillery in the 1950s after they were exiled from Cuba. It's now the world's largest distillery, able to produce 100,000 gallons of spirits a day, which translates to 21 million cases a year. Book a mixology class or rum-tasting tour; both include a welcome cocktail at the pavilion and a trolley ride through the property. A ferry is available from Pier 2 (50¢), but then you'll have to Uber, or you can drive. ✉ *Bay View Industrial Park, Rte. 165, Km 2.6, at Rte. 888, Cataño* ☎ *787/788–8400* 🌐 *www.visitcasabacardi.com* 🎫 *$75 (mixology class or rum tasting).*

Guaynabo

Guaynabo is a mix of residential and industrial areas and is worth visiting for its historical importance—Juan Ponce de León established the island's first settlement here in Caparra, and you can visit the ruins of the original fortification.

Sights

Ruinas de la Casa de Juan Ponce de León (*Caparra Archaeological Site*)
RUINS | In 1508, Ponce de León established the island's first settlement here. The Caparra Ruins—just a few crumbling walls—are all that remain of an ancient fort. The small **Museo de la Conquista y Colonización de Puerto Rico** (Museum of the Conquest and Colonization of Puerto Rico) contains historical documents, exhibits, and excavated artifacts, although you can see the museum's contents in less time than it takes to say its name. Both the ruins and the museum are maintained by the Puerto Rican Institute of Culture. ✉ *Rte. 2, Km 6.4, Guaynabo* ☎ *787/781–4795* 🎫 *Free* ⏲ *Closed weekends.*

Shopping

MARKETS AND MALLS

San Patricio Plaza
SHOPPING CENTER | Off Avenida John F. Kennedy, about 15 minutes south of San Juan, San Patricio Plaza has a T.J. Maxx and a Bed Bath & Beyond, a movie theater, and several restaurants. For the best dining in the area, head to Bottles or Avocado. ✉ *100 Av. San Patricio, at Av. Franklin Delano Roosevelt, Guaynabo* ☎ *787/792–5328* 🌐 *www.sanpatricio.com.*

Bayamón

Just to the west of Guaynabo, Bayamón is a busy, sprawling suburb of San Juan (it's actually the second-largest city in Puerto Rico). Although it's home to a giant shopping mall and a distinctive rum distillery, most visitors who make it out this far are probably just passing through en route to Isabela and Rincón.

Sights

★ **Ron del Barrilito**
DISTILLERY | Although Ron del Barrilito's handcrafted Puerto Rican rum isn't often seen outside the island, it's a local favorite that has been around since 1880. A visit to its distillery, which only produces about 14,000 cases a year, offers a more authentic experience than a trip to larger operations. It's also a great way to ensure you take home a truly special island souvenir. The rum's four varieties are differentiated by how long they're aged. Most places only carry the two- and three-star bottles; the rarer four-star version is aged up to 20 years, and the extremely limited five-star variety spends 35 years in oak casks. Although you can sample rum at the visitor center, for a more in-depth look at things, book a Heritage Tour, Rum Tasting Tour, or mixology class. ✉ *Hacienda Santa Ana, Carretera 5, Km 5.5, Bayamón* ☎ *787/415–8601* 🌐 *rondelbarrilito.com* 🎫 *$30–$60, depending on tour* ⏲ *Closed Sun.*

Shopping

MARKETS AND MALLS

Plaza del Sol
SHOPPING CENTER | Plaza del Sol has Old Navy, Bed Bath & Beyond, Home Depot, and H&M, among other stores. It's about 30 minutes west of San Juan. ✉ *725 Av. Principal Oeste, Bayamón* ☎ *787/778–8724.*

Chapter 4

EL YUNQUE AND THE NORTHEAST

Updated by
Jennifer Ruiz Garay

Sights	Restaurants	Hotels	Shopping	Nightlife
★★★★★	★★★★☆	★★★★☆	★☆☆☆☆	★☆☆☆☆

WELCOME TO EL YUNQUE AND THE NORTHEAST

TOP REASONS TO GO

★ **Take a hike:** Take in the spectacular waterfalls of El Yunque, the only rain forest within the U.S. National Forest system.

★ **Take a dip:** Relax at Luquillo Beach, one of the prettiest beaches in Puerto Rico and a family favorite.

★ **Take a seat:** Hang with locals at one of the dozens of outdoor seafood kiosks on the highway before you get to Luquillo Beach.

★ **Hit the links:** Tee off on the tree-lined fairways of one of the area's golf courses, especially at St. Regis Bahia Beach.

If you seek an alternative to the hectic urban environs of San Juan, head to the pristine coastal towns and charming inland locales along Puerto Rico's northeast corridor. Easily reached by car, El Yunque and northeast Puerto Rico are convenient enough for a quick day trip, but they offer enough exploration for at least two days. Kayak the lagoon in Piñones, take a surf lesson in Luquillo, horseback ride in the foothills of El Yunque, or tee off in Humacao—the list of exciting and relaxing activities in this region goes on and on.

1 Piñones. A popular destination among locals, this coastal town between Isla Verde and Río Grande comes alive on weekends, when food kiosks and roadside stands sell all manner of fried Puerto Rican snacks, many of them stuffed with freshly caught seafood. Grab one for yourself, and sit along the shore, contemplating the vast Atlantic.

2 Río Grande. Río Grande is home to Puerto Rico's most popular natural attraction, El Yunque, North America's only tropical rain forest. There's not much in the town beyond that, but its proximity to Luquillo Beach and Ceiba, the departure point for ferries to Vieques and Culebra, makes it a bustling town.

3 El Yunque. Puerto Rico's most visited site is this tropical rain forest, a lush green palette. It was heavily damaged by Hurricane Maria, though, so before making the trip, check on current conditions and accessibility in the parts of the forest that interest you.

4 Luquillo. With an expansive beach that is postcard-perfect thanks to its neat row of coconut palms, lively Luquillo attracts people from across the island.

5 Fajardo. While Fajardo has more development, nearby Ceiba (just to the south) is now the point of departure for ferries that make daily trips to the outlying islands of Vieques and Culebra.

6 Naguabo. Boats that travel around Monkey Island, where rhesus monkey research is conducted, depart from here.

7 Humacao. Golfers take note: this coastal town has some of the island's best greens.

EL YUNQUE NATIONAL FOREST

El Yunque is the only tropical rain forest in the U.S. National Forest system, spanning 28,000 acres, reaching an elevation of more than 3,500 feet, and receiving an estimated average of 200–240 inches of rain each year.

Prior to Hurricane Maria, the forest's 13 hiking trails were extremely well maintained. The hurricane damaged much of the forest and work crews are still clearing trails; not all are open to the public as of this writing. Check with your hotel concierge or an El Yunque tour operator about the current status of trails. When open and clear of hurricane debris, most trails in the park are easy to navigate and less than 1 mile (1.6 km) long. If you prefer to see the sights from a car, as many people do, simply follow Route 191 as it winds into the mountains, and stop at several observation points along the way.

WHEN TO GO

It's about 73°F here year-round, so weather isn't much of a factor for seasonal planning. For easier parking and fewer crowds, be sure to arrive early in the day—although the park rarely gets crowded, by national park standards. Expect rain nearly every day, but keep your eyes peeled post-showers for the best bird-watching.

PARK HIGHLIGHTS

Flora and Fauna. Each year more than half a million visitors from all over the world come to El Yunque to experience the rain forest's ecological treasures. Rivers and streams provide habitats for freshwater snails, shrimp, and crabs, while approximately 66 species of migratory birds either winter in or pass through El Yunque. Sonorous coquí frogs (tree frogs endemic to Puerto Rico), 14 different lizard species, and more than 1,200 insect species—ranging from ants to beetles to flies—all inhabit the forest.

Four major forest types, roughly stratified by elevation, are home to thousands of native plants including 150 fern species and 240 tree species (88 of which are endemic or rare, and 23 exclusively found here). Two of the island's highest peaks rise out of this forest: El Toro and El Yunque, both at more than 3,500 feet.

El Yunque doesn't have larger wildlife species like monkeys, large cats, and poisonous snakes, but hundreds of small creatures have found their ecological niche here. Many of these species exist nowhere else on the planet, such as the endangered Puerto Rican green parrot, Puerto Rican boa, and Puerto Rican sharp-shinned hawk. If you're interested in bird-watching, pack your binoculars, because Puerto Rican todies, Puerto Rican lizard cuckoos, five species of hummingbird, flycatchers, and warblers are commonly spotted.

La Coca waterfall

Puerto Rico Spindalis

El Portalito HUB Visitor Center. This temporary visitor center is the place to stop before entering the park itself if you want to pick up a map and speak with a ranger.

Cascada La Coca. The first spectacular sight you're likely to see in El Yunque is Cascada La Coca (La Coca Falls), which plunges 85 feet down a flat sheet of solid rock. The waterfall is inches from the road, so it's visible from your car. The gate to the park, which opens at 9 am and closes at 4:30 pm, is just before the falls.

BEST WAYS TO EXPLORE

Hiking. At present, work crews continue to clear debris left by Hurricane Maria. Check at El Portalito HUB to confirm which trails are currently open and to ask about conditions of each.

Driving. A leisurely drive-through may not be as immersive as a hike, but you'll still encounter beautiful waterfalls, hibiscus, banana and orchid plants, lizards, and the occasional vista over the forest out to the Atlantic Ocean. The main and most direct route to El Yunque, Route 3, is a multilane highway dotted with places to stop for cold drinks and typical Puerto Rican snacks. Obey the speed limit, as rental cars are

Hiking in El Yunque is a great way to explore the rainforest.

frequently pulled over. From the highway, hop onto Route 191, the only road through the preserve. When hurricanes and mudslides haven't caused portions of the road to be closed, you can drive straight from the entrance to Km 13, the base of Pico El Yunque. A stop at El Portalito HUB will teach you everything you need to know about your majestic surroundings. Make another quick stop to climb the winding stairs of Yokahú Tower for breathtaking views of the rain forest and the island. Take note that drivers don't always recognize common road courtesies, such as slow cars to the right, stop signs, and signals.

Ziplining. This adrenaline-fueled, half-day activity enables visitors to take a tree-to-tree canopy tour via a network of platforms, cables, and pulleys. Step off a platform more than 80 feet up, and fly through the air as you take in bird's-eye views of the northern limit of El Yunque National Forest and El Yunque and Este peaks. For more information, contact Yunke Zipline Adventure (787/242–3368) or Rain Forest Zip Line Corp (787/370–1010).

STAY THE NIGHT

If you're thinking about a second day at El Yunque, book a room nearby instead of schlepping back to San Juan. (There is no lodging within the national forest.) The St. Regis Bahia Beach Resort and Meliá Coco Beach are both within a 10-minute drive in Río Grande, but the two cottages at Sue's Place in Barrio Sabana, above the town of Luquillo, cannot be beat (www.rainforestrental.com). For a taste of local flavor, visitors leaving the area may want to consider stopping off at the *friquitines* (seafood kiosks) lining Route 3 west of the beach turnoff. Frequented by locals and visitors alike, the kiosks are open all day and serve everything from cold drinks to stuffed lobsters, plates of fried fish (head and tail attached), and fritters (usually codfish or corn) to bagels and lox or Spanish-style tapas.

BEST ONE-DAY ITINERARY

Start at **El Portalito HUB.** Driveto **La Coca Falls**—one of the best photo ops in the park. View it from your car or climb up slippery rocks to the base of the falls. Then drive about half a mile to **Torre Yokahú** (Yokahú Observation Tower), a lookout with vistas of 1,000-year-old trees, exotic flowers, and birds in flight. (The tower has restrooms.) Continue just beyond the halfway point to the **Area de Pasadías Palma de Sierra.** Rangers here have information on closures, trail conditions, and daily activities. The center and the next two parking lots, Caimitillo and Palo Colorado, have trailheads to both **El Yunque summit** (a half-day adventure) and **La Mina Falls.** Casual hikers should follow the moderate **Big Tree Trail** to reach the falls (a half-hour hike). Bring a swimsuit for the falls, and water shoes or sandals to navigate the slippery rocks. More advanced hikers can follow **La Mina Falls Trail.** It's only 0.7 miles (1.1 km) long, but climbs to 2,132 feet. (Plan 30–45 minutes each way.) A little more than a mile up the road is one more trail, **Baño de Oro,** which offers a peaceful, quarter-mile walk on fairly flat ground along the river. It's less visited, and you may not see another soul on your walk.

Did You Know? El Yunque has had many names. President Theodore Roosevelt named it Luquillo Forest Reserve in 1903, and President Franklin Roosevelt changed its name to the Caribbean National Forest. In 2007 the area officially became El Yunque National Forest.

The Atlantic east coast is edged with sandy, palm-lined shores that are occasionally cut by rugged stretches. Some of these beaches are quiet, isolated escapes. Others—such as Luquillo and Seven Seas near Fajardo—are jammed with water-loving families, especially on weekends and during the Easter holidays. Known as "La Capital del Sol" (sun capital) and "La Riviera de Puerto Rico" (Puerto Rico's Riviera), Luquillo is beloved for its towering palm trees and shimmering sand. Its public beaches are among the nicest in the San Juan area, making it a popular stop on the coastal highway. Fajardo has a vibrant boating community with many hotels and inns. Snorkelers revel in Fajardo's crystal clear waters and, at night, its bioluminescent lagoon. In Piñones you can find solitary coastline. The surf here is strong, and swimming—especially in winter—can be dangerous at some beaches.

Tree frogs, rare parrots, and wild horses only start the list of northeastern Puerto Rico's offerings. The backdrops for encounters with an array of flora and fauna include the 28,000 acres of El Yunque tropical rain forest, the seven ecosystems in the Reserva Natural Las Cabezas de San Juan, and Laguna Grande, where tiny sea creatures appear to light up the waters.

As the ocean bends around the northeastern coast, it laps onto beaches of soft sand and palm trees, crashes against high bluffs, and almost magically creates an amazing roster of ecosystems. The beautiful beaches at Luquillo are complemented by more rugged southeastern shores. Inland, green hills roll down toward plains that once held expanses of coconut trees, such as those still surrounding the town of Piñones, or sugarcane, as evidenced by a few surviving plantations near Naguabo and Humacao.

The natural beauty and varied terrain continue in the area's other towns as well: Río Grande, which once attracted immigrants from Austria, Spain, and Italy; Naguabo, which overlooks what were once immense cane fields; and Cayo Santiago, where the only residents are monkeys.

You can golf, ride horses, hike marked trails, and plunge into water sports throughout the region. In many places, green hills cascade down to the ocean. On the edge of the Atlantic, Fajardo serves as a jumping-off point for diving, fishing, and catamaran excursions. Luquillo is the site of a family beach so well equipped that there are even facilities enabling wheelchair users to enter the sea.

MAJOR REGIONS

The Northeastern Coast. As you head east from San Juan, you'll first come to Piñones and its popular open-air eateries. Loiza is next, with a scenic beach displaying the largest drum in Puerto Rico. After, you'll come to Río Grande, which is the closest developed area to the rain forest and home to several restaurants and popular resorts, as well as long strips of pristine beach. Its closest neighbor is the region's magnificent natural wonder, El Yunque, a park you can explore in the air-conditioned comfort of a car in a matter of hours or hike in for days without seeing all the greenery, waterfalls, and views. Nearby in Luquillo, Balneario de Luquillo (Luquillo Beach) beckons. At the island's eastern end, the Reserva Natural Las Cabezas de San Juan and Fajardo are worth exploring.

The Eastern Coast. Below Fajardo on your way to Humacao is Ceiba. You may be flying or traveling through the city by ferry or plane. Be sure to check out the natural waterslides at Las Tinajas before heading south to Naguabo. This town is said to be the birthplace of the *pastelillo de chapín*, a popular dish that consists of trunkfish wrapped inside deep-fried flour dough. Farther south and west is Humacao, home of the island's exceptional Wyndham Candelero Beach Resort.

Planning

When to Go

In general, the northeast coast—preferred by those seeking abandoned beaches and nature reserves rather than casinos and urban glitz—tends to be less popular than San Juan. Exceptions include Easter and Christmas, when Luquillo and Fajardo become crowded with local sun worshippers, merrymakers, and campers. Island festivals also draw crowds, but planning a trip around one of them will give you a true sense of the region's culture. Be sure to make reservations well in advance if you're visiting during high season (December 15–April 15).

Getting Here and Around

AIR

Air Flamenco, Cape Air, and Vieques Air Link offer flights between San Juan, Vieques, and Culebra. Flights are also offered from Ceiba, and they're even shorter than those departing from San Juan.

CONTACTS Air Flamenco. ☎ *787/724–1818* 🌐 *www.flyairflamenco.com.* **Cape Air.** ☎ *800/227–3247* 🌐 *www.capeair.com.* **Vieques Air Link.** ☎ *787/741–8331, 888/901–9247* 🌐 *www.viequesairlink.com.*

BUS

Públicos (a cross between a privately owned taxi and a small van or bus) travel between San Juan and Fajardo, stopping en route at the ferry terminal in Ceiba. The full journey can take up to four hours, depending on where you board, frequency of stops, traffic, and where you are dropped off. However, the fare is a huge bargain at about $26 (pay the driver as you board). To get to Fajardo or Ceiba, simply flag down a público anywhere along Route 3.

Within cities and towns, local buses pick up and discharge at marked stops. Enter and pay at the front (35¢–50¢, exact fare required), and exit at the front or the back.

CAR

Unless you are planning to hop directly onto a ferry to Vieques or Culebra, you should consider renting a car in eastern Puerto Rico. Even the destination resorts are fairly isolated, and you may appreciate the mobility if you want to get out and have a meal away from the resort or explore El Yunque or some of the great beaches. Rates start at about $40 per day, but it may be possible to rent directly from your hotel, so ask about packages. And keep in mind that most of these resorts do charge a daily fee for parking.

From San Juan the east coast is accessible via Route 3, or Route 187 if you want to visit Piñones and Loíza. At Fajardo the road intersects with Route 53, which continues down the coast. Route 3 also continues along the coast, providing a more scenic, if slower, trip.

TAXI

You can flag cabs down on the street, but it's faster and safer to have your hotel call one for you. Make sure it's clear whether you'll pay a flat rate or a meter will determine the fare. Instead of renting a car, consider taking a taxi to Fajardo; the cost from the San Juan area should be about $80 for up to five people.

CONTACTS Humacao Taxi. ☎ *787/307–3933.*

Hotels

East coast lodgings range from small inns and guesthouses in the mountains to large, lavish resorts along the coast. Government-approved *paradores* are also available. A kind of country inn, paradores offer affordable Puerto Rican hospitality and the cozy comforts of home outside the San Juan metro area. These small, privately owned properties are usually quite picturesque and can be found throughout the interior and in more remote coastal towns. If you wish to get away from it all with a neatly packaged trip, eastern Puerto Rico has some of the island's top resorts: the St. Regis Bahia Beach Resort and El Conquistador, an iconic resort and the only hotel on the island with its own water park. You'll also find extensive facilities and services at large, self-contained complexes like the Wyndham Grand Río Mar and the Hyatt Regency Grand Reserve Puerto Rico, making the list of regional offerings more than complete.

Restaurants

Some restaurants carry the tourism board's *mesón gastronómico* designation. Such establishments specialize in typical island food. The eastern region has both formal restaurants, where reservations are necessary, and casual beachside eateries, where you can walk in unannounced in beach attire and have a fine meal of fresh fish. The bill generally doesn't include a service charge, so a 15% tip is customary and expected. Most restaurants are open for dinner from late afternoon until about 10 pm.

HOTEL AND RESTAURANT PRICES

⇨ *Restaurant and hotel reviews have been shortened. For full information, visit Fodors.com.*

What It Costs in U.S. Dollars

	$	$$	$$$	$$$$
RESTAURANTS	under $12	$12–$20	$21–$30	over $30
HOTELS	under $150	$150–$250	$251–$350	over $350

Packing for El Yunque

When you come to El Yunque, bring binoculars, a camera (preferably with a good zoom function), bottled water, and sunscreen; wear a hat or visor, good walking shoes, and comfortable clothes. Although daytime temperatures rise as high as 80°F (27°C), wear long pants, because some plants can cause skin irritations. There are no venomous snakes native to the forest (or the island as a whole), but bugs can be ferocious, so a strong repellent is a must. And remember: this is a rain forest, so bring a poncho, and be prepared for frequent showers.

Safety

Although crime isn't as high in the island's eastern areas as it is in San Juan, use prudence. Avoid bringing valuables with you to the beach; if you must do so, be sure not to leave them in view in your car. It's best to keep your car locked while driving, and steer clear of out-of-the-way beaches after sunset.

If You Like

Great Food

In the east, you'll find fine fare of all types. On the traditional side, look for the deep-fried snacks (often stuffed with meat or fish) known as *frituras*, as well as numerous dishes laced with coconut. Plantains are the star ingredient in the hearty mofongo, a seafood-stuffed dish, and also appear as tostones (fried plantain chips). For a healthier option try the *pana* tostones made from breadfruit. Fresh fish is commonly prepared with tomatoes, onions, and garlic, or some combination of the three. These days, island chefs are experimenting with flavor and texture, putting modern spins on classic dishes. Throughout the island, you'll find a blend of old and new cooking styles and techniques that will suit all palates.

Golf

There's something to be said for facing a rolling, palm-tree-lined fairway with the distant ocean at your back. And then there are the ducks, iguanas, and pelicans that congregate in mangroves near some holes. That's what golf in eastern Puerto Rico is all about. The Arthur Hills–designed course at El Conquistador is one of the island's best. The Flamboyán course, a Rees Jones creation at Palmas del Mar Golf Club, consistently gets raves, as do the courses at Wyndham Grand Río Mar and at St. Regis Bahia Beach Resort, where Robert Trent Jones Jr. oversaw construction of an eco-friendly green that overlooks the meeting place of the Espíritu Santo River and the Atlantic Ocean.

Visitor Information

Cities usually maintain information offices connected to the city hall, and most are open on weekdays during regular business hours.

CONTACTS Fajardo Tourism Office. ✉ *6 Calle Dr. Lopez, Fajardo* ☎ *787/863–4013* 🌐 *www.fajardopr.org.* **Naguabo Tourism Office.** ✉ *Playa Húcares Malecón, Naguabo* ☎ *787/874–5904.* **Río Grande Office of Tourism and Culture.** ✉ *Calle San José, Plaza de Recreo, Río Grande* ☎ *787/887–2370.*

Piñones

16 km (10 miles) east of San Juan.

Funky Piñones is little more than a collection of open-air seaside eateries. Sand floors, barefoot patrons, and tantalizing seafood—traditionally washed down with icy beer—have made it popular with locals, especially on weekend evenings. Chilled *agua de coco* is served right from the coconut. During the day you can rent a bike and follow the marked seaside trail that meanders 11 km (7 miles) through the mangrove forest and along the northern coastline. It takes about two hours to bike from one end and back, but allow some time to stop and take pictures, grab something to eat, and explore the scenic beach areas.

The area has grown as a nightlife destination, too, as fancier establishments, some with live music, have opened up. As midafternoon turns into evening and people begin to leave the beach for refreshments, the air is thick with smoke from grilled fish, beef and chicken kebabs (called *pinchos* here), and the kettles of oil used to fry codfish and crab fritters. When the giant orange Caribbean

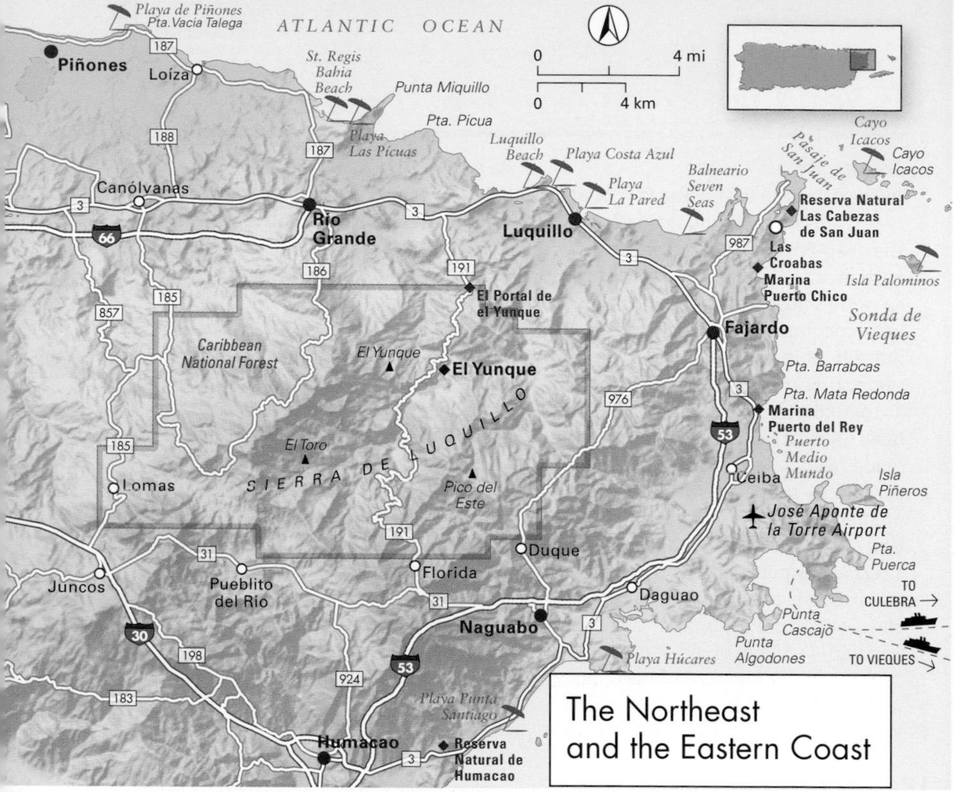

The Northeast and the Eastern Coast

sun starts to fall behind the San Juan skyline, salsa and merengue—not to mention reggae and Latin pop—start to blare from jukeboxes and sound systems at dozens of ramshackle establishments dotting Route 187, the main drag. Traffic on the two-lane road into and out of the area is daunting on Friday and Saturday nights, when many of these open-air bars host merengue combos, Brazilian jazz trios, or reggae bands.

GETTING HERE AND AROUND

The approach to Piñones from San Juan is simple. Take Route 26 east or Route 37 east, follow signs for the Balneario de Carolina, then go straight on Route 187 and cross Punta Cangrejos. Door to door, the trip should take about 15 minutes. You can also get a taxi to Piñones, or take the bus for about 75¢ (via C45)—but the latter can take more than an hour. To avoid getting stranded, prearrange a pickup time for your taxi driver to return.

TAXI CONTACTS AA American Taxi, Inc. ☎ *787/982–3466.* **Astro Taxi.** ☎ *787/727–8888.*

Sights

Paseo Piñones

PROMENADE | One of the most enjoyable ways to pass the time in Piñones is walking along its *paseo,* a 10½-km (6½-mile) boardwalk that traverses sand dunes and crosses lagoons and mangrove forests. All the while, a line of coconut palms shades you from the sun. You'll share the path with bikers, joggers, and in-line skaters. Food kiosks abound. ✉ *Rte. 187, Piñones.*

Great Itineraries

If You Have 1 Day

If you have only a day (or even less) to visit eastern Puerto Rico, make a beeline for **El Yunque** (Route 3 is the quickest way). This rain forest has hiking trails of various lengths leading to secluded waterfalls and mountaintop towers with spectacular views. It's wonderful to explore even if you never get out of your car. If you are staying overnight, your best bet is nearby **Río Grande.**

If You Have 3 Days

To avoid the unrelenting string of strip malls along Route 3, take the winding, coastal Route 187. Stop for lunch at one of the seafood kiosks that line the beach at **Piñones.** Spend your afternoon in **Loíza** shopping for masks and other locally made artwork. If you're there on the weekend, attend a *bomba* dancing class on the beach. Otherwise, head to Cueva Maria de la Cruz, a tall and historic cave. Spend the night in or near **Río Grande**, a town that makes a good base for exploring the region. On your second day, get up early to beat the crowds to **El Yunque.** Bring binoculars so you can spot the rare Puerto Rican green parrot. On Day 3, head to **Luquillo**, which has one of the island's prettiest beaches. Stop for lunch in one of the food kiosks on Route 3 just before you reach the town.

If You Have 5 Days

If you have five days, follow the three-day itinerary above. On Day 4 head east along Route 3 to the coastal city of **Fajardo**, which has plenty of accommodations in every price range. Make sure you have called ahead to reserve a spot on a tour of Reserva Natural Las Cabezas de San Juan. If there's no moon, sign up for a nighttime excursion to the reserve's bioluminescent bay. On Day 5, take a snorkeling trip from the Fajardo marina to see surrounding coral reefs at sites like Cayo Icacos, or go for a dip in a natural pool in **Naguabo** or **Ceiba**.

Beaches

Playa de Piñones

BEACH | You'll find Playa de Piñones right in front of the cluster of food kiosks built by the government for resident cooks. A large barrier reef blocks the strong currents and serves as the foundation for the large bathing pools in front of a sandy beach. **Amenities**: food and drink; parking. **Best for**: swimming. ✉ *Route 187, Km 8, Piñones.*

Restaurants

El Kiosko Boricua

$ | **PUERTO RICAN** | **FAMILY** | Forget McDonald's and Taco Bell; in Puerto Rico, a beachside kiosk like this one is *the* place to go for fast food. El Kiosko Boricua ticks all the boxes for fried Puerto Rican goodies, with *alcapurrias*, arepas, and *bacalaítos* among the items on offer. **Known for:** fast food, Puerto Rican style; ultracasual setting; cash only. $ *Average main: $8* ✉ *Rte. 187, Piñones* ☎ *787/596–1684* ▭ *No credit cards* ⊙ *Closed Mon.*

El Nuevo Acuario

$$ | **PUERTO RICAN** | One among the ever-changing cast of restaurants along Route 187, the New Aquarium, like its neighbors, won't win any awards for decor and design. The setting here is decidedly laid-back, with plastic tables and chairs serving as the humble backdrop for some stellar seafood. **Known**

Lagoons, dunes, and mangroves await on Paseo Piñones. Coconut palms offer shade; food kiosks provide sustenance.

for: fresh seafood; ultracasual setting; good service. *Average main: $12* *Punta Cangrejos, off Rte. 187, Piñones* *787/662–8258* *Closed Tues. and Sun.*

El Parrilla

$$ | PUERTO RICAN | Like its neighbors along Route 187, which fronts the Atlantic, El Parrilla specializes in seafood. Trunkfish fritters and seafood empanadillas are tasty starters, while the hearty seafood stew called *asopao* is the main event, and flan with fresh coconut can't be missed. **Known for:** the freshest seafood; traditional Puerto Rican–style asopao; cash only. *Average main: $12* *Rte. 187, Loíza* *787/876–3191* *No credit cards* *Closed Mon.–Wed.*

Shopping

ART

Artesanías Castor Ayala

SOUVENIRS | Just east of Piñones is the town of Loíza, where you can find authentic coconut *vejigante* masks, dubbed "Mona Lisas" because of their elongated smiles. Craftsman Raúl Ayala Carrasquillo has been making these pieces for nearly half a century, following in the footsteps of his late father. Collectors prize these wild masks, most with tentaclelike horns. His one-room shop, in a shack that was painted yellow many years ago, is on the road between Loíza and Río Grande. *Rte. 187, Km 6.6, Loíza* *787/564–6403.*

Estúdio de Arte Samuel Lind

ART GALLERIES | At his studio on a short, dusty lane across the street from the Artesanías Castor Ayala, artist Samuel Lind sculpts, paints, and silk-screens images that are quintessentially Loízano. Lind's work is displayed in the two floors of his latticework studio. Of special note are his colorful folk-art posters inspired by everyday Puerto Rican life. *Rte. 187, Km 6.6, Loíza* *787/876–1494* *www.estudiodeartesamuellind.com.*

Activities

Piñones is bordered by a 16-km (10-mile) strip of beaches along the coast, which winds to a bluff called Vacía Talega, a once infamous lovers' lane with a wonderful view of an unspoiled coast lined with dense palm groves and towering sea grapes. The area has some fine surf, and several spots have become favorites of local and visiting surfers. You'll also find good fishing, snorkeling, and scuba opportunities. Away from the coast is Torrecilla Baja, one of the largest mangrove swamps on the island.

The Outlet 66 Mall

STORE/MALL | FAMILY | This outlet mall and entertainment center features activities that are fun for families, including a bowling alley, movie theater, arcade, and go-karts. They also have an indoor obstacle course and NASCAR simulator as part of the Sector Sixty6 complex with a reloadable card you can use to purchase admission to each of the games and attractions. ✉ *18400 Autopista Roberto Sánchez Vilella, Canóvanas* ☎ *787/256–7040* 🌐 *theoutletmall66.com* 🎟 *Varies by activity.*

BICYCLING

The area's big outdoor attraction is a bike path that follows swaying coconut palms on a quiet, breezy stretch, sometimes crossing the main roadway but mostly running parallel to it. Along most of its 11 km (7 miles), it's a wooden boardwalk for bicycles.

COPI (Cultural and Ecotouristic Center of Piñones)

BIKING | Bike rentals are available to explore the Piñones Bicycle Trail in the Piñones State Forest and Nature Reserve. Rentals, including helmets for children and adults, bicycles with baby seats, and double bikes are $10 an hour. Be sure to inspect your equipment before you set out; some bikes are in better condition than others. COPI also rents double kayaks for $15 an hour per person; these can be taken out on the nearby Torrecilla Lagoon. ✉ *Rte. 187, Km 4.2, Piñones* ☎ *787/253–9707* 🌐 *www.copipr.com.*

DIVING AND FISHING TRIPS

Locals go fishing and crabbing right off the coast, and it's likely the crab fritters you eat in any beachfront shack are local as well.

Cangrejos Yacht Club

FISHING | Charter-operated boating, deep-sea fishing, and scuba-diving trips are run out of the marina right below the bridge from Isla Verde. Call the yacht club to be referred to a captain who is appropriate for your trip. ✉ *Rte. 187, Km 3.8, Piñones* ☎ *787/791–1015* 🌐 *www.cangrejosyachtclub.com.*

Río Grande

35 km (21 miles) southeast of San Juan

This urban cluster of about 54,000 residents proudly calls itself "The City of El Yunque," as it's the closest community to the rain forest and most of the reserve falls within its municipal borders. Two images of the rare green parrot, which makes its home in El Yunque, are found on the city's coat of arms; another parrot peeks out at you from the town's flag.

Río Espíritu Santo, which runs through Río Grande, begins in El Yunque's highest elevations. It was once used to transport lumber, sugar, and coffee from plantations, and immigrants flocked to the region to take advantage of the employment opportunities.

GETTING HERE

Only 30 minutes from San Juan, Río Grande is easy to reach. From the city, take Route 26 toward Carolina until you reach Route 3. Then take Route 3 toward Fajardo for approximately 20 minutes until you see signs for Río Grande.

Sights

Museo de Arte Popular José Hernández
ART MUSEUM | The museum is devoted to various popular arts, but the highlights of the collection are posters dating from the 1950s. There are more than 200 pieces by 35 artists, including many eye-popping posters created for island festivals and art exhibits. ✉ *37 Calle Pimentel, El Centro, Río Grande* ☎ *787/887–2370* 🎟 *Free* ⏲ *Closed weekends.*

Restaurants

Degree 18 Juice Bar
$ | VEGETARIAN | A rare vegan find on the island, this outdoor eatery features healthy smoothies, fresh juices, acai bowls, vegan burgers, and more. The setting is an outdoor garden with board games and hammocks. **Known for:** vegan empanada; parcha (passion fruit) smoothie; freshly made hummus. 💲 *Average main: $8* ✉ *16 Calle Principal, Palmer, Río Grande* ☎ *787/534–6645* 🌐 *degree-18juice.com.*

Ekelekua
$$ | EUROPEAN | Best known for their brunch, the cuisine here is a blend of Puerto Rican and European influences. The arepa Benedict is a welcome twist on a well-known dish, and options like the guava French toast boast island flavors. **Known for:** guava French toast; arepas Benedict; coffee (ask for the special of the day). 💲 *Average main: $15* ✉ *PR-3 Bo. Jiménez, Río Grande* ☎ *787/953–0303* 🌐 *www.ekelekuapr.com* ⏲ *Closed Tues.*

Las Picuas 123 Seafood
$$$ | SEAFOOD | This seafood restaurant serves fresh-caught fish and is recommended during lobster season for a larger-than-life stuffed Caribbean spiny lobster. They have outdoor seating available with scenic swinging seats, as well as a bar on-site making popular concoctions from sangria to mojitos. **Known for:** whole Caribbean lobster; mofongo; sangria. 💲 *Average main: $25* ✉ *PR-968 s/n, Río Grande* ☎ *787/953–4200.*

Lluvia Deli Bar and Artefacto
$$ | PUERTO RICAN | This restaurant is locally owned and family run. They have a popular brunch menu with hearty meal options and recently completed an outdoor expansion to include a taco bar and pizza oven. **Known for:** breakfast burritos (various); tacos al pastor; deviled eggs. 💲 *Average main: $12* ✉ *52 Calle Principal, Río Grande* ☎ *787/657–5186* 🌐 *www.lluviapr.com.*

Palio
$$$$ | ITALIAN | Northern Italian dishes—such as veal marsala or fillet of beef with a caramelized shallot Barolo reduction—are the star attractions at this top-notch restaurant, where the staff is attentive and amiable. The dining room, with its black-and-white checkerboard floor and dark-wood paneling, is elegant and refined. **Known for:** Caesar salad prepared tableside; great ocean views, particularly at sunset; attentive service. 💲 *Average main: $35* ✉ *Wyndham Grand Río Mar*

It's da Bomb(a)

The *bomba*—a musical and dance style for which the northeastern coast is famous—can be traced to the Kongo people of West Africa. Sometimes wearing a flouncy white dress, the woman of a dancing couple moves in a relatively fixed pattern of steps while her partner improvises to the drumbeat. A lead singer and a choir perform a call-and-response song—recounting a local story or event—while percussionists play maracas, *fuás* (wooden sticks that are smacked against a hard surface), *buleadores* (low-timbre, barrel-shape drums), and *subidores* (higher-pitch drums).

Beach Resort & Spa, 6000 Río Mar Blvd., Río Grande ☎ *787/888–6000* 🌐 *www.wyndhamriomar.com* ⊗ *No lunch.*

Richie's Café

$$$ | SEAFOOD | Perched on a mountaintop, this restaurant—a convenient option for Wyndham Grand Río Mar guests who don't want to dine on-site but are willing to pay resort prices—has a pair of open-air dining rooms with views to Vieques on a clear day. The atmosphere is festive; there's often a game playing on one of the big screens or a local band jamming on the weekend. **Known for:** fresh seafood, especially whole red snapper; fried plantains stuffed with seafood; ocean views. $ *Average main: $25* ✉ *Rte. 968, Km 2.0, Río Grande* ☎ *787/887–1435* 🌐 *www.richiesrestaurantpr.com.*

Hotels

Casa Alternavida

$$$$ | ALL-INCLUSIVE | This all inclusive wellness retreat center features morning movement classes, nature outings, three organic meals a day prepared by an in-house chef, and additional services like team building and rapid transformation coaching. **Pros:** personalized service and retreat experience; transportation available; delicious, healthy meals. **Cons:** cannot book just the room; no alcohol; no smoking on the property. $ *Rooms from: $780* ✉ *PR 968 Km 0.87, Río Grande* ☎ *855/850–0855* 🌐 *casaalternavida.com* *7 rooms* *All-Inclusive.*

Hyatt Regency Grand Reserve Puerto Rico

$$$$ | RESORT | FAMILY | This massive resort on a stretch of pristine coastline does a decent job of being all things to all people, with oversized suites, many of which have plunge pools or patio Jacuzzis, spread among two-story bungalows and even larger suites that have features like an adults-only pool and private check-in. **Pros:** beautiful setting; lovely pool area; short walk to beach. **Cons:** scarce parking; blank and uninviting facade; iguanas near pool bother some guests. $ *Rooms from: $500* ✉ *200 Coco Beach Blvd., Río Grande* ☎ *787/809–1770* 🌐 *www.hyatt.com* *579 suites* *No Meals.*

★ St. Regis Bahia Beach Resort, Puerto Rico

$$$$ | RESORT | Between El Yunque National Forest and the Río Espíritu Santo, this luxurious, environmentally aware property, with 3 km (2 miles) of pristine private beach, is an oasis of calm that hums with local wildlife. **Pros:** privacy; impeccable service; luxurious amenities. **Cons:** isolated location; slim off-property restaurant selection; very, very expensive. $ *Rooms from: $1300* ✉ *Rte. 187, Km 4.2, Río Grande* ☎ *787/809–8000* 🌐 *www.stregisbahiabeach.com* *174 rooms* *No Meals.*

Wyndham Río Mar Golf & Beach Resort

$$$$ | RESORT | FAMILY | This sprawling resort offers a host of outdoor activities, including championship golf and tennis as well as hiking in the nearby rain forest. **Pros:** expansive beachfront; good restaurants; casino. **Cons:** expensive resort fee; occasionally long lines at check-in; far from off-site restaurants. $ *Rooms from: $450* ✉ *6000 Río Mar Blvd., Río Grande* ☎ *787/888–6000* 🌐 *www.wyndhamriomar.com* *400 rooms* *No Meals.*

Nightlife

Wyndham Grand Río Mar Resort & Spa

GATHERING PLACES | Pick a game—Caribbean stud poker, blackjack, slot machines—and then head to the Las Vegas–style casino at the Wyndham Grand Río Mar Resort & Spa. If all that betting makes you thirsty, step into the Players Club Bar, which is connected to the gaming room. ✉ *Wyndham Grand Río Mar Resort & Spa, 6000 Río Mar Blvd., Río Grande* ☎ *787/888–6000.*

Water recreation options abound in the enormous pools of the Wyndham Grand Río Mar Beach Resort & Spa.

Activities

Activities in the Río Grande region are mostly oriented around the area's resorts, Wyndham Grand Río Mar Resort & Spa and Hyatt Regency Grand Reserve Puerto Rico, as well as St. Regis Bahia Beach Resort.

GOLF

★ St. Regis Bahia Beach Resort Golf Course

GOLF | Designed by Robert Trent Jones Jr., this tranquil 18-hole course meanders alongside the island's Río Espíritu Santo and overlooks the Atlantic Ocean. Environmentally respectful (it boasts a golden certification from Audubon International), this challenging course traipses past scenic lakes, deep-rooted mangroves, and spectacular residences, blending into the area's rain-forest surroundings, while ocean breezes add a degree of difficulty to lush, rolling fairways. Greens fees vary seasonally; rates and times are available on request. ✉ *Rte. 187, Km 4.2, Río Grande* ☎ *787/957–1510* 🌐 *www.stregisbahiabeach.com* 💵 *From $165* 🏌 *18 holes, 7014 yards, par 72.*

The Wyndham Grand Río Mar Beach Resort & Spa

GOLF | The Río Mar Country Club portion of the resort features two of the region's more luxurious golf courses. The Ocean Course, designed by Tom and George Fazio, has slightly wider fairways than its sister course. Iguanas can usually be spotted sunning themselves near the 4th hole, but contrary to its name it has only one isolated ocean hole: the par-three 16th. River Course, designed by Greg Norman, has challenging fairways that skirt the Mameyes River. Either way, at the end of a round you can enjoy the spacious modern clubhouse with a pro shop and two restaurants where you can grab a sit-down lunch or a quick beverage and a bite. If you're not a resort guest, be sure to reserve tee times at least 24 hours in advance. Fees include discounts for resort guests and twilight times with club and shoe rentals available. ✉ *6000 Río Mar Blvd., Río Grande*

☎ *787/888–6000* 🌐 *www.wyndhamriomar.com* 🎫 *9 holes from $130; 18 holes from $195* ⛳ *Ocean Course: 18 holes, 6782 yards, par 72; River Course: 18 holes, 6945 yards, par 72.*

HORSEBACK RIDING

Carabalí Rainforest Park

HORSEBACK RIDING | FAMILY | A family-run operation, this hacienda is a good place to jump in the saddle and ride one of Puerto Rico's Paso Fino horses. Hour-long rides take you around the 600-acre ranch, while two-hour treks take you to a river where you and your horse can take a dip. If you prefer something more high-tech, rent a four-wheeler for an excursion through the foothills of El Yunque. ✉ *Rte. 3, Km 31.6, Luquillo* ☎ *787/889–4954* 🌐 *www.carabalirainforestpark.com.*

TENNIS

Río Mar Tennis Club

TENNIS | These tennis facilities are the best in the area. In addition to 13 courts with spectacular views, the center offers lessons for everyone from novices to old pros. ✉ *Wyndham Grand Rio Mar Resort & Spa, 6000 Río Mar Blvd., Río Grande* ☎ *787/888–7066* 🌐 *www.wyndhamriomar.com* 🎫 *Court rentals from $25 per hr; ½-hr private lessons from $45.*

Shopping

Caribbean Trading Company

SOUVENIRS | This store features locally crafted artwork in various mediums, as well as souvenirs like coffee, hot sauce, picture frames, and clothing. ✉ *4 Calle Principal, Río Grande* ☎ *787/888–2762* 🌐 *caribbeantrading.com.*

El Yunque

11 km (7 miles) southeast of Río Grande, 43 km (26 miles) southeast of San Juan.

⇨ *For more information on El Yunque, see the special feature at the beginning of this chapter.*

The temperature in the U.S. Forest Service's only tropical rain forest—an easy and popular day trip from San Juan—is about 73°F year-round, so seasonality isn't an issue. It can't be said enough, though: come prepared for rain. Showers are a factor every day. Indeed, the park receives an estimated 200–240 inches of rain annually.

Prior to Hurricane Maria, when the forest was fully operational, it had more than a million visitors each year. Ongoing post-storm restoration and a gradual return to normal operations have led to a drop in visitations, but the forest can still get crowded, with fewer areas open to accommodate those who do come. If you're driving yourself, try to book a morning timed-entry slot (🌐 *recreation.gov*), and arrive early to readily find parking. If you're taking a guided tour, book a morning departure to avoid larger crowds.

GETTING HERE AND AROUND

You can take a taxi from San Juan to El Yunque (metered rates outside the city run about $36 per hour), but to get the most out of the rain forest, it's best to rent a car, even if you have only a few hours to explore. From the greater San Juan area, take the Airport Expressway, Highway 26 (Baldorioty de Castro Avenue) and follow signs east to Carolina; once you are on the expressway (PR-66), follow it approximately 22½ km (14 miles) to the end. At the final exit (Carolina), turn right onto Route 3 east. Once you enter the town of Río Grande, turn right at the light onto Route 955, and then take the first left onto Route 191, which leads into the forest. (You should also see directional signs to El Yunque once you are in Río Grande.) When mudslides haven't caused portions of the forest's road to be closed, you can drive straight from the entrance to the base of Pico El Yunque (Km 13).

A couple of driving notes: check ahead on forest-road conditions, and be sure

Puerto Rican Green Parrot

The Taíno Indians called it the *iguaca*, Spanish speakers refer to it as the *cotorra*, and scientists know it as *Amazona vittata*. Whatever moniker it takes, the Puerto Rican green parrot—the only one native to the island—is one of the world's rarest birds. It nests primarily in the upper levels of El Yunque and in nearby Sierra de Luquillo. The bird is almost entirely green, though there are touches of blue on its wings, white rings around its eyes, and a red band just above its beak. It's only about 12 inches long, and its raucous squawk belies its delicate appearance. The parrots mate for life. In February (the rain forest's driest month), they build nests within tree hollows and lay three to four eggs. Both parents feed the young.

When the Spanish arrived, the parrot population was an estimated 1 million, between the main island, Vieques, and Culebra. But deforestation, hurricanes, and parasites decimated the population (parrot hunting was common before being outlawed in 1940)—by 1967 there were only 19 birds, and a 1975 count totaled only 13. Prior to Hurricane Maria, which ripped through Puerto Rico in 2017, scientists estimated 75 cotorras lived in the wild, but this population was wiped out by the hurricane.

Fortunately, a 240-strong captive population—part of a breeding program—survived the hurricane and was released into the wild. If you're very observant (and very lucky), you just might spot one. You can also see them at El Portal de el Yunque.

to obey the speed limit (rental cars are frequently pulled over here). Also, drive defensively: other motorists don't always employ safe-driving practices, such as using turn signals, keeping to the right when driving slowly, or being mindful of stop signs.

TOUR OPERATORS

Many companies in San Juan and Río Grande offer excursions to El Yunque, an alternative if you don't want to drive yourself. Check with your hotel concierge about which companies are currently offering tours.

ESSENTIALS

Admission Fees. You will need to make a reservation for timed entry online at 🌐 *www.recreation.gov/ticket/facility/300017*. Only one reservation is required per vehicle, and there is a fee of $2.

Admission Hours. The road into El Yunque opens daily at 7:30 am and closes at 6 pm.

Emergencies. If you witness an accident or an unlawful act or felony, or if you see something happening that looks wrong or suspicious, please contact the Law Enforcement and Investigation Patrol, at ☎ *787/888–5675* (office), ☎ *787/888–1880* (VHF radio paging), or ☎ *787/549–0075* (mobile).

Restrooms. There are picnic areas with sheltered tables and bathrooms as well as several basic eateries along the road through the rain forest.

Sights

El Portal de el Yunque

VISITOR CENTER | FAMILY | El Portal de El Yunque, located at the entrance to the rain forest, is the newly renovated visitor center for El Yunque. Here, you can pick

Look closely at the small tree branches along El Yunque's nature trails and you may spot creatures such as the mountain garden lizard.

up maps and ask for information about current conditions in the rain forest. They have art exhibits made of reclaimed wood from the hurricanes, local artist shows, and daily ranger talks explaining unique aspects of the forest. ✉ *Rte. 191, Km 4.0, Río Grande* ☎ *787/888–1880* 🌐 *www.fs.usda.gov/detail/elyunque* 🎫 *$8 for anyone over 15.*

★ El Yunque

FOREST | FAMILY | Oversized flora, rushing streams, and powerful cascades are just some of what you'll find in El Yunque, which gets 100 billion gallons of precipitation annually. Two of the island's highest *picos* (peaks), El Toro and El Yunque, are also here, rising over 3,500 feet amid the more than 28,000 lush acres that encompass four major forest types, roughly stratified by elevation.

These ecosystems are home to thousands of native plants, including 150 fern and 240 tree species—88 of them rare and endemic, 23 of them found here exclusively. There are no monkeys or large cats (and no poisonous snakes, either). Rather, El Yunque is populated with small creatures, some of which—like the *cotorra* (the island's greatly endangered green parrot) and the *culebrón* (Puerto Rican boa)—exist nowhere else on Earth.

The bird-watching is especially good after a shower, so, in addition to a rain poncho, pack binoculars to spot some of the forest's 68 types, including the Puerto Rican tody, lizard cuckoo, and sharp-shinned hawk, as well as five species of hummingbirds. Rivers and streams provide aquatic habitats for freshwater snails, shrimp, and crabs. The forest's 1,200 species of insects—from ants to beetles to flies—provide food for some of the 14 different types of lizards, geckos among them. In the evening, millions of inch-long coquís (tree frogs) begin their calls.

The best way to experience all this nature is on a hike. The forest's 13 official trails are short and easy to navigate. Although not as immersive as a hike, a leisurely drive-through is also gratifying. Along the way, you'll encounter beautiful waterfalls;

Did You Know?

El Yunque is divided into four forest types according to their elevations. At 2,500 feet above sea level, the cloud forest is the highest and receives nearly constant rainfall.

Take in the views of El Yunque National Rainforest at the Yokahù observation tower.

hibiscus, banana, and orchid plants; and the occasional vista. Be sure to stop and climb the winding stairs of Yokahu Tower for breathtaking views of the rain forest and the islands. **■ TIP→ Advanced reservations are required.** *Rte. 191, Km 4, off Rte. 3, Río Grande* *787/888–1880* *www.fs.usda.gov/main/elyunque/home* *Rain forest free; reservation $2; visitor center $8.*

Activities

HIKING

Some of El Yunque's 13 trails are closed due to damage by Hurricane Maria; those that are open are fairly easy and suitable for both beginning adult hikers and children. Most are short and paved.

HORSE RACING

Hípodromo Camarero

HORSE RACING | Try your luck with *exactas* and *quinielas* at this large thoroughbred racetrack about 20 minutes east of San Juan. Post time is at 2:30 pm every day except Tuesday and Thursday. There's an air-conditioned clubhouse and restaurant (open at 12:30 pm on race day), as well as a bar where people occasionally dance to live rumba music. Parking and admission to the grandstand and clubhouse are free. *Rte. 3, Km 15.3, Canóvanas* *787/641–6060* *www.hipodromo-camarero.com.*

Luquillo

13 km (8 miles) northeast of Río Grande, 45 km (28 miles) east of San Juan.

Known as the Sun Capital of Puerto Rico, Luquillo has one of the island's best-equipped family beaches. It's also a community where fishing traditions are respected. On the east end of Balneario de Luquillo, past the guarded swimming area, fishermen launch small boats and drop nets in open stretches between coral reefs.

Like many other Puerto Rican towns, Luquillo has its own signature festival—in this case, the Festival de Platos Típicos (Festival of Typical Dishes), a late-November or early-December culinary event that revolves around one ingredient: coconut. During the festivities, many of the community's 20,000 residents gather in the Plaza de Recreo to sample treats rich with coconut or coconut milk. There's also plenty of free entertainment, including folk shows, troubadour contests, and salsa bands.

GETTING HERE AND AROUND

Públicos run between San Juan and Fajardo and will let travelers off at Luquillo (about a 45-minute ride). Driving takes about the same amount of time. From San Juan, head out Route 3, get off at Route 193, and follow signs for Luquillo. If you want to explore the town (it's small but well worth the time), a car is helpful. Take note not to park in places where the curb is painted yellow—it's a parking violation.

Beaches

Luquillo Beach (*Balneario La Monserrate*)
BEACH | FAMILY | Signs refer to this gentle beach off Route 3 as "Balneario La Monserrate," but everyone simply calls it Luquillo Beach. Lined with lifeguard stations and shaded by soaring palm trees, it's a magnet for families and has picnic areas and more than 60 kiosks serving fritters and drinks—making it a local hangout. Lounge chairs and umbrellas are available to rent, as are kayaks and Jet Skis. One very distinctive feature here is the *Mar Sin Barreras* (Sea Without Barriers), a gradual ramp into the water that allows wheelchair users to take a dip. On busy days, the beach can be crowded and characterized by a party atmosphere. **■ TIP→ There is a nominal fee for using the shower facilities, so bring small bills for this purpose. Amenities:** food and drink; lifeguards; parking (fee); showers; toilets; water sports. **Best for:** partiers; swimming; walking. ✉ *Off Rte. 3, Luquillo* ☎ *787/889–5871* 🎟 *$4 plus tax, per car (cash only).*

Playa Costa Azul
BEACH | Waving palm trees and fishing boats add charm to the small Playa Costa Azul, although the ugly residential buildings along the water make an unattractive backdrop. The water here is good for swimming, and the crowds are thinner than elsewhere, but there are no facilities. **Amenities:** none. **Best for:** swimming. ✉ *Off Rte. 193, near Rte. 3, Luquillo.*

Playa La Pared
BEACH | Playa La Pared (literally, "The Wall Beach") is a surfer haunt. Numerous local competitions are held here throughout the year, and several surfing shops are close by in case you need a wet suit or wax for your board. The waves here are medium-range. It's very close to Luquillo Beach, but has a separate entrance. There are no facilities. **Amenities:** none. **Best for:** partiers, surfing. ✉ *Off Rte. 3, Luquillo.*

Restaurants

Brass Cactus
$$ | STEAKHOUSE | This steak-and-chop eatery attracts so many English-speaking tourists that management doesn't bother printing a Spanish menu. Nearly every dish on the expansive menu is made to be washed down with beer. **Known for:** great steaks and burgers; fun sports-bar atmosphere; reasonably priced cocktails and beer. $ *Average main: $18* ✉ *Off Rte. 3, near main entrance to Luquillo, Luquillo* ☎ *787/980–9659* ⏲ *Closed Wed.*

La Parrilla
$$$ | SEAFOOD | FAMILY | There are dozens of *kioskos,* or food stands, along Route 3 on the way to Luquillo Beach, most offering humble local fare, much of it fried. This full-service restaurant raises the bar for its culinary counterparts. **Known for:** good grilled seafood; alfresco dining; steaks for the non-fish eaters. $ *Average*

Best Luquillo Food Kiosks

Off Route 3, just before the exit for pristine Luquillo Beach, something of a culinary renaissance is occurring. Here you'll find dozens of food shacks or *kioskos*, some with CIA-trained (Culinary Institute of America) chefs, offering everything from burgers to ceviche to stuffed lobster. Stop in for breakfast, lunch, dinner, or cocktails. Take some time to weigh your options at establishments ranging from no-frills takeout counters to full-service restaurants. Once you've made your decision, pull up a seat and get ready to feast—these kioskos are turning out some of the island's best eats.

Each kiosk is numbered. Here are a couple of our favorites:

No. 2, La Parrilla. Head here for the original kiosko experience and indulge in a lobster or steak as big as your head.

No. 38, Ceviche Hut. Fresh ceviches and classics like *pescado a lo macho* (fish in Peruvian seafood sauce) are all solid choices.

main: $28 ✉ *Luquillo Beach, Rte. 3, Kiosk 2, Luquillo.*

Latin Gyros

$$ | **MEDITERRANEAN** | Offering the best lamb gyros on the island, this is a casual breakfast and lunch spot serving Mediterranean dishes with a Puerto Rican flair. From falafel to baklava, there are large portions to ensure you don't leave hungry. **Known for:** Greek breakfast; baklava; gyros (chicken, lamb, falafel, churrasco). *Average main: $15* ✉ *352 Cll Fernández Garcia, Luquillo* ☎ *787/889–4801* 🌐 *latingyros.com/.*

Lolita's

$$ | **MEXICAN** | When it comes to Mexican food, this place is the real deal. For lunch, grab a few tacos (soft or crispy), or try one of the classic Mexican entrées. **Known for:** authentic Mexican cuisine; generous portions; good (and large) margaritas. *Average main: $15* ✉ *Rte. 3, Km 41.3, Luquillo.*

Hotels

The Yunque Mar Hotel & Parador

$ | **HOTEL** | This cute little hotel is just west of the popular Luquillo Beach, but the hotel's own strand is nearly as nice and almost always deserted. **Pros:** on a lovely beach; friendly owners; nice pool. **Cons:** bland decor; no in-room safe; building is on a crowded street. *Rooms from: $145* ✉ *Playa Fortuna, 6 Calle 1, Luquillo* ☎ *787/889–5555* 🌐 *www.hotelyunquemar.com* *15 rooms, 2 suites* *No Meals.*

Fajardo

11 km (7 miles) southeast of Luquillo, 55 km (34 miles) southeast of San Juan.

Fajardo, founded in 1772, was once notorious as a piratical pit stop. It later developed into a fishing community and an area where sugarcane flourished. Today, it's a hub for yachts that use its marinas; divers who head to its good offshore sites; and day-trippers who travel by catamaran, ferry, or plane to

The calm waters of Luquillo Beach are a draw for families and beachgoers looking for a relaxing ocean dip.

the islands of Culebra and Vieques from nearby Ceiba. With the most significant docking facilities on the island's eastern side, Fajardo is a bustling city of 37,000—so bustling, in fact, that its unremarkable and somewhat battered downtown is often congested and difficult to navigate. Much of the tourist activity in Fajardo centers on the northern reaches of Las Croabas, near the gigantic Conquistador Resort.

GETTING HERE AND AROUND

Getting around Fajardo is tricky without a car, especially if you plan on visiting several of the sights. Thrifty has an office at the Fajardo Inn. Ferries to Vieques and Culebra now leave from a new terminal in Ceiba, about 8 km (5 miles) south of Fajardo. Tickets must be purchased in advance online at 🌐 *www.porferry.com.*

CAR RENTAL Thrifty Car Rental. ✉ *Parcelas Beltrán 52, Puerto Real, Fajardo* ☎ *787/860–2030* 🌐 *www.thrifty.com.*

FERRY CONTACTS Ceiba Ferry Terminal. ✉ *Marina Dr., Roosevelt Roads, Ceiba* 🌐 *www.porferry.com.*

Sights

Hacienda Chocolat

FARM/RANCH | This international award-winning farm cultivates locally grown cacao, from bar to bean. Guests can go on a walking tour of the property or sign up for special tasting events, like whiskey and chocolate pairings. ✉ *Carretera 984, Cam. Los Polacos, Fajardo* ☎ *787/637–5666* 🌐 *www.haciendachocolatpr.net* 🎫 *Tours start at $34* 🕑 *Closed weekdays* ✍ *Reservations required.*

Las Croabas

NATURE SIGHT | **FAMILY** | A few miles north of Fajardo is this fishing area, where seafood is sold in open-air restaurants along the ocean. A small park in the middle of town has a lovely waterfront walk, and it's easy to find outfitters for any kind of ocean adventure, from kayak

Pack a picnic and hire a boat or a book a tour for a day of sun and snorkeling at Cayo Icacos.

excursions to sailing trips. ✉ *Rte. 3, Km 51.2, Fajardo.*

Marina Puerto Chico

MARINA/PIER | This lively marina off Route 987 is home to a cadre of glistening fishing boats and the offices of Kayaking Puerto Rico. ✉ *Rte. 987, Fajardo* ☎ *787/863–0834* 🌐 *www.gcmarinas.com.*

Marina Puerto del Rey

MARINA/PIER | Home to 1,000 slips, Puerto del Rey claims to be the Caribbean's largest marina. This is the place to hook up with a scuba-diving group, arrange an excursion to one of the bioluminescent bays, or charter a fishing boat. The marina, located south of Fajardo, also has several restaurants and boating-supply stores. ✉ *Rte. 3, Km 51.4, Fajardo* ☎ *787/860–1000* 🌐 *www.puertodelrey.com.*

★ Reserva Natural Las Cabezas de San Juan

NATURE PRESERVE | The 316-acre reserve on a headland north of Fajardo is owned by the nonprofit Conservation Trust of Puerto Rico. You ride in open-air trolleys and wander down boardwalks through seven ecosystems, including lagoons, mangrove swamps, and dry-forest areas. Green iguanas skitter across paths, and guides identify other endangered species. A half-hour hike down a wooden walkway brings you to the mangrove-lined Laguna Grande, where bioluminescent microorganisms glow at night. The restored Fajardo Lighthouse is the final stop on the tour. Its Spanish colonial tower has been in operation since 1882, making it Puerto Rico's second-oldest lighthouse. The first floor houses ecological displays, and a winding staircase leads to an observation deck. The only way to see the reserve is on a guided tour; reservations are required and can be made through the trust's website. ✉ *Rte. 987, Km 6, Fajardo* ☎ *787/722–5882* 🌐 *www.paralanaturaleza.org* 🎟 *$12.*

Beaches

Balneario Seven Seas

BEACH | FAMILY | One of Puerto Rico's prized Blue Flag beaches, this long stretch of powdery sand near the Reserva Natural Las Cabezas de San Juan has calm, clear waters that are perfect for swimming. There are plenty of picnic tables, as well as restaurants just outside the gates. **Amenities:** food and drink; parking (fee); showers (fee); toilets. **Best for:** swimming. ✉ *Rte. 195, Km 4.8, Las Croabas* ☎ *787/863–8180* *Parking $5.*

★ Cayo Icacos

BEACH | Cayo Icacos is one of about 10 small islands that make up the Cordillera Nature Reserve just off the coast of Puerto Rico. It's a beautiful beach with good snorkeling offshore. Icacos can only be reached by a 15- to 20-minute boat ride, so pack whatever you might need for the day. Several tour operators in Fajardo offer day trips here, or you can hire a boat in Las Croabas. **Amenities:** none. **Best for:** snorkeling; solitude; swimming; walking. ✉ *La Cordillera Nature Reserve, Las Croabas* ⊕ *Off the coast 15 to 20 mins by boat from Las Croabas.*

Restaurants

Calizo

$$$ | SEAFOOD | There's a string of seafood shacks in the village of Las Croabas, all serving delicious fried fish. This open-air eatery, with tables covered with straw umbrellas and anchored by a bustling square bar, takes things up a notch or two. **Known for:** good fresh seafood; alfresco dining; rather high prices. [$] *Average main: $29* ✉ *Rte. 987, Km 4.6, Las Croabas* ☎ *787/863–3664* ⊙ *Closed Tues.–Thurs.*

Cremaldi

$ | DESSERTS | This ice cream shop has more than 30 flavors available and is home of the fried ice cream. The chairs are swings and the walls are coated with newspaper clippings and pictures of famous guests over the years, chronicling its long history in the community. **Known for:** banana splits; made-to-order waffle cones; fried ice cream. [$] *Average main: $4* ✉ *Calle Union 62, Fajardo* ☎ *787/801–1770.*

★ La Estación

$$$ | PUERTO RICAN | This laid-back spot has elevated Puerto Rican street food to an art form, thanks to two New Yorkers (one Puerto Rican) with restaurant pedigrees who decided to leave the big city and open a new spot dedicated to barbecue in an old gas station outside the Conquistador Resort. Highlighting products obtained from local fishermen and farmers, and smoking their own meats in an outdoor kitchen, Idalia García and Kevin Roth's awesome joint is one of Puerto Rico's don't-miss culinary treats. **Known for:** locally sourced produce and meats; delicious barbecue; friendly service. [$] *Average main: $28* ✉ *Rte. 987, Km 4, Las Croabas* ☎ *787/863–4481* 🌐 *www.laestacionpr.com* ⊙ *Closed Tues. and Wed.*

Las Vistas Cafe

$$ | CARIBBEAN | This rooftop cafe boasts 360-degree views, shaded by patio umbrellas and located by the water. With gluten-free options and the owner herself greeting guests upon arrival, it is a personable and surprisingly healthy find. **Known for:** basil lemonade; locally sourced fruit platter; coco-banana pancakes. [$] *Average main: $14* ✉ *83 2nd St., Las Croabas* ☎ *787/655–7053* 🌐 *www.lasvistascafepr.com* ⊙ *Closed Tues. and Wed.*

Pasión por el Fogón

$$$ | CARIBBEAN | FAMILY | At this beloved Fajardo restaurant, chef Myrta Pérez Toledo transforms traditional dishes into something special. Succulent cuts of meat and fish are presented in unexpected ways. **Known for:** contemporary Caribbean cuisine; fresh seafood; great desserts. $ *Average main: $28 ✉ Rte. 987, Km 2.3, Fajardo ☎ 787/863–3502 🌐 www.pasionporelfogon.net ⏲ Closed Mon. and Tues.*

Hotels

El Conquistador Resort
$$$$ | RESORT | FAMILY | El Conquistador is back after Hurricane Maria, and it's more inviting than ever. **Pros:** bright, spacious rooms; unbeatable views of nearby islands; good dining options. **Cons:** large-scale, post-hurricane renovation in progress; long waits at funicular running between levels; hidden fees including parking and kids' club (and you need a car). $ *Rooms from: $400 ✉ 1000 Av. El Conquistador, Fajardo ☎ 787/863–1000, 888/543–1282 🌐 www.conquistadorresort.com 🛏 299 rooms 🍽 Free Breakfast.*

Fajardo Inn
$ | HOTEL | FAMILY | The buildings that make up this hilltop hotel offer lovely views of islands poking out of the Atlantic Ocean. **Pros:** pretty grounds; family-friendly environment; good value. **Cons:** not on the beach; motel-like rooms; lacks amenities. $ *Rooms from: $130 ✉ 52 Parcelas Beltrán, Rte. 195, Beltrán Sector, Fajardo ☎ 787/860–6000, 888/860–6006 🌐 www.fajardoinn.com 🛏 125 rooms 🍽 No Meals.*

Nightlife

Most of the evening action takes place in El Conquistador's lounges, but there are a few neighborhood bars where locals drink beer.

Activities

DAY SAILS

Several reputable catamaran and yacht operators in Fajardo make excursions to the reefs and sparkling blue waters surrounding a handful of small islets just off the coast. Two of the most popular of these are Cayo Icacos and Isla Palominos, both of which are in La Cordillera Nature Reserve. Many of the trips include transportation to and from San Juan–area hotels.

Whether or not you're staying in Fajardo, if you take a day trip on the water you'll see classic Caribbean scenes of coral reefs rife with sea life, breathtakingly clear water, and palm-fringed, deserted beaches. The day sails, with stops for snorkeling, include swimming breaks at deserted beaches and picnic lunches. Most of the craft are outfitted for comfort, with quality stereo systems, bathrooms, deck showers, and full-service bars.

Many competent operators offer nearly identical experiences, so your selection will probably be based on price and which operators serve your San Juan hotel or which operate out of the marina you're visiting in Fajardo. Prices run $55–$95 per person, depending on whether you join a trip in San Juan or in Fajardo and on what is included in the cost. Although they are often standard features, ask if picnic lunches and a full-service bar are included.

East Island Excursions
SAILING | This outfit operates 45- to 65-foot catamarans, three of which are powered to cut down on travel time to outlying islands. Trips may include offshore snorkeling, stops at isolated beaches, and a lunch buffet. Trips are offered to Cayo Icacos and Isla Palomino, within La Cordillera Nature Reserve. An evening excursion to Vieques to see the bioluminescent bay includes dinner at a local restaurant. All of the plush craft are outfitted with swimming decks, freshwater showers, and full-service bars. *✉ Marina Puerto del Rey, Rte. 3, Km 51.4, Fajardo ☎ 787/860–3434, 877/937–4386 🌐 www.eastislandpr.com.*

Spread Eagle II

SAILING | The *Spread Eagle II* is a 51-foot catamaran that heads out to isolated beaches on the islands off Fajardo. The trip includes an all-you-can-eat buffet and a complimentary piña colada. To top it off, you get a free snorkel to bring home. The boat is comfortable and well equipped with a bathroom and freshwater deck shower so you can rinse off salt and sand. Sunset and moonlight cruises are also available. ✉ *Dock J, Villa Marina Harbor, Rte. 987, Fajardo* ☎ *787/887–8821, 888/523–4511* 🌐 *www.snorkelpr.com.*

DIVING

Aqua Adventure

SCUBA DIVING | Aqua Adventure focuses its scuba and snorkeling activity on the islets of Palomino, Lobos, and Diablo in Fajardo, but also offers trips to Culebra. ✉ *El Conquistador Resort, 1000 Av. El Conquistador, Fajardo* ☎ *787/860–3483* 🌐 *www.scubapuertorico.net* 🎟 *Diving from $99; snorkeling from $69.*

Sea Ventures Pro Dive Center

SCUBA DIVING | Here you can get diving certification, arrange dive trips to 20 offshore sites, including Culebra and Vieques, and organize boating and sailing excursions. ✉ *Safe Harbor Puerto del Rey, 4900 State Rd. 3, Km 51.4, Fajardo* ☎ *787/863–3483, 800/739–3483* 🌐 *www.divepuertorico.com.*

FISHING

787 Fishing Puerto Rico

FISHING | Sail away on one of Captain Marcos Hanke's 22- or 26-foot sportfishing boats for deep-sea, light-tackle, or fly-fishing excursions. Tarpon, snook, bonefish, and kingfish can be caught inland year-round, while game fish like marlin, sailfish, wahoo, tuna, and mahimahi await just offshore. Half-day charters are typically for four hours, full-day charters for eight hours (the latter on the 26-foot boat). Sunset fishing charters are also available. ✉ *Marina Puerto Chico, Slips 4 and 6, Fajardo* ☎ *787/347–4464* 🌐 *www.787fishing.com* 🎟 *Half-day charters from $450; full-day charters from $950.*

GOLF

Arthur Hills Golf Course at El Conquistador

GOLF | Named for its designer, this 18-hole course is famous for mountainous terrain with elevation changes of more than 200 feet—a rarity in the Caribbean. From the highest spot, on the 15th hole, you have great views of the surrounding mountains and rain forest. Trade winds challenge every shot—as if the gorgeous views, strategic bunkering, and many water hazards aren't distracting enough. You are also likely to spot the harmless and generally timid iguana that populate the area. ✉ *El Conquistador Resort, 1000 Av. El Conquistador, Fajardo* ☎ *787/863–6784* 🌐 *www.conquistadorresort.com* 🎟 *From $60 for non–hotel guests* ⛳ *18 holes, 6746 yards, par 72.*

KAYAKING

Kayaking Puerto Rico

WATER SPORTS | **FAMILY** | This adventure outfitter has an excursion for all types of water (and kayak) lovers. They offer a host of day and night trips—such as kayaking the glowing waters of Fajardo's bioluminescent lagoon, paddling along Culebra's reefs, snorkeling with local turtles, and piloting an eco-friendly, inflatable speedboat across crystal clear waters. Group rates and specials can be found online. ✉ *PR-987, Km 5, Las Croabas, Fajardo* ☎ *787/245–4545* 🌐 *www.kayakingpuertorico.com* 🎟 *From $59.*

Naguabo

18 km (11 miles) southwest of Fajardo.

In this municipality's downtown, pastel buildings give the main plaza the look of a child's nursery: a golden-yellow church on one side faces a butter-yellow city hall, and a pink-and-blue amphitheater anchors one corner. It's a good spot for people-watching until the heat drives you to the beach.

Offshore, Cayo Santiago (aka Monkey Island) is the site of some of the world's most important rhesus monkey research. A small colony of monkeys was introduced to the island in the late 1930s, and since then scientists have been studying their habits and health, especially as they pertain to the study of diabetes and arthritis. You can't land at Cayo Santiago, but Captain Frank López sails a small tour boat, *La Paseadora,* around it.

GETTING HERE AND AROUND

Naguabo is about an hour's drive from San Juan, just south of Fajardo along Route 31, off Route 53. From Route 31, turn down Calle Garzot to reach the town square. Although públicos run to and from Naguabo, public transportation within Naguabo is extremely limited, so a rental car is your best option.

Beaches

Playa Húcares

BEACH | Playa Húcares is *the* place to be. Although the strip is a little run-down and the beach itself can be a bit messy, an authentic vibe permeates the casual outdoor eateries and funky little shops that vie with the water for your attention. Locals sell ice out of trucks, and the heavy bass of reggaetón music thumps from the windows of passing cars. Two Victorian-style houses anchor one end of the waterfront promenade, a dock with excursion boats anchors the other, and a red, green, and blue–painted bridge connects both sides of the town. **Amenities:** food and drink. **Best for:** sunset. ✉ *Off Rte. 3, south of Naguabo, Naguabo.*

Hotels

Casa Cubuy Ecolodge

$ | B&B/INN | El Yunque's southern edge is the setting for this eco-friendly hotel where guest rooms are simple (no phones or TVs) but comfortable, with tile floors, rattan furniture, and windows that show off one of the island's best views. **Pros:** spectacular setting; close to some of the island's best hiking trails; doting staff. **Cons:** basic rooms; access roads are often affected by landslides; lower-level rooms are small. $ *Rooms from: $130* ✉ *Rte. 191, Km 22, Naguabo* ☎ *787/874–6221* 🌐 *www.casacubuy.com* *10 rooms* *Free Breakfast.*

Activities

WATER TOURS

La Paseadora

SAILING | For more than 20 years, Captain Frank López has been sailing visitors from Naguabo's Malecón around Cayo Santiago aboard his boat, *La Paseadora.* López, a charming, well-informed guide, tailors outings to the group, and over the course of three hours you'll motor around and watch the monkeys at Monkey Island—one of the world's oldest primate colonies. Plan to make some fishing and snorkeling stops in local waters using onboard gear. ✉ *Playa Húcares, Rte. 3, Km 66.6, Naguabo* ☎ *787/316–0441.*

Humacao

15 km (9 miles) southwest of Naguabo, 55 km (34 miles) southeast of San Juan.

Travelers flock to the Humacao area for one reason: the sprawling resort community called Palmas del Mar and its two world-class golf courses, the Flamboyán and the Palm. Although it's not thought of as a tourist destination, Humacao does have a handful of interesting neocolonial buildings along its traffic-clogged downtown streets. These are worth a peek if you're stuck here on a rainy day.

GETTING HERE AND AROUND

Humacao is served by two highways and one toll expressway. Route 30 serves as the main highway coming from points west (Caguas and Las Piedras), while Route 53 serves origins to the north (Fajardo and Naguabo). Route 3, the main highway following the eastern coastline from San Juan, passes through Humacao.

Sights

Plaza de Recreo de Humacao

PLAZA/SQUARE | Downtown's broad square is anchored by Concatedral Dulce Nombre de Jesús (Sweet Name of Jesus Cathedral), which dates from 1869. It has a castlelike facade, and even when its grille door is locked, you get a peek at the sleek altar, polished floors, and stained-glass windows dominated by blues. Across the plaza, four fountains splash under the shade of old trees. People pass through feeding the pigeons, children race down the promenade, and retirees congregate on benches to chat. ✉ *Calle Font Martelo at Calle Ulises Martinez, Humacao.*

Reserva Natural de Humacao

NATURE PRESERVE | As you travel from Naguabo to Humacao, you'll pass stretches of beach and swaths of undeveloped land, including the swamps, lagoons, and forested areas of the Reserva Natural de Humacao. Walk along the trail to discover abandoned military bunkers and murals amidst the wilderness. This nature reserve has an information office, restrooms, and campsites. No pets are allowed. ✉ *Rte. 3, Km 74.3, Humacao* ☎ *787/852–4440* 🌐 *www.paralanaturaleza.org.*

Restaurants

Bocata by Campillo

$$ | SPANISH | This Spanish-style tapas restaurant has a variety of menu items and daily specialties. They pride themselves on a robust wine menu and have a selection of decadent desserts. **Known for:** wine selection; paella; jamon Iberico. [$] *Average main: $15* ✉ *PR-3 441 Ste. 1, Humacao* ☎ *787/850–4429* ⏲ *Closed Mon.*

Chez Daniel

$$$$ | FRENCH | Chef Daniel Vasse's French country-style dishes are some of the island's best. The Marseille-style bouillabaisse is full of fresh fish and bursts with the flavor of a white garlic sauce. **Known for:** French country cuisine; extensive wine cellar; upscale setting and experience. [$] *Average main: $33* ✉ *Palmas del Mar, 1 Country Club Dr., Humacao* ☎ *787/850–3838* 🌐 *www.chezdanielpr.com* ⏲ *Closed Mon. No lunch.*

Pura Vida

$$ | PUERTO RICAN | Humacao and its neighboring towns have plenty of humble spots where you can pull up at a table and order traditional Puerto Rican fare. While the name is more evocative of Costa Rica than Puerto Rico, the menu's heavy emphasis on all things plantain will reassure you of your Caribbean location. **Known for:** fresh fish; any kind of mofongo, casual setting. [$] *Average main: $20* ✉ *295 Palmas Inn Way, Humacao* ☎ *787/914–0316* ⏲ *Closed Mon.*

Hotels

Wyndham Candelero Beach Resort

$$ | HOTEL | Amid acres and acres of condo developments and golf courses, the Wyndham Candelero is surprisingly modest in scale, given its opulent surroundings, but it does have a beautiful pool area. **Pros:** access to all the amenities at Palmas del Mar; outgoing staff; free Wi-Fi. **Cons:** uninspired architecture; some ongoing construction; no sea views from any rooms. [$] *Rooms from: $160* ✉ *170 Candelero Dr., Humacao* ☎ *787/247–7979* 🌐 *www.wyndhamhotels.com* *107 rooms* *No Meals.*

Did You Know?

The Palmas del Mar Golf Club features the Rees Jones–designed Flamboyán course.

Nightlife

Wyndham Candelero Beach Resort

GATHERING PLACES | The small casino at the Wyndham Candelero Beach Resort offers everything from blackjack to slot machines. The action is liveliest on weekends. ✉ *170 Candelero Dr., Humacao* ☎ *787/247–7979.*

Activities

FISHING

Maragata Charters

FISHING | This company takes anglers out from Palmas del Mar on a 38-foot power catamaran. Snorkeling and combination trips to Monkey Island, Vieques, and Culebra are also available. ✉ *Palmas del Mar, Anchor's Village Marina, Slip 14, Humacao* ☎ *787/850–7548, 787/637–1802 (mobile)* 🌐 *www.maragatacharters.com* 🎫 *4-hr tours from $70; 8-hr tours from $200.*

GOLF

Palmas Athletic Club

GOLF | Palmas Athletic Club has two good golf courses. The Rees Jones–designed **Flamboyán** course was named for the nearly six dozen flamboyants (aka flame trees) that pepper its fairway. You begin play among villas, but the back nine ventures into forest and hills. It is considered one of the tougher courses in Puerto Rico. The older Gary Player–designed **Palm** course is a bit shorter in more of a resort style of play, with the 14th and 16th holes affording some wonderful Caribbean vistas. ✉ *Palmas del Mar, Rte. 906, Humacao* ☎ *787/656–3000* 🌐 *www.palmaspac.com* 🎫 *From $100* ⛳ *Flamboyán: 18 holes, 7117 yards, par 70; Palm: 18 holes, 6675 yards, par 71.*

Chapter 5

VIEQUES AND CULEBRA

Updated by
Jennifer Ruiz Garay

Sights	Restaurants	Hotels	Shopping	Nightlife
★★★★★	★★☆☆☆	★★☆☆☆	★☆☆☆☆	★☆☆☆☆

WELCOME TO VIEQUES AND CULEBRA

TOP REASONS TO GO

★ **Puerto Mosquito:** Kayak after dark on the astounding bioluminescent bay of Vieques.

★ **Playa Flamenco:** Catch some rays on this Culebra bay, consistently ranked as one of the world's best white-sand beaches.

★ **Refugio Nacional de Vida Silvestre de Culebra:** Bird-watch and hike in one of Puerto Rico's oldest nature refuges.

★ **Comida Criolla:** Sample traditional Puerto Rican fare with the locals at colorful roadside restaurants, seafood shacks, and other non-touristy spots.

★ **Playa Carlos Rosario:** Stroll right into the waters off this deserted Culebra beach to snorkel a fabulous coral reef.

Vieques is 33½ km (21 miles) long and 6½ km (4 miles) wide, and has two small communities. On the northern shore is Isabel Segunda, the main town, where the ferry docks. On the southern shore is the village of Esperanza, a string of low-cost bars, restaurants, and hotels along a waterfront promenade. Nearby is the world-famous bioluminescent bay, Puerto Mosquito. Most of the island consists of the Vieques National Wildlife Refuge, where you'll find dozens of beaches with names such as Caracas, Pata Prieta, and Chiva, as well as many more that have no official names, found off unpaved side roads.

At 11 km (7 miles) long and 6½ km (4 miles) wide, Culebra is much smaller and less developed than Vieques. There's only one community: the tiny town of Dewey.

1 Vieques. Two-thirds of this island is a wildlife refuge, and it's a fabulous destination for active travelers who like bicycling, kayaking, and fishing. It is fringed by gorgeous beaches, and a visit to the bioluminescent bay is an unforgettable experience. The island has several boutique hotels, trendy restaurants, and upscale resorts.

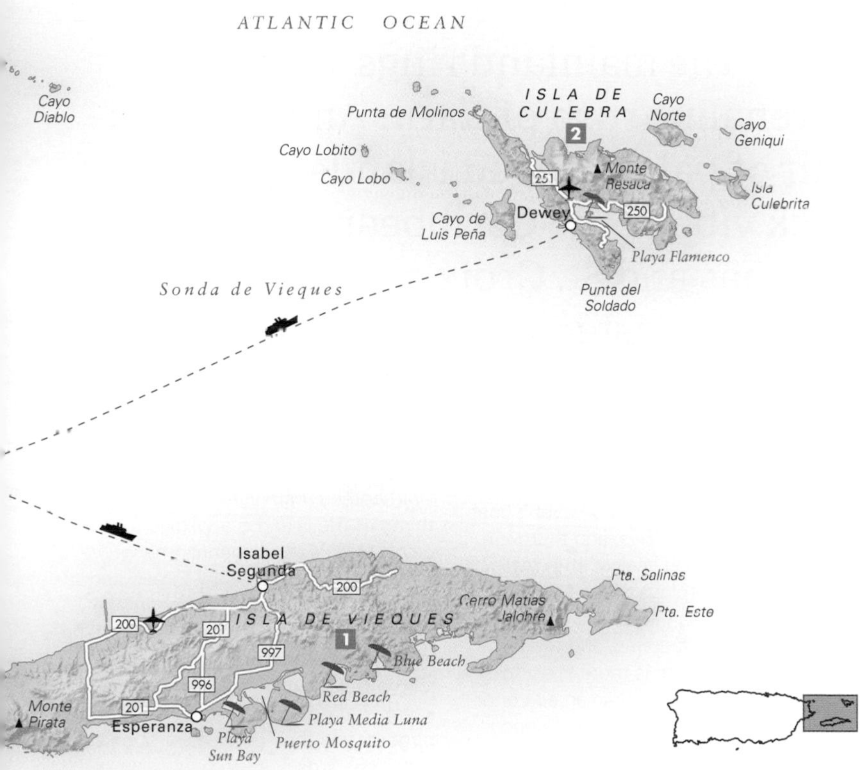

2 Culebra. The island is mostly unspoiled, a quality that brings many people back year after year. People come to Culebra to laze on the stunning, white-sand Playa Flamenco, as well as lesser-known but also sensational sandy stretches. Snorkeling and diving on the cays surrounding Culebra are rated world-class.

Although the islands of Vieques and Culebra (known as the "Spanish Virgins") are only a few miles off the coast of Puerto Rico, they feel like another world. While the mainland rings with the adrenaline rush of Latin America, this pair of palm-fringed islands has the laid-back vibe of the Caribbean—indeed, St. Thomas and St. Croix are clearly visible from the eastern edges of Culebra.

Vieques and Culebra are alike in many ways. Neither has much traffic—in fact, you won't find a single traffic light on either island; high-rise hotels haven't cast a shadow on the beaches; and there are no casinos, fast-food chains, strip malls, or most other trappings of modern life. "Barefoot" is often part of the dress code at casual restaurants, and the hum you hear in your room is more likely to come from a ceiling fan than an air conditioner. Things happen here *poco a poco*: slowly, at an islander's easy pace.

Beautiful beaches abound on both islands. Many of the best stretches of sand on Vieques—Chiva, Caracas, and Punta Arenas, to name a few—are on land that was once part of a U.S. naval base. This means that resort development hasn't reared its ugly head. It also means there are few, if any, amenities, so bring plenty of water and a picnic lunch. Most accommodations provide guests with beach chairs, towels, and coolers for the day; some will even pack guests' lunches to take to the beach. The beaches on Culebra are just as unspoiled; marine turtles are perfectly comfortable coming ashore to lay eggs.

Wild horses roam Vieques, where two-thirds of the island is a wildlife refuge protecting coastal lagoons, mangrove wetlands, subtropical dry forest, and islands—ecotourism is a key draw. Fishing in the turquoise flats just offshore is fantastic. And the island seems tailor-made for exploring by bicycle and/or kayak. Off Culebra, several cays delight birders with their colonies of boobies and other seabirds.

Some of the best snorkeling and diving in the Caribbean can be found in the waters surrounding Vieques and Culebra. You can sign up for a half- or full-day excursion to nearby coral reefs that teem with colorful fish. It's also possible to grab a mask and snorkel and simply wade out a few yards to see what you can see. Playa Esperanza, on the southern coast of Vieques, is a good place for beginners. More experienced snorkelers will prefer La Chiva (Blue Beach) or Punta Arenas (Green Beach).

MAJOR REGIONS

Vieques is 26 km (16 miles) southeast of the ferry port of Ceiba. **Isabel Segunda** is the major town, on the north shore. The other town is **Esperanza,** on the south shore. **Elsewhere on Vieques** are most of the best beaches, as well as the island's bioluminescent bay, popular restaurants, and a scattering of hotels.

Culebra is 38 km (24 miles) east of Ceiba. It's also considerably smaller (less than half the size of Vieques). Many of the island's restaurants and guesthouses are concentrated in **Dewey,** but there are places all over the island.

Planning

When to Go

High season runs roughly December 15–April 15. Puerto Ricans flock here at Christmas and Easter, when Vieques and Culebra are packed with families enjoying the sun and sand. Be sure to make reservations well in advance if you're visiting during the holidays. The shoulder season, when prices are a bit lower, is a good option, but keep in mind that both islands are popular weekend getaways for mainland Puerto Ricans, so reservations are always advisable. And do note that some restaurants and hotels are closed during low season. The only time you might want to avoid is late August to late October, when hurricanes can strike the area.

Getting Here and Around

AIR

Most international travelers fly from San Juan's Aeropuerto Internacional Luis Muñoz Marín (SJU) or from nearby Aeropuerto Fernando L. Ribas-Dominicci (SIG; more commonly known as Aeropuerto Isla Grande), which is cheaper. You can also fly from Ceiba's Aeropuerto José Aponte de la Torre (RVR), about 61 km (38 miles) southeast of San Juan's SJU.

Air Flamenco flies to Vieques and Culebra daily from San Juan's Isla Grande Airport and offers charters to both islands from Luis Muñoz Marín. The airline also offers daily flights from Ceiba. Cape Air is another carrier with daily flights year-round between Luis Muñoz Marín and Vieques and Culebra.

Taxi Aereo is essentially an air taxi service. Missed your flight to Culebra or Vieques? Don't want to be limited by scheduled flights? As long as you have a maximum of four passengers, you can walk into Ceiba airport and request on-the-spot service for $360 (one-way) The service is also available out of Isla Grande Airport, though rates are considerably higher.

Vieques Air Link flies to both islands daily from San Juan's Luis Muñoz Marín and Isla Grande airports, as well as Ceiba's municipal airport. Charters are also available. Flights from San Juan take 20–30 minutes, and one-way fares are $75–$135. Flights from Ceiba are about 10 minutes, and one-way fares $36–$46. Small propeller planes that hold up to nine passengers are used.

CONTACTS Air Flamenco. ☎ *787/724–1818* 🌐 *www.flyairflamenco.com.* **Cape Air.** ☎ *800/227–3247* 🌐 *www.capeair.com.* **Taxi Aereo.** ✉ *Aeropuerto José Aponte de la Torre, Ceiba* ☎ *787/602–7605* 🌐 *www.taxiaereopr.travel.* **Vieques Air Link.** ☎ *888/901–9247* 🌐 *www.viequesairlink.com.*

CAR

It's nearly impossible to see either island without renting a car. You cannot rent a car on mainland Puerto Rico and ferry it across; you'll need to rent from local agencies, all of which specialize in SUVs. Most also rent golf carts, although they're not ideal for getting around if you want to explore the beaches. Road conditions and local driving habits are spotty. Rates are expensive ($50–$95 per day), so it's often cheaper to book a hotel–rental car package. Be sure to read Culebra and Vieques rental car companies' rules, as off-pavement driving is prohibited by many companies, and violations will result in a fine. Both islands' rental car companies also impose fees for excessive sand and/or water inside the vehicle.

FERRY

The Puerto Rico Ports Authority runs passenger ferries to Vieques and Culebra from the terminal in Ceiba, roughly a 90-minute drive southeast of San Juan. Some ferries carry cars, but rental agencies won't let you take their vehicles between the mainland and islands. (A municipal parking lot next to the terminal costs $5–$7 per day.) Fares are cheap: $2 per person from Ceiba to Vieques and $2.25 to Culebra, with discounts for children and seniors (those over age 75 ride for free). You must reserve tickets online, in advance.

On fast ferries, trips take 30 minutes (Vieques) or 45 minutes (Culebra). No ferries link the two islands at present. Schedules often change, and ferries can be cancelled due to rough seas, so call ahead to confirm. Also note that there's limited ferry seating: arrive at least an hour ahead of the departure time (more on busy weekends, particularly for the early-morning departures and midafternoon returns).

CONTACTS Ceiba Ferry Terminal. ✉ *Roosevelt Roads, Marina Dr., Ceiba* ☎ *787/497–7740* 🌐 *www.puertoricoferry.com.*

Beaches

Vieques and Culebra are where you'll find Puerto Rico's most serene shores. Ideal for romantic strolls or family swims, the calm waters and long, unspoiled stretches here are what you probably had in mind when you envisioned a Caribbean beach paradise.

Many of the beaches around Vieques were once named by the U.S. Navy, which assigned them random colors: Red Beach, Blue Beach, and Green Beach—most have since been renamed in Spanish by locals. Islanders know Sun Bay as Sombé. Those within the Vieques National Wildlife Refuge are open from 6 am to sunset. Of more than three dozen beaches on Vieques, Sun Bay east of Esperanza is easily the most popular. Although the island's beaches are favored for their comparative isolation, crowds can gather on weekends at the most popular spots. On weekdays, however, it's not uncommon for large swaths of shore to be sparsely populated.

Hotels

Vieques has a wide variety of lodgings, from surf shacks across from the beach to boutique hotels high up on secluded hillsides. There's something here for everyone. Looking for tropical splendor? Try Hacienda Tamarindo. Interesting architecture? There's El Blok or Hix Island House. An intimate inn where you'll meet fellow travelers? Head to Casa de Amistad.

Culebra has fewer options. Dewey, the island's only town, has a handful of small inns that are easy on the wallet. Scattered around the island are a couple of more luxurious lodgings plus villa rentals. Nothing remotely resembles a chain hotel, and that's how the locals like it.

PRIVATE VILLA RENTALS

One good way to visit Vieques is to rent one of the beautiful vacation homes that have been built in the hilly interior or along the coasts. These are concentrated in three major areas: Bravos de Boston, Esperanza, and Pilón. Several local real-estate agents deal in short term rentals of at least a week. While you can always use Airbnb or Homeaway to find a rental, the services of an experienced management company with broad local knowledge are always helpful.

Rainbow Realty
A list of rental properties is available from this gay-friendly company. ✉ *278 Calle Flamboyán, Esperanza* ☎ *787/741–4312* 🌐 *www.viequesrainbowrealty.com.*

Restaurants

Seafood is on the menu at almost every eatery. Not only is it truly fresh—your red snapper supper was probably splashing around in the Caribbean that very morning—but you can also order it any number of ways. Many chefs are experimenting with European and Asian cooking techniques, so you may find your fish smoked or in a sushi roll. Regardless of a restaurant's culinary specialty, you can be sure that mangoes, papayas, and other tropical fruits will make an appearance on its menu.

Even the most formal restaurants on the islands are on covered terraces or in open-air dining rooms, so there's not a single establishment where you'll be frowned upon for wearing shorts. Pack a couple of nice shirts, and you'll be set. Most restaurants are open for dinner from about 6 until about 10. Bills often include service; if not, a 15% tip is customary.

HOTEL AND RESTAURANT PRICES

⇨ *Restaurant and hotel reviews have been shortened. For full information, visit Fodors.com.*

What It Costs in U.S. Dollars

	$	$$	$$$	$$$$
RESTAURANTS				
	under $12	$12–$20	$21–$30	over $30
HOTELS				
	under $150	$150–$250	$251–$350	over $350

Packing

Hospitals on Vieques and Culebra were destroyed by Hurricane Maria and have not been rebuilt, so both medical services and supplies are extremely limited. Stock up on everything you need—allergy medications, contact-lens solution, or feminine supplies—before heading to the islands, and don't forget to bring insect repellent.

Safety

Drug-related violent crime has recently increased on Vieques. Tourists are largely unaffected, but it pays to be on your guard. Avoid bringing valuables to the beach, and don't leave any personal items in your car. Rental agencies advise that you leave your car unlocked when parked at a beach so thieves won't break the windows to get inside. There's very little crime on Culebra, but again, don't leave valuables in your car.

Visitor Information

Note that the islands' tourism offices have spotty office hours. The Culebra Tourism Office is near the ferry dock in front of Banco Popular. The staff will help you as best they can, even recommending restaurants that are off the beaten path. The Vieques Tourism Office is across the main square in Isabel Segunda. If you need portable information, ask them to print out a complete list of local businesses. In addition, local maps for both islands are available at most hotels and restaurants.

CONTACTS Culebra Tourism Office. ✉ *250 Calle Pedro Marquez, Dewey* ☎ *787/742–1033.* **Vieques Tourism Office.** ✉ *449 Calle Carlos Lebrón, Isabel Segunda.*

Vieques

13 km (8 miles) southeast of Fajardo.

Looking for a place to play Robinson Crusoe? Well, here you can wander along almost any stretch of sand and rarely see another soul. You can also while away the hours underneath coconut palms, wade in the warm water, or get a mask and snorkel and explore coral reefs that ring the island.

For many years the island was known mostly for the conflict between angry islanders and aloof federal officials. Over the course of six decades, the U.S. Navy used two-thirds of Vieques, mostly on the island's eastern end, as a bombing range, and the western tip as an ammunition dump. After an April 1999 bombing accident took the life of one resident, waves of protests brought the maneuvers to a standstill, and political pressure from the island's governor helped force the military to leave on May 1, 2003.

Ironically, the military presence helped keep the island pristine by keeping resort developers away. Today, the military's former holdings have been turned into Vieques National Wildlife Refuge. The island's woodsy western end is laced by trails that offer fabulous cycling around the base of Monte Pirata, the island's highest peak. More and more of the eastern area is being opened every year, granting access to stupendous beaches shelving into calm turquoise waters. The park also protects Puerto Mosquito, a flask-shape bay populated by microscopic organisms that glow when disturbed at night—a thrilling experience for kayakers.

Just because Vieques is sleepy doesn't mean there's nothing to do besides hit the beach. In its two communities—Isabel Segunda and Esperanza—you can dine at a variety of excellent restaurants, stock up on supplies, or book a kayaking trip.

GETTING HERE AND AROUND

Isabel Segunda is the transportation hub of Vieques. The ferry drops off passengers at the town's dock, and propeller planes deposit passengers at Aeropuerto Antonio Rivera Rodríguez (VQS), a 10-minute cab ride from Isabel Segunda, 15 minutes from Esperanza. Route 200 leads from the airport to Isabel Segunda, and Route 997 leads from Isabel Segunda to Esperanza. For a longer but more scenic drive, take Route 200 west from Isabel Segunda to Route 201 south; then, after about 1½ km (1 mile), take Route 996 to Esperanza.

If you want to rent or gas up a car, you need to make a trip to Isabel Segunda. Try Vieques Car Rental or Maritza's Car Rental.

You can flag down taxis on the street, but it's faster and safer to have your hotel call one for you. Either way, agree on the cost of the trip before you climb inside, as many drivers are prone to charge tourists exorbitant fares.

■ TIP→ If you plan to rent a car, make sure you reserve it in advance, especially during high season. Rental agencies have limited stock, and when they're out of cars, you're out of luck.

AIRPORT CONTACTS Aeropuerto Antonio Rivera Rodríguez. ✉ *Rte. 200, Km 2.6* ☎ *787/741–0515.*

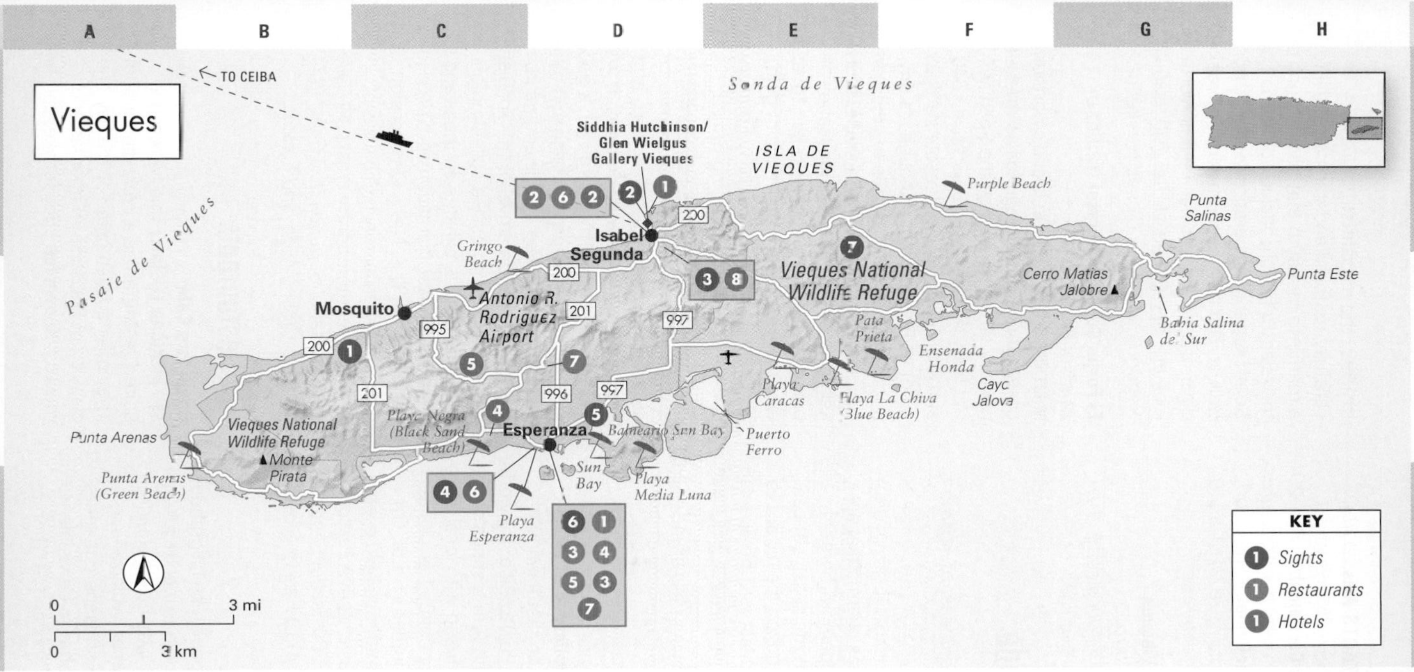

Sights

1 Crab Island Rum Distillery B2
2 El Faro Punta Mulas D1
3 El Fortín Conde de Mirasol D1
4 Malecón D2
5 Puerto Mosquito Bioluminescent Bay D2
6 Vieques Conservation & Historical Trust D2
7 Vieques National Wildlife Refuge E1

Restaurants

1 Bananas D2
2 Coqui Fire Cafe D1
3 Duffy's D2
4 El Quenepo D2
5 Placita Restaurant at El Blok Hotel D2
6 Rising Roost D1
7 Tin Box D2

Hotels

1 Bravo Beach Hotel D1
2 Casa de Amistad D1
3 El Blok Hotel D2
4 Hacienda Tamarindo C2
5 Hix Island House C2
6 Malecón House D2
7 Puertas at El Quenepo D2
8 Sea Gate Hotel D1

CAR RENTAL CONTACTS Avis. ✉ *Rte. 200, Km 5* ☎ *787/397–2533* 🌐 *www.avis.com.* **Maritza's Car Rental.** ✉ *Rte. 201* ☎ *787/741–0078* 🌐 *www.maritzascarrental.com.* **Vieques Car Rental.** ✉ *Rte. 200, Km 0.8, Monte Santo* ☎ *787/412–8540* 🌐 *www.viequescarrental.com.*

FERRY CONTACTS Vieques Terminal. ✉ *Calle Morropo* ☎ *787/494–0934* 🌐 *vieques.com/passenger-cargo-ferry-guide.*

Isabel Segunda

29 km (18 miles) southeast of Fajardo by ferry.

Isabel Segunda (or Isabel II, as it's often labeled on maps) has charms that are not immediately apparent. There's a lovely lighthouse on the coast just east of the ferry dock, and, on the hill above town, you'll find the last fort the Spanish constructed in the New World. The town also has lodgings that range from funky to fancy.

Sights

Crab Island Rum Distillery

DISTILLERY | This is the first handcrafted-rum distillery in Puerto Rico. They offer tours that come with rum tastings at the end. Their rum is infused with local ingredients like orange or coffee from Lajas. You can purchase bottles on-site. On Saturdays, they sometimes hold events that include live music. ✉ *Ave Pedro Albizu Campos PR-200, Isabel Segunda* 🌐 *crabislandrum.com* 🎫 *Free* 🕓 *Closed Sun. and Mon.*

El Faro Punta Mulas

LIGHTHOUSE | This Spanish-built lighthouse above the ferry dock in Isabel Segunda dates from 1895. It was built to guide vessels into the harbor, which is surrounded by a chain of dangerous reefs. Its red light is rumored to be visible from as far away as St. Croix and St. Thomas. In 1992, the elegant structure was carefully restored and transformed into a maritime museum that traces much of the island's history, including the visit by South American liberation leader Simón Bolívar. The tiny museum is open weekdays, but the lighthouse itself is worth a look any day. ✉ *End of Rte. 200, Isabel Segunda* 🎫 *Free* 🕓 *Closed weekends.*

El Fortín Conde de Mirasol (*Count of Mirasol Fort*)

MILITARY SIGHT | On the island's northern coast, above Isabel Segunda, is the last military structure built by the Spanish in the New World. It was erected in 1840 at the order of Count Mirasol, then governor of Puerto Rico. Although it's tiny, it took more than a decade to complete, which meant Mirasol had to repeatedly ask for more money. (Queen Isabel, on being petitioned yet again, asked Mirasol whether the walls were made of gold.) The hilltop fort helped solidify Spanish control of the area, keeping British, French, Dutch, and Danish colonists away and dissuading pirates from attacking Isabel Segunda. In 1991, after sitting empty for several decades, it was transformed into a museum with a good array of artifacts from the Taíno and other cultures that thrived on this and nearby islands before the arrival of the Spanish. It also has an impressive collection of small arms, plus exhibits on the island's years as a sugar plantation and its occupation by the U.S. Navy. On occasion, it presents temporary exhibitions of works by contemporary artists. ✉ *Calle El Fuerte, Isabel Segunda* ☎ *787/741–1717* 🎫 *$2* 🕓 *Closed Mon. and Tues.*

Restaurants

Coqui Fire Cafe

$$ | **MEXICAN FUSION** | This Mexican-inspired restaurant is a lively dinner spot. They offer a fresh catch of the day and classic cocktails like margaritas and mojitos. **Known for:** cheesecake; carnitas;

Great Itineraries

If You Have 1 Day

If you are headed to one of the islands for an overnight excursion, your best bet is **Vieques.** Get here by plane, either from San Juan or Ceiba, to maximize your time. Spend the day exploring the beaches, especially the half moon–shape **Sun Bay.** In the evening, dine at one of the ocean-front restaurants in Esperanza, then head off for an excursion to **Puerto Mosquito,** a bay filled with glow-in-the-dark dinoflagellates. Spend the night in Esperanza or Isabel Segunda.

If You Have 3 Days

Three days will allow you to see most of Vieques. Start your first day in Isabel Segunda, where you can take a few snapshots of **El Faro Punta Mulas,** then explore the hilltop **Fortín Conde de Mirasol.** Head off for an after-noon by the ocean, perhaps at **Punta Arenas** (aka Green Beach) or one of the delightfully deserted beaches in the north. Enjoy happy hour at **Duffy's,** by far the most popular bar in Esperanza. In the cool of the evening, have dinner in one of the chic eateries nearby. On your second day, after booking a tour of Puerto Mosquito for later in the evening, go for an early-morning mountain-bike ride in the western portion of **Vieques National Wildlife Refuge,** a swath of wilderness that was once a naval base. Pack a picnic and head off to **Playa Media Luna** or another of the beautiful southern coast beaches. After dinner, head out on your tour of **Puerto Mosquito.** Spend your third day kayaking, snorkeling, and/or fishing.

If You Have 5 Days

With a few more days, you can see both Vieques and Culebra. Follow the itinerary above, and then head to Culebra on your fourth day. (A 10-minute flight between the islands is the only way to travel between them directly.) Your destination should be **Playa Flamenco,** a long, curving beach of talcum-white sand and turquoise water; the mountains beyond make a striking backdrop. Dine that evening at **Susie's** in the island's only town: diminutive Dewey. On your last day, try snorkeling in **Refugio Nacional de Vida Silvestre de Culebra,** a lovely nature preserve. One of the best places for a morning boat trip is **Isla Culebrita,** an islet dominated by a lighthouse built in 1882, abandoned in 2003, and slated for restoration.

catch of the day (seafood like mahimahi or snapper). *$ Average main: $15 ✉ Calle Carlos Lebrum 443, Esperanza ☎ 787/741–0401 ⏲ Closed weekends.*

Rising Roost

$ | **AMERICAN** | Part café and part boutique, Rising Roost is where early risers can get their caffeine or green-juice fix. It has a cute back patio and two street-side tables that are great for people-watching, and it serves healthy breakfast options including oatmeal, açai bowls, and avocado toast in addition to cold-pressed juices, smoothies, and espresso drinks. **Known for:** quirky souvenirs and gifts; omelets and eggs; vegan and vegetarian options. *$ Average main: $10 ✉ 110 Calle Muñoz Rivera, Isabel Segunda 🌐 www.facebook.com/risingroost ⏲ Closed Sat.–Mon.*

Did You Know?

El Faro Punta Mulas, a lighthouse built in 1895, is now a small museum exhibiting Vieques historical items.

Hotels

Bravo Beach Hotel

$$ | **HOTEL** | **FAMILY** | Several blocks north of the ferry dock in Isabel Segunda, this simple but attractive hotel makes a good home base for island exploration. **Pros:** gorgeous building; beautiful pools; friendly management. **Cons:** out-of-the-way location in residential neighborhood; can't swim on property's beach; no on-site restaurant. *Rooms from: $210* *1 North Shore Rd., Isabel Segunda* *787/741–1128* *www.bravobeachhotel.com* *11 rooms* *No Meals.*

Casa de Amistad

$ | **B&B/INN** | If you're looking for a budget-friendly property in the town center, this groovy little guesthouse not far from the ferry dock in Isabel Segunda is perfect. **Pros:** gay-friendly; funky furnishings; access to common kitchen. **Cons:** drive to beaches; cheaper rooms lack en suite bathrooms; no elevator. *Rooms from: $130* *27 Calle Benito Castaño, Isabel Segunda* *787/247–1017* *www.casadeamistad.com* *9 rooms* *No Meals.*

Sea Gate Hotel

$ | **HOTEL** | This hilltop hotel—the oldest on Vieques—overlooks the island's picturesque, historic fort and is about 10 minutes by foot (downhill) from Isabel Segunda. **Pros:** friendly and helpful owner-manager; complimentary pickup at ferry or airport; continental breakfast included. **Cons:** small rooms; no restaurant; presence of farm animals and dogs might be problematic for some. *Rooms from: $125* *Barrio Fuerte, Isabel Segunda* *201/450–8238* *www.seagatehotel.com* *15 rooms* *Free Breakfast.*

Shopping

Most residents do their shopping on the mainland, so there are very few shops on Vieques. You'll find mostly clothing stores that lean toward beach attire, as well as a few art galleries.

Siddhia Hutchinson / Glen Wielgus Gallery Vieques

ART GALLERIES | Since the mid-1980s, this gallery has showcased pastel watercolor prints of Caribbean scenes, as well as limited-edition ceramic dinnerware. The gallery is a hip, sophisticated place for Caribbean artists to see and be seen, hosting openings of local artists, and it features a number of island artworks. Shoppers looking for more affordable wares or smaller souvenirs and locally made jewelry won't be disappointed. *Hotel Carmen, Calle Muñoz Rivera, Isabel Segunda* *787/556–5409* *www.hutchinsonwielgusgallery.com.*

Activities

Various outfitters offer trips to Puerto Mosquito, the island's celebrated bioluminescent bay. Most excursions are made in single-person kayaks, which can be a challenge if you lack experience or endurance. Many people prefer electric-powered boats—gas-powered engines harm the environment.

Black Beard Sports

WATER SPORTS | This five-star PADI dive center in downtown Isabel Segunda is a one-stop shop. In addition to renting snorkeling and diving gear, the team arranges dive trips; PADI certification courses; and kayaking, biking, snorkeling, and hiking ecotours. Their 2½-hour, bio-bay excursions ($55 per person) feature clear-bottom kayaks and include pick up and drop off. *53 Calle Benítez Guzmán, Isabel Segunda* *787/207–4222* *www.blackbeardsports.com.*

Popular with local fisherman, the gentle waters of Esperanza Beach are ideal for small boats.

Esperanza

10 km (6 miles) south of Isabel Segunda.

The only time there's a traffic jam in Esperanza is when one of the wild horses frequently seen on the nearby beaches wanders into the road. This community, once a down-at-the-heels fishing village, now hosts a string of bars, restaurants, and small hotels on the waterfront drag. All of them overlook Playa Esperanza, a shallow stretch of sand made all the more picturesque by the presence of a tiny islet called Cayo Afuera.

Sights

Malecón

PROMENADE | In the evening, there's no better way to enjoy the sunset than a stroll along Esperanza's 200-yard-long Malecón, a waterfront walkway running the length of the beach. ✉ *107 Calle Flamboyan, Esperanza.*

Vieques Conservation & Historical Trust

OTHER MUSEUM | **FAMILY** | The Vieques Conservation & Historical Trust was established to help save Puerto Mosquito, one of the last remaining bioluminescent bays in the world. The small museum, located on the main drag in Esperanza, has interesting information about the bay, as well as the island's flora and fauna and history. A little pool lets kids get acquainted with starfish, sea urchins, and other denizens of the not-so-deep. There's also a tiny gift shop, the profits from which are funneled back into the foundation. Call ahead if you're coming at lunchtime, as the place is sometimes closed for an hour or more. If you're interested in history and architecture, ask about a guided tour of the Playa Grande sugar mill ruins. ✉ *138 Calle Flamboyán, Esperanza* ☎ *787/741–8850* 🌐 *www.vcht.org* *Suggested donation $3* ⏲ *Closed Sun.*

Beaches

Balneario Sun Bay

BEACH | **FAMILY** | Just east of Esperanza, this mile-long stretch of sand skirts a perfect crescent-shape bay. Dotted with picnic tables, this beach gets packed on holidays and weekends. On weekdays, when crowds are thin, you might see wild horses grazing among the palm trees. There is a small fee for parking, but often there is no one at the gate to take your money. **Amenities:** food and drink; parking (fee); showers; toilets. **Best for:** snorkeling; swimming; walking. ✉ *Rte. 997, Esperanza* ☎ *787/741–8198* 🎫 *Parking $2.*

Playa Esperanza

BEACH | People staying in any of the inexpensive accommodations in Esperanza can simply walk across the road to this beach. There's good snorkeling across the bay around Cayo Afuera, an uninhabited islet, and by the derelict pier. Manatees are occasionally spotted here, as well as barracudas and nurse sharks. If you're looking for swimming or sunbathing, keep moving; there are much better beaches nearby. **Amenities:** none. **Best for:** snorkeling; walking. ✉ *Esperanza Malecón, Esperanza.*

Playa Media Luna

BEACH | Ideal for families because the water is calm and shallow, this is also a good spot to try snorkeling. There are no facilities. **Amenities:** none. **Best for:** snorkeling; swimming. ✉ *Off Rte. 997* ✣ *East of Balneario Sun Bay.*

Playa Negra (Black Sand Beach)

BEACH | About 2½ km (1½ miles) east of Esperanza, Playa Negra is a narrow, black-sand beach backed by cliffs. Often deserted, it's one of the most ruggedly beautiful beaches on the island, with sparkling turquoise water and soft sand. There's neither shade nor facilities, so bring water and sunscreen. The beach is accessed by an easy 15-minute hike through a riverbed surrounded by jungle, so be sure to wear mosquito repellent and waterproof shoes (or go barefoot), as the trail is often muddy. **Amenities:** none. **Best for:** solitude; swimming; walking. ✉ *Rte. 201* ✣ *2½ km (1½ miles) east of Esperanza, next to Oro Vieques.*

Restaurants

Bananas

$$ | **CARIBBEAN** | Overlooking the Caribbean in Esperanza and geared to tourists, this longtime, open-air favorite has playful rain-forest murals climbing its walls. Claim a spot at one of the curvy, teal-colored, concrete tables or under an umbrella out front, and order the red snapper sandwich (popular at lunchtime) or the jerk chicken. **Known for:** party atmosphere; excellent salads; deep-fried bananas with hot honey sauce. Ⓢ *Average main: $12* ✉ *142 Calle Flamboyán, Esperanza* ☎ *787/741–8700* 🌐 *www.bananasvqs.com.*

Duffy's

$$ | **CARIBBEAN** | At some point during your time in Vieques, you should end up at Duffy's, the island's most popular hangout, where customers tend to sit elbow-to-elbow around the bar (the owner is a real character, and locals love to to chew the fat with him). Don't dismiss the food, though: in addition to burgers, fries, and other standards, there are chalkboard specials like conch fritters, scallop ceviche, grilled rib eye, or pan-seared pork loin—all a cut above the usual beach fare. **Known for:** good bar food; lively atmosphere and waterfront location; cheap drinks. Ⓢ *Average main: $12* ✉ *140 Calle Flamboyán, Esperanza* ☎ *787/435–6585* 🌐 *www.duffysesperanza.com* ⏲ *Closed Sun. and Mon.*

★ El Quenepo

$$$ | **ECLECTIC** | This elegant yet unpretentious spot (the owners, Scott and Kate Cole, don't mind if you show up in anything from a dripping wet bikini with a cover-up to a ball gown) brings fine dining and a touch of class to the Esperanza waterfront. Local herbs and fruits, such as quenepas and breadfruit, appear in artfully prepared dishes that the Coles call "fun, funky island food." Scott is the chef, known for seafood specials highlighting the daily catch, as well as dishes you're unlikely to find elsewhere in Puerto Rico, such as braised goat masala. **Known for:** fresh fish and seafood; excellent service; good choice of wine and cocktails. *$ Average main: $30 ✉ 148 Calle Flamboyán, Esperanza ☎ 787/741–1215 🌐 www.elquenepovieques.com ⏲ Closed Sun. No lunch.*

★ Placita Restaurant at El Blok Hotel
$$ | **PUERTO RICAN** | The inviting bar and restaurant on the ground floor of the trendy Blok Hotel is one of the island's most sophisticated and design-forward eateries. The menu is simple and spectacular, full of carefully selected, internationally inspired, tapas-sized dishes—including grilled fish, ceviche, and steak—made with a Puerto Rican twist. **Known for:** grilled octopus; fresh salads; local spiny lobster. *$ Average main: $12 ✉ El Block Hotel, 158 Calle Flamboyan, Esperanza ☎ 787/741–6020 🌐 www.elblok.com.*

Hotels

El Blok Hotel
$$ | **HOTEL** | This boutique hotel, which has received rave reviews for its unique architecture and design (minimalist concrete, open-air common spaces), is a great place to unplug and relax. **Pros:** continental breakfast included; rooftop plunge pool; on-site restaurant. **Cons:** can be noisy; may be too minimalist for some tastes; no TVs or phones in rooms and poor Wi-Fi. *$ Rooms from: $220 ✉ 158 Calle Flamboyán, Esperanza ☎ 787/741–6020 🌐 www.elblok.com 🛏 30 rooms 🍴 No Meals.*

★ Hacienda Tamarindo
$$$ | **HOTEL** | Taking its name from a centuries-old tamarind tree rising more than three stories through the center of its main building, this plantation-style property—with a barrel-tile roof and wood-shuttered windows—was once a dance hall but is now one of the island's prettiest hotels. **Pros:** beautiful views; nicely designed rooms; excellent breakfast included. **Cons:** must drive to beaches; no full-service restaurant; no elevator. *$ Rooms from: $265 ✉ Rte. 997, Km 4.5, Esperanza ☎ 787/741–8525 🌐 www.haciendatamarindo.com 🛏 17 rooms 🍴 Free Breakfast.*

Malecón House
$$ | **B&B/INN** | Raising the bar for Vieques lodging are posh boutique hotels like this immaculate seaside escape, where rooms are decorated with rich wood furniture, luxurious stone flooring, and high-end linens. **Pros:** affordable waterfront property; tasty breakfast; welcoming hosts. **Cons:** in-town location not for those seeking seclusion; rather small pool; surrounding area can be noisy. *$ Rooms from: $200 ✉ 105 Calle Flamboyán, Esperanza ☎ 939/239–7113 🌐 www.maleconhouse.com 🛏 13 rooms 🍴 Free Breakfast.*

★ Puertas at El Quenepo
$$ | **B&B/INN** | This luxurious B&B sits above El Quenepo restaurant and has a handful of rooms named after local fruits and plants. **Pros:** local artwork; room service from El Quenepo restaurant when they're full; large showers. **Cons:** minimum two-night stay; adults only; noise from adjacent nightlife. *$ Rooms from: $250 ✉ 148 Calle Flamboyan, Esperanza ☎ 787/436–4709 🌐 www.puertasvieques.com 🛏 4 rooms 🍴 Free Breakfast.*

Nightlife

Bananas

BARS | Bananas is the place for burgers and beer—and not necessarily in that order. There's occasional live music and dancing, and a Monday happy-hour special on bottles of Medalla, the local brew. ✉ *142 Calle Flamboyán, Esperanza* ☎ *787/718–6349* 🌐 *www.bananasvqs.com.*

Duffy's

BARS | Hands down, Duffy's is the most popular bar on the island, thanks to live music, daily specials, and a prime location on Esperanza's Malecón—not to mention the jawboning of owner Michael Duffy. ✉ *140 Calle Flamboyán, Esperanza* ☎ *787/435–6585* 🌐 *www.duffysesperanza.com.*

Activities

BOATING AND KAYAKING

Various outfitters offer trips to Puerto Mosquito, the island's celebrated bioluminescent bay. Most trips are made in single-person kayaks, which can be a challenge if you lack experience or endurance. A better option for many people is an electric-powered boat—gas-powered engines harm the environment.

Abe's Snorkeling and Bio-Bay Tours

KAYAKING | Abe is one of Vieques's most animated characters, so it's no surprise that his kayaking tours to Puerto Mosquito are the most popular. Over the course of two hours, guests kayak into the glowing bay for a once-in-a-lifetime experience. For an entire day on the water, Abe's All-in-One Tour involves kayaking through mangrove lagoons, snorkeling coral reefs, watching the sunset on a secluded beach, and visiting the bio-bay after dark. Lunch is provided. ✉ *278 Calle Flamboyan, Esperanza* ☎ *787/435–1362* 🌐 *www.abessnorkeling.com* 🎫 *Night tours from $60, 5-hr tours from $150.*

FISHING

Vieques Sport Fishing

FISHING | Captain J. Ferguson has been a charter fisherman since 1989, and off Vieques's coast he navigates a 26-foot boat into waters laden with tuna, mahimahi, dorado, kingfish, and marlin. He offers four-hour deep-sea fishing trips. ✉ *103 Calle Hucar, Esperanza* ☎ *787/502–3839* 🌐 *www.viequessportfishing.com* 🎫 *From $350.*

HORSEBACK RIDING

★ Esperanza Riding Company

HORSEBACK RIDING | If you've ever dreamed of riding a horse on the beach, splashing through waves and under palm trees, Esperanza Riding Company can make your dreams come true. Morning and afternoon rides are offered and typically include a route that takes riders into the hills and down to Playa Negra, sometimes even riding in the water. Group rides are $80 per person, or you can book a private ride for $125. Go online to make reservations. All experience levels are welcome. ✉ *Rte. 996 at Rte. 201* ☎ *787/435–0073* 🌐 *esperanzaridingcompany.com.*

Elsewhere on Vieques

Isabel Segunda and Esperanza are just a tiny portion of Vieques. Most of the island—more than two-thirds of it, in fact—was commandeered by the military until 2003. It's now a nature preserve that draws thousands of visitors each year.

Sights

★ Puerto Mosquito Bioluminescent Bay

NATURE SIGHT | East of Esperanza, Puerto Mosquito is one of the world's best spots for a glow-in-the-dark experience with undersea dinoflagellates—microorganisms that light up when the water around

Continued on page 177

BIOLUMINESCENT BAYS

Plankton Pyrotechnics in Puerto Rico

Puerto Rico's bioluminescent bays are beautiful. The slightest stirring of these waters, whether from the swish of a stick or droplets of rain, produces tiny bursts of teal-blue light. The darker the night, the better the bright; a moonless sky affords the most gorgeous marine moments in these wondrous bays.

by Francesca Drago

It's estimated that there are only 12 bio bays in the world, but it's difficult to determine exactly because the phenomenon occurs sporadically in warm seas. Puerto Rico has three. **Puerto Mosquito** in Vieques is the most spectacular bay. It won a Guinness World Record for most outstanding bioluminescent bay in the world. **Lagunas Grande** in Fajardo is not as bright, but convenient to see from San Juan. **Bahía de Fosforescente** in La Parquera's deserves an honorable mention even though water pollution, primarily from gas- and diesel-powered tourist boats, has darkened its luster.

Positively glowing! Puerto Rico's bio bays will literally have you beaming with joy.

EXPLORING THE BAYS

Kayaks are an environmentally friendly way to explore the bays.

Seeing your oars glow as they blade through the water is a magical experience. Go with an operator that uses glow sticks to illuminate the stern of each kayak (for minimal light interference) and reviews safety practices at the start. Never book a tour with an operator who is unlicensed or uses gas- or diesel-powered boats. Ask your hotel concierge for assistance. On Vieques all hotels listed in our Where to Stay section will help arrange tours of Puerto Mosquito Bay.

RECOMMENDED OUTFITTERS IN VIEQUES

Island Adventures runs nightly bio bay tours and an educational tour aboard an open-air electric boat. (Prone to motion sickness? Be advised that a 45-minute cruise on a catamaran and 15-minute bus ride on a rough, unpaved road is part of this trip.) **Aqua Frenzy Kayaks** and **Abe's Snorkeling & Bio Bay Tours** both provide sturdy kayaks and knowledgeable guides for day and night trips to Puerto Mosquito.

IN FAJARDO

The two-hour night tour at Las Cabezas Nature Reserve (see Exploring, Fajardo, chapter 3) takes you on a winding boardwalk through mangroves to the water's edge. Strike the dark lagoon with a stick and marvel at the flashing wakes, or stir the water to "draw" with light.

For more information on recommended outfitters, see Boating & Kayaking in this chapter.

KNOW BEFORE YOU GLOW

- Paddling through the long, dark mangrove channel to reach Mosquito Bay is exciting but also challenging. Kayaking can be strenuous and requires teamwork; book with small groups, if possible, because crowds with varying experience and endurance can lead to exasperation and delay.
- People with little or no kayak experience, or with small children, may prefer a pontoon trip that provides an easy and safe way to swim in luminescent water.
- Puerto Mosquito is aptly named. Wear a hat, water shoes, and nylon pants as protection from bites. A lightweight, waterproof windbreaker worn over a bathing suit is ideal.
- Jellyfish are sometimes present but cannot be seen in the dark water. Look carefully.

NEW MOON

Bioluminescence is best experienced on a cloudy or moonless night. The darkest nights occur during the new moon phase, when its face is in shadow. Ask your tour guide what the moon phase will be and when it will rise, as a full moon may not appear in the sky until after your planned excursion.

PUERTO MOSQUITO: A BAY IN BALANCE

Dinoflagellates occur sporadically in tropical waters around the world, but the highest concentration on earth can be found in Puerto Mosquito Bay in Vieques. Billions of dinos dwell here because their habitat is balanced by a number of ecological features and protections.

Puerto Mosquito Bay

❶ Puerto Mosquito Bay is a **designated wildlife preserve**. This special zoning prevents rampant development, pollution, and destruction of the surrounding forest, which acts as a natural barrier against strong winds and rain.

❷ Salt-tolerant **mangrove trees** are vital for healthy coastal ecosystems. Their pronged roots stabilize the silt-rich shoreline, helping to filter sediments and reduce erosion, while leaves and bark fall into the water, where they rot and provide food and nutrients essential to the dinos' diet (e.g., vitamin B12). Moreover, the mangroves absorb carbon dioxide and store carbon in their sediments, which makes them a vital resource for reducing greenhouse gasses in the atmosphere.

❸ The long, **narrow channel leading to the ocean** acts as a buffer that minimizes how much seawater flows into the bay daily and limits the amount of dinoflagellates (and nutrients) that are swept out with the tides. This enables the dinos to concentrate in the bay's shallow refuge.

❹ The **channel exit** at the windward end of the bay allows sufficient water exchange with the sea to keep it from overheating or stagnating. The water in Puerto Mosquito remains calm and warm, creating the ideal environment for dinoflagellates to thrive in.

WHAT'S IN THE WATER?

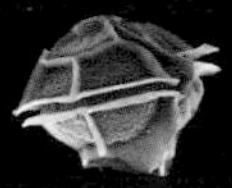

The undersea shooting stars are produced by microscopic algae called dinoflagellates, or "dinos." They convert chemical energy into light energy and emit tiny flashes when the water is disturbed. Scientists have theorized that their sudden sparks are a defense mechanism—a way to startle and disorient a predator and perhaps attract a larger predator to eat the first one.

A bio bay's brightness is a measure of its health. Dinoflagellates use the energy from sunlight to photosynthesize. Their luminescence is influenced by circadian rhythms, meaning their brightness depends on the light-dark conditions over a 24-hour period. One full day of sunshine and no clouds will result in two nights of plankton brilliance—with the second night brighter than the first. A cloudy day may still produce a bright night, but the following night won't be as spectacular. Artificial and ambient light will disrupt the fragile cycles of these "living lanterns" and erase their natural bioluminescence. Preservation of bio-bay brightness depends on public awareness about the harmful effects of light pollution and thoughtful planning for future land development.

The species of dinoflagellate Pyrodinium Bahamenese, found in Puerto Mosquito, is only 1/500 of an inch

PROTECTING THE BAYS

Destruction of mangroves, dredging, land development, and overuse of the bays' waters endanger the bio bays. Light pollution is especially harmful, since artificial and ambient light suppress the luminescence of the dinoflagellates. The Vieques Conservation and Historical Trust (VCHT) held its first symposium in the fall of 2008, convening expert scientific and technical authorities to discuss conservation of the bio bays. The goal, said Trust marine expert Mark Martin, was to "involve everybody," including government and the public, and rally commitments and resources to ensure the continuous scientific monitoring of Puerto Mosquito. The VCHT wants to name Puerto Mosquito a UNESCO World Biosphere Reserve to preserve it for future generations.

Here's what you can do to help maintain the pristine condition of this precious natural resource:

- Book with licensed operators who use kayaks or electric boats only.
- Swimming is banned in all the bio bays but Puerto Mosquito. Shun those operators who ignore the law.
- Dinoflagellates absorb basic chemicals directly from the water. Bug repellents containing DEET will kill them. Rinse off any remnants of suntan lotion, perfume, and deodorant before swimming.
- Do not throw any objects in the water or litter in any way.
- Support the conservation efforts of the VCHT.

them is agitated. Local operators offer kayak trips or excursions on nonpolluting boats to see the bay's light show. Look behind your boat at the twinkling wake. Even the fish that swim through and jump from the water bear an eerie glow. The high concentration of dinoflagellates sets the bay apart from other spots (including in Puerto Rico) that are home to these microorganisms. The experience is best when there's little or no moonlight; rainy nights are beautiful, too, because drops hitting the water produce ricochets that shimmer like diamonds. Note that licensed operators are prohibited from leading tours on the day before, during, and after a full moon. ✉ *Unpaved roads off Rte. 997.*

Vieques National Wildlife Refuge

WILDLIFE REFUGE | A portion of the west and the entire eastern end of the island is administered by the U.S. Fish and Wildlife Service as the Vieques National Wildlife Refuge. With almost 18,000 acres, it's Puerto Rico's biggest protected natural reserve; in 2015, it was voted the fourth-best refuge in the entire Fish and Wildlife system. Many of the beaches on the northern and southern coasts—where an asphalt road leads to six of them—are open to the public. Hiking, biking, and horseback riding are allowed on designated trails. Fishing (both shore and from kayak), swimming, snorkeling, and diving are also permitted in designated zones. Much, though not all, of the eastern region is pristine, astonishingly beautiful, and well forested, with a hilly center region overlooking powder-white sandy beaches and a coral-ringed coastline. Some of the refuge—including 900 acres that once served as a naval bombing range—remains off-limits to visitors, though, as authorities continue to search for unexploded munitions and contaminants, the byproducts of the area's 60 years as a military base. ✉ *Rte. 997, Km 3.2* ☎ *787/741–2138* 🌐 *www.fws.gov/refuge/vieques.*

Beaches

★ Pata Prieta (*Secret Beach*)

BEACH | The not-so-secret Secret Beach is a heavenly cove for those seeking privacy. This tiny yet beautiful horseshoe-shape stretch of sand, reached via a rambling dirt road, is calm and secluded. You can find yourself completely alone or in the company of just a few couples embracing in the crystal clear water. **Amenities:** none. **Best for:** solitude; snorkeling; swimming. ✉ *Off Rte. 997, east of Playa Caracas.*

Playa Caracas (*Red Beach*)

BEACH | One of the first stretches of sand east of Esperanza, this well-maintained beach boasts covered cabañas for lounging. Less rustic than other nearby beaches, it is sheltered from waves. **Amenities:** parking (no fee); toilets. **Best for:** snorkeling; swimming; walking. ✉ *Off Rte. 997.*

Playa La Chiva (*Blue Beach*)

BEACH | Some consider this the most beautiful beach on Vieques. It has a handful of covered cabañas with individual parking spots, so guests can claim their own personal stretch of sand and survey an expansive, tranquil horizon. Beware of strong surf in some spots. **Amenities:** none. **Best for:** solitude; walking. ✉ *Off Rte. 997, 4 km (2½ miles) east of Esperanza.*

Punta Arenas (*Green Beach*)

BEACH | On the western edge of the island, at the end of a long unpaved road marred by potholes, this beach faces the Vieques Passage. Miles of coral reef just offshore attract snorkelers and divers, but caution is required due to strong currents. From the shore you can catch a glimpse of El Yunque on the mainland. **Amenities:** none. **Best for:** snorkeling; solitude. ✉ *Off Rte. 200, at western end of Rte. 994.*

Vieques Libre

For nearly six decades, the U.S. Navy had a stranglehold on Vieques. It controlled the island's eastern half and western end and exerted enormous influence over the destiny of the civilian area in between. Though long protested, the bombing, shelling, and amphibious landings continued. When an off-target bomb killed a civilian on naval land in April 1999, opposition transformed the island's placid beaches into political hotbeds.

Protesters camping out on the bombing range kept it shut down from 1999 to 2000. Hundreds of Puerto Rican residents were arrested for trespassing on naval land during war games. They were joined by celebrity protesters from the United States, including environmental lawyer Robert F. Kennedy Jr. (who gave his son Aiden the middle name Vieques), the wife of Reverend Jesse Jackson, and Reverend Al Sharpton, all of whom were arrested for trespassing on the bombing range. For much of 2000 and 2001, protests were so commonplace that there were semipermanent encampments of opponents. Songs such as "Paz Pa' Vieques" (Peace for Vieques) began to surface, as did bumper stickers and T-shirts with protest slogans. Latin pop celebrities like singer-songwriter Robi Draco Rosa (who wrote Ricky Martin's "Livin' la Vida Loca"), actor Edward James Olmos, singer Millie Corretjer, and protest singer Zoraida Santiago, as well as other actors, painters, doctors, and lawyers later added to the fanfare.

President Bill Clinton finally agreed that residents could vote on whether to continue to host the navy. A nonbinding referendum held in 2001 found that 68% of the island's voters wanted the military to leave immediately. Although some members of Congress argued that the navy should stay indefinitely—a faction whose cries grew louder after September 11, 2001, when even local protesters called for a moratorium on civil disobedience—the government ultimately capitulated. The navy finally withdrew from its Atlantic Fleet training grounds in May 2002, and in 2003 the installation was officially closed. By the end of 2005, much of the former military base was transformed into the Vieques National Wildlife Refuge. Today, there are concerns that the sustained bombing activity produced high levels of contamination that are linked to health issues such as higher cancer rates among residents. Visitors who may be concerned about potential risks associated with travel to the area should check the Centers for Disease Control website (*cdc.gov*) for the latest information.

Restaurants

★ Tin Box

$$ | **BARBECUE** | **FAMILY** | Tin Box is, quite literally, a tin box serving barbecue platters and po'boys piled high with smoked chicken, pork, fried shrimp, or ribs, served with classic sides like coleslaw, baked beans, and cornbread. A sushi bar rounds out the offerings—you can't go wrong with one of the rolls made with local spiny lobster. **Known for:** watermelon margaritas and martinis; house-cured bacon; best sushi and barbecue on the island. *Average main: $18* *Rte. 996 at Rte. 201* *787/435–6064* *www.facebook.com/tinboxvqs* *Closed Mon. and Tues.*

Hotels

Hix Island House

$$$ | **HOTEL** | Constructed entirely of concrete and set in a tropical forest, the four buildings of this luxurious hotel echo the granite boulders strewn around Vieques, blending with the surroundings. **Pros:** acclaimed eco-friendly architecture; very secluded setting; friendly staff. **Cons:** the lack of window screens means bugs get in; no air-conditioning, TVs, or phones; no Wi-Fi in rooms (although it's free in public areas). *Rooms from: $300 ✉ Rte. 995, Km 1.5 ☎ 787/435–1590 🌐 www.hixislandhouse.com 🛏 19 rooms 🍴 Free Breakfast.*

Shopping

★ Oro Vieques

ART GALLERIES | This art gallery, event space, and boutique is dedicated to Puerto Rican artists and designers, with monthly events and ongoing exhibits. Stop by before or after your visit to Playa Negra to browse affordable paintings and photographs by local artists, or check the calendar for upcoming artist dinners and other events while you're in town. *✉ Rte. 997 ✣ Next to Playa Negra 🌐 www.orovieques.com.*

Culebra

28 km (17 miles) east of Fajardo by ferry.

"Open some days, closed others," reads the sign on a food kiosk near the canal that cuts through a part of this island. It's a pretty good motto for most of Culebra, which—if you can imagine it—is even more laid-back than Vieques. Visitors don't come here for highbrow entertainment. They come for one thing: beaches. Culebra is known around the world for its curvaceous coastline. Playa Flamenco, the tiny island's most famous stretch of sand, is considered one of the top 10 best beaches in the world. If Playa Flamenco gets too crowded, as it often does around Easter or Christmas, many other neighboring beaches will still be nearly deserted. And if it's complete privacy you're after, hire a motorboat to take you to one of the nearby islets, such as Isla Culebrita or Cayo Luis Peña. It won't be difficult to find a little cove that you can have all to yourself.

Archaeological evidence shows that Taíno and Carib peoples lived on Culebra long before the arrival of the Spanish in the late 15th century. The Spanish didn't bother laying claim to it until 1886; a lack of freshwater made it an unattractive location for a settlement. The U.S. Navy and Marine Corps, however, thought it was a very valuable piece of real estate. Although President Theodore Roosevelt created a wildlife refuge here in 1909, the military later used this island, as well as nearby Vieques, for target practice and amphibious assault training, beginning in WWII. Despite having a smaller population than Vieques, the residents of Culebra staged a number of sit-ins and succeeded in ousting the military in 1975.

GETTING HERE AND AROUND

AIR

Culebra's airport is a no-frills affair, with bathrooms, airline counters, and a small café inside, and chickens pecking the ground outside. The airport is about three minutes from downtown Dewey. Route 250 leads east and south of the airport; Route 251 leads northeast to Playa Flamenco. Two car rental companies have facilities directly across the street from the airport, a two-minute walk at most.

CONTACTS Aeropuerto Benjamin Rivera Noriega (CPX). *✉ Rte. 250 at Rte. 251.*

CAR

Renting a Jeep or at least a golf cart is imperative for getting around Culebra. Carlos Jeep Rental, a quick walk from the

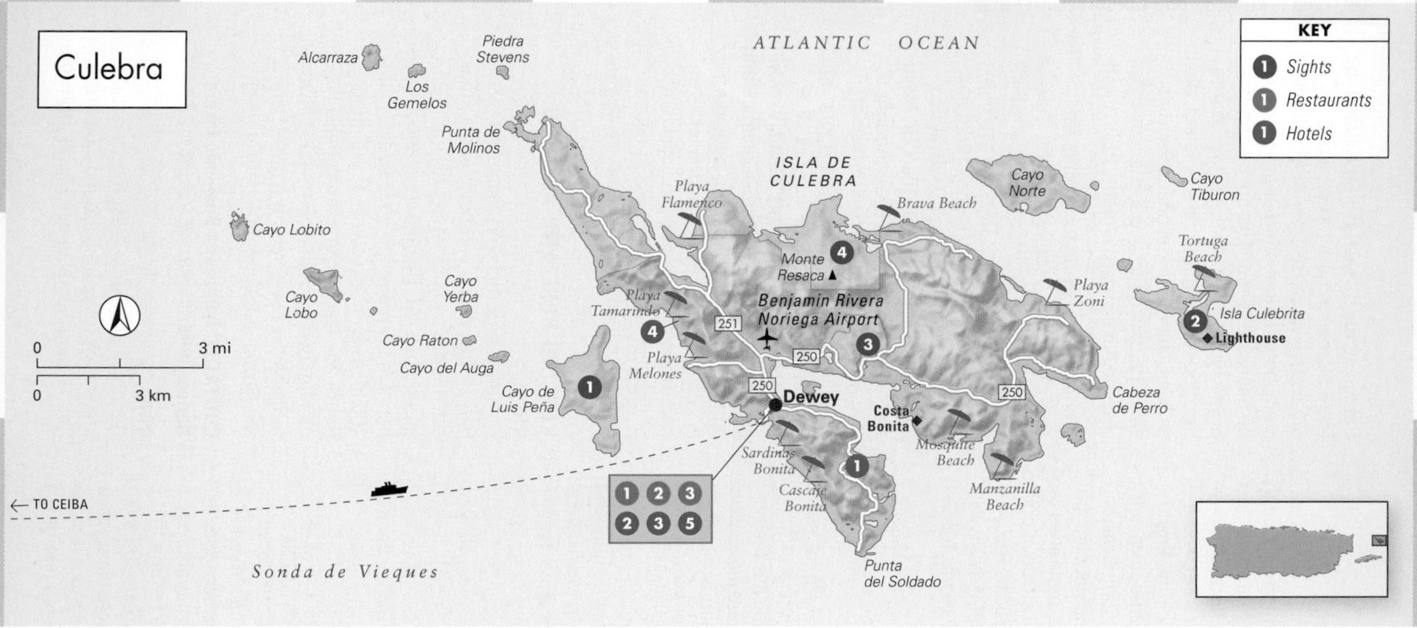

Sights	
1 Cayo Luis Peña	D2
2 Isla Culebrita	G2
3 Museo El Polvorín	E2
4 Refugio Nacional de Vida Silvestre de Culebra	E2

Restaurants	
1 Dinghy Dock	E2
2 Mamacita's Bar & Grill	E2
3 Moncho's BBQ	E2

Hotels	
1 Club Seabourne	E3
2 Mamacita's	E2
3 Posada La Hamaca	E2
4 Tamarindo Estates	D2
5 Villa Boheme	E2

airport, is a good place to choose your steed. Daily rates range from $27, for a four-passenger golf cart, to $50. Customers arriving by ferry can request courtesy round-trip shuttle service.

Directly across from Culebra's airport, Jerry's Jeep Rental is the most convenient car rental spot on the island, but advance reservations are recommended year-round and are imperative during high season. In addition to a fleet of Jeeps, Jerry's has golf carts; both types of vehicles are available for rentals as short as a few hours or as long as a month.

CONTACTS Carlos Jeep Rental. ✉ *Aeropuerto Benjamin Rivera Noriega* ☎ *787/742–3514* 🌐 *www.carlosjeeprental.com.* **Jerry's Jeep Rental.** ✉ *Rte. 251, directly across from the airport* ☎ *787/742–0526* 🌐 *www.jerrysjeeprental.com.*

Sights

Almost everything about Culebra is diminutive. The island's only community—named for U.S. Admiral George Dewey (locals resent the association, preferring to call it simply "el pueblo" instead)—is set along a single street leading from the ferry dock. You can explore the few shops along Calle Pedro Márquez in a half hour. The one-room airport is 1 km (½ mile) to the north. Except for one resort, few hotels have more than a dozen rooms.

Cayo Luis Peña

ISLAND | A kayak is a great way to reach Cayo Luis Peña, an islet just off the western edge of Culebra. There are a handful of protected beaches where you can soak up the sun and not run into a single soul. Cayo Luis Peña is also part of the Refugio Nacional de Vida Silvestre de Culebra (Culebra National Wildlife Refuge).

★ Isla Culebrita

ISLAND | Part of the Refugio Nacional de Vida Silvestre de Culebra, uninhabited Isla Culebrita is clearly visible from the northeast corner of Culebra. An essential day-trip excursion, this islet is a favorite destination for sunbathers, snorkelers, and boating enthusiasts. Isolation amid a palette of crystalline, turquoise waters, and dewy, lush greens makes for a one-of-a-kind natural experience. On weekends and holidays however, the island can get crowded. On the northern shore there are several tidal pools, snuggling into one of them is like taking a warm bath. Snorkelers and divers love that they can reach the reef from the shore and carouse with sea turtles, rays, and schools of colorful fish. Bring your sneakers: in about 20–30 minutes you can hike to the islet's peak, where the spectacular ruins of an old lighthouse await. Views of the surrounding Caribbean are sublime from the top of the structure, but you may not be able to climb its 54 steps; the lighthouse is currently being restored. Several tour operators offer excursions to the island. 🌐 *www.paralanaturaleza.org.*

Museo El Polvorín

MILITARY SIGHT | If the collection of this museum underwhelms, take a close look at the photo album next to the visitor log to see how much community spirit and sweat went into the restoration of El Polvorín, a former U.S. military munitions building, constructed in 1905. It reopened in 2008 as a museum, but not without an enormous amount of effort; the structure was little more than a shell. Today, it houses a small but interesting collection of objects and photos that tell the island's history (don't miss the story of Puerto Rico's first female mayor), along with several TVs with interesting oral history–based documentaries on loop. ✉ *Rte. 250* ☎ *787/617–8517* 🎫 *$1.*

Did You Know?

Like Culebra, the even more diminutive Isla Culebrita has stunning, curvaceous beaches. Vibrant shore reefs and warm tidal pools make it popular with day-trippers.

★ Refugio Nacional de Vida Silvestre de Culebra

WILDLIFE REFUGE | Commissioned by President Theodore Roosevelt in 1909, the Culebra National Wildlife Refuge is one of the nation's oldest. The total protected area comprises some 1,500 acres of the island. It's a lure for hikers and bird-watchers: Culebra teems with seabirds, from laughing gulls and roseate terns to red-billed tropic birds and sooty terns. Maps of trails in the refuge are hard to come by, but you can stop by the U.S. Fish and Wildlife Service office east of the airport to find out about trail conditions and determine whether you're headed to an area that requires a permit. The office also can tell you whether the leatherback turtles are nesting. From mid-April to mid-July, volunteers help monitor and tag these creatures, which nest on nearby beaches, especially Playa Resaca and Playa Brava. ✉ *Rte. 250, north of Dewey* ☎ *787/742–0115* 🌐 *www.fws.gov/refuge/culebra.*

Beaches

★ Playa Flamenco

BEACH | **FAMILY** | Consistently ranked one of the most beautiful beaches in the world, this stretch has snow-white sands, turquoise waters, and lush hills rising on all sides. During the week, it's pleasantly uncrowded; on weekends it fills up with day-trippers from the mainland. With kiosks selling simple dishes and vendors for lounge-chair and umbrella rentals, it's easy to make a day of it. There's great snorkeling past the old dock. Tanks on the northern end of the beach are a reminder that the area was once a military base. **Amenities:** food and drink; parking (no fee); showers; toilets. **Best for:** snorkeling; swimming; walking. ✉ *Rte. 251, west of the airport* ☎ *787/742–0700.*

Playa Melones

BEACH | Just west of Dewey, this is a favorite spot for snorkelers. The reef that runs around the rocky point is easy to reach from shore. Locals swear this is the best place for sunsets, too. To get here, head uphill on the unmarked road behind the church. **Amenities:** none. **Best for:** snorkeling; sunset; swimming. ✉ *Camino Vecinal, west of town, Dewey.*

Playa Zoni

BEACH | On the island's northeastern end, this beach is long and narrow—perfect for afternoon strolls. From the shore you can catch a glimpse of Isla Culebrita, as well as St. Thomas and St. Croix. Leatherback turtles nest here. Note that there is a gravel parking lot, but it's small; it won't fit more than a dozen Jeeps at a time. **Amenities:** parking (no fee). **Best for:** swimming; walking. ✉ *End of Rte. 250, 11 km (7 miles) northeast of Dewey.*

Restaurants

Dinghy Dock

$$ | **SEAFOOD** | This restaurant takes its name from the nearby site of Culebra's heaviest traffic—the arrival and departure of the water taxi. The menu leans toward grilled meats, from hamburgers and wraps to sirloin steaks. **Known for:** creole-style seafood; burgers and other bar food; laid-back atmosphere. $ *Average main: $20* ✉ *Calle Fulladoza, Dewey* ☎ *787/742–0233.*

Mamacita's Bar & Grill

$$ | **CARIBBEAN** | Pull your dinghy up to the dock, and watch the resident iguanas plod past this simple, open-air, tin-roof restaurant on a rough-plank deck beside the Dewey canal. Tarpon cruise past, and the to-and-fro of boaters completes the show at Culebra's favorite watering hole and gringo hangout. **Known for:** grilled seafood; lunchtime burgers; casual setting. $ *Average main: $18* ✉ *66 Calle Castelar, Dewey* ☎ *787/742–0090.*

Moncho's BBQ

$ | **PUERTO RICAN** | This unassuming lunch spot is a favorite for locals. They serve classic Puerto Rican dishes from a

A tank—left to the whims of the elements and graffiti artists—recalls Playa Flamenco's days as a military site.

takeout counter with generous servings at an affordable price. **Known for:** pernil; arroz guisado (with gandules, longaniza, chorizo, or jamonilla); roasted chicken. *Average main: $10 15 Calle Pedro Marquez 787/366–4993 Closed weekends.*

Hotels

VILLA RENTALS

Lovely vacation homes are scattered around Culebra.

★ Club Seabourne

$$ | **HOTEL** | The most sophisticated place in Culebra is an assemblage of lovely plantation-style cottages on a picturesque hilltop overlooking Fulladoza Bay. Though just a five-minute drive south of Dewey, it feels completely isolated—in a good way. **Pros:** lush gardens; nice pool; airport or ferry transfers included. **Cons:** some steps to negotiate; no full-service on-site restaurant; spotty Internet and mobile phone reception. *Rooms from: $249 Rte. 252, northwest of town 787/742–3169 www.clubseabourne.com 13 rooms Free Breakfast.*

Mamacita's

$ | **HOTEL** | The best rooms in Mamacita's venerable guesthouse have balconies overlooking the canal, but this is a decidedly no-frills establishment suitable for budget-minded travelers. **Pros:** friendly staff; pickup point for water taxis; popular restaurant and bar in guesthouse. **Cons:** basic rooms; no elevator; on a narrow street. *Rooms from: $89 66 Calle Castelar, Dewey 787/742–0090 11 rooms No Meals.*

Posada La Hamaca

$ | **HOTEL** | This building, which shares Mamacita's mangrove-lined canal, has spick-and-span guest rooms—as simple as they come—with louvered windows and calming color schemes. **Pros:** walk to shops and restaurants; laid-back atmosphere; cheap rates. **Cons:** some rooms are small; constant clunking noises from adjacent bridge; no parking. *Rooms from: $100 68 Calle Castelar, Dewey*

☎ *787/742–3516* 🌐 *www.posada.com* ⇌ *12 rooms* 🍽 *No Meals.*

Tamarindo Estates
$$ | APARTMENT | A few of the one- and two-bedroom cottages at this 60-acre estate, hidden away on Culebra's western coast, sit directly on a long, sandy beach; most cottages, however, are a bit farther inland, though they have great coastal views from covered verandas. **Pros:** peaceful location; pretty pool area; all apartments have full kitchens. **Cons:** short walk to the beach; isolated, far from dining options; no housekeeping service. 💲 *Rooms from: $169* ✉ *Off Rte. 251* ☎ *787/742–3343* 🌐 *www.tamarindoestates.com* ⇌ *12 cottages* 🍽 *No Meals.*

Villa Boheme
$ | B&B/INN | Colorful and breezy, this Spanish-style guesthouse is centrally located, next to the popular Dinghy Dock restaurant–bar. **Pros:** expansive view of the bay; walk to restaurants and shops; on-site kayak and paddleboard rentals. **Cons:** basic furnishings; no elevator; few on-site amenities. 💲 *Rooms from: $125* ✉ *368 Calle Fulladoza, Dewey* ☎ *787/742–3508* 🌐 *villaboheme.com* ⇌ *11 rooms* 🍽 *No Meals.*

Nightlife

Mamacita's
BARS | The island's favorite gringo watering hole is always jumping, with a weekday happy hour (4–6) and Saturday night's live music jam. Don't miss the bar's signature drink: the frozen Bushwhacker—a delicious but deadly mix of rum, vodka, Bailey's, amaretto, Kahlua, and coconut. ✉ *66 Calle Castelar* ☎ *787/742–0090.*

Shopping

Culebra is smaller than Vieques, but has much better shopping. Dewey has several shops on its main drag that sell trendy jewelry, clothing, and souvenirs that range from the tacky to the terrific.

Estudio Arte Fango
CRAFTS | The island's best place for gifts is right above the popular Dinghy Dock restaurant. Local artist Jorge Acevedo paints scenes of island life and Culebra's natural tableaux of mangroves and seascapes. Be sure to browse his one-of-a-kind works and original T-shirts, as well as his wife's handmade jewelry. If you happen to be around on a Saturday, follow him downstairs to the Dinghy Dock, where he plays conga music. ✉ *Above Dinghy Dock restaurant, Dewey* ☎ *787/435–6654* 🌐 *www.artefango.com.*

La Cava
OTHER SPECIALTY STORE | Forgot your snorkel? Left your bathing suit at home? Need a new pair of flip-flops or a souvenir for your favorite cousin? La Cava is the perfect place to meet all of those needs. ✉ *138 Calle Escudero, Dewey* ☎ *787/742–0566.*

Activities

DIVING AND SNORKELING

Aquatic Adventures
BOATING | Captain Taz Hamrick takes guests out on snorkeling and PADI-certified scuba trips, as well as charters to the surrounding keys. Two-tank dive trips start at $110. ✉ *372 Sector Fulladoza, Dewey* ☎ *515/290–2310.*

Culebra Divers
SCUBA DIVING | The island's premier dive shop caters to scuba newbies and old hands alike. The company's 25-foot cabin cruisers travel to more than 50 local sites to see spotted eagle rays, octopus, moray eels, and turtles. You can also rent a mask and snorkel to explore on your own. Two-tank dive trips start at $125. ✉ *4 Calle Pedro Márquez, Dewey* ☎ *787/742–0803* 🌐 *www.culebradivers.com.*

Chapter 6

THE NORTH COAST AND THE CORDILLERA CENTRAL

Updated by
Adriana Mercado

Sights	Restaurants	Hotels	Shopping	Nightlife
★★★★☆	★☆☆☆☆	★★☆☆☆	★☆☆☆☆	★☆☆☆☆

WELCOME TO THE NORTH COAST AND THE CORDILLERA CENTRAL

TOP REASONS TO GO

★ **Bosque Estatal de Toro Negro:** Hike to the island's highest lake and explore its tallest mountain.

★ **Indigenous culture:** Dorado's Museo de Arte e Historia has intriguing artifacts highlighting indigenous coastal communities. The towns of Utuado and Jayuya were both named after Taíno chiefs and have fascinating sites related to the Taíno people.

★ **Hacienda La Esperanza:** Tour a restored sugar plantation to learn more about the commodity's role in Puerto Rican history.

★ **Karst country:** In some areas, limestone deposits have been shaped by erosion into astounding formations and caves.

The North Coast and Cordillera Central are two distinct regions, each with its own gorgeous geography (and, thus, its own road conditions). Highways 22 and 2 lead west out of San Juan, unspooling in a smooth, fast ribbon across the northern shore. Below the region's limestone (karst) formations sit Puerto Rico's famous caves. Head south on any secondary road to cut into the core of the island, through which the Cordillera Central runs east to west; these are typically two-lane roadways that wind through mountainous terrain.

1 Dorado. Just west of the San Juan metro area is this laid-back beach town.

2 Arecibo. This town—a good jumping off point for deeper exploration of the central mountain region—was once best known as the site of the world's largest radio telescope. The telescope is now closed, but the Science and Visitor Center is still open!

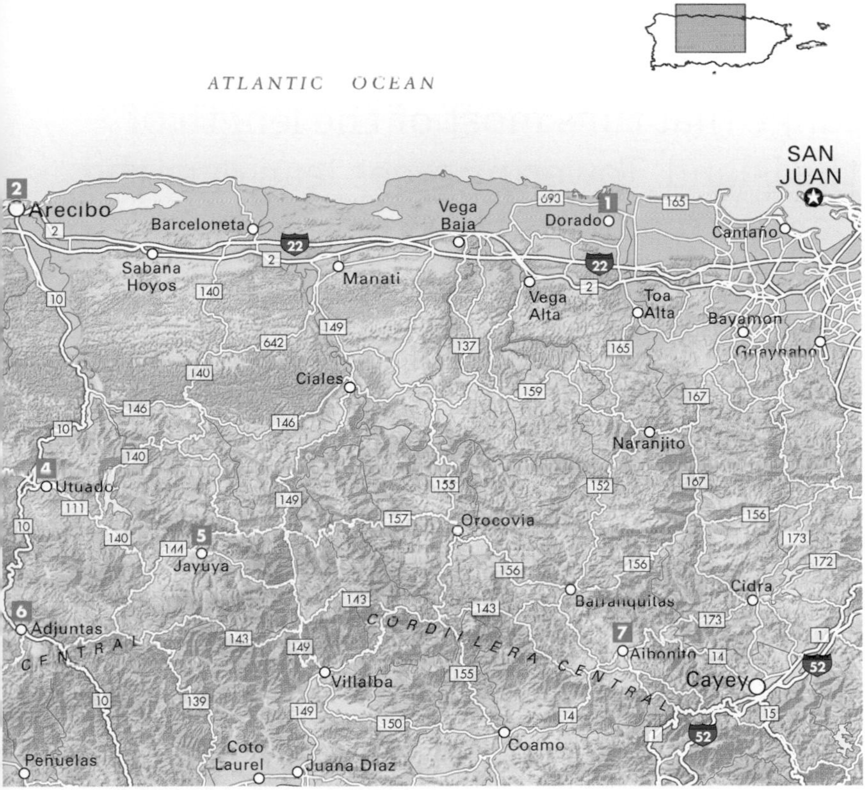

3 Lares. Amid the region's limestone karst country, this town makes a good side trip—for its history and its geology—from either Arecibo or Utuado.

4 Utuado. This mountain town has coffee fields, rivers, and indigenous parks to explore.

5 Jayuya. Learn more about Taíno culture at Jayuya's Museo El Cemí, a uniquely shaped structure with symbolic significance.

6 Adjuntas. In Adjuntas, a gateway to Puerto Rico's coffee culture, you can stay in a small parador on the grounds of a coffee plantation.

7 Aibonito. Several legends attempt to explain the town's name; regardless of which one you choose to believe, Aibonito is "bonito"—especially during its annual flower festival.

There's more to Puerto Rico than beautiful beaches, as anyone who lives on the island will tell you. Locals escape the heat by heading to the Cordillera Central, an incredibly lush mountain range that runs most of the length of the island. Towering trees lean over the narrow roadways that crisscross the region. In the shade below, impatiens in shades of pink and purple bloom in profusion.

Agriculture is very important to the economy of the Cordillera Central. Bananas, pineapples, and plantains are grown throughout the region. Coffee was once a dominant crop along the hillsides near Utuado, and it has enjoyed a resurgence of late. You can now visit coffee plantations and a coffee museum; time your visit right, and you might even catch one of the island's many coffee festivals. A few of the old plantation homes have become quaint country inns, all of them stocked with plenty of blankets for cool evenings, when temperatures—especially in higher elevations—can drop into the 40s.

In the east you'll find a number of attractive colonial towns, such as Aibonito. Farther west is karst country—terrain built up by limestone deposits in which erosion has produced fissures, sinkholes, and underground streams and rivers. The peaks above are often astounding, and visitors love the kinds of photo ops provided by aboveground caves like the popular Cueva Ventana. Along the Cordillera Central, the road threads in and out of the Bosque Estatal de Toro Negro, where the island's highest peak, Cerro de Punta, rises 4,398 feet above sea level. It may not measure up to many around the world, but on this island it seems as tall as Mt. Everest.

All too often, visitors to the Cordillera Central zoom right past the northern coast's many appealing attractions. In Dorado, there's the natural rock formation Ojo del Buey (Bull's Eye) right on the beach; it's believed to have held significance for the people who lived on the island before the arrival of Columbus, as quite a few artifacts have been found there. Many of them are displayed in the town's Museo de Arte e Historia (Museum of Art and History). West of Dorado, you'll find the Reserva Natural Laguna Tortuguero, a natural recreation area with diverse habitat and an array of birds and other wildlife. Just south of the reserve is the Hacienda Don Carmelo, home of the School of Equestrian Art. One highlight is a 130-year-old tree that is the setting for a magical tree house with cathedral-esque windows and a series of porches, making this a popular wedding destination.

Arecibo was once home to the world's largest radio telescope. Sadly, it fell out of operation but still has a thriving Science and Visitor Center that's perfect for kids and families. Another great spot is Parque de las Cavernas del Río Camuy—the world's third-largest underground cave system. After a series of hurricanes, not all caves are safe for walking, but local tour guides can still show you around this once-in-a-lifetime experience.

Planning

When to Go

The temperate climate of the mountainous central zone makes it a pleasure to visit year-round, and outdoor activities abound in any season. Locals especially like to head up to this area in summer, when Aibonito holds its flower festival (late June or July), but there are fun local festivals nearly every month, celebrating everything from handmade lace to coffee. It gets hot in August and September, but North Coast beaches help everyone stay cool. Note that during busy times some hotels require a two- or three-night minimum stay on weekends.

Getting Here and Around

Highways 22 and 2 head west out of San Juan. These are frequently congested with commuters heading into and out of the capital. Local roads to Dorado, Arecibo, and other points west, north, and south, are accessible via exits off these two highways.

Transportation options include car rentals in all airports and local taxi companies. Uber is not widely available, but larger towns, such as Arecibo and Dorado, do have the option.

Hotels

High-class resorts aren't limited exclusively to San Juan and the eastern coast. On the North Coast, for example, travelers who aren't constrained by a budget will find Dorado Beach, a Ritz-Carlton Reserve, sitting on 1,400 acres, much of it prime beachfront. For the most part, however, paradores and other modest lodgings are the norm in the small towns, especially in the Cordillera. Towns in this part of the island seldom have more than two or three options. Sometimes there's just one hotel, take it or leave it—and you'd better take it, especially if you're traveling on a weekend. The best lodgings, rustic retreats set beside a river or on acres of lush forest, are often booked solid. Make sure to call ahead, as it's a long way between towns.

Restaurants

Traditional Puerto Rican cooking is the norm in this part of the island. Many of the ingredients on your plate—breadfruit, coconuts, plantains, mangoes, root vegetables, and the *ají* pepper, to name a few—are sold at roadside stands throughout the region, and they are served at humble eateries along the highways and secondary roads. With a couple of exceptions, don't expect upscale dining or international influences in these regions. Do expect down-home cooking and memorable meals, especially along Route 184, where you'll find a number of restaurants serving slow-roasted *lechón* (suckling pig), a local delicacy cooked outdoors over coals.

HOTEL AND RESTAURANT PRICES

⇨ *Hotel and restaurant reviews have been shortened. For full information visit Fodors.com.*

What It Costs in U.S. Dollars

	$	$$	$$$	$$$$
RESTAURANTS				
	under $12	$12–$20	$21–$30	over $30
HOTELS				
	under $150	$150–$250	$251–$350	over $350

Safety

For the most part, the biggest hazards are traffic and rough patches of road. Still, the same common sense you use anywhere else applies here, too. Don't leave valuables exposed in your rental car or your hotel room. Be aware of your surroundings, especially if walking alone at night or using an ATM. And keep your receipts if you're using a credit or debit card, as fraud is an occasional (but not widespread) problem.

Visitor Information

Arecibo, Jayuya, and Utuado have tourism offices in their town halls. All are open weekdays during normal business hours.

CONTACTS Arecibo City Hall. ✉ *100 Av. José de Diego, Arecibo* ☎ *787/882–2770.* **Jayuya.** ✉ *Carr No. 144, Km 4.8, Jayuya* ☎ *787/828–0900.* **Utuado.** ✉ *8–26 Calle Dr. Betances, Utuado* ☎ *787/894–3505.*

Dorado

27 km (17 miles) west of San Juan.

This small and tidy town is one of the oldest vacation spots on the island, having gotten a boost in 1955, when Laurance Rockefeller bought the pineapple, coconut, and grapefruit plantation of Dr. Alfred Livingston and his daughter Clara and built a resort on the property. Sadly, the Hyatt Dorado Beach Resort & Country Club closed in 2005. Its excellent golf courses—among the best-known in Puerto Rico—are still open, however, and the property has been redeveloped as a private residential resort. Those looking for upscale accommodations evoking the erstwhile golden age still have an option here, thanks to the Dorado Beach, a Ritz-Carlton Reserve. The town of Dorado itself is fun to visit; its winding road leads across a bridge to a main square, with small bars, restaurants, and shops nearby. Most visitors, however, don't stray too far from the beach.

GETTING HERE AND AROUND

As is the case throughout most of Puerto Rico, the best means of getting to and around Dorado and the surrounding towns is by car. In any case, a map and a sense of adventure will be your greatest assets.

Sights

Hacienda Don Carmelo

FARM/RANCH | Hacienda Don Carmelo means different things to different people. To couples getting married, it's a gorgeous backdrop for a dream wedding. To jockeys and horse lovers, it's a school of equestrian art and a venue for the finest horse shows on the island. To visitors who stop by on the first Saturday of the month, it's a pleasant opportunity to take a break from the traffic on a walk through a 60-acre property with views of the Atlantic Ocean. The branches of a 130-year-old tree hold a beautiful tree house. If the property looks vaguely familiar, you might have seen it before: the hacienda appeared on Anthony Bourdain's *No Reservations*. You will, however, need to make a reservation if you want to access the property and go on a tour of its grounds. ✉ *Rd. 670, Km 8.2, Vega Baja, about 15 miles west of Dorado* ☎ *787/991–7044* 🌐 *hdc.events* 🎫 *Tours $20* 🕒 *Tours only on the 1st Sat. of each month, must be booked ahead.*

Great Itineraries

If You Have 1 Day
If you feel like escaping San Juan for a day, head to one of the resorts in Dorado. Because so many *sanjuaneros* do just that, this pretty little town has amazing restaurants. For a dose of history or culture, squeeze in a guided tour of Hacienda La Esperanza, a restored sugar plantation just a short drive from Dorado.

If You Have 2 Days
Head to the town of Guavate via Route 184, where you'll find a string of open-air eateries serving lechón. On weekends the roads are jammed with people from San Juan and Ponce sampling Puerto Rican comfort food. Spend the night in Barranquitas, a mountain town just northwest of Aibonito. On Day 2, you can visit Cañón Las Bocas Natural Reserve in Barranquitas to catch a glimpse of the island's waterfalls, trails, and diverse wildlife.

Visit the Cañón de San Cristóbal and the Bosque Estatal de Toro Negro. Stop for photos along the way, pulling over at one of the *miradores*, or lookout points.

Hacienda La Esperanza

FARM/RANCH | One of several Conservation Trust properties around the island is a restored sugar plantation with a functioning steam engine that once powered the sugarcane press, increasing production fourfold. Listed on the National Register of Historic Places, the hacienda requires an appointment for tours, but visitors with a little time will find it a worthwhile opportunity to learn a great deal about the bittersweet role of sugar in Puerto Rican and Caribbean history. ✉ *616 Calle La Esperanza, Manatí, about 40 km (25 miles) west of Dorado* ☎ *787/552–9515, 787/722–5834 (ext. 261)* 🌐 *www.paralanaturaleza.org/en/hacienda-la-esperanza* 🎫 *Tours $12* 🕓 *Tours not offered every day and must be booked ahead.*

Reserva Natural Laguna Tortuguero

NATURE PRESERVE | Puerto Rico has incredible geographic diversity for such a small island, from the rain forest of El Yunque to the dry forest of Guánica. But along the northern coast, there are all sorts of micro-habitats, including marshes and lagoons and flat stretches of grasslands that have reclaimed their territory after their use as sugarcane fields for much of the 20th century. If you're speeding past in a car, they're hard to appreciate, so stop at this nature reserve, which is crisscrossed with mountain-biking trails and has a kayak launch point. Marsh and coastal birds, as well as an occasional caiman, can be spotted here. ✉ *Rd. 687, Km 2.1, Vega Baja* ☎ *787/4622373* 🎫 *Free* 🕓 *Closed Mon. and Tues.*

Beaches

Playa Breñas

BEACH | This exceptional strand is known for surfing, but adventurous swimmers also enjoy the waves. The beach itself is crescent-shape, and its light golden sands are a popular backdrop for local photo shoots. **Amenities:** none. **Best for:** surfing. ✉ *Rte. 693, Km 10.8* 🎫 *Free.*

Playa Cerro Gordo

BEACH | The 2,500-foot-long beach, one of Puerto Rico's government-administered *balnearios*, is a crescent-shape stretch of groomed sand lined with cliffs. It's very popular and can get crowded on weekends. Take care if you intend to scramble around on the rocks; currents here are strong, and it's not uncommon

The tiny Dorado Beach, a Ritz-Carlton Reserve resort, was originally developed by Laurance Rockefeller, who opened it as the Caribbean's first eco-resort on an expansive 1,400-acre former plantation in 1958.

for crashing waves to wash over the rocks unexpectedly. This beach also has a large camping area and some facilities, including food kiosks that tend to be open only on busy days. **Amenities**: food and drink; toilets. **Best for**: walking. ✉ *End of Rte. 90* 🎫 *Free.*

Playa Los Tubos

BEACH | This beach is popular for both swimming and surfing, but take care with the strong current. There's a summer festival with live music and water-sports competitions here, normally the first week of July. Lots of local scuba instructors hold classes and do dive certifications here as well. **Amenities**: parking (no fee). **Best for**: snorkeling; surfing; swimming. ✉ *Rte. 687, Vega Baja* 🎫 *Free.*

★ Playa Mar Chiquita

BEACH | This beach is only a short drive from Dorado, and it matches the unique look of the natural pools surrounded by limestone walls one finds along Puerto Rico's northern coast. This half-moon shaped, natural pool is one of the island's most visited, and the crashing waves are a spectacular sight. Food trucks selling all of PR's fave fried goodies are always set up here, and arts vendors come out on the weekends when the beach is busier. The water gets rough in the winter months, so swimming may not always be a good idea. **Amenities:** food and drink; parking (no fee). **Best for:** snorkeling; swimming; walking. ✉ *Playa Mar Chiquita, Manatí* ✥ *End of Rte. 684; 21 miles west of Dorado* 🎫 *Free.*

Playa Sardinera

BEACH | This Dorado beach—not to be confused with a beach by the same name in the northwestern town of Isabela—is suitable for swimming and has shade trees, changing rooms, and restrooms, although it's certainly not top-of-class among North Coast beaches. **Amenities**: food and drink; lifeguards; parking (fee); showers; toilets. **Best for**: swimming. ✉ *End of Rte. 697* 🎫 *Free.*

★ **Poza de las Mujeres**

BEACH | About a 30-minute drive outside of Dorado you can find Poza de las Mujeres, another natural North Coast swimming hole protected by rock formations, which split the beach almost in two. On the left, the water is shallow, calm, and protected from the rougher waters outside the natural barricade. On the right, the rocks do not form a protective barrier and the water is much rougher year-round. **Amenities:** parking (no fee). **Best for:** snorkeling; swimming; walking. ✉ *Tierras Nuevas Poniente, Manatí* ✣ *22 miles west of Dorado* *Free.*

Restaurants

El Ladrillo

$$$ | **STEAKHOUSE** | This popular restaurant is named for its floor-to-ceiling brick walls covered in original painting. It's known primarily for steaks—and offers an excellent filet mignon—but given its coastal location, there's also a wide selection of fresh seafood. **Known for:** filet mignon; ample wine cellar; zarzuela. $ *Average main: $28* ✉ *334 Calle Mendéz Vigo, Dorado* ☎ *787/796–2120* 🌐 *www.elladrillorest.com* ⏲ *Closed Mon. and Tues.*

★ **Grappa**

$$$ | **ITALIAN** | Dorado's most charming restaurant—and perhaps the most appealing one on the North Coast—Grappa is spectacular, both in design and on the plate. Specializing in Italian fare, the kitchen staff makes pasta by hand, and it's served with fruits of the sea or delicious, tender beef. **Known for:** fresh seafood; house-made pastas; romantic setting. $ *Average main: $27* ✉ *247 Calle Mendéz Vigo, Dorado* ☎ *787/796–2674* 🌐 *www.grappapr.com* ⏲ *Closed Mon. and Tues.*

Hotels

★ **Dorado Beach, a Ritz-Carlton Reserve**

$$$$ | **RESORT** | Luxurious accommodations, spectacular golf courses, and 5 km (3 miles) of exquisite coast are among the many draws at this resort, set on 1,400 acres that were once part of Laurance Rockefeller's estate. **Pros:** all rooms are beachfront; activities galore; excellent spa and gourmet dining. **Cons:** $150 daily resort fee; exceedingly expensive; occasional service lapses. $ *Rooms from: $2,500* ✉ *100 Dorado Beach Dr., Dorado* ☎ *787/626–1100* 🌐 *www.ritzcarlton.com* *114 rooms* 🍽 *No Meals.*

Embassy Suites by Hilton Dorado del Mar Beach Resort

$$$ | **HOTEL** | **FAMILY** | This beachfront resort is much like an Embassy Suites anywhere else in the world, offering a consistent, quality experience but little local flavor. **Pros:** on a gorgeous beach; breakfast and happy hour included; suites have kitchenettes. **Cons:** $35 resort fee; noisy common areas; limited on-site food options. $ *Rooms from: $280* ✉ *201 Dorado del Mar Blvd., Dorado* ☎ *787/796–6125* 🌐 *www.hilton.com/en/hotels/dorpres-embassy-suites-dorado-del-mar-beach-resort/* *174 suites* 🍽 *Free Breakfast.*

Hyatt Residence Club Dorado, Hacienda del Mar

$$$ | **HOTEL** | This Hyatt-branded vacation club features studio, one-, and two-bedroom condos, but don't worry: all are about the same price as other nearby resorts. **Pros:** lots of peace and quiet; beachfront setting; great golf. **Cons:** too isolated; need to drive off-site for additional dining options; $20 resort fee added for each night's stay. $ *Rooms from: $305* ✉ *301 Rte. 693, Dorado* ☎ *787/796–3000* 🌐 *www.hyatt.com* *82 suites* 🍽 *No Meals.*

The name says it all: Cueva Ventana truly provides a window on the world.

Shopping

Puerto Rico Premium Outlets

OUTLET | FAMILY | About 20 minutes from Dorado via Highway 22 at Exit 55 in the town of Barceloneta is Puerto Rico's first factory-outlet mall. Puerto Rico Premium Outlets is a pastel village of more than 40 stores selling discounted merchandise from such familiar names as Polo Ralph Lauren, Calvin Klein, The Gap, Nautica, Perry Ellis, Puma Outlet, and Tommy Hilfiger. ✉ *Hwy. 2, Km 54.8, Barceloneta* ☎ *787/846–5344, 787/846–5300* 🌐 *www.premiumoutlets.com/outlet/puerto-rico.*

Activities

GOLF

TPC Dorado Beach

GOLF | Two 18-hole, regulation courses blend Caribbean luxury and great golf at this iconic property with a storied tradition. These courses, which are exclusive to club members and Ritz Carlton Hotel guests, were designed by Robert Trent Jones Sr. and renovated by his son in 2011. The famous **East** course is secluded along 3 km (2 miles) of northeasterly shore within the former Rockefeller estate. A plantation course—the challenging **Sugarcane**—completes the offerings. ✉ *5000 Plantation Dr., Dorado* ☎ *787/262–1100* 🌐 *www.tpc.com* 🎫 *East Course $325, Sugarcane Course $245; Members or resort guests only* ⛳ *East Course: 18 holes, 7200 yards, par 72; Sugarcane: 18 holes, 7119 yards, par 72.*

Arecibo

60 km (38 miles) west of Dorado.

The town of Arecibo was founded in 1515 and is known as the Villa of Capitán Correa because of a 1702 battle fought here by Captain Antonio Correa and a handful of Spanish soldiers to repel a British sea invasion. Today, it's a busy manufacturing center that makes a good jumping-off point for deeper exploration of the central mountain region. For one of the best ocean drives on the island, get off the main road at Barceloneta and take Route 681 through Arecibo's waterfront district.

The city once attracted visitors interested in touring the Arecibo Observatory, which is currently only open as a Science and Visitor Center. Another area site, the Parque de las Cavernas del Río Camuy, has partially opened some caverns after the passing of several hurricanes over the area.

You can also visit the Cueva Ventana; although more commercial than the park, it still offers a taste of the region's unique caves. If you're more intrepid, head southwest of Arecibo to Lares for a tour (booked through Puerto Rico Interior Tours) of the Cueva Encantada.

GETTING HERE AND AROUND

From San Juan, take Highway 2 or 22 west toward Arecibo.

Sights

Cueva Ventana

CAVE | For years this cave was known among locals only, but thanks to social media, their well-kept secret is out. The attraction has since become a bit commercialized, and now a local landowner charges admission. Still, many travelers find the view worthwhile—it's not called "Window Cave" for nothing (be sure to bring your camera). ✉ *Rd. 10, Hato Viejo, Arecibo* ☎ *787/322–3554* 🌐 *www.cuevaventanapr.com* 🎟 *$19.*

Faro de Arecibo (*Arecibo Lighthouse*)

LIGHTHOUSE | **FAMILY** | A beautiful example of Spanish colonial architecture, the Faro de Arecibo is one of the loveliest lighthouses on the island. Dating from 1897, it sits on a bluff high above Arecibo. Although the museum inside the lighthouse has maritime treasures that will interest everyone in your group, the rest of the park is strictly kid stuff. There are scaled-down replicas of Christopher Columbus's *Niña, Pinta,* and *Santa María,* as well as replicas of the huts used by the island's original inhabitants, the Taíno Indians. On weekends, groups in traditional costumes play live music; you can watch the revelry from the sitting area of the café. ✉ *End of Rte. 655, off Rte. 681, Arecibo* ✣ *Follow signs from Hwy. 2* ☎ *787/880–7540* 🌐 *www.arecibolighthouse.com* 🎟 *$12; $3 parking fee* ✍ *Groups of 15-plus must make reservation.*

Observatory Science and Visitor Center

SCIENCE MUSEUM | **FAMILY** | This scientific haven was once attached to the world's largest radio telescope, which has sadly been pronounced defunct recently. However, over 100,000 visitors check out the science center every year, with information about the radio telescope's history, accomplishment, and ultimate ending. Besides all the valuable information here, the way up to the center is a steep climb with some of the most beautiful views Arecibo has to offer. This is a must-do for folks in STEM and for families with children interested in the field! ✉ *Rte. 625, Bo. Esperanza, Arecibo* ☎ *787/878–2612* 🌐 *www.naic.edu/ao/visitor-center/overview* 🎟 *$15* ⏲ *Closed June, July, and Dec. 14–Jan. 16* ✍ *Tickets must be purchased online.*

Parque de las Cavernas del Río Camuy

CAVE | The 268-acre Parque de las Cavernas del Río Camuy contains one of the world's largest cave networks. The guided tour of the caverns will lead you on foot through the 170-foot-high cave, which is teeming with wildlife. You're likely to see blue-eyed river crabs and long-legged tarantulas. More elusive are the more than 100,000 bats that make their home in the cave; they don't come out until dark, but you can feel the heat they generate at the cave's entrance (and you can certainly smell their presence). The cavern trails are wheelchair accessible, so anybody can join in on the fun! There is a mile-long walk from the visitor center to the cave entrance (with a ride offered for people with disabilities, senior citizens, and parents with young children), and each tour is about an hour and a half. Make sure to get here early, as this is a popular destination for locals as well. There's a picnic area, cafeteria, and gift shop in the visitor center. ✉ *Rte. 129, Km 18.9, Camuy* ☎ *787/898–3100, 787/898–3136* 🎫 *$18* ⏲ *Closed Mon. and Tues.*

Restaurants

El Buen Cafe

$$ | PUERTO RICAN | Often packed with locals, especially on weekends, this diner near Hatillo makes a good pit stop to refuel. You can sit at the curvy counter or at one of the cozy booths. **Known for:** carne mechada; red snapper with rice and beans; breakfast. [$] *Average main: $15* ✉ *Parador El Buen, 381 Hwy. 2, Km 84, Hatillo* ☎ *787/898–1000* 🌐 *elbuencafepr.com.*

Gustitos Criollos

$$ | PUERTO RICAN | This popular restaurant specializes in value-priced Puerto Rican favorites, including daily specials ranging from *sancocho* (root-vegetable stew) to pork chops with plantains and rice and beans. Portions are generous, service is attentive, and the atmosphere is ultra-casual. **Known for:** large portions; casual setting; great coffee. [$] *Average main: $12* ✉ *Hwy. 2, Km 65.9* ☎ *787/815–0804* ⏲ *Closed weekends. No dinner* 👔 *Casual.*

Shopping

OUTLETS

Plaza del Norte

MALL | FAMILY | This shopping center is only 10 minutes outside of Arecibo, with plenty of food options and standard stores for all your shopping needs. There's a great mix of both American chain stores and local vendors offering everything from apparel, jewelry, and food to trinkets and house goods. ✉ *506 Calle Truncado, Hatillo* ☎ *787/878–0700.*

Lares

39 km (24 miles) southwest of Arecibo, 29 km (18 miles) northwest of Utuado.

It may not look like it today, as you drive through what seems to be a quiet, slow-paced town, but Lares was once a hotbed of resistance, the birthplace of the 19th-century movement to break free from Spanish colonial rule. Today, it attracts visitors less for this history than for its natural features. One of the town's key features is the Cordillera's karst landscapes, characterized by fascinating limestone formations and caves.

Sights

Cueva Encantada

CAVE | This cave earns the "charming" part of its name because of the river that runs along the cave bed. Guides from Puerto Rico Interior Tours will lead you through the cave on a trip that's made for adventure lovers: be prepared to rappel, wade in waist-deep water, and shimmy through small openings. ✉ *Rte. 111, Km 22.1, Lares* ☎ *787/487–7815* 🎫 *$10.*

Restaurants

Heladería Lares

$ | ICE CREAM | FAMILY | This ice cream shop has some of the most unique flavor you'll ever have in a frozen treat. Popular varieties include rice and beans, codfish, avocado, and garlic, but don't worry; there are classic flavors if you're not feeling quite so adventurous. **Known for:** rice and sausage ice cream; garlic ice cream; corn ice cream with cinnamon. [$] *Average main: $4* ✉ *10 Cll Vilella* ☎ *787/378–4288* 👔 *Casual.*

The Parque Ceremonial Indígena de Caguana has ancient Taíno bateyes (ball courts) and stone monoliths carved with petroglyphs.

Utuado

32 km (20 miles) south of Arecibo, 29 km (18 miles) southeast of Lares, 24 km (15 miles) northwest of Jayuya.

The name Utuado comes from the Taíno word for "in between mountains," *Otoao*. This makes perfect sense, as this beautiful town sits surrounded by mountains and dotted with blue lakes. The drive along Route 10 between Arecibo and Utuado is an experience—imposing brown limestone cliffs flank the road, and clouds often hover above surrounding hills. Utuado's narrow and sometimes busy streets lead to a double-steepled church on the main plaza. The best sights, however, are outside town along winding side roads.

■ TIP→ Give yourself plenty of time when navigating the Ruta Panorámica (Panoramic Route), which runs through the Cordillera Central. Almost all segments of the route are marked by hairpin curves and bridges originally built for horse-drawn carts.

GETTING HERE AND AROUND

As with almost everywhere in Puerto Rico, the best way to get to and around Utuado is by car. Public transportation is all but nonexistent, commonly difficult, and unreliable, especially for visitors. Uber and taxi services are also difficult, if not impossible, to come by in mountainous regions.

Sights

Parque Ceremonial Indígena de Caguana
OTHER ATTRACTION | FAMILY | This 13-acre site was used more than 800 years ago by the Taíno tribes for worship and recreation, including a game—thought to have religious significance—that resembles modern-day soccer. Today you can see a dozen *bateyes* (ball courts) of various sizes, as well as some large stone monoliths carved with petroglyphs. Archaeologists believe this may have been one of the most important ceremonial sites for the Taíno people. ✉ *Rte. 111, Km 12.3, Utuado* ☎ *787/894–7325* 🎟 *$5.*

Restaurants

Bier Garden
$$ | **CARIBBEAN** | **FAMILY** | This family-friendly restaurant has a modern twist and Caribbean food that's sure to please everyone in your party. As the name suggests, they have quite a variety of local and foreign beers, and lots of fried and hearty foods that pair beautifully with their brews. **Known for:** variety of stuffed mofongos; fried pork; huge variety of local and imported beers. *Average main: $20 Carr 123 Barriada Nueva #11, Utuado 787/966–9600.*

Activities

HIKING

Expediciones Tanamá
HIKING & WALKING | This company leads half- and full-day excursions into the Río Tanamá underground-cave system. Guides speak limited English but are friendly and eager. Lunch is included. There's a free camping site adjacent to the office, which provides electricity and bathrooms. *Rte. 111, Km 14.5, Barrio Angeles 787/462–4121 www.tanamariveradventures.com From $65.*

Jayuya

24 km (15 miles) southeast of Utuado.

Jayuya is a small town in the foothills of the Cordillera Central, Puerto Rico's tallest mountain range. Cerro de Punta, the island's highest peak, looms to the south of the town center. Named after the Taíno chief Hauyua, Jayuya is known for preserving its Indian heritage, drawing people from all over the island for its yearly Indigenous Festival in November, which features crafts, exhibits, parades, music, and dancing. Coffee is still grown in the area—look for the locally produced Tres Picachos.

GETTING HERE AND AROUND

As with other areas outside of metropolitan San Juan, it's best to get to and around Jayuya by car. The Puerto Rico Travel Map, free and available at most hotels, should be adequate to get you to the town. Online GPS can be used, but keep in mind signals can get spotty in the more mountainous regions.

Sights

Bosque Estatal de Toro Negro (*Toro Negro State Forest*)
The main attraction of the 7,000-acre "Black Bull" State Forest is the island's crowning glory: 4,398-foot Cerro de Punta. Toro Negro also has the island's highest lake, Lago Guineo, as well as an impressive waterfall, the 200-foot Salto de Doña Juana. The best place to start is at the ranger station on Route 143. Ask the friendly staffers for a map; the trails—like the one that leads from the ranger station to an observation tower with views of the northern and southern sides of the island—are not always well marked. There are more trails east of the ranger station, at the Area Recreacional Doña Juana. Keep an eye out for exotic birds, such as the Guadalupe woodpecker. The reserve also contains a huge swimming pool (often out of service) built into a mountainside. Note that some trails have not been fully cleared or restored following Hurricane Maria's devastation in 2017. *Rte. 143, Km 32.4 787/999–2200 Free.*

La Piedra Escrita (*Written Stone*)
RUINS | This huge boulder with a handful of highly visible Taíno petroglyphs is located in a stream among several other large rocks. There are several viewing areas and a shady spot for a picnic lunch. Don't worry: the boulder in the parking lot painted a lurid shade of blue is *not* La Piedra Escrita. Also remember wet rocks are slippery, so for your own safety do not jump from the stones or climb them after dark. *Rte. 144, Km 7.8 Free.*

Did You Know?

The Toro Negro State Forest has the island's highest mountain, the 4,398-foot Cerro de Punta; the island's highest lake, Lago Guineo; and its most impressive waterfall, the 200-foot Doña Juana Falls.

Did You Know?

In late June or early July, Aibonito, known as the City of Flowers, hosts a festival honoring its renowned blooms.

Museo El Cemí (*Cemí Museum*)
RUINS | **FAMILY** | This could be the oddest building in Puerto Rico. Named for a Taíno artifact believed to have religious significance, the tiny structure resembles the snail-like *cemí*—you enter through its mouth. The collection, however, is only mildly interesting; it consists of religious and ceremonial objects of the Taíno found on the island. ✉ *Rte. 144, Km 9.3* ☎ *787/828–1241* 🎫 *$1.*

Hotels

Parador Hacienda Gripiñas
$ | **B&B/INN** | **FAMILY** | Built on the grounds of a coffee plantation, this 19th-century inn is surrounded on all sides by mountain peaks. **Pros:** set amid coffee fields; interesting, historic building; restaurant on property. **Cons:** isolated location; Wi-Fi doesn't reach all rooms; accommodations are simple and rustic. [$] *Rooms from: $102* ✉ *Rte. 152, Km 1.7* ☎ *939/274 8936* *17 rooms* *No Meals.*

Adjuntas

27 km (17 miles) southwest of Jayuya.

The coffee-growing town of Adjuntas sits north of Puerto Rico's Ruta Panorámica. It's also the world's leading producer of citron, a fruit whose rind is processed here and then shipped for use in sweets.

GETTING HERE AND AROUND

A rental car is really the only way to get to and around Adjuntas and neighboring towns. Town trolleys are great for getting a sense of the local landscape, but they aren't viable modes of transportation.

Sights

Bosque Estatal de Guilarte (*Guilarte State Forest*)
FOREST | **FAMILY** | Hiking trails surrounded by wild impatiens lead up to the 3,900-foot Pico Guilarte and elsewhere in this state forest. Bird-watchers have 26 different species to look for, including the carpenter bird. If your interest is botany, you can find a variety of trees, such as candlewood, trumpet, Honduran mahogany, and Honduran pine.

⚠ **Many trails have been affected by recent hurricanes, so hike with caution.** ✉ *Rte. 518 at Rte. 131, Adjuntas* ☎ *787/999–2200* 🎫 *Free.*

Restaurants

Hacienda Maribó
$$$ | **BARBECUE** | **FAMILY** | You can find this Argentinean-inspired slice of heaven in the mountains of Adjuntas, surrounded by sprawling greenery and livestock. Their specialty is barbecue meats, but their wine selection leaves nothing to be desired. **Known for:** good selection of wines; parrillada, with sausage, steak, and chicken; churrasco con chimichurri (skirt steak). [$] *Average main: $30* ✉ *Km 28, PR 10, Adjuntas* ☎ *787/202–4305* *Closed Mon.–Wed.*

Hotels

Parador Villas Sotomayor
$ | **RESORT** | If you're looking for a natural setting in which to relax and forget about the stress of city life, look no further than these cabinlike villas amid 14 lush acres of rolling hills. **Pros:** friendly staff; great for kids; gym offers Spin and dance classes. **Cons:** many bugs; noise from neighboring villas; an additional fee is charged for use of the pool. [$] *Rooms from: $126* ✉ *Carretera 123, Km 56, at Int. 522, Km 0.2, Adjuntas* ☎ *787/829–1717* 🌐 *paradorvillassotomayor.com* *34 villas* *No Meals.*

Aibonito

78 km (48 miles) east of Adjuntas.

Legend has it that Aibonito got its name when a Spaniard exclaimed, "*¡Ay, que bonito!*" (Oh, how pretty!) upon seeing the valley where the town now stands. At 1,896 feet above sea level, it's Puerto Rico's highest city. A double-steepled cathedral graces the charming town square. Local guides organize outings to the nearby Cañón de San Cristóbal. Aibonito is known as "The Queen of Flowers" because flowering plants thrive in its temperate climate. The city hosts a flower festival every year, usually in late June or July, and gives awards for blossoms and garden design.

GETTING HERE AND AROUND

Aibonito is best explored by car. Forego any promises made by public transportation, and take the reins yourself.

Sights

Cañón de San Cristóbal

NATURE SIGHT | FAMILY | The canyon may be difficult to find, but it's well worth the effort. Trails of tropical vegetation lead to a breathtaking waterfall. Tour guides can take you straight to the action while you learn about the plants and animals that inhabit this stunning region. ✉ *Rte. 725, Km 5.1, Aibonito* ☎ *787/722–5882* 🌐 *www.paralanaturaleza.org* 🎫 *$12* ✍ *Tour must be reserved in advance.*

Mirador Piedra Degetau (*Degetau Lookout Rock*)

VIEWPOINT | FAMILY | Degetau Lookout Rock is a scenic point near Aibonito. From the tower, use the telescope to get a closer look at the surrounding mountains. You'll find picnic tables under gazebos and a playground nearby. The tower is currently closed for renovation and safety concerns, so views are limited to those in the surrounding hill area. ✉ *Rte. 7718, Km 0.7, Aibonito* ☎ *787/735–3880* 🎫 *Free.*

Restaurants

El Balconcito Criollo

$ | CARIBBEAN | FAMILY | This family-friendly restaurant serves classic Puerto Rican food, with a menu that varies slightly based on the house specials. Typical meals like rice and beans, fried pork, and various forms of plantains are a staple you can find at any time. **Known for:** stuffed chicken breasts; cafeteria-style food; criollo meals. $ *Average main: $10* ✉ *Carr No. 7718, Km 3.1, Aibonito* ☎ *787/735–2005.*

Hotels

Hacienda Margarita

$ | HOTEL | Simple, clean, bright, affordable: this small property in the mountains just northwest of Aibonito in Barranquitas ticks a lot of boxes. **Pros:** affordable; clean; scenic mountain setting. **Cons:** remote; limited services; no on-site restaurant. $ *Rooms from: $89* ✉ *Rte. 152, Km 1.7, Barranquitas* ☎ *939/484–2662* *21 rooms* 🍽 *No Meals.*

Chapter 7

RINCÓN AND THE PORTA DEL SOL

Updated by
Paulina Salach Antonetti

Sights	Restaurants	Hotels	Shopping	Nightlife
★★★★★	★★★☆☆	★★★★☆	★☆☆☆☆	★★☆☆☆

WELCOME TO RINCÓN AND THE PORTA DEL SOL

TOP REASONS TO GO

★ **Catch a wave at Playa Tres Palmas:** Challenge the waves here or at any of Rincón's world-famous surfing spots.

★ **Visit Cabo Rojo:** This region of beaches along the Caribbean Sea ends at a peninsula with a beautiful lighthouse on the island's southwestern tip.

★ **Savor the area's delicious eateries:** From food trucks to farm-to-table restaurants to simple roadside stands, the west has great dining and snacking options.

★ **Delight your palate at the "Golden Mile":** Sample fresh seafood at any of the oceanfront eateries in Joyuda.

★ **Explore Desecheo Island or Mona Island:** Enjoy snorkeling, diving, or fishing around these spectacular islands.

The speedy Route 22 and the more meandering Route 2 head west from San Juan and swing around the northwestern part of the island. After Arecibo, Route 2 continues along the coast, where the ragged shoreline holds some of the island's best surfing beaches; a steady contingent of surfers in Aguadilla and Rincón gives the area a laid-back atmosphere. Past Mayagüez, Route 100 leads to the region known as Cabo Rojo, where you'll find small beach towns like Joyuda, Boquerón, and El Combate.

1 Isabela. You can surf, hike, golf, or just bake on the beach in this small town on the island's northwest coast and en route from San Juan to Rincón.

2 Aguadilla. Like Rincón just to the south, Aguadilla is a surfing mecca. It's also a regional air-travel gateway: surfers from all over the world fly in here to ride some of the island's best waves at Wilderness, Crashboat, and Gas Chamber beaches.

3 Rincón. The first World Surfing Championships in 1968 put Rincón on the map, and its laid-back vibe and epic waves have kept it there. Paddle out to one of the town's 15 surf spots, or experience horseback riding on the beach and fishing in the crystal Caribbean waters. One of Rincón's greatest attractions is the diving and snorkeling at nearby Desecheo Island.

4 Mayagüez. Stroll the marble-paved square of Plaza Colón, where a statue of Christopher Columbus commemorates the site where he allegedly disembarked. Experience an artistic performance at the Teatro Yagüez, which dates from 1909. Savor the flavor of Mayagüez by sampling traditional *brazo gitano* (gypsy arm) jelly rolls baked at the century-old Ricomini Bakery.

5 Joyuda. This small fishing village in the Cabo Rojo region is known for its fresh seafood and incredible ocean views. The sunsets are breathtaking.

6 Boquerón. After a day on Playa Buyé in tiny, laid-back Boquerón, also in the Cabo Rojo region, head to one of the many oceanfront eateries.

7 Morrillos Peninsula. Locals flock to the island's southwestern tip to soak up the sun at beaches like Playa Sucia and El Combate.

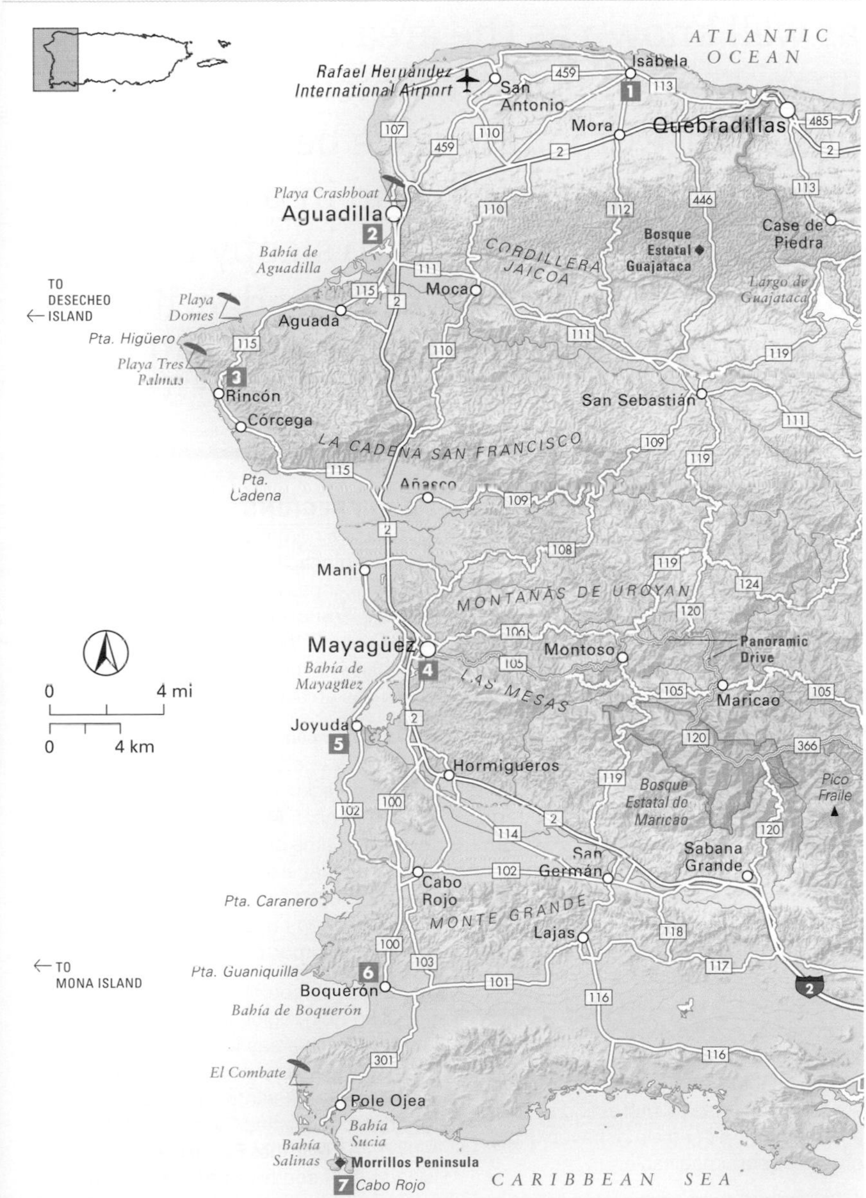

ATLANTIC OCEAN
Rafael Hernández International Airport
San Antonio
Isabela
Mora
Quebradillas
Playa Crashboat
Aguadilla
Bahía de Aguadilla
CORDILLERA JAICOA
Bosque Estatal Guajataca
Case de Piedra
Largo de Guajataca
TO DESECHEO ISLAND
Playa Domes
Aguada
Moca
Pta. Higüero
Playa Tres Palmas
Rincón
Córcega
San Sebastián
LA CADENA SAN FRANCISCO
Pta. Cadena
Añasco
Mani
MONTAÑAS DE UROYAN
Mayagüez
Bahía de Mayagüez
Montoso
Panoramic Drive
LAS MESAS
Maricao
0 4 mi
0 4 km
Joyuda
Hormigueros
Bosque Estatal de Maricao
Pico Fraile
Sabana Grande
San Germán
Cabo Rojo
Pta. Caranero
MONTE GRANDE
Lajas
TO MONA ISLAND
Pta. Guaniquilla
Boquerón
Bahía de Boquerón
El Combate
Pole Ojea
Bahía Sucia
Bahía Salinas
Morrillos Peninsula
Cabo Rojo
CARIBBEAN SEA

"La Porta del Sol" is how tourism officials describe the island's western coast—but the Gateway to the Sun is still not nearly as well known as the area around San Juan. Even in Rincón, which has the lion's share of lodging, the beaches are delightfully deserted. And in places like Aguadilla and Isabela, two sleepy towns on the island's northwestern edge, it's easy to find a stretch of shoreline all to yourself.

Since the time of Christopher Columbus, adventurers have been drawn to the jagged coastline of northwestern Puerto Rico. Columbus first stopped here on his second voyage to the Americas in 1493. His exact landing point is the subject of ongoing dispute: both Aguadilla, on the northernmost tip of the coast, and Aguada, just south of Aguadilla, claim the historic landing, and both have monuments honoring the explorer.

Less than a century ago, western Puerto Rico was still overwhelmingly rural, with a few large fruit plantations along the coast and coffee *fincas* (farms) dotting inland hills. The slow pace of agrarian life began to change in the mid-20th century, as new roads brought development to once-isolated towns. They also brought international surfers, who were amazed to find some of the world's best waves in Rincón, Isabela, and Aguadilla. Now there are top-notch hotels, interesting natural areas to explore, and almost every kind of water sport imaginable.

MAJOR REGIONS

The island's northwestern coast has less developed beaches with modest hotels that have appealed historically to local families. Some say the waves here are better than to the south in Rincón itself. The major destinations are **Aquadilla,** which has an airport, and **Isabela.**

Although **Rincón** is Puerto Rico's surfing capital, it also attracts other travelers, from backpackers to families to honeymooners. **Mayagüez** was once a textile and tuna-processing center, two industries that are long gone now. Today, the city is better known for its university and interesting historical sights. It also has a small airport.

In the island's southwestern corner, the Cabo Rojo region is known for its low-key beach areas (including **Joyuda** and **Boquerón**), inexpensive hotels, waterfront restaurants, and opportunities for outdoor activities. Also part of this region, the **Morrillos Peninsula,** at the island's very southwestern tip, is equally enchanting with beaches like Playa Sucia and El Combate.

Planning

When to Go

Winter brings the best weather—plus it's the height of the surfing season—so you'll need to book well in advance. Between December and March, you may get a glimpse of humpback whales off the coast. In summer, the weather gets hot, especially in August and September, and many family-oriented hotels fill up with *sanjuaneros* escaping the city for the weekend. Although some hotels require a two-night stay, larger resorts normally drop their rates by at least 10% during this time of year.

Getting Here and Around

AIR

Aguadilla's Aeropuerto Internacional Rafael Hernández (BQN) is a convenient gateway to western Puerto Rico, thanks to several daily international flights, including United Airlines from Newark (EWR), Spirit from Fort Lauderdale (FLL), and JetBlue from Orlando (MCO) or New York–JFK. Cape Air flies between San Juan and the small, public-use Aeropuerto Eugenio María de Hostos (MAZ), which is just north of the central business district in Mayagüez. There's little inside this airport besides car-rental counters and an ATM.

Transfers: There are no airport shuttles in either Aguadilla or Mayagüez. A taxi from either airport into town is about $10, but if you are going any farther, you should rent a car.

AIRLINES Cape Air. ☎ *800/227–3247* 🌐 *www.flycapeair.com.* **JetBlue.** ☎ *800/538–2583* 🌐 *www.jetblue.com.* **Spirit Airlines.** ☎ *801/401–2200* 🌐 *www.spirit.com.* **United Airlines.** ☎ *800/525–0280* 🌐 *www.united.com.*

AIRPORTS Aeropuerto Eugenio María de Hostos. (*MAZ*) ✉ *Rte. 2, Km 148.7, Mayagüez* ☎ *787/833–0148.* **Aeropuerto Internacional Rafael Hernández.** (*BQN*) ✉ *Hangar Rd. between Rtes. 110 and 107, off Rte. 2, Km 148.7, Aguadilla* ☎ *787/891–2286, 787/890–6075.*

BUS AND VAN

There is no easy bus network linking the towns of the Porta del Sol region as there is in San Juan. Renting a car is easy and relatively inexpensive if booked in advance.

CAR

You really need a car to see northwestern Puerto Rico, especially the areas in the mountains. From San Juan, the toll road, Route 22, turns into Route 2 just after Arecibo, travels along the island's northwestern edge, then heads south to Mayagüez. If you don't rent in San Juan, major agencies are represented at the airports in both Aguadilla and Mayagüez.

TAXI

Taxis can be hailed near the main plaza in Mayagüez, but they may be hard to come by in smaller towns. The staff at hotels or restaurants may be able to call one for you.

Hotels

The western part of the island near Rincón has everything from furnished villas geared toward families to beachfront hotels ideal for honeymooners. Although some of the newer accommodations resemble Spanish villas, elsewhere interior design seems stuck in the 1970s (faux wood, sun-bleached photographs, floral bedding, white linoleum). Smaller beach cottages, especially in Rincón, usually have "adopted" dogs or cats roaming the premises, so guests with allergies may want to inquire ahead of time.

VILLA RENTALS

Because many people come for a week or more to surf, find a secluded spot on the beach, or just hang out, renting a villa in Rincón makes perfect sense. Guests can make the place their own, without worrying about their noisy kids bothering the people in the next room or leaving sandy shoes outside the door. In the long run, it might also be a money-saver for those who like to cook at home rather than dine out. There are several local chefs who will prepare gourmet dinners for large groups in private villas.

There are a few things to keep in mind, however. If you're looking for a secluded location, you won't find it on such a crowded part of the coast; it's likely that your neighbor will be within shouting distance. In addition, few villas are actually on the ocean, and those that are go for a premium price. Many are within walking distance of the water, but others require a drive to reach the shore—if a beachfront location is important to you, make that clear. Finally, where you stay might depend on whether or not you're a surfer. Those who like to ride the waves favor the northern coast, while those who want to snorkel, scuba dive, or swim prefer the calmer southern shore.

Island West Properties
Around for years, this office rents villas in Rincón by the day, week, or month. (They're also real estate specialists who can help you find your dream property should you fall in love with the area and decide to stay.) ✉ *Rte. 413, Km 0.7, Rincón* ☎ *787/823–2323* 🌐 *www.rincon-realestateforsale.com.*

Restaurants

If you like seafood, do as locals from across the island do: head to the Cabo Rojo region in the southwest. Throughout the northwest you'll find wonderful *comida criolla* (Puerto Rican creole) cuisine, and most local eateries serve deep-fried tapas, commonly called *frituras* (fritters). A trip to Puerto Rico is not complete without sampling the island's most iconic dish, *mofongo relleno,* made from fried, seasoned, and mashed plantain or yuca stuffed with your choice of seafood or meat.

As a rule, the farther south along the coast you go, the more limited your options will be. If you tire of fried food, you may have to ask the chef to grill or sauté your fish. That said, dozens of foreign-owned eateries offer relief by serving everything from hamburgers to sushi to Thai. In Rincón, more places are catering to wellness-oriented visitors, too, by offering vegeterian options.

When it comes to beverages, locals usually drink rum and Coke or rum with fresh-squeezed juice. You'll also see people sipping on Medalla Light, Puerto Rico's most popular and affordable beer. All restaurants are nonsmoking. Gratuity is not usually included in the bill, but it's always wise to double-check; unless it is, tip the customary 15%–20%.

HOTEL AND RESTAURANT PRICES

⇨ *Hotel and restaurant reviews have been shortened. For full information visit Fodors.com.*

What It Costs in U.S. Dollars

$	$$	$$$	$$$$
RESTAURANTS			
under $12	$12–$20	$21–$30	over $30
HOTELS			
under $150	$150–$250	$251–$350	over $350

Safety

Unless you're camping in a recreational area, it's best to visit forest reserves during daylight hours only. Outside metro areas there's little crime, but you should take normal precautions: remember to lock your car, and don't leave valuables unattended.

For Surfers: The waves near Rincón range from gentle, low waves suitable for novices to expert-only breaks. It's a good idea to talk with other surfers about which beaches would be suitable for your skill level.

Visitor Information

The Puerto Rico Tourism Company has an office at the airport in Aguadilla. The Cabo Rojo branch is open weekdays 8–4:30. Rincón's tourism office is open weekdays 8–4. Mayagüez has a tourism office in the city hall.

CONTACTS **Cabo Rojo Tourism Office.** ✉ *Galleria 100, Rte. 100, Km 7.6, Cabo Rojo* ☎ *787/851–7070.* **Isabela Tourism Office.** ✉ *Inside Alcaldía, 124 Calle Manuel Corchado Juarbe, Isabela* ☎ *787/872–2100.* **Mayagüez City Hall.** ✉ *Calle Peral, Mayagüez* ☎ *787/834–8585.* **Puerto Rico Tourism Company.** ✉ *Rafael Hernández Airport, 405 Hangar Rd., Aguadilla* ☎ *787/890–3090* 🌐 *www.discoverpuertorico.com.* **Rincón Tourism Office.** ✉ *Sunset Village, Calle Cambija, next to Balneario de Rincón, Rincón* ☎ *787/823–5024.*

Isabela

113 km (70 miles) west of San Juan, 20 km (13 miles) northeast of Aguadilla, 37 km (23 miles) northeast of Rincón.

Founded in 1819 and named for Spain's Queen Isabella, this small town on the northwestern edge of the island skirts tall cliffs that overlook the rocky shoreline. Locals have long known of the area's natural beauty, and, lately, more offshore tourists have been drawn to this niche, which offers secluded hotels, sprawling golf courses, fantastic beaches, excellent surf, and hiking through a forest reserve.

GETTING HERE AND AROUND

If you are driving to the town of Isabela from San Juan, take Route 2 west to Route 112 north to the intersection with Route 4466, Isabela's coastal road. To eliminate this two-hour drive, consider flying directly to the region via Aguadilla's Aeropuerto Internacional Rafael Hernández (BQN), just 15 minutes from Isabela. Direct flights from Newark are available through United Airlines; JetBlue flies from Orlando or New York. There are several rental-car companies at Aguadilla's airport.

Sights

Guajataca Forest Reserve

NATURE PRESERVE | Explore karst topography and subtropical vegetation at the 2,357-acre Guajataca State Forest, between the towns of Quebradillas and Isabela. On more than 46 walking trails you can see 186 species of trees, like royal palm and ironwood, and 45 species of birds—watch for red-tailed hawks and Puerto Rican woodpeckers. Bring a flashlight and descend into the **Cueva del Viento** (Cave of the Wind) to find stalagmites, stalactites, and other strange formations. At the forest entrance there's a small ranger station where you can pick up a decent hiking map (get here early, as the rangers don't always stay until closing time). ✉ *Rte. 446, Km 10, Isabela* ☎ *787/872–1045* *Free* *Ranger station closed weekends.*

Palacete Los Moreau

HISTORIC HOME | In the fields south of Isabela toward the town of Moca, a French family settled on a coffee and sugar plantation in the 1800s. The grand two-story house was immortalized in the novel *La Llamarada,* written in 1935 by Puerto Rican novelist Enrique A. Laguerre. In the novel, about conditions in the sugarcane industry, the house

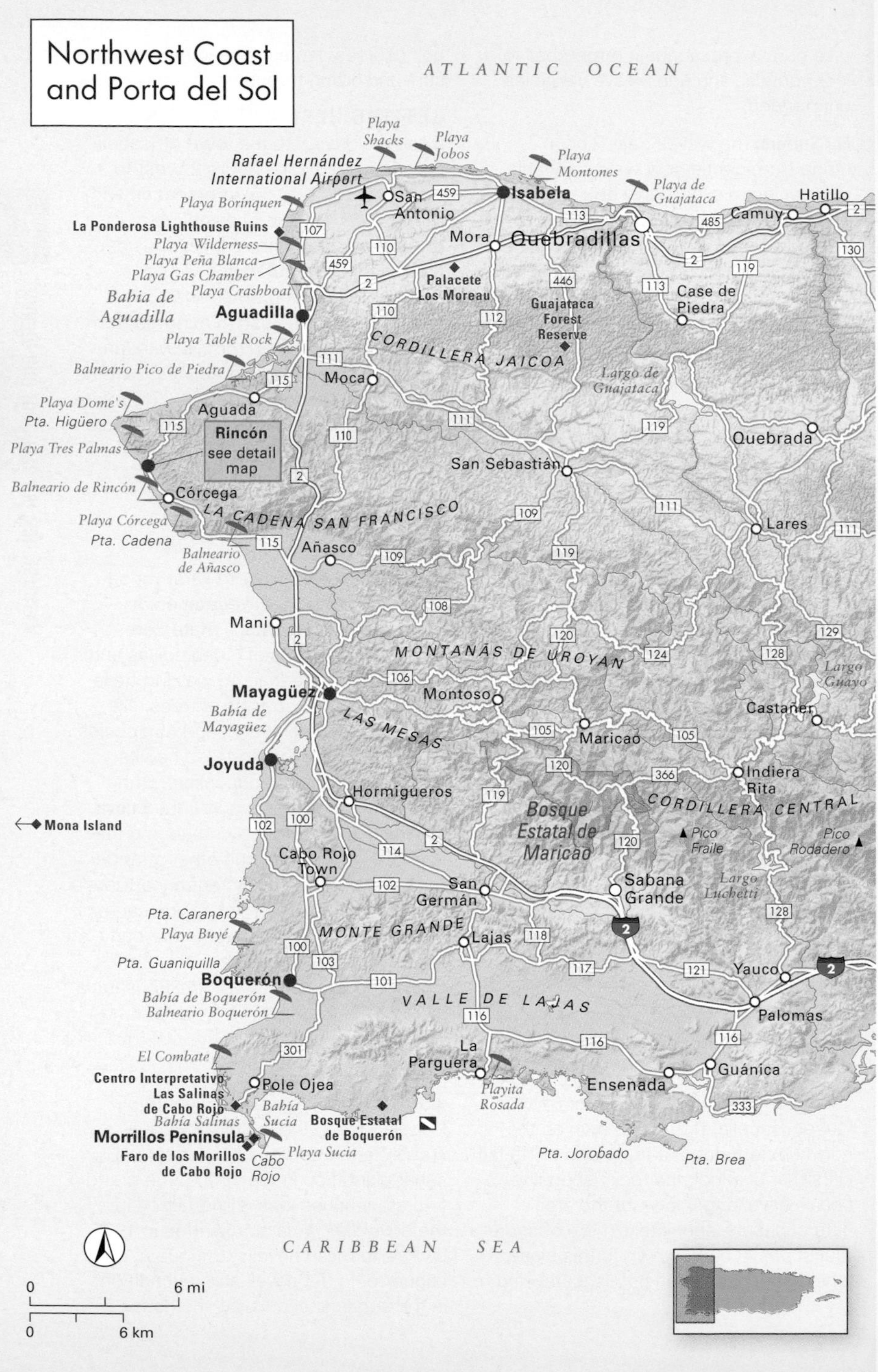

Northwest Coast and Porta del Sol
ATLANTIC OCEAN
CARIBBEAN SEA
Rafael Hernández International Airport
Playa Shacks
Playa Jobos
Playa Montones
Playa de Guajataca
Playa Borínquen
La Ponderosa Lighthouse Ruins
Playa Wilderness
Playa Peña Blanca
Playa Gas Chamber
Playa Crashboat
Bahia de Aguadilla
Aguadilla
Playa Table Rock
Balneario Pico de Piedra
Playa Dome's
Pta. Higüero
Playa Tres Palmas
Balneario de Rincón
Playa Córcega
Pta. Cadena
Balneario de Añasco
Rincón see detail map
San Antonio
Isabela
Mora
Quebradillas
Camuy
Hatillo
Palacete Los Moreau
Guajataca Forest Reserve
Case de Piedra
CORDILLERA JAICOA
Largo de Guajataca
Moca
Aguada
Córcega
LA CADENA SAN FRANCISCO
San Sebastián
Quebrada
Lares
Añasco
Mani
MONTANÃS DE UROYAN
Largo Guayo
Mayagüez
Bahía de Mayagüez
Montoso
Castañer
LAS MESAS
Maricao
Joyuda
Indiera Rita
CORDILLERA CENTRAL
Hormigueros
Bosque Estatal de Maricao
Mona Island
Pico Fraile
Pico Rodadero
Cabo Rojo Town
San Germán
Sabana Grande
Largo Luchetti
Pta. Caranero
Playa Buyé
MONTE GRANDE
Lajas
Pta. Guaniquilla
Boquerón
Bahía de Boquerón
Balneario Boquerón
VALLE DE LAJAS
Yauco
Palomas
El Combate
La Parguera
Playita Rosada
Ensenada
Guánica
Centro Interpretativo Las Salinas de Cabo Rojo
Pole Ojea
Bahía Salinas
Bahía Sucia
Bosque Estatal de Boquerón
Morrillos Peninsula
Faro de los Morillos de Cabo Rojo
Cabo Rojo
Playa Sucia
Pta. Jorobado
Pta. Brea
2
100
101
102
103
105
106
107
108
109
110
111
112
113
114
115
116
117
118
119
120
121
124
128
129
130
301
333
366
446
459
485
0
6 mi
0
6 km

Make sure to see the Cueva del Viento (Cave of the Wind) while hiking through the Guajataca Forest.

belonged to his fictional family, the Moreaus. Although it doesn't have many furnishings, you can walk through the house and also visit Laguerre's personal library in the mansion's basement. ✉ *Rte. 2, Km 115.9, Isabela* ☎ *787/830–4475* 🎫 *Free* ⏲ *Closed Tues. and Wed.*

Beaches

Playa de Guajataca

BEACH | Near this beach is El Tunel de Guajataca, part of an old tunnel used by a train that once connected the towns of Isabela and Quebradillas and transported sugarcane. Just before El Tunel is El Merendero de Guajataca, a picnic area with cliff-side trails. This is not a swimming beach due to strong currents, but it's a great place for walks and photo ops. **Amenities**: none. **Best for:** walking. ✉ *Off Rte. 113, Isabela.*

Playa Jobos

BEACH | Famous for surfing, this beach also has a couple of restaurants with oceanfront decks. Down the road, the gorgeous dunes and long stretches of golden sand are great for walks or runs. Route 466 runs parallel to the shore, and there's parking and beach access along the way. ⚠ **Next to the large rock formation is a strong riptide that drags people out to sea. The water is only about thigh high, but when the wind changes, the current is like a raging river.** There are no lifeguards, no signs, and no roped-off areas, so be sure to stay close to shore. **Amenities**: none. **Best for**: partiers; surfing; walking. ✉ *Rte. 466, Isabela.*

Playa Montones

BEACH | Not far from Playa Jobos, this is a beautiful beach for swimming; it has a protected natural pool perfect for children. **Amenities**: none. **Best for**: swimming; walking. ✉ *Rte. 466, in front of Villas del Mar Hau, Isabela.*

Playa Shacks

BEACH | Known for its surfing and horseback riding, this secluded spot also has an area called the Blue Hole that's popular with divers. It is east of the Villa Montaña beach resort, where you can

Hike for hours on some of the many trails at the Guajataca Forest Reserve.

stop in for a great meal at the oceanfront restaurant, The Eclipse. **Amenities:** none. **Best for**: snorkeling; surfing; swimming; walking. ✉ *Rte. 4446, Isabela.*

Restaurants

The Eclipse

$$$ | **ECLECTIC** | Beautiful beachfront dining, farm-to-table ingredients, and fantastic service are worth the drive from San Juan. The setting is rustic yet elegant, and the view is unbeatable. **Known for:** great pizza; weekend brunch; unbeatable beachfront location. *Average main: $28 ✉ Villa Montaña, Rte. 4466, Km 1.9, Isabela ☎ 787/872–9554 www.villamontana.com.*

Ola Lola's Tiki Bar

$ | **CARIBBEAN** | The owners have maximized their residence, which boasts "the friendliest wave on the island," by converting the garage into overflow seating for this garden bistro. With fairy lights, beach chairs, and Latin music, the no-frills setting complements the simple menu of burgers, sandwiches, and signature dips. **Known for:** peanut-butter burgers (you gotta try one); "Tropical Dreamsicle" piña coladas; cash only. *Average main: $10 ✉ Playa Shacks, Rte. 4466, Km 2.1, Isabela ☎ 787/872–1230 www.olalolaspr.com No credit cards.*

Restaurant at La Casa

$$$ | **ECLECTIC** | Many things stand out at this picturesque resort restaurant: the emerald-green golf course in the foreground, the majestic cliffs on the coast, and the roaring ocean in the background. A fair amount of the fruits and vegetables used in the dishes here are grown at Royal Isabela's River Farm and Gatehouse Garden; all the fish is caught offshore. **Known for:** freshest seafood; Caribbean lobster specials; farm-to-table approach. *Average main: $30 ✉ Royal Isabela, 396 Av. Noel Estrada, Isabela ☎ 787/609–5888.*

Uma's Playa Jobos

$$ | **EUROPEAN** | This family-run restaurant, a Rockaway Beach (New York City) outpost on Playa Jobos, serves Euro-Asian cuisine with a tropical twist. You can sip a creative cocktail on the wooden deck and chow down on unique dishes like Korean carrot and green papaya salad, pumpkin *manti,* or Hawaiian poke bowl with local yellowfin tuna. **Known for:** great Caribbean-inspired, Euro-Asian fare; perfect beachfront location; live reggae on Saturday. *Average main: $13 ✉ Playa Jobos, Rte. 4466, Km 72, Isabela ☎ 917/865–6261.*

Hotels

★ Royal Isabela

$$$$ | **RESORT** | The area's most luxurious property, this 2,200-acre paradise is a must for anyone remotely interested in golf—it has one of the best courses in Puerto Rico. **Pros:** great views; luxurious accommodations; access to a private beach. **Cons:** luxury isn't cheap; 15-minute drive from other dining options; long walk to the beach. *Rooms from: $700 ✉ 396 Av. Noel Estrada, Isabela ☎ 787/609–5888 www.royalisabela.com 20 casitas No Meals.*

Villa Montaña

$$$ | **RESORT** | **FAMILY** | This cluster of villas, on a deserted stretch of beach between Isabela and Aguadilla, feels like its own little town, one where you can leave the car in your garage, and then head upstairs to an airy studio or one-, two-, or three-bedroom suite with hand-carved mahogany furniture and canopy beds. **Pros:** bikes and playground; secluded beach; great restaurant on-site. **Cons:** a bit pricey for some dated rooms; far from off-site restaurants; airplane noise. *Rooms from: $350 ✉ Rte. 4466, Km 1.9, Isabela ☎ 787/872–9554 www.villamontana.com 71 units No Meals.*

Villas del Mar Hau

$$ | **HOTEL** | One-, two-, and three-bedroom cottages—painted in cheery pastels and trimmed with gingerbread—are the heart of this simple beachfront hotel. **Pros:** laid-back vibe; protected swimming cove that's great for children; good restaurant. **Cons:** very basic rooms; may be too kitschy for some; late check-in (4 pm). *Rooms from: $179 ✉ Rte. 466, Km 8.3, Isabela ☎ 787/872–2045 www.hauhotelvillas.com 46 cottages No Meals.*

Activities

GOLF

★ Golf Links at Royal Isabela

GOLF | Mixing luxurious service, ecological sensitivity, and an incomparable setting, this 18-hole course is considered one of the Caribbean's best. Designed and developed by Stanley and Charlie Pasaroll with assistance from course architect David Pfaff, it can play to as much as 7,667 yards and a par of 72 or 73, depending upon how you play the fork-in-the-road 6th. The course has many signature moments—from the 6th to the island green at No. 9 to the carry over the sea at No. 12. Carts are available, although walking is encouraged and caddies are mandatory. Note too that the course is open to guests staying at the Royal Isabela. *✉ 396 Av. Noel Estrada, Isabela ☎ 787/609–5888 www.royalisabela.com $250 (guests $125); caddie $90 for 2 players 18 holes, 7667 yards, par 73.*

HORSEBACK RIDING

Tropical Trail Rides

HORSEBACK RIDING | **FAMILY** | Group rides depart Playa Shacks, one of the region's prettiest beaches. The two-hour tours cost approximately $100 per person and take you along the beach and through a forest of almond trees. At the end you have a chance to take a dip in the ocean.

The company also offers hiking trips to the limestone caves at Survival Beach. ✉ *400 Bo Bajuras, Rte. 4466, Km 1.9, Isabela* ☎ *787/872–9256* 🌐 *www.tropical-trailrides.com.*

SURFING

Hang Loose Surf Shop

SURFING | For surf lessons, Hang Loose Surf Shop offers a two-hour basic course and has board rentals. Lessons are usually held at Playa Jobos, a great surfing spot where you can reward yourself with a refreshing drink from one of the beach shacks. Lessons start at $100. ✉ *Rte. 446, Km 1.2, Isabela* ☎ *787/560–0181.*

Wave Riding Vehicles

SURFING | Surfboard rentals and one-hour surfing lessons are offered through this surf shop and board factory. They also rent stand-up paddleboards and bodyboards. ✉ *Playa Jobos, Carretera 4466, Isabela* ☎ *787/669–3840* 🌐 *www.waveridingvehicles.com* *Rentals from $20 per hr, lessons from $35.*

Aguadilla

20 km (13 miles) southwest of Isabela, 18 km (12 miles) north of Rincón.

Resembling a fishing village, downtown Aguadilla has narrow streets lined with small wooden homes. Weathered but lovely, the faded facades recall the city's long and turbulent past. Officially incorporated as a town in 1775, Aguadilla subsequently suffered a series of catastrophes, including a devastating earthquake in 1918 and strong hurricanes in 1928 and 1932. Determined to survive, the town rebuilt after each disaster, and, by World War II, it had become known for the sprawling Ramey Air Force Base—an important link in the U.S. defense system throughout the Cold War. Ramey was decommissioned in 1973, and today this area has small businesses, a golf course, a university, and the region's most important airport. As a result of tourism, the north end of town is budding with international restaurants, surf shops, and even an outdoor mall.

Perhaps the town's greatest draw is its surfing at local spots like Playa Wilderness, Playa Crashboat, and Playa Gas Chamber. Famous for their right-hand barrels, these beaches have hosted a variety of amateur and professional surfing events, including the 1968 and 1988 International Surfing Association (ISA) World Championships and the 2010 Association of Surfing Professionals (ASP) World Tour.

GETTING HERE AND AROUND

Most people arrive in Aguadilla either by car from San Juan or by flying directly into Aguadilla's Aeropuerto Internacional Rafael Hernández. United Airlines offers daily flights from Newark to Aguadilla, and JetBlue has service from Orlando or New York. Rental cars ($35–$65 per day) are available from companies operating out of the Aguadilla airport. To reach Aguadilla by car from San Juan, head west on Route 22 (toll road), which turns into Route 2. Continue on Route 2 until it intersects with Route 111, leading to the center of town.

CAR RENTAL CONTACTS Avis. ✉ *Aeropuerto Internacional Rafael Hernández, Hangar Rd., Aguadilla* ☎ *787/890–3311.* **Enterprise.** ✉ *Aeropuerto Internacional Rafael Hernández, Hangar Rd., Aguadilla* ☎ *787/890–3732.* **Hertz.** ✉ *Aeropuerto Internacional Rafael Hernández, Hangar Rd., Aguadilla* ☎ *787/890–5650.* **Allied Rent a Car.** ✉ *Ramsey Base, 333 Wings Rd., Aguadilla* ☎ *787/890–3010* 🌐 *www.alliedcarrentalpr.com.*

Sights

La Ponderosa Lighthouse Ruins

RUINS | Along Route 107—an unmarked road crossing through Punta Borinquen Golf Club—you'll find the ruins of La

The fascinating ruins of La Ponderosa Lighthouse are remnants of Spanish colonial architecture.

Ponderosa, an old Spanish lighthouse, as well as its replacement, Punta Borinquen, at Puerto Rico's northwesternmost point. The original lighthouse was built in 1889, destroyed by an earthquake in 1918, and rebuilt in 1920 by the U.S. Coast Guard. Just beyond the ruins is a local surf spot, **Playa Wilderness.** ✉ *Rte. 107, Aguadilla.*

Beaches

★ Playa Borínquen

BEACH | This big, beautiful stretch of white sand leads to large rocks and a cliff that juts into the sea. The water can be too rough and choppy for swimming in the winter, but the summer months are great for swimming and snorkeling. During low tide, you'll find a small cave at the far end. **Amenities:** parking (free). **Best for:** snorkeling; swimming; walking. ✉ *Av. Borínquen, Aguadilla.*

Playa Crashboat

BEACH | Named for the rescue boats used when nearby Ramey Air Force Base was in operation, this beach has soft, sugary sand, water as smooth as glass, and the sort of colorful fishing boats pictured on postcards. A food stand serves the catch of the day with cold beer. **Amenities:** food and drink; parking (free); showers; toilets. **Best for:** partiers; snorkeling; swimming. ✉ *End of Rte. 458, off Rte. 107, Aguadilla.*

Playa Gas Chamber

BEACH | Just north of Playa Crashboat, this beach with big sucking barrels is favored by surfers. There is limited parking and no beach area, just coral. On a good surf day, this is where you come to watch the pros charge the waves. **Amenities**: none. **Best for**: surfing. ✉ *Rte. 107, north of Playa Crashboat, Aguadilla.*

★ Playa Peña Blanca

BEACH | Swimming in the crystal clear waters of Peña Blanca is best in the summer months during low tide. In the winter months, the waters reach the rocks around the beach, eliminating the already fairly small shoreline. Regardless, the views here are stunning. **Amenities:**

Did You Know?

Playa Crashboat is named for the boats that were used for search and rescue of downed airmen when Ramey Air Force Base was in operation. Now brightly painted fishing boats line its shore.

PR.1831FF

parking (free in winter, fee in summer when it's busy). **Best for:** snorkeling; walking. ✉ *Calle Wishin Wells, Aguadilla.*

Playa Wilderness

BEACH | This undeveloped beach near La Ponderosa ruins is recommended only for experienced surfers, as it can have dangerous breaks. The long rights, and difficulty in reaching the break, make it popular with locals. To get here, take Route 107 through the Punta Borinquen Golf Club. **Amenities**: none. **Best for**: surfing. ✉ *Rte. 107, north of Playa Gas Chamber, Aguadilla.*

Restaurants

CINCO

$$$ | PUERTO RICAN | FAMILY | Although the menu at this family-friendly restaurant includes pizza and pasta dishes, it's a good place to dine on hearty Caribbean fare, including Puerto Rican specialties like mofongo, churrasco, and *bistec encebollado*. The wine list is short but well curated, and the cocktails are creative and affordable. **Known for:** mofongo; churrasco; friendly staff. *$ Average main: $22 ✉ Rte. 110, Km 32, Aguadilla ☎ 787/658–6078.*

The Coffee Spot

$ | BAKERY | You'll love the chill vibe at this café, where you can sip on a latte, use Wi-Fi, and enjoy a creative sandwich. Most dishes and drinks are named after famous composers and classical pieces, and sometimes there's live piano music. **Known for:** great coffee; good spot for breakfast; friendly service. *$ Average main: $9 ✉ Rte. 110, Km 4.6, Aguadilla ☎ 787/996–7340 ⏲ No dinner.*

D'Rose Chocolate Factory

$ | CAFÉ | This truffle treasure hidden in a nondescript strip mall has a reputation for fantastic coffee. The aroma of chocolate entices passersby into the sweet shop with its pink candy-striped walls and chocolate-tone tables. **Known for:** excellent coffee; large variety of chocolates; baked goods. *$ Average main: $6 ✉ Rte. 107, Km 2.1, Aguadilla ☎ 787/891–0552.*

Flora

$$$ | MODERN AMERICAN | Farm to table is the focus at Flora. Upscale, well-thought-out dishes are presented in a casual setting. **Known for:** creative, rotating menu; vegetarian friendly; farm to table. *$ Average main: $25 ✉ Maleza Alta, Carr 110, Km 32.1, Aguadilla.*

Levain Bakery

$ | BAKERY | FAMILY | This small bakery across the street from the airport makes some of the best breads and croissants on the island. They also serve lattes and breakfast items such as cinnamon buns, as well as sandwiches and quiche for lunch. **Known for:** great coffee; excellent fresh breads and croissants; weekend brunch. *$ Average main: $10 ✉ 333 Wing Rd., Aguadilla ☎ 787/658–6220 🌐 www.levainpr.com ⏲ No dinner; Closed Mon. and Tues.*

Mister Harry

$$ | THAI | FAMILY | Locals come from as far as San Juan to get a taste of the Thai dishes at Mister Harry. The short yet tasty menu features a selection of curries. **Known for:** curries; Thai cuisine; local favorite. *$ Average main: $20 ✉ Carr 110, Gate 5 Plaza, Aguadilla ⏲ Closed Mon.–Thurs.*

Zazones

$$$ | PUERTO RICAN | FAMILY | Here you'll find everything from mofongo to catch of the day, pastas, and steaks. The varied menu makes it a good place to dine with family. **Known for:** great service; Puerto Rican cuisine; family friendly. *$ Average main: $22 ✉ 2066.5 Av. Dr Pedro Albizu Campos, Suite 6, Aguadilla 🌐 www.zazones.com.*

Hotels

Courtyard by Marriott Aguadilla

$$ | **HOTEL** | A former military hospital has been transformed into this hotel, which appeals to both business executives and vacationing families. **Pros:** near the airport; nice pool area; free coffee. **Cons:** airplane and casino noise; not on the beach; chain-hotel feel. *Rooms from: $199* *West Parade, off Cliff Rd., Aguadilla* *787/658–8000* *www.marriott.com* *150 rooms* *No Meals.*

El Faro Parador

$ | **HOTEL** | **FAMILY** | This family-friendly hotel isn't very close to the lighthouse from which it takes its name, but it's a good place to keep in mind if you're driving along the coast and need to stop for the night (keep a sharp eye out for the "Parador" sign on Route 107, as it's easy to miss). **Pros:** reasonable rates; pretty pool areas; children's playground. **Cons:** no beach; rather secluded location; motel-like feel. *Rooms from: $125* *Rte. 107, Km 2.1, Aguadilla* *787/882–8000* *www.farohotels.net* *69 rooms* *No Meals.*

Activities

DIVING AND SNORKELING

Aquatica Dive and Surf

DIVING & SNORKELING | Near Gate 5 of the old Ramey Air Force Base, Aquatica offers scuba-diving certification courses (starting at $325), as well as snorkeling, stand-up paddleboarding, and surfing trips. There's a great selection of surfboards and paddleboards for rent. For a memorable adventure, try the two-hour stand-up paddleboard tour down the Río Guajataca. *Rte. 110, Km 10, Gate 5, Maleza Alta, Aguadilla* *787/890–6071* *www.aquaticapr.com.*

GOLF

Punta Borinquen Golf Club

GOLF | The 18-hole Punta Borinquen Golf Club, on the former Ramey Air Force Base, was a favorite of President Dwight D. Eisenhower. Now a public course, the beachfront course is known for its tough sand traps and strong crosswinds. Membership is not required to play, but some say the course needs better upkeep and repairs since Hurricane Maria. *Rte. 107, Km 2, Aguadilla* *787/890–2987* *www.puntaborinquengolfclub.org* *From $25, including cart* *18 holes, 6633 yards, par 72.*

Rincón

18 km (12 miles) south of Aguadilla, 150 km (93 miles) southwest of San Juan.

Jutting out into the ocean along the rugged western coast, Rincón ("corner" in Spanish) may have gotten its name because it's tucked into a bend of the coastline. Some, however, trace it to Gonzalo Rincón, a 16th-century landowner who let poor families live on his land. Whatever the history, the name suits the town, which is like a little corner of the world unto itself.

Larger hotels in the region include Rincón of the Seas and Rincón Beach Resort, but rentals and small inns are the norm. Although Rincón is a mecca for wave seekers—particularly those from the East Coast of the United States, who like the relatively quick New York–Aguadilla flight—the laid-back town also appeals to budget-conscious families and honeymooners.

The pace picks up October to April, when the waves are at their best, but tourists can be found here year-round, and many American mainlanders have settled here. Budget travelers will most likely find discount accommodations in

Sights

1 Desecheo Island........ **A2**

2 Parque Pasivo El Faro....... **A3**

Restaurants

1 Café 413..... **B5**

2 Cafe 2 Go ... **B5**

3 The English Rose......... **B3**

4 Estela........ **B4**

5 Jack's Shack **B2**

6 La Cambija.. **B5**

7 La Copa Llena at the Black Eagle **A4**

8 La Sirena Sushi & Tiki Bar ... **B5**

9 Mangia Mi............ **C5**

10 Mimosa Brunch Farm to Table...... **D1**

11 Parrilleria Vacas Gauchas **C6**

12 Reina Mora **D3**

13 Sana Farm to Table...... **C4**

14 Shipwreck Bar & Grill .. **B4**

15 Tamboo **B2**

Hotels

1 Aqua Marina Beach Club.......... **B4**

2 Casa Isleña.. **B2**

3 Dos Angeles del Mar Bed and Breakfast ... **B2**

4 The English Rose......... **B3**

5 Lazy Parrot Inn........... **B3**

6 Mar Azul Villas......... **B3**

7 Rincón Beach Resort....... **D9**

8 Rincón of the Seas **B6**

9 Tamboo Beside the Pointe... **B2**

10 Tres Sirenas..... **B6**

11 Villa Cofresí **B6**

12 Villa Tres Palmas...... **A4**

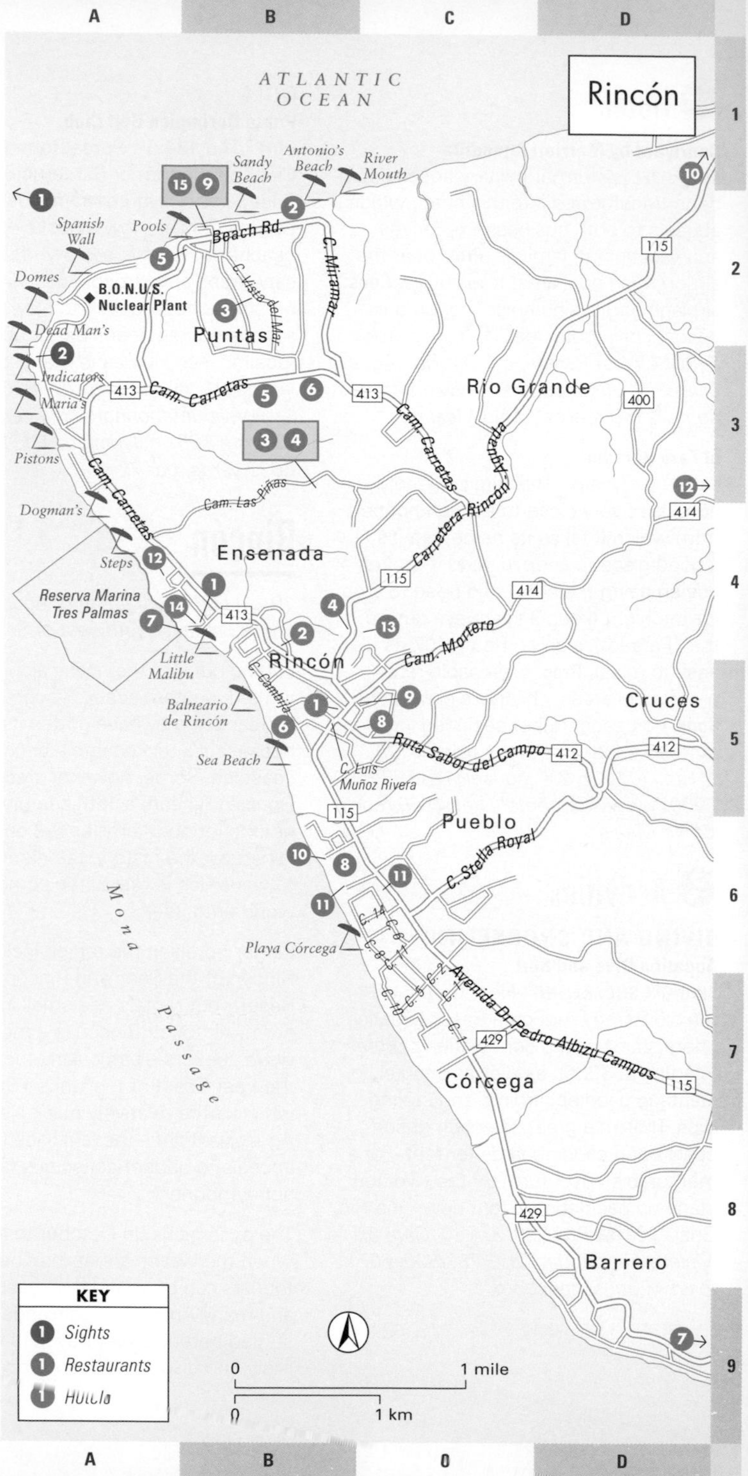

August and September, when tourism is slow. Hurricane season runs June to November, bringing occasional swells for the surf crowd.

GETTING HERE AND AROUND

Rincón itself is a spread-out labyrinth of unmarked streets without any apparent logic to its layout. The city is built on a hillside, so most streets are narrow and steep, weaving erratically through the intermingled residential–business zones. There are three main highways to keep in mind. Route 115 cuts through the middle of "downtown" (the administrative center) and runs north to the Aguadilla airport and south to the Mayagüez airport. Route 413 snakes along the hillsides, past villas and local restaurants. The smaller Route 4413 follows the water, past Punta Higuero Lighthouse, and ends at the Bonus Thermonuclear Energy Plant.

AIR

San Juan's international airport is the most commonly used on the island and is approximately two hours from Rincón. The closest airports, however, are in Aguadilla and Mayagüez—only 20 minutes' drive north or south respectively. An Uber from either airport into town costs around $30, but the best option is to rent a car at the airport, since you'll need it for transportation during your trip.

BUS AND VAN

Amigos Tours & Travel has private transfers from Aguadilla's airport to Rincón and to most hotels in the Porta del Sol for $80 per van (limit five passengers).

CAR

To reach Rincón from San Juan, take Route 22, which merges with Route 2 after Arecibo. Follow it past the northwestern tip of the island, just beyond Aguadilla. Then take Route 115 southwest past Aguada until you reach Rincón's Route 413, "the Road to Happiness."

TIMING

Occupying a total area of 36 square km (14 square miles), Rincón is easily traversable in a single afternoon. Nevertheless, to fully embrace its laid-back vibe you'll want to leave yourself three to five days for surfing, diving, fishing, or just relaxing at the beach.

Sights

Desecheo Island

ISLAND | Protected by the U.S. Fish and Wildlife Service, this uninhabited island—about 20 km (13 miles) off the coast of Rincón—is home to lizards, rats, and rhesus monkeys, first introduced in 1967 from Cayo Santiago. Among divers, it's known for abundant reef and fish life. The main draw here is "Candyland," a rocky bottom that rims the island and slopes to 120 feet. Long tunnels and caverns covered with purple hydrocoral distinguish one formation known as Yellow Roof. With visibility of 150 feet, this is also a popular snorkeling spot. Other sites have plentiful fish and coral in shallower water just off Rincón's shores. ✉ *Rincón.*

Parque Pasivo El Faro

CITY PARK | Surrounding the Faro de Punta Higuero (Rincón's lighthouse), Parque Pasivo El Faro has small kiosks at the water's edge. If you're lucky, you may spot a whale in the distance. (Have patience, though, as it could take days to see one.) You can also glimpse the rusty, mint-color dome of the defunct Bonus Thermonuclear Energy Plant from here; it has been closed since 1968. The park—complete with benches and a refreshment stand—is a nice place to take in sunsets. The lighthouse is closed to the public, but it's hard to walk away without taking a photo of the stately white structure. ✉ *End of Rte. 413, Rincón* *Free.*

Named for the futuristic-looking structures of a nearby power plant, Domes Beach is a surfing favorite.

Beaches

The waters of northwestern Puerto Rico have long played a siren song for traveling surfers. Spared the trade winds that limit surf in other areas, the region has some of the best waves in the world, especially in winter. But you don't have to be a big-wave rider to enjoy the beaches here.

The best beaches are north of Rincón. Follow Route 413 and Route 4413 (the road to the lighthouse). South of town, the only beach worth noting is Playa Córcega, off Route 115. As with many other beaches in the Caribbean, there are often urchins, riptides, undertows, and rocky reefs below the surface—never swim alone.

Balneario de Rincón

BEACH | **FAMILY** | Families enjoy the tranquil waters, playground, and shelters for seaside picnics. The beach is within walking distance to the center of town. **Amenities:** parking (no fee); showers; toilets. **Best for:** sunset; swimming. ✉ *Calle Cambija, Rincón.*

Domes

BEACH | Named for the eerie green domes on a nearby power plant, this beach is extremely popular with surfers, with its consistent rights and occasional lefts. On a good surf day, arrive early if you want a spot on the sand. Though not recommended for swimmers because of the rocks, it's a great whale-watching spot in winter. The dirt road leading to the parking area is rather steep and difficult to exit. There are no facilities here, so plan accordingly. **Amenities:** none. **Best for:** surfing. ✉ *Rte. 4413, north of the lighthouse, Rincón.*

Maria's

BEACH | This surf spot, south of Domes, can get crowded when the waves are high. When waves are small, it serves as a schoolhouse for surf lessons. It's popular with locals, as much for its breaks as for its proximity to the Calypso Café. To get here, look for the street sign reading

"Surfer crossing." **Amenities:** none. **Best for:** sunsets; surfing. ✉ *Rte. 4413, south of the lighthouse, Rincón.*

Playa Córcega

BEACH | The long stretch of yellow sand in front of Villa Cofresí is considered one of the best swimming beaches in Rincón. It's also perfect for relaxing and stand-up paddleboarding. **Amenities:** none. **Best for:** swimming; walking. ✉ *Rte. 115, Km 12, Rincón.*

Steps (*Tres Palmas*)

BEACH | This beach, which takes its name from the mysterious concrete steps at the water's edge, is home to the Tres Palmas Marine Reserve. It's a good place to find sea glass; on calm days, it's also an excellent snorkeling spot. At other times, the waves can be huge. Indeed, on a handful of days each year, the waters deliver epic rides that draw surfers from around the globe. A small food truck serves coconut water, fish tacos, empanadas, and other treats. The beach is hard to find—look for the turnoff at a whale-shape sign reading "Playa Escalera." **Amenities:** none. **Best for:** snorkeling; sunsets. ✉ *Rte. 413, north of turnoff for Black Eagle Marina, Rincón.*

Restaurants

Café 413

$$ | **ECLECTIC** | **FAMILY** | This multicuisine dining locale is coffee shop, restaurant, and bar all in one. Conveniently located right on the town square, it's a great place for a latte, smoothie, wrap, or even a full breakfast or dinner. **Known for:** breakfast; family-friendly dining; gluten-free and vegan choices. *$ Average main: $14 ✉ 157 Calle Progreso, Rincón ☎ 939/697–8188 ⏲ Closed Wed.*

Cafe 2 Go

$ | **CAFE** | For the best coffee in town, make your way to this tiny food cart off Route 413. Owner Aaron makes an awesome latte using local Puerto Rican coffee. **Known for:** Puerto Rican coffee; açaí bowls; made-to-order fruit smoothies. *$ Average main: $4 ✉ Rte. 413, Km 0.5, Rincón ⏲ Closed June–Oct.*

★ The English Rose

$ | **CAFÉ** | **FAMILY** | Open for breakfast only, this quaint bed-and-breakfast has a spectacular view of the valley spilling into the sea. If terrace seating is not available, indoor dining is equally charming, with walls colorfully adorned by the work of local artisans. **Known for:** eggs Benedict; house-baked breads and croissants; beautiful views. *$ Average main: $10 ✉ Rte. 413, Km 2, Rincón ☎ 787/823–4032 🌐 theenglishroserincon.com ⏲ Closed Sept. and Oct. Closed Mon.–Wed. May–Aug.*

★ Estela

$$$ | **CARIBBEAN** | On weekends, patrons come from as far as San Juan to dine at this cozy restaurant. Operated by husband-and-wife team Juan and Nerylu, it's found a niche in Rincón offering dishes made using locally sourced ingredients—you may even see a fisherman pull up with a giant yellowfin tuna. **Known for:** fresh seafood; farm-to-table dining; good wine list. *$ Average main: $25 ✉ Rte. 115, Km 14, Rincón ☎ 787/823–1795 ⏲ Closed Sun. and Mon. No lunch.*

Jack's Shack

$ | **VEGETARIAN** | **FAMILY** | This popular food cart across from Pool's Beach serves healthy breakfasts and lunches featuring seasonal ingredients and the catch of the day. The fish tacos are popular, though the menu also has veggie burgers and quinoa salads. **Known for:** fish tacos; breakfast burritos; fresh-pressed juices. *$ Average main: $10 ✉ Across from Pools Beach, Rte. 413 Ramal, Rincón ☎ 939/274–8066 ⏲ No dinner.*

La Cambija

$ | **SEAFOOD** | **FAMILY** | You'll find some of the freshest seafood in town at this casual roadside restaurant. Order an

Great Itineraries

If You Have 1 Day

If you have only a day for the Porta del Sol, head to **Joyuda** in the Cabo Rojo region for some of Puerto Rico's freshest seafood. You probably won't be the only one driving from San Juan for this feast.

If You Have 3 Days

If you have a few days to explore the region, start in **Rincón,** where you'll find accommodations for every taste, from compact inns to sprawling resorts. There isn't too much to see, other than the lighthouse at Parque Pasivo El Faro, but you will find plenty of beautiful beaches. The secret's out about many of them, but you can still often find complete solitude on beaches near **Aguadilla** or **Isabela.** On Day 2, drive south to the Cabo Rojo region. Your first stop should be **Joyuda,** where you can choose from dozens of seaside restaurants. After lunch, continue past **Boquerón** to the **Morrillos Peninsula.** This is the end of the line, quite literally: the road ends at the Faro de los Morrillos de Cabo Rojo, a lighthouse that once warned sea captains about the treacherous waters around the island's southwestern tip. On Day 3 you can explore more of this windswept landscape.

If You Have 5 Days

After spending three days along the western coast, you may be tempted to sail off to one of the nearby islands. On Day 4, head out on an overnight trip to **Mona Island,** a 14,000-acre paradise known as the "Galápagos of the Caribbean." You'll have to camp on this deserted island, but the view from the 200-foot cliffs on the northern shore makes it all worth it.

■ TIP→ Trips to Mona Island must be arranged weeks in advance.

assortment of grilled fish skewers, choosing from tuna, mahimahi, grouper, wahoo, rainbow runner, and more. **Known for:** grilled fish skewers; house-made empanadas; happy-hour drink prices all day. *$ Average main: $10 ✉ Calle Cambija, at Calle B, Rincón ☎ 787/823–1118.*

La Copa Llena at the Black Eagle

$$ | CARIBBEAN | Join patrons from across the island for spectacular sunsets at this restaurant right on the beach. Whether you choose one of the small plates or an entrée, fresh seafood is always your best bet. **Known for:** fresh seafood; sunset drinks; great outdoor deck. *$ Average main: $20 ✉ Black Eagle Rd., off Rte. 413, Km 1.0, Ensenada, Rincón ☎ 787/823–0896 ⏲ Closed Sun., Mon., Sept., and Oct. No lunch.*

Mangia Mi

$$ | ITALIAN | FAMILY | Chef Rebecca White of Food Network's *Cooks vs. Cons* whips up Italian creations at her newest venture in Rincón. The open kitchen allows you to see the staff meticulously preparing each dish amid strands of hanging, freshly made pasta. **Known for:** homemade pastas; good wine list by the bottle; grilled artisanal pizzas. *$ Average main: $15 ✉ 4 Muñoz Rivera St. E, Rincón ☎ 787/823–4812 🌐 www.facebook.com/mangiamirincon ⏲ Closed Wed. No lunch.*

Mimosa Brunch Farm to Table

$$ | AMERICAN | FAMILY | Breakfast and brunch are served all day at this popular restaurant in Aguada. Perfectly cooked eggs Benedict and creative dishes like pancakes can be found on the menu.

Did You Know?

You can't enter Rincón's Faro del Punta Higuero, but its exterior is picture-perfect, and the surrounding park is a great place to enjoy sea views (especially at sunset) and maybe even spot a whale.

Known for: farm to table; fantastic service; brunch served all day. *Average main: $19 ✉ Barrio Malpaso, Carr. 417, Km 2.0, Aguada.*

Parrilleria Vacas Gauchas
$$$ | **ARGENTINE** | **FAMILY** | Excellent cuts of meat—from filet mignon and rib eye to pork loin—are the draws here. Splurge-worthy dry-aged porterhouse and kurobuta pork are also likely to be on the menu. **Known for:** family-friendly restaurant; great meats; fantastic service. *Average main: $30 ✉ Rte. 115, Km 11.8, Rincón ☎ 787/529–1200 Closed Mon.*

La Sirena Sushi & Tiki Bar
$$ | **SUSHI** | One of only a few sushi restaurants on the west coast, the former Pool Bar Sushi attracts visitors from as far away as San Juan. The menu rivals that of any high-end Japanese restaurant, with mango tuna rolls, eel maki, shumai, and wakame seaweed salads. **Known for:** sushi rolls; fish tacos for lunch; movie night. *Average main: $20 ✉ 15 Calle Comercio, Rincón ☎ 787/823–2583.*

Reina Mora
$$$$ | **CONTEMPORARY** | Located on the Rincón–Aguada border, this supper club run by a husband-and-wife team has a multicourse menu that changes weekly and highlights locally sourced and grown food (add a bag of produce from area farms to take home). Vegan and vegetarian options are available upon request, and it's BYOB. **Known for:** supper club; seasonal, farm-to-table menu; by reservation only. *Average main: $50 ✉ Rte. 414, Km 6, Aguada ☎ 404/431–1587 www.reinamorapuertorico.com.*

Sana Farm to Table
$ | **VEGETARIAN** | This charming restaurant specializes in vegan, vegetarian, and pescatarian dishes. The summer rolls are made with veggies from local farms, and the fish in the poké bowl features the catch of the day. **Known for:** green juices; vegetarian food; healthy eats. *Average main: $9 ✉ PR-413, Km 4.1, Rincón ☎ 787/823–7621 No dinner.*

Shipwreck Bar & Grill
$$$ | **CARIBBEAN** | **FAMILY** | This pirate-themed restaurant has a laid-back vibe and a friendly staff who are always ready with a smile or a joke. Don't be surprised to see local fishermen making their way to the kitchen with their still-flapping catch. **Known for:** fresh seafood and steaks; kid-friendly dining environment; large portions. *Average main: $22 ✉ Black Eagle Marina, Black Eagle Rd., off Rte. 413, Rincón ☎ 787/823–0578 www.rinconshipwreck.com No lunch weekdays.*

Tamboo
$$ | **CARIBBEAN** | The best thing about this bar and grill is its beachfront location. The open-air venue serves a mean mojito, and the deck is a great place to watch novice surfers wipe out on the beach. **Known for:** guava barbecue ribs; fish sandwiches; drinks on the deck. *Average main: $20 ✉ Beside the Pointe, Rte. 413, Km 4.4, Rincón ☎ 787/823–8550 Closed Sept.*

Hotels

Aqua Marina Beach Club
$$ | **B&B/INN** | The walled garden that surrounds this little inn makes it seem miles away from civilization, but it's actually within walking distance of several bars and restaurants. **Pros:** gorgeous gardens and pool; use of common kitchen; extremely private. **Cons:** not on the beach; some noise from nearby restaurant; a long walk to town. *Rooms from: $250 ✉ 556 Black Eagle Rd., off Rte. 413, Rincón ☎ 787/823–2593 www.aquamarinabeachclub.com 8 rooms No Meals.*

Casa Isleña

$$ | **B&B/INN** | With its barrel-tiled roofs, walled gardens, and open-air dining room, Casa Isleña might remind well-traveled souls of a villa on the coast of Mexico. **Pros:** beautiful beach; friendly staff; walking distance to great restaurants. **Cons:** books up quickly; somewhat dated decor; rooms are very basic. *Rooms from: $200 Rte. 413, Km 4.8, Rincón 787/823–1525, 888/289–7750 www.casaislena.com Closed Oct. 9 rooms Free Breakfast.*

Dos Angeles del Mar Bed and Breakfast

$$ | **B&B/INN** | On a quiet hillside overlooking the ocean, this no-frills guesthouse is about as clean and comfortable as it gets. **Pros:** friendly staff; great breakfast; peaceful haven. **Cons:** morning rooster crows; uphill climb from the beach; far from town. *Rooms from: $169 Calle Vista del Mar, Rincón 787/823–1378, 787/431–6057 www.dosangelesdelmar.com 5 rooms Free Breakfast.*

The English Rose

$$$ | **B&B/INN** | Nestled in the hills of Rincón, this charming inn—with a pale blue exterior and white plantation shutters—has some of the best views of the Caribbean. **Pros:** excellent breakfast; all rooms have kitchens; friendly staff. **Cons:** somewhat isolated with a breakfast-only restaurant; not on the beach; reservations taken only online. *Rooms from: $350 Rte. 413, Km 2, Rincón theenglishroserincon.com Closed Sept. and Oct. 3 apartments Free Breakfast.*

Lazy Parrot Inn

$$ | **HOTEL** | **FAMILY** | Though its guest rooms are more subdued, this mountainside hotel—painted in eye-popping tropical hues and with an open lobby featuring colorful murals of its namesake bird—makes a statement without taking itself too seriously. **Pros:** in-room microwaves; beautiful pool; good on-site restaurant. **Cons:** not on the beach; stairs to climb; some may consider the whimsical style tacky. *Rooms from: $200 Rte. 413, Km 4.1, Rincón 787/823–5654, 800/294–1752 www.lazyparrot.com 22 rooms No Meals.*

Mar Azul Villas

$ | **APARTMENT** | Set in a tropical garden behind Mar Azul Surf Shop (the best in town), these charming little apartments have all the comforts of home. **Pros:** spotless rooms; friendly owners; walking distance to restaurants. **Cons:** limited ocean view; foot traffic from attached surf shop; not on the beach. *Rooms from: $95 Rte. 413, Km 4.4, Rincón 787/214–7224, 787/823–5692 www.puertoricosurfinginfo.com 2 apartments No Meals.*

Rincón Beach Resort

$$ | **RESORT** | **FAMILY** | It's a bit off the beaten path, but that's part of the allure of this oceanfront resort, which sits on a great swimming beach and offers bountiful activities. **Pros:** beautiful pool area; laid-back vibe; children's playground. **Cons:** far from restaurants; decor is slightly dated; halls echo. *Rooms from: $230 Rte. 115, Km 5.8, Añasco 787/589–9000 www.rinconbeach.com 112 rooms No Meals.*

Rincón of the Seas

$$ | **RESORT** | **FAMILY** | Tucked away at the end of a palm-lined drive, this high-rise hotel feels as if it could be in Miami Beach: a gently curving facade and elegant balcony railings give it a vaguely art deco feel. **Pros:** lush gardens; nice pool area; Wi-Fi in common areas. **Cons:** on a slender beach; loud music blares from pool area all day; rooms need a makeover. *Rooms from: $200 Rte. 115, Km 12.2, Rincón 787/823–7500 www.rinconoftheseas.com 112 rooms No Meals.*

Rincón is an extremely popular surfing and watersports town.

Tamboo Beside the Pointe

$$ | **HOTEL** | This perennial favorite sits right on Sandy Beach, where the waves are big but not too large for novice surfers. **Pros:** social atmosphere; popular restaurant; great views from some rooms. **Cons:** noise from restaurant; not all rooms have ocean views; no elevator. *Rooms from: $200 Rte. 413 at Km 4.4, Rincón 787/823–8550 www.visittamboo.com Closed Sept. 8 rooms No Meals.*

★ Tres Sirenas

$$$ | **B&B/INN** | Waves gently lap against the shore at the "Three Mermaids" (a nod to the original owners' daughters), a boutique inn set in a luxurious two-story villa on one of Rincón's calmer beaches. **Pros:** beachfront; spotless; tastefully decorated. **Cons:** often fully booked far in advance; pricey in high season; long walk to restaurants. *Rooms from: $350 26 Seabeach Dr., Rincón 787/823–0558 www.tressirenas.com 5 rooms Free Breakfast.*

Villa Cofresí

$$ | **HOTEL** | **FAMILY** | On one of the best swimming beaches in town, Villa Confresí is Rincón's oldest hotel, making it extremely popular with Puerto Rican families. **Pros:** good restaurant; family-friendly environment; some rooms have kitchenettes. **Cons:** standard rooms lack ocean views; not enough parking; lots of noise from pool area. *Rooms from: $200 Rte. 115, Km 12, Rincón 787/823–2450 www.villacofresi.com 107 rooms Free Breakfast.*

Villa Tres Palmas

$$$ | **HOUSE** | Not all beach houses are created equal, as Villas Tres Palmas makes clear. **Pros:** full kitchen; near many good restaurants; great location for surfers. **Cons:** only the bedrooms have air-conditioning; not on a bathing beach; two rooms share a bath. *Rooms from: $300 Off Rte. 413, Rincón 787/539–3519 www.trespalmasvillas.com 6 rooms No Meals.*

Nightlife

Rincón attracts a younger crowd, so there are plenty of options for fun after dark.

Calypso Café
GATHERING PLACES | On weekends the Calypso Café often has live music. The open-air establishment has a daily sunset happy hour and is a good place to grab fresh ceviche, grilled fish, or a juicy burger after you've had your fill of the beach. ✉ *Maria's Beach, Rte. 4413, Rincón* ☎ *787/823–1626.*

Rincón Beer Company
BREWPUBS | This microbrewery on the town square serves a great selection of local and craft beers. The food is also good, especially the fish tacos. There's live music on Thursday night during the Art Walk. ✉ *15 Calle Muñoz Rivera, Rincón* ☎ *787/823–2538* 🌐 *rinconbeer.company.site.*

Tamboo Tavern
BARS | A casual beachfront restaurant by day, Tamboo becomes a fun, loud hangout after dark. A DJ spins every Friday night, and there is live music every Saturday. Stop in for happy hour (daily 5–9). ✉ *Beside the Pointe, Rte. 413, Km 4.4, Rincón* ☎ *787/823–8550* 🌐 *www.visittamboo.com.*

Shopping

CLOTHING

★ Ocean State of Mind
MIXED CLOTHING | This beach boutique sells an array of carefully curated clothing and accessories. ✉ *4 Calle Progreso, Rincón* ☎ *808/384–1950* 🌐 *www.oceanstateofmindshop.com.*

The Uncharted Studio
MIXED CLOTHING | This shop in the main town square makes eco-friendly screen-printed T-shirts using their own ocean-inspired designs. ✉ *Rincón Plaza, 6 Calle Sol, Rincón* ☎ *939/697–8177* 🌐 *www.theunchartedstudio.com.*

GIFTS AND SOUVENIRS

Tinto Wine Shop
WINE/SPIRITS | Just off the main square, this small, family-run shop has a fantastic selection of wines. Enjoy a glass with snacks while you browse. Wine tastings happen weekly, and charcuterie are available for sale. ✉ *176 Calle Sol, Rincón* ☎ *787/823–4773* 🌐 *www.tintowineshop-rincon.com.*

SURF GEAR

Desecheo Surf & Dive Shop
SPORTING GOODS | In addition to selling swimwear, sandals, sunglasses, and surf gear, this shop rents bodyboards, a variety of short and long surfboards, and snorkeling equipment. The staff can also organize surfing lessons. ✉ *Rte. 413, Km 2.5, Maria's Beach, Rincón* ☎ *787/823–0390.*

Playero
SPORTING GOODS | With a great selection of surfboards, clothing, swimwear, and accessories, this brand-new surf shop has everything you need for your beach vacation. ✉ *Rt. 413, Km 0.7, Rincón* ☎ *787/609–7500* 🌐 *www.playero.com.*

Activities

DIVING AND SNORKELING

Most of the region's dive operators also run fishing charters around Desecheo Island and whale-watching trips in season.

Taíno Divers
DIVING & SNORKELING | Taíno Divers has all-day snorkeling and diving trips that include lunch. They also offers daily trips to Desecheo Island, winter whale-watching trips, and scuba certification courses. ✉ *Black Eagle Marina, Black Eagle Rd., off Rte. 413, Rincón* ☎ *787/823–6429* 🌐 *www.tainodivers.com* 🎫 *From $89.*

HORSEBACK RIDING

Pintos R Us

HORSEBACK RIDING | Pintos R Us has two-hour horseback riding tours ($90 per person) along the beach to the lighthouse, as well as full-moon tours and riding lessons. The horses are spirited but gentle enough for novices. Reservations are a must. ✉ *Rte. 413, Km 4.7, Rincón* ☎ *787/516–7090* 🌐 *www.pintosrus.com.*

PADDLEBOARDING

Rincon Paddleboards

WATER SPORTS | FAMILY | In addition to renting paddleboards, this company offers morning and sunset paddle tours (from $60 per person). ✉ *Black Eagle Marina, Rincón* ☎ *787/546–9545* 🌐 *www.rinconpaddleboards.com.*

SAILING

Katarina Sail Charters

SAILING | Set sail in the morning for a day in the sun, or in the late afternoon for unobstructed sunset views. The catamaran sails from Black Eagle Marina, except mid-August–mid-November (hurricane season). Sailing adventures start at $65 per person. ✉ *Black Eagle Marina, Black Eagle Rd., off Rte. 413, Rincón* ☎ *787/823–7245* 🌐 *sailrinconpr.com.*

SURFING

After hosting the World Surfing Championship in 1968, Rincón became a popular surfing destination. Today, locals and tourists flock to this small, laid-back town every winter to catch the season's best waves. But you don't need to be a pro to vacation in Rincón. There are several surfing schools that offer lessons for beginners, and the town's chill vibe is the perfect place to unwind, relax, and soak up the sun.

Mar Azul

SURFING | One of the best surf shops on the entire island has Rincon's finest selection of performance surfboards and stand-up paddleboards to buy or rent. Rent a board for $30 a day or $150 for an entire week. ✉ *Rte. 413, Km 4.4, Rincón* ☎ *787/823–5692* 🌐 *www.puertoricosurfinginfo.com.*

Puntas Surf School

SURFING | With more than a decade of surf-coaching experience, Puntas is a great surf school for beginners and kids. ✉ *Rincón* ☎ *787/366–1689* 🌐 *www.puntassurfschool.com.*

Rincón Surf School

SURFING | This popular surf school offers private and group lessons. ✉ *Rte. 413, Km 4.4, Rincón* ☎ *787/823–0610* 🌐 *www.rinconsurfschool.com.*

Surf Lessons Puerto Rico

SURFING | Ex–pro surfer Ramse Morales has been conducting high-quality surfing classes since 2000. ✉ *Maria's Beach, Rincón* ☎ *787/617–4731* 🌐 *www.surflessonspuertorico.com* 🎫 *From $75 for private 2-hr lessons.*

YOGA

Barefoot Yoga PR

YOGA | Enjoy a beachfront yoga session ($20) hosted under a canopy of almond trees. ✉ *Sandy Beach, Rte. 413 Interior, Km 4.8, Rincón* ☎ *787/234–8124* 🌐 *www.barefootyogapr.com.*

Centro La Paz

YOGA | This studio hosts yoga, Pilates, and meditation classes. You can book a massage or a facial as well, and the on-site café, Passiflora, offers a tasty vegan menu; most dishes are organic and made with locally sourced ingredients. Group yoga and mat Pilates classes are $15. ✉ *Next to Island West Properties, Rte. 115, Km 14.1, Rincón* ☎ *787/823–2885* 🌐 *www.lapazrincon.com.*

Mayagüez

24 km (15 miles) southeast of Rincón.

"Me encanta" is what most people from Puerto Rico say when you ask them about Mayagüez. However, the city is home to 12,000 university students, several casinos, and the largest shopping mall on the west coast, and you are less likely to be enchanted by its traffic-clogged streets, especially with so many more charming communities in every direction. Still, if you have some spare time, the city known as the "Sultan of the West" has some worthwhile attractions. Its tree-lined main square, Plaza Colón, is dominated by a large statue of Christopher Columbus, and surrounding streets contain the domed Teatro Yagüez, which dates from 1902, as well as a mishmash of neoclassical, baroque, and art deco buildings.

Mayagüez isn't famous for its beaches—you'll find better in Rincón, about 25 minutes north—but Balneario de Añasco (aka Tres Hermanos Beach) is 10 minutes north of town via Route 2 and Routes 115 and 401. Dotted with palm trees, it's good for swimming and has changing facilities and restrooms.

GETTING HERE AND AROUND

AIR

The small Aeropuerto Eugenio María de Hostos (MAZ), just north of Mayagüez on Route 2, has flights from San Juan on Cape Air. Cars rented at the airport cost $35–$65 per day.

CAR

Driving in Mayagüez can be complicated, especially in the high-trafficked town center, where the city grid is made up of one-way streets. Nevertheless, a rental car is your best option for getting around town. From Route 2 you can reach downtown by taking Route 105 (Calle McKinley) or Route 106 (Calle Méndez Vigo); either will take you to the heart of the city.

CAR RENTAL Avis. ✉ *Mayagüez Mall, 975 Av. Eugenio Maria de Hostos, Mayagüez* ☎ *787/805–5911* 🌐 *www.avis.com.* **Enterprise.** ✉ *Rte. 2, Km 158.9, Mayagüez* ☎ *844/794–8596* 🌐 *www.enterprise.com.* **Thrifty.** ✉ *Aeropuerto Eugenio María de Hostos, off Rte. 2, Mayagüez* ☎ *787/834–1590* 🌐 *www.thrifty.com.*

TAXI TRAVEL

In Mayagüez taxis charge flat rates—no meters—by location. A one-way trip to or from San Juan costs about $120.

Sights

Yagüez Theatre

NOTABLE BUILDING | The Teatro Yagüez is an extravagant yellow-and-white theater dating from 1902 that's famed throughout the island for its lavish, columned facade, impressive chandeliers, and domed roof. The structure, a little over-the-top, is still the main venue for theater in Mayagüez. ✉ *Calle McKinley, 1 block from Plaza Colón, Mayagüez* 🎫 *Free* 🕒 *Closed weekends.*

Restaurants

De Raiz

$$$ | CARIBBEAN | Chef Juan Camacho's newest venture brings him to the college town of Mayaguez. Here, he elevates the dining scene in town. 💲 *Average main: $25* ✉ *60 Calle Ernesto Ramos Antonini, Mayagüez* 🌐 *www.deraizpr.com.*

Ricomini Bakery

$ | CAFÉ | Open daily 5 am–midnight, this popular bakery is a good spot to try one of the city's trademark delicacies: the *brazo gitano* (gypsy arm), a gigantic jelly roll filled with anything from guava to sweet cheese. There are also tasty pastries like flan, tres leches cake, mallorcas, and cheesecake, as well as freshly baked bread and a selection of sandwiches. **Known for:** brazo gitano jelly rolls; Fido's sangria; sandwiches for lunch. *Average main: $6* *101 Calle Méndez Vigo, Mayagüez* *787/832–0565* *www.ricominipr.com* *No dinner.*

Hotels

Holiday Inn Mayagüez & Tropical Casino
$$ | **HOTEL** | They've managed to shoehorn nearly everything into this big box on the northern edge of Mayagüez, where the sound of slot machines is impossible to escape in the extremely popular casino adjacent to the lobby. **Pros:** great staff; pretty pool area; family-friendly. **Cons:** not on the beach; motel-style rooms; continental breakfast free for executive rooms only. *Rooms from: $165* *2701 Rte. 2, Km 149.9, Mayagüez* *787/833–1100* *www.ihg.com* *141 rooms* *No Meals.*

Mayagüez Resort & Casino
$$ | **HOTEL** | **FAMILY** | The center of the city's social life, on weekends, this old-fashioned hotel is packed with elegantly dressed men and women—some trying their luck in the casino, some dancing the tango in the lounge, and some sipping cocktails on the long, sweeping terrace. **Pros:** lovely pool area; best casino on this coast; surrounded by gardens with an aqua park. **Cons:** not on the beach; guests must wear identity wristbands; time for a renovation. *Rooms from: $200* *Rte. 104, Km 0.3, off Rte. 2, Mayagüez* *787/832–3030, 888/689–3030* *www.facebook.com/MayaguezResort* *140 rooms* *No Meals.*

Shopping

Small stores and pharmacies dot downtown Mayagüez.

Mayagüez Mall
MALL | Offering heavy-duty shopping, the Mayagüez Mall has local stores; a food court; movie theaters; and stateside chains like Old Navy, Walmart, and Marshalls. *975 Av. Eugenio María de Hostos, Mayagüez* *787/834–2760.*

The Golden Mile

Anyone interested in seafood must visit La Milla de Oro del Buen Comer (Gourmet Golden Mile), along Route 102 in the small fishing village of Joyuda. This string of more than 15 restaurants serves the best fish on the island. The seafood here is the freshest—caught daily from the Caribbean or Laguna Joyuda.

Activities

MULTISPORT OUTFITTERS

AdvenTours
LOCAL SPORTS | The Mayagüez-based AdvenTours offers bird-watching, biking, and kayaking trips. *1102 Calle Uroyán, Mayagüez* *787/530–8311* *www.adventourspr.com.*

Joyuda

21 km (14 miles) south of Mayagüez.

Known as the La Milla de Oro (Golden Mile) because of its string of more than 15 seaside restaurants, the community of Joyuda is a must for seafood lovers. The same can't be said for those in search of a beautiful beach, as erosion has taken a terrible toll: in some places, all that's left is a sliver of sand. But that doesn't stop hordes of local families from making a beeline to the bit of beach that's left.

GETTING HERE AND AROUND

From Mayagüez, take Route 2 south to Route 100 south, and then head west on Route 102. Most of the area's restaurants and hotels dot a 3-km (2-mile) stretch on Route 102, making this a convenient town to explore on foot.

Sights

Mona Island

ISLAND | About 80 km (50 miles) off the Morrillos Peninsula, at the island's very southwestern tip, Mona Island sits brooding in the ocean. Known as the "Galápagos of the Caribbean," the 14,000-acre island has long been a destination for adventurous travelers. It's said to have been settled by the Taíno Indians and visited by both Christopher Columbus and Juan Ponce de León. Pirates were known to have used it as a hideout, and legend has it that there is still buried treasure to be found there. Today, however, Mona's biggest lure is its distinctive ecosystem. It is home to a number of endangered species, such as the Mona iguana and the leatherback sea turtle, as well as a number of seabirds, including the red-footed booby. Off its coast are reefs filled with 270 species of tropical fish, black coral, and purple sea fans. On land, you can explore 200-foot cliffs on the island's north side or an abandoned lighthouse to the south. The only way to get here is by boat—planes aren't permitted to land. Several tour operators in Joyuda, Boquerón, Mayagüez, and Rincón offer camping trips and will help arrange permits from the Puerto Rico Department of Natural and Environmental Resources.

⚠ **You need to reserve at least a few weeks ahead for an overnight stay.** ✉ *Joyuda* ☎ *787/722–1726 Departamento de Recursos Naturales y Ambientales (DRNA).*

Restaurants

El Bohío

$$ | **SEAFOOD** | Watch seagulls dive for their food while you dine on a covered deck extending out into the bay. The long list of seafood is prepared in a variety of ways: shrimp comes breaded, stewed, or skewered; conch is served as a salad or cooked in a butter-and-garlic sauce; and the lobster can be prepared just about any way you can imagine. **Known for:** fresh seafood; idyllic waterfront setting; lobster prepared many ways. $ *Average main: $20* ✉ *Milla de Oro, Rte. 102, Km 13.9, Joyuda* ☎ *787/851–2755* 🕑 *Closed Oct.*

Activities

DIVING AND SNORKELING

Several reef-fringed cays lie off the Cabo Rojo area near walls that drop to 100 feet. A mile-long reef along Las Coronas, better known as Cayo Ron, has a variety of hard and soft coral, reef fish, and lobsters.

Boquerón

5 km (3 miles) south of Joyuda.

Once a quiet fishing village, Boquerón still has its share of seaside shanties. Its narrow streets are quiet during the week but come alive on the weekend, when vendors appear with carts full of clams and oysters you can slurp down on the spot and when bars and restaurants throw open their doors—if they have any, that is. Many of the establishments here are open to the breeze, making this a Puerto Rican party spot where the music (and the people) can be heard until 2 in the morning. Boquerón is also a water-sports center; many companies operate from or near the docks of the imposing Club Nautico de Boquerón, which is easy to find at the end of Route 100.

GETTING HERE AND AROUND

To reach Boquerón from Joyuda, take Route 2 south to Route 100. The small town can easily be explored on foot.

Beaches

Balneario Boquerón

BEACH | FAMILY | The long stretch of sand at this beach off Route 101 is a favorite with islanders, especially on weekends. This is a Blue Flag beach, meaning it is recognized for its adherence to high environmental standards. **Amenities:** lifeguards; parking (no fee); showers; toilets. **Best for:** swimming. ✉ *Off Rte. 101, Boquerón.*

Playa Buyé

BEACH | Crystal clear water laps this white-sand beach that's lined with swaying palm and almond trees for shade. It's a bit hard to find and very crowded on weekends, so visit during the week or during the off-season. In high season, some kiosks with food and drink are open. Parking along Calle Buyé is free, but you'll pay $3 to park at the Buyé Beach Resort. **Amenities**: parking (no fee); showers; toilets. **Best for**: swimming; walking. ✉ *Rte. 307, Km 4.8, north of Boquerón, Boquerón.*

Restaurants

Downtown by José Carles

$$$ | SEAFOOD | FAMILY | Former executive chef of the Royal Isabela resort, José Carles, is now the proprietor of this restaurant in his home town. His menu focuses on seafood, most of which he catches himself, and dishes might include fish crudo with passion fruit, grilled lobster, blackened shrimp, or octopus risotto. **Known for:** fresh seafood; family-friendly atmosphere; crudo specials. $ *Average main: $23* ✉ *9 Calle José de Diego, Boquerón* ☎ *787/366–6166* ⏲ *Closed Mon. and Tues.*

101 West Kitchen & Bar

$$ | AMERICAN | This casual restaurant serving new American cuisine is a must when visiting Boquerón. Sit on the patio and indulge in tasty dishes like lobster mac 'n' cheese, pork sliders, and key lime pie. **Known for:** lobster mac 'n' cheese; good drinks from the bar; Sunday brunch. $ *Average main: $20* ✉ *Rte. 101, Km 5.7, Boquerón* ☎ *787/649–4320* ⏲ *Closed Mon. and Tues.*

Hotels

Aquarius Vacation Club

$$ | RESORT | FAMILY | As Boqueron's largest resort, this high-rise offers one-, two-, and three-bedroom suites, each with a private balcony. **Pros:** family-friendly; calm beach; full kitchens and laundry in every unit. **Cons:** hotel is often full; congested lot with a lot of double parking; rooms need an update. $ *Rooms from: $200* ✉ *Rte. 101, Km 18, Boquerón* ☎ *787/254–5400* 🌐 *www.aquariusvacationclub.com* *88 rooms* *No Meals.*

Morrillos Peninsula

3 km (2 miles) south of Boquerón.

Welcome to the end of the Earth—or the end of the island, anyway: this peninsula on the southwest corner of Puerto Rico is a bit removed from everything. The travel industry hasn't figured out how to market the area quite yet, so they've left it mostly to the locals, who have built small but elaborate weekend homes—some with grandiose touches like fountains. On the road closest to the beach is a cluster of seafood shacks. The more prosperous among them have added second stories.

GETTING HERE AND AROUND

From Route 101, head south on Route 301 to Km 7.8, where the road intersects with Route 3301. The five-minute drive west on Route 3301 ends at El Combate Beach, where a cluster of restaurants and hotels line the main strip (Calle 3). To reach Cabo Rojo Lighthouse and the salt flats, bypass Route 3301 and continue south on Route 301 until the road ends. This paved road soon turns into a bumpy

Surrounded by rugged coastline, the Faro de los Morrillos de Cabo Rojo is best reached with four-wheel drive.

one with potholes dotting the dusty course (if you're heading here, it's best to have a four-wheel-drive vehicle). The trek is well worth the effort, however, as jutting mangroves and crystal waters welcome travelers to Puerto Rico's southwestern tip.

Sights

Centro Interpretativo Las Salinas de Cabo Rojo

VISITOR CENTER | The Cabo Rojo Salt Flats Interpretive Center has two-hour guided tours along nature trails and a small display about the salt flats. The best part of the center is a massive observation tower that lets you scan the outline of Cabo Rojo itself. Next to the main building is an audiovisual center where presentations on marine ecosystems and bird migration are offered. ✉ *Rte. 301, Km 11, Cabo Rojo* ☎ *787/254–0115* 🌐 *www.ccpsai.org* 🎫 *Center free, tours $6.*

Faro de los Morrillos de Cabo Rojo

LIGHTHOUSE | The area's most popular attraction is this neoclassical lighthouse, dating from 1881. The magnificent structure, built on a limestone cliff, has amazing views of the Caribbean Sea. It is open to the public, and you are free to hike around the rugged terrain or relax on La Playuela or one of the other pink-sand beaches nearby.

■ TIP→ There are no facilities here, so bring water, food, and sunscreen. ✉ *End of Rte. 301, Cabo Rojo* ☎ *787/255–1560* 🎫 *Free* 🕓 *Closed Wed.*

Beaches

El Combate

BEACH | This great beach draws large crowds on weekends to its rustic waterfront eateries and calm waters. You can rent small boats and kayaks here. **Amenities:** food and drink. **Best for:** partiers; swimming. ✉ *End of Rte. 3301, Cabo Rojo.*

Did You Know?

Golden-brown, white, and turquoise—Cabo Rojo's salt flats are responsible for intriguing and colorful vistas like this one near Playa Sucia.

★ **Playa Sucia** (*La Playuela*)
BEACH | The crescent-shape strand is the most secluded, and beautiful, of the area's beaches. It's commonly referred to as "Playa Sucia" (Dirty Beach) by locals, because of the blankets of seaweed that drift to shore during winter months. The label is rather unfitting for the white sand and turquoise waters that mark the island's southwestern corner, reachable by way of a dirt road lined with mangroves. **Amenities:** none. **Best for:** swimming. ✉ *End of Rte. 301, past the vast salt flats, Cabo Rojo.*

Restaurants

Annie's Place
$$ | **SEAFOOD** | A dining room facing the ocean is a fitting place to try some of the southwest coast's best seafood. You can snack on *empanadillas* (fritters), then move on to red snapper with rice and beans or mofongo relleno. **Known for:** fresh red snapper; waterfront dining with great ocean views; empanadillas. *$ Average main: $20 ✉ Rte. 3301, Km 3, at Calle 3, Cabo Rojo ☎ 787/254–2553.*

Buena Vibra
$$ | **PUERTO RICAN** | Located right on Route 308, this no-frills Puerto Rican restaurant has an inviting, relaxed vibe. Friendly staffers serve local specialties like stuffed avocado, churrasco, and mofongo. **Known for:** fresh seafood; stuffed avocado; family-friendly atmosphere. *$ Average main: $19 ✉ Rte. 308, Km 7.1, Cabo Rojo ☎ 787/718–0024 ⏲ Closed Mon. and Tues.*

Hotels

Parador Combate Beach
$ | **HOTEL** | **FAMILY** | On a quiet side street near the beach, this nicely renovated little hotel is one of the best in the area and is a good value. **Pros:** quiet neighborhood; recently remodeled; complimentary breakfast. **Cons:** isolated location; patios face the parking lot; not on the beach. *$ Rooms from: $130 ✉ Rte. 3301, Km 2.7, Cabo Rojo ☎ 787/254–2358 🌐 www.combatebeachresort.com 🛏 18 rooms 🍴 Free Breakfast.*

Chapter 8

PONCE AND THE PORTA CARIBE

8

Updated by
Adriana Mercado

Sights ★★★★★ | Restaurants ★★★★☆ | Hotels ★★★★☆ | Shopping ★★☆☆☆ | Nightlife ★☆☆☆☆

WELCOME TO PONCE AND THE PORTA CARIBE

TOP REASONS TO GO

★ **Parque de Bombas:** Marvel at Ponce's century-old firehouse whose red-and-black color scheme has inspired thousands of photographers.

★ **Bosque Estatal de Guánica:** Hike where the cactus may make you think you're in the American Southwest.

★ **Hacienda Buena Vista:** Sample a cup of the local brew on a tour of the historic, beautifully restored coffee plantation outside Ponce.

★ **San Germán:** Stroll cobblestone streets lined with architectural treasures, then dine on fine Puerto Rican cuisine high above the main plaza.

★ **Casa Cautiño:** Step back in time to a colonial-era residence in the community of Guayama.

Ponce is the region's dynamic center, with a surrounding metropolitan area that includes a slew of vibrant attractions and sophisticated restaurants and hotels rivaled only by those in San Juan. Southeast of Ponce, the shoreline is rugged and the villages more rural and isolated. Seaside inns and some of the island's best seafood can be found here. Slightly inland are charming colonial towns and the beautiful historic city of San Germán, one of Puerto Rico's oldest settlements.

1 Ponce. Reminiscent of Old San Juan before cruise ships, Ponce has a yesteryear charm and an increasingly cosmopolitan vibe that delight many visitors.

2 Juana Díaz. This small town is worth at least a pit stop for its most famous drink, *maví*, a fermented beverage made from the ironwood tree.

3 Coamo. Puerto Ricans come from all over the island to Coamo, where thermal baths offer a promise of relaxation.

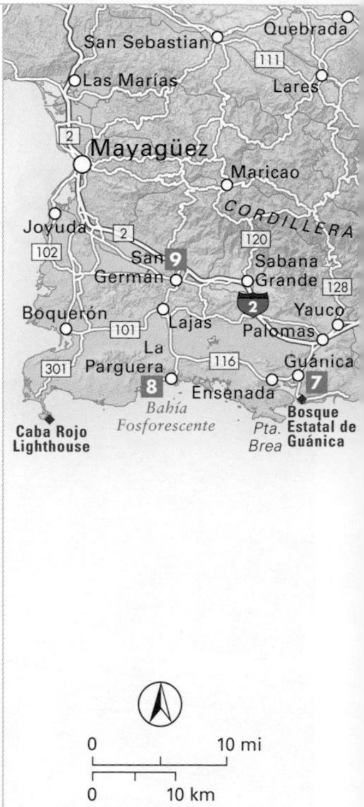

4 Salinas. Just off the main highway leading from San Juan to Ponce, Salinas is a destination for seafood lovers.

5 Guayama. A stop in Guayama should include Casa Cautiño, a 19th-century home that tells the story of the colonial period in Puerto Rico.

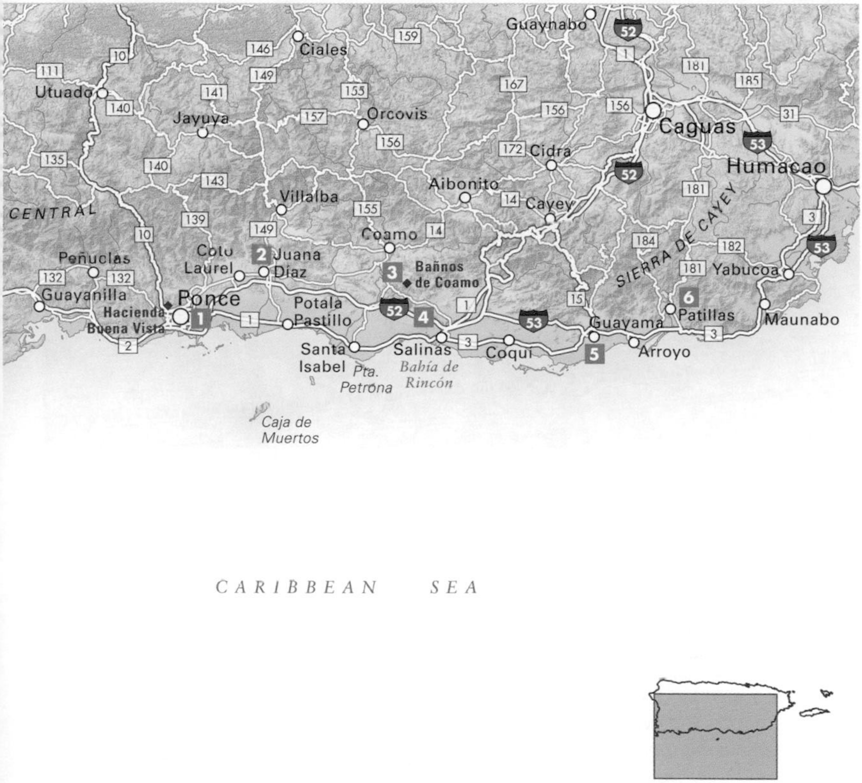

6 Patillas. Puerto Rico's "emerald of the south" is so named because of its green mountains to the north. It is also, though, a beach town, and its sunsets are stellar, so time your visit accordingly.

7 Guánica. This unassuming town is believed to be the spot where Columbus landed when he arrived in 1493; it's also where U.S. troops arrived to wrest Puerto Rico from the Spanish in the Spanish–American War.

8 La Parguera, Lajas. This lively southern coastal town is home to one of Puerto Rico's three bioluminescent bays, best seen when there's no moon.

9 San Germán. Architecture buffs won't want to bypass this historic town, whose squares and surrounding neighborhoods offer examples of every kind of architectural style.

THE MASKS OF PUERTO RICO

Puerto Rico's masks are true expressions of folk art, following a tradition that dates back to early-17th-century Spain.

During the Fiestas de Santiago Apóstol (St. James Festivals), brightly dressed *vejigantes* (pronounced "veh-hee-GAN-tays") represented the devil in a battle between good and evil. Their costumes consisted of long robes and grotesque masks, and they would wave cow bladders, or *vejigas,* on long sticks at anyone they passed. Parading as devils, their intention was to frighten sinners into returning to church for Lent.

Today, balloons and plastic bottles have replaced the cow bladders, and the now more playful masks have become one of Puerto Rico's most distinguished forms of artistic expression. One week before Ash Wednesday, vejigantes—wearing long, colorful robes and brightly painted horned masks—turn the normally placid city of Ponce into a hotbed of rowdiness. The masked mischief-makers prowl city streets, scaring and fascinating anyone in their path.

ISLAND ART

The best hand-designed masks in Puerto Rico come from three parts of the island: Ponce, Loíza (just east of San Juan), and Hatillo (on the north-west coast). Mask making is a family tradition in these towns, and styles are passed down for generations. For a fine souvenir and a memorable experience, head to one of the local workshops. Small masks cost \$20–\$30; larger ones by well-known artisans may cost more than \$1,000.

PONCE

Ponce's vejigante masks are made of papier-mâché and are most prominent during the February carnival. Many have African and indigenous elements; it's even possible to detect influences from ancient Greece and Rome. All masks have at least two horns, but most have several protruding from the forehead, chin, and nose. Some antique masks have more than 100 horns. At the beginning of the 20th century, masks were usually painted red with yellow dots or vice versa; today, they come in every imaginable color and pattern.

Where to Go: One of the best-known mask-making families is the Caraballo family from Playa de Ponce near El Ancla restaurant.

To purchase a mask, check social media for artisans offering commissions or ready-made pieces. The Caraballo family is nationally recognized for their vejigante masks, made to order but also available at Mi Coquí Arts and Crafts, right in the heart of Ponce. Masks are more readily available in stores around February, leading up to Ponce's carnival

Caraballo Family. ✉ *24 San Tomas, Playa de Ponce* ✉ *artesaniascaraballo@gmail.com.*

LOÍZA

Founded by freed and escaped African slaves, Loíza is known as the island's Capital of Traditions for its bomba and plena music and dance and its traditional Taíno and African cuisine.

Loíza's masks are created from coconut husks, and the individual shape of each determines the face and placement of the nose and lips. The teeth are made of bamboo, and the tongue is made of coconut shell.

Where to Go: For generations the Ayala family, whose workshop sits just east of town, has been the most renowned of Loíza's mask makers. Their masks appear during the St. James Festival of Loíza each July.

Artesanias Castor Ayala. ✉ *Rte. 187, Km 6.6, Barrio Mediana Alta* ☎ *787/564–6403.*

HATILLO

Hatillo was founded in 1823 by settlers from the Canary Islands. These *isleños,* in honor of King Herod's soldiers, the first Christian martyrs or Holy Innocents, would dress head to toe in costumes with a cape, hat, and mask made of fine metallic screening meant to resemble the face of a Spaniard. Today, the masked performers run through surrounding neighborhoods, joined by children, singing and dancing. The annual mask festival, Día de las Máscaras, is held every December 28.

Where to Go: Plaza Del Norte. ✉ *506 Calle Truncado.*

Not as popular as San Juan or Vieques, the south is a region full of underrated attractions, fine food, and a laid-back, authentic vibe that is hard to come by elsewhere. From lush tropical mountains to arid coastal plains, Puerto Rico's southern region lets you sample the island from a local's perspective.

Though rich in history, the area also provides ample opportunities for golf, swimming, hiking, and cave exploration. Snaking roads between major highways reveal a glimpse of how enjoyable rural living can be in Puerto Rico. Every mile or so you'll see a café or bar, which is the local social center. Traffic jams are a rare occurrence along the old roads, so smooth riding is basically guaranteed.

At the center of everything is Ponce, the "Pearl of the South," founded in 1692 by farmers attracted to the area's rich soil, which was perfect for growing sugarcane. Evidence found at the Tibes Indian ceremonial site, just north of the city, suggests that people have inhabited the region since 400 BC. Many residents still carry the last names of the dozens of European families who settled here during the 19th century. The region's largest city is also home to some of the island's most interesting architecture, excellent restaurants, and one of its most important art museums. To the west, San Germán, the second-oldest city in Puerto Rico, is known for its two historic main squares, which exhibit well-preserved examples of a wide variety of architectural styles.

On the southeast coast, Guayama and Patillas show off their splendor as little-known destinations for beachgoers. But the real party is on the southwest coast at La Parguera, which attracts a young and lively crowd. If you're willing to explore beyond the casinos, high-rises, and daily traffic congestion of the island's capital, the south is a great escape from Puerto Rico's usual tourist fare. Don't be surprised by the help many of its residents will offer, whether you ask for it or not—*puertorriqueños* in these parts are known for their friendliness in addition to their own brand of southern hospitality.

MAJOR REGIONS

Ponce, on the south coast of Puerto Rico, is the most populous city outside the greater San Juan region and has been an important city since Spanish colonial times.

The **Southeastern Coast** is one of the least-visited areas of Puerto Rico by tourists, but it's popular with locals, including such towns as Juana Díaz, Coamo, Salinas, Guayama, and Patillas.

The **Southwestern Coast** is where you'll find Guánica, home to a fascinating tropical dry forest as well as the spot where Columbus may have landed; La Parguera, one of Puerto Rico's three bioluminescent bays; as well as San Germán, a historic town famous for its architecture.

Planning

When to Go

The towns of Patillas, Guánica, and Lajas are popular with Puerto Ricans during Easter, Christmas, and summer, when children are out of school. Ponce's spirited pre-Lenten carnival, held the week before Ash Wednesday, draws many visitors. For the rest of the year, much of the south is quiet and receives only a fraction of the visitors that other parts of the island do, though the weather is equally superb, and most facilities remain open. Still, the southwestern region is the number 1 destination for internal tourism.

Hotels tend to lower their rates May to November, so do look around for any deals. Some *paradores* (small, government-sponsored inns) and hotels require a minimum two- or three-night stay on weekends.

Getting Here and Around

AIR

JetBlue flies from New York (JFK) and Orlando (MCO) to Ponce's Aeropuerto Internacional Mercedita (PSE).

Transfers: Taxis at the airport use meters; expect to pay about $10–$12 to get to downtown Ponce. Some hotels have shuttles to and from the airport, but you must make arrangements in advance.

AIRLINE CONTACTS JetBlue. ☎ *800/538–2583* 🌐 *www.jetblue.com.*

AIRPORT CONTACTS Aeropuerto Internacional Mercedita. (*PSE*) ✉ *Rte. 506, off Rte. 52, Ponce* ☎ *787/842–6292.*

BUS

There's no easy network of buses linking the towns in southern Puerto Rico with San Juan or with each other. Some municipalities and private companies operate buses or *públicos* (usually large vans) that make many stops. Be sure to call ahead; although reservations aren't usually required, you'll need to check schedules, which change frequently. The cost of a público from Ponce to San Juan is about $20–$25; agree on the price beforehand.

CAR

Getting around southern Puerto Rico without a car can be quite frustrating. You can rent cars at the Luis Muñoz Marín international airport and other San Juan locations. There are also car-rental agencies in some of the larger cities along the south coast, including Ponce, which has several at its Mercedita airport. Rates run about $35–$65 per day. A road map is essential in southern Puerto Rico. So is patience: allow extra time for twisting mountain roads and wrong turns. Many roads, especially in rural areas, aren't plainly marked.

TAXI

In Ponce, you can hail taxis in tourist areas and outside hotels. In smaller towns, it's best to call a taxi. You can also hire a car service (make arrangements through your hotel); often you can negotiate a lower rate than with a taxi.

Hotels

Modest, family-oriented establishments near beaches or in small towns and the occasional restored colonial hacienda or mansion are the most typical accommodations. Southern Puerto Rico doesn't have the abundance of luxury hotels and resorts found to the north and east; however, the Hilton Ponce Golf & Casino Resort and Copamarina Beach Resort and Spa are self-contained complexes with a dizzying array of services.

What It Costs in U.S. Dollars			
$	$$	$$$	$$$$
RESTAURANTS			
under $12	$12–$20	$21–$30	over $30
HOTELS			
under $150	$150–$250	$251–$350	over $350

Restaurants

Not all the hot spots are in San Juan—in fact, people from the capital drive to Ponce or Guánica to scan the culinary horizon. Some of the more ambitious restaurants in this part of Puerto Rico are experimenting with Asian and Latin fusion cuisines, which means you might find pork with tamarind glaze or guava sauce or snapper in a plantain crust. But mostly what you'll find are open-air eateries serving simple, filling fare. The southern coast is known for seafood, particularly in Salinas and Ponce, both of which have a string of popular seaside restaurants. A 15%–20% tip is customary; most restaurants won't include it in the bill, but it's wise to check.

HOTEL AND RESTAURANT PRICES
⇨ *Hotel and restaurant reviews have been shortened. For full information visit Fodors.com.*

Safety

For the most part, the south is safe. You won't encounter big-city crime, but you should take a few simple precautions. Don't wear flashy jewelry outside tourist areas. Keep an eye on your belongings at the beach, don't leave valuables locked in your car for all to see, and avoid out-of-the-way beach areas after dark.

Tours

CONTACTS Isla Caribe Tours. ✉ *6953 Calle Isabel Muñoz Rivera, Ponce* ☎ *939/265-5691* 🌐 *www.islacaribepr.com.* **VIP Tours.** ☎ *787/536-4683.*

Visitor Information

In Ponce the municipal tourist office is open weekdays 8–4:30, as is the small information desk in the Parque de Bombas. Smaller cities generally have a tourism office in the city hall, open weekdays 8–noon and 1–4.

CONTACTS Ponce Municipal Tourist Office. ✉ *Located in City Hall (Alcaldía), Plaza de las Delicias, Ponce* ☎ *787/284-4141* 🌐 *www.visitponce.com.*

Ponce

129 km (80 miles) southwest of San Juan.

"Ponce is Ponce and the rest is parking" is the adage used by residents of Puerto Rico's second-largest city (population 166,000) to express their pride in being *ponceños.* The rivalry with the island's capital began in the 19th century, when European immigrants from England, France, and Spain settled here. Because the city limits extend from the Caribbean to the foothills of the Cordillera Central, it's a lot hotter in climate than San Juan. Another contrast is the neoclassical architecture of the elegant homes and public buildings that surround the main square.

Many of the 19th-century buildings in Ponce Centro, the downtown area, have been renovated, and the Museo de Arte de Ponce—currently undertaking renovations as well—is considered one of the Caribbean's finest art museums. Just as

Great Itineraries

If You Have 1 Day

Many residents of San Juan think nothing of a day trip to **Ponce.** If you head south on Route 52, you'll be there in less than two hours. There's plenty to do here, including a tour of the Museo de Arte de Ponce, one of the island's top art collections. The best way to spend an hour or two is to stroll around the lovely Plaza de las Delicias. Make sure to dine in one of the area's outstanding restaurants and have ice cream at King's Cream, which features tropical flavors.

If You Have 3 Days

From San Juan, head south on Route 52 until you reach **Ponce,** the "Pearl of the South." Spend the afternoon strolling around the Plaza de las Delicias, peeking into the beautiful Catedral de Nuestra Señora de Guadalupe and the striking Parque de Bombas. On the following day, visit some of the other attractions in and around the city, perhaps the Museo de Arte de Ponce, the Castillo Serrallés, or Hacienda Buena Vista. Dedicate your final day to **Guánica,** where you'll find wonderful beaches and deserted cays; spend the night here before heading back to San Juan. If you are in the mood for hiking, check out Bosque Estatal de Guánica, a dry forest.

If You Have 5 Days

Make a leisurely trip south from San Juan on Route 52, stopping for a half or full day at Albergue Olímpico, a massive sports complex that features, among other installations, two family-friendly water parks and Puerto Rico's Olympic Museum. Spend the night in **Coamo,** a town whose hot springs were thought by some to be Ponce de León's Fountain of Youth. Soak in them, and feel the years melt away before continuing on your second day to **Ponce** for two days of exploring. Travel west along the coast and settle at a waterfront hotel in **Guánica.** In the evening, take a boat trip to the bioluminescent bay in **La Parguera.** On your last day, explore the beautifully preserved colonial city of **San Germán;** don't miss the lovely colonial-era chapel known as the Capilla de Porta Coeli.

famous is Ponce's pre-Lenten carnival. The colorful costumes and vejigante (mischief-maker) masks worn during the festivities are famous throughout the world. The best dining in Ponce is just west of town. Seafood restaurants line the highway in an area known as Las Cucharas, named for the spoon-shape bay you'll overlook as you dine.

GETTING HERE AND AROUND

The fastest route through the region is the Luis A. Ferré Expressway (Route 52), a toll road that runs from San Juan to Ponce, crossing the island's central mountain range. The trip from Condado or Old San Juan takes about two hours. Route 2, also a toll road, connects to San Germán, Mayagüez, and the western part of the island.

Car rental is typical for most visitors to Ponce and makes exploring the surrounding region considerably easier. Most hotels have parking lots, and metered parking is easy to come by in the town center.

CAR RENTAL Avis. ✉ *Aeropuerto Mercedita, Rte. 506, off Rte. 52, Ponce* ☎ *787/842–6154* 🌐 *www.avis.com.*

Sights

1 Catedral de Nuestra Señora de Guadalupe.. **B3**
2 Museo de la Historia de Ponce.... **C3**
3 Museo de la Música Puertorriqueña .. **C3**
4 Parque de Bombas..... **B3**
5 Teatro La Perla..... **C3**

Restaurants

1 Diverso...... **B3**
2 King's Cream Helados..... **B3**
3 Lola Eclectic Cuisine...... **B3**
4 Sabor y Rumba **B3**

Hotels

1 The Fox Hotel......... **B3**
2 Hotel Bélgica...... **B3**
3 Meliá Century Hotel Ponce....... **B3**
4 Ponce Plaza Hotel & Casino....... **B3**

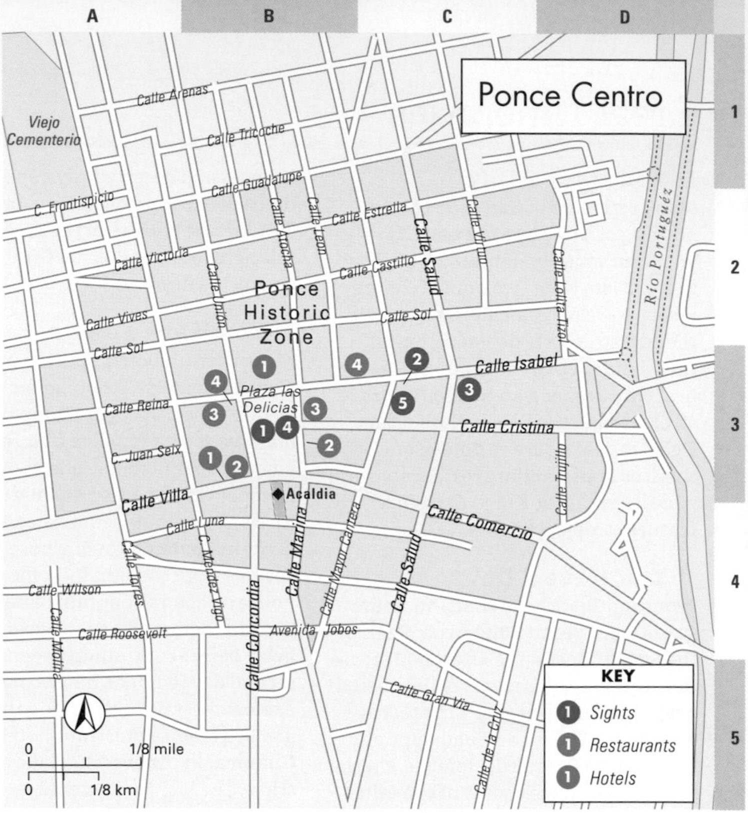

Budget. ✉ *Aeropuerto Mercedita, Rte. 506, off Rte. 52, Ponce* ☎ *787/848–0907* 🌐 *www.budget.com.* **Enterprise.** ✉ *1023 Av. La Ceiba, Ponce* ☎ *844/794–8595* 🌐 *www.enterprise.com.*

Ponce Centro

At the heart of Ponce Centro is Plaza de las Delicias, with trees, benches, and the famous lion fountain. Several interesting buildings are on this square and adjacent streets, making the area perfect for a leisurely morning or afternoon stroll. This plaza was once a popular site for music, dancing, and it still is the background for all of Ponce's amazing festivals and celebrations.

Sights

Catedral de Nuestra Señora de Guadalupe

RELIGIOUS BUILDING | This pale blue cathedral has always been one of the city's jewels, but it regained much of its luster after a complete renovation in 2007. Dedicated to the Virgin of Guadalupe, it is built on the site of a 1670 chapel destroyed by earthquakes. Part of the current structure, where Mass is still held, dates from 1835. After another earthquake in 1918, new steeples and a roof were put on and neoclassical embellishments were added to the facade. Inside, you'll see stained-glass windows and two alabaster altars. A festival to honor its patron saint, La Virgen Guadalupe, is held every year, complete with music, food, and altars. ✉ *Plaza de las Delicias, Ponce* *Free.*

Named for Juan Ponce de León y Loayza—great-grandson of the famed conquistador—Ponce has adopted the león (lion) as a symbol.

Museo de la Historia de Ponce

HISTORY MUSEUM | FAMILY | Housed in two adjoining neoclassical mansions, this museum includes 10 rooms with exhibits covering the city's residents, from the indigenous Taíno people to Spanish settlers to the mix of the present. Guided tours in English and Spanish give an overview of the city's history. Although descriptions are mostly in Spanish, displays of clothing from different eras are interesting. ✉ *53 Calle Isabel, at Calle Mayor, Ponce* ☎ *787/844–7071* 🎫 *Free* 🕒 *Closed weekends.*

Museo de la Música Puertorriqueña

OTHER MUSEUM | At this museum you'll learn how Puerto Rican music has been influenced by African, Spanish, and Native American cultures. On display are dozens of instruments, such as the *tres* (a small string instrument resembling a banjo), as well as memorabilia of local composers and musicians. The small museum takes up several rooms of a neoclassical former residence, which alone is worth the trip. ✉ *Calle Isabel at Calle Salud, Ponce* ☎ *787/848–7016* 🎫 *Free* 🕒 *Closed Mon. and Tues.*

★ **Parque de Bombas**

NOTABLE BUILDING | FAMILY | After El Morro in Old San Juan, this distinctive red-and-black-striped building may be the second-most-photographed structure in Puerto Rico. Built in 1882 as a pavilion for an agricultural and industrial fair, it was converted the following year into a firehouse. In 1990, it took on new life as a small museum tracing the history—and glorious feats—of Ponce's fire brigade. Kids love the antique fire truck on the lower level. Short tours in English and Spanish are given on the hour starting at 10; if the trolley is running, you can sign up for free tours of the historic downtown here, too. Helpful tourism officials staff a small information desk inside. ✉ *Plaza de las Delicias, Ponce* ☎ *787/284–3338* 🌐 *www.visitponce.com* 🎫 *Free.*

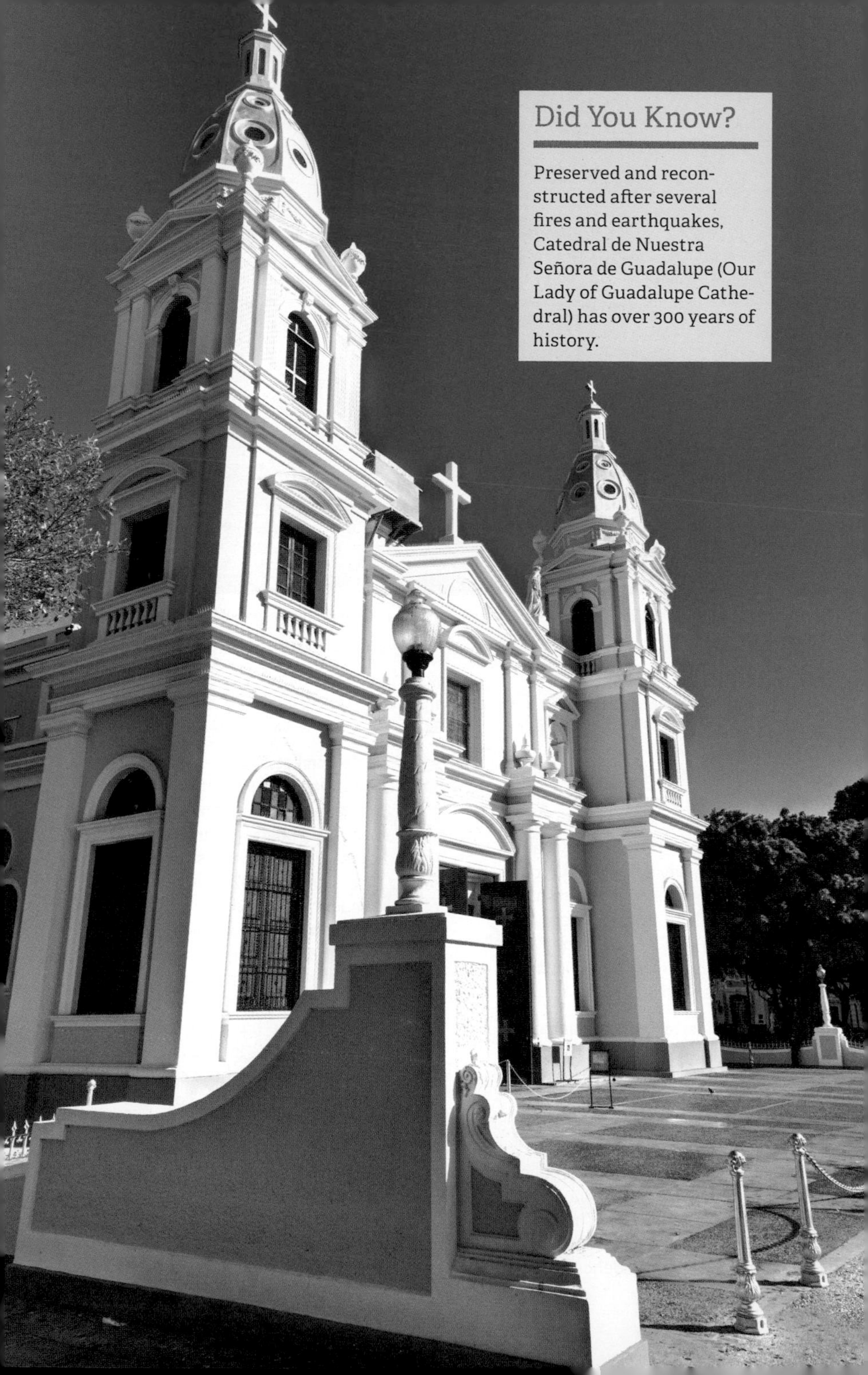

Did You Know?

Preserved and reconstructed after several fires and earthquakes, Catedral de Nuestra Señora de Guadalupe (Our Lady of Guadalupe Cathedral) has over 300 years of history.

A Good Walk: Ponce Centro

Start on the tree-lined Plaza de las Delicias (you'll find parking nearby on Calle Marina, Calle Isabel, and Calle Reina). Dominating it is the **Catedral Nuestra Señora de Guadalupe,** dating from 1835. Right behind the Cathedral you'll find the eye-catching black and red striped **Parque de Bombas,** complete with a functioning antique fire truck!

From the intersection of Calles Marina and Cristina, take Calle Cristina a block east to one of the city's first restoration projects, **Teatro La Perla,** at the corner of Calles Cristina and Mayor. One block north of the theater, at Calles Mayor and Isabel, is a former home that's now the **Museo de la Historia de Ponce.** A block east, at the corner of Calles Salud and Isabel, is the **Museo de la Música Puertorriqueña.** Four blocks west (you'll go by Plaza de las Delicias again; Calle Isabel will turn into Calle Reina) is the Casa Wiechers-Villaronga, a 1911 architectural masterpiece that's home to the **Museo de la Arquitectura Ponceña.** For more early-20th-century architecture, continue west on Calle Reina, where you'll see examples of *casas criollas*, wooden homes with spacious front balconies that were popular in the Caribbean during the early 1900s.

Companies like Isla Caribe Tours offer in-depth walking tours around the town center and other nearby sites.

Timing

Although it's possible to see Ponce Centro in a single morning or afternoon, it's best to devote a full day and evening. Explore the streets and museums during daylight, and then head to the plaza at night, when the lion fountain and streetlamps are illuminated and townspeople are out on a stroll. With police officers on nearly every corner, this area is very safe to explore.

■ TIP→ Two of the city's most popular museums—Museo de la Arquitectura Ponceña and the Museo de la Música Puertorriqueña—are not air-conditioned, so they close early when the weather is hot. If you want to see these sites, make sure to arrive before 11 am. Also note, most of the museums in Ponce are closed Monday and Tuesday.

Teatro La Perla

PERFORMANCE VENUE | This theater was restored in 1941 after an earthquake and fire damaged the original 1864 structure. The striking interior contains seats for 1,047 and has excellent acoustics. It's generally open for a quick peek on weekdays. Tickets for plays and events taking place here can be found via the TicketCenter website. ✉ *Calle Mayor at Calle Cristina, Ponce* ☎ *787/284–4141* 🎫 *Free* ⏲ *Closed weekends.*

Restaurants

Diverso

$$$ | PUERTO RICAN | This new restaurant in the heart of Ponce prides itself, as the name suggests, on having a wide and diverse food variety. The owner not only serves high-quality, unique meals, but she also makes stunning chocolate bonbons in a huge variety of flavors. **Known for:** osso buco with guanciale gnocchi; unique atmosphere; chocolate bonbons and desserts. $ *Average main: $25* ✉ *124 Calle Villa, Ponce* ☎ *939/992–9170* ⏲ *Closed Mon.–Thurs.*

Did You Know?

Built as a pavilion for an industrial fair (1882) and subsequently used as a firehouse, Ponce's distinctive, black-and-red-striped Parque de Bombas is at the ready for its close-up—from any angle, day or night.

★ King's Cream Helados

$ | CAFÉ | FAMILY | An institution since it opened in 1964, King's Cream Helados, across from Plaza de las Delicias, is *the* place for ice cream in Ponce. It serves 12 varieties—from tamarind, peanut, and passion fruit to classics like chocolate and vanilla. **Known for:** tropical fruit flavors; cash only; long hours. *$ Average main: $5 ✉ 9223 Calle Marina, Ponce ☎ 787/843–8520 ▭ No credit cards.*

Lola Eclectic Cuisine

$$$ | ECLECTIC | This trendy bistro in the heart of downtown has an eclectic menu to match the decor. Grab a seat in a green-velvet booth, and start off with their delicious tuna tartare *taquitos,* beef bruschetta, and fried plantains. **Known for:** blackened ahi tuna served with seaweed; Quenepatini (Don Q Cristal, guava juice, cranberry juice, quenepa liquor); showcase for local artists. *$ Average main: $27 ✉ Ponce Plaza Hotel & Casino, Calle Reina, at Calle Union, Ponce ☎ 787/813–5033 ⊕ www.lolacuisine.com ⏲ Closed Mon. and Tues. No lunch.*

Sabor y Rumba

$$ | PUERTO RICAN | The short menu of this alfresco dining spot allows the kitchen to focus on its specialties, which include tostones, ceviche, and skirt steak. But even more than the food, many guests love the vibe of Sabor y Rumba, whose name alludes not only to its tasty flavors, but also its fun-loving spirit. **Known for:** churrasco; mofongo; live music and dancing on weekends. *$ Average main: $16 ✉ 66 Calle Isabel, Ponce ☎ 787/843–3003 ▭ No credit cards ⏲ Closed Sun.*

Hotels

The Fox Hotel

$$ | HOTEL | FAMILY | The Fox has lived many lives in the heart of Ponce. **Pros:** lively lobby atmosphere; lots of bars, food, and snacks nearby; in the heart of Ponce. **Cons:** elevators don't work, still under renovation; very loud at night; not all rooms have windows or mirrors. *$ Rooms from: $150 ✉ Calle Isabel, Ponce ☎ 787/429–8385 ⊕ thefoxponce.com ⇨ 30 rooms 🍴 No Meals.*

Hotel Bélgica

$$ | HOTEL | Near the central square, this hotel dating from 1872 is both comfortable and economical, with rooms featuring hardwood floors, high ceilings, and wrought-iron beds. **Pros:** a taste of old Ponce; on-property restaurant; friendly staff. **Cons:** front-facing rooms are noisy; some rooms don't have windows; lots of steps and no elevator. *$ Rooms from: $185 ✉ 122 Calle Villa, Ponce ☎ 787/844–3255 ⊕ www.hotelbelgica.com ⇨ 20 rooms 🍴 No Meals.*

Meliá Century Hotel Ponce

$$ | HOTEL | In the heart of the city, this family-owned hotel has been a local landmark for more than 125 years; in fact, it claims to be the island's oldest hotel. **Pros:** great location on the main square; good dining options nearby; budget-friendly. **Cons:** under construction; front rooms can be noisy; Internet service is often spotty. *$ Rooms from: $155 ✉ 75 Calle Cristina, Ponce ☎ 787/842–0260 ⊕ www.meliacenturyhotel.com ⇨ 65 rooms 🍴 No Meals.*

Ponce Plaza Hotel & Casino

$ | HOTEL | On the main square, in a stunningly restored building that dates from 1882, this hotel has six dazzling rooms that preserve a 19th-century design, with black-and-white tiles, hand-carved furniture, and wooden balconies; rooms in the more modern wing are a bit bland by comparison. **Pros:** excellent location; lively bar and restaurant; suites have historic charm. **Cons:** regular rooms are basic; small pool gets foot traffic from attached restaurant. *$ Rooms from: $140 ✉ Calles Reina at Calle Unión, Ponce ☎ 787/813–5050 ⊕ www.ponceplazahotelandcasino.com 🍴 No Meals.*

Nightlife

BARS AND CLUBS

Velada

BARS | This jazz bar right in the center of Ponce will make you feel transported into a James Bond movie. The elegant ambiance and skilled bartenders keep this spot feeling classy but still accessible and fun. There's also full menu options, but it really comes alive at night when the rest of the town begins to liven up. ✉ *Plaza Muñoz Rivera No. 84, Ponce* ☎ *787/472–7272* 🌐 *veladajazzbar.com.*

Shopping

On holidays and during festivals, artisans sell wares from booths in Plaza de las Delicias. During Christmas, limited-time kiosks open up dedicated to selling toys for the holiday season. There are a few souvenir and gift shops in the area around the plaza, and Paseo Atocha, a pedestrian mall with shops geared to residents, runs north of it.

Mi Coquí

CRAFTS | Explore shelves filled with carnival masks, colorful hammocks, freshly ground coffee, and bottles and bottles of rum. ✉ *9227 Calle Marina, Ponce* ☎ *787/841–0216.*

Utopía

CRAFTS | Utopía sells clothes, jewelry, carnival masks, carved figurines, and other crafts. There's also a café inside the store with delicious local coffee and locally sourced baked goods you have to try. ✉ *78 Calle Isabel, Ponce* ☎ *787/848–5441.*

Greater Ponce

The greater Ponce area has some of Puerto Rico's most notable cultural attractions, including one of the island's finest art museums and its most important archaeological site. Cars are necessary to travel outside the town center, as public transportation isn't available here.

Sights

Centro Ceremonial Indígena de Tibes (*Tibes Indigenous Ceremonial Center*)

RUINS | **FAMILY** | This archaeological site, discovered after flooding from a tropical storm in 1975, is the island's most important. Dating from AD 300–700, it includes nine playing fields used for a ritual ball game that some think was similar to soccer. The fields are bordered by smooth stones, some of which are engraved with petroglyphs that might have ceremonial or astronomical significance. In the eye-catching Plaza de Estrella (Plaza of the Star), stones are arranged in a pattern resembling a rising sun, perhaps used to chart the seasons. A village with thatched huts has been reconstructed. Visit the small museum before taking a walking tour of the site. Last entry varies from day to day, so call ahead to confirm. ✉ *Rte. 503, Km 2.5, Barrio Tibes* ☎ *787/840–5685, 787/840–2255* 🌐 *www.nps.gov/nr/travel/prvi/pr15.htm* 🎟 *$3* ⏲ *Closed Mon.*

Cruceta del Vigía

VIEWPOINT | **FAMILY** | At the top of Cerro Vigía—a hill where the Spanish once watched for ships, including those of marauding pirates—is this colossal concrete cross. You can climb the stairs or take a glass elevator to the top of the 100-foot cross for a panoramic view across the city. Purchase tickets at nearby Castillo Serrallés. ✉ *17 El Vigía, across from Castillo Serrallés, El Vigía* ☎ *787/259–1770* 🌐 *www.museocastilloserralles.com* 🎟 *$10* ⏲ *Closed Mon. and Tues.*

★ **Hacienda Buena Vista**

FARM/RANCH | **FAMILY** | Built by Salvador de Vives in 1838, this was one of the area's largest coffee plantations. It's a technological marvel: water from the nearby

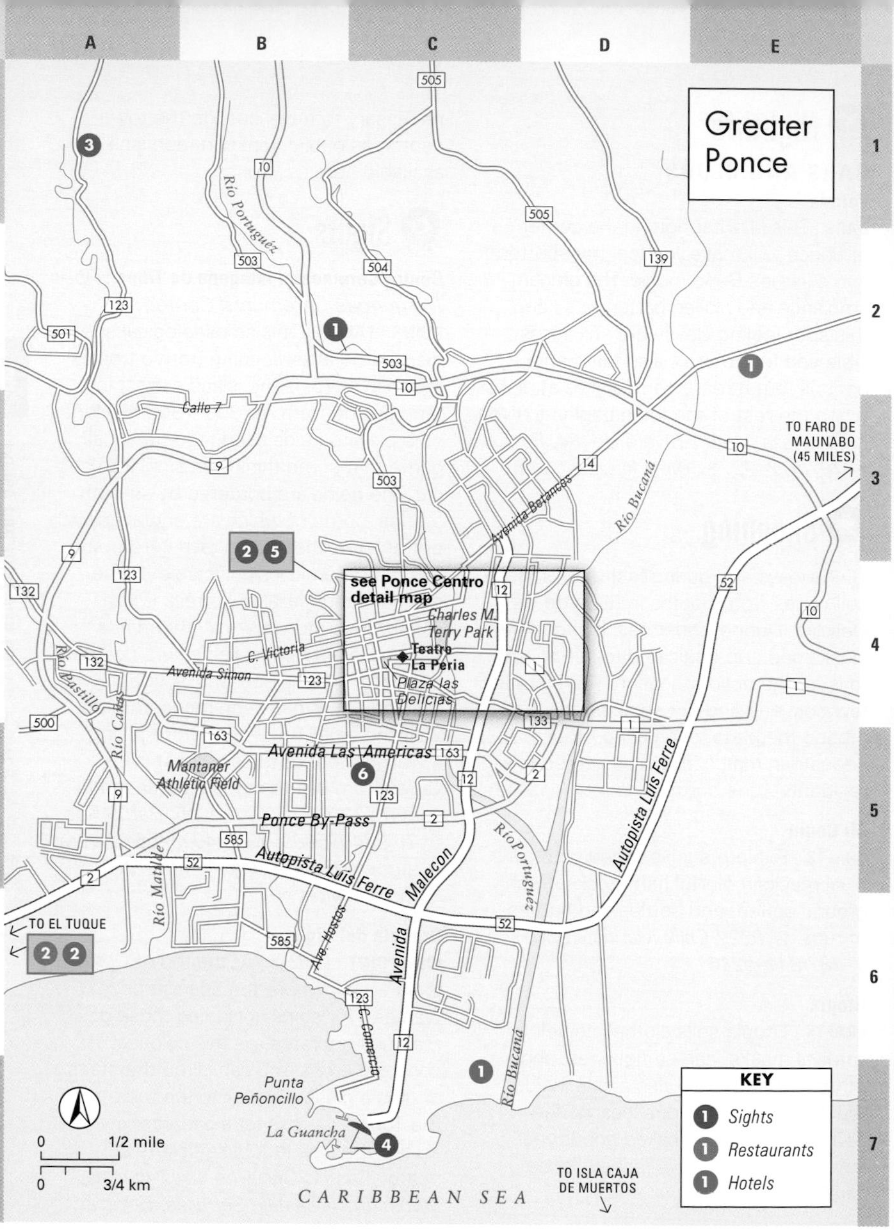

Sights

1 Centro Ceremonial Indígena de Tibes....... **B2**

2 Cruceta del Vigía........ **B4**

3 Hacienda Buena Vista **A1**

4 La Guancha de Ponce... **C7**

5 Museo Castillo Serrallés................. **B4**

6 Museo de Arte de Ponce.................. **C5**

Restaurants

1 El Negocio de Panchi ... **E2**

2 Santorini Ocean Lounge........... **A6**

Hotels

1 Hilton Ponce Golf & Casino Resort.......... **C7**

2 Holiday Inn Ponce & Tropical Casino.......... **A6**

The Spanish-style Castillo Serrallés dates from the 1930s, having been buit for the city's wealthiest family, the makers of Don Q rum.

Río Canas was funneled into narrow brick channels that could be diverted to perform any number of tasks, like turning the waterwheel. Seeing the two-story wheel slowly begin to turn is fascinating, especially for kids. Nearby is the two-story manor house, with a kitchen dominated by a massive hearth and furniture that hints at life on a coffee plantation nearly 150 years ago. In 1987, the plantation was restored by the Puerto Rican Conservation Trust, which leads several tours each day (at least one in English; by reservation only, call several days in advance or reserve online). A gift shop sells coffee beans and other souvenirs. ✉ *Rte. 123, Km 17.3, Sector Corral Viejo* ☎ *787/284–7020 weekdays* 🌐 *www.paralanaturaleza.org* 🎫 *$12.*

La Guancha de Ponce

PROMENADE | FAMILY | Encircling the cove of a working harbor, the seaside boardwalk features a small lookout tower and kiosks where vendors sell local food and drink. The adjacent park has a large children's area filled with playground equipment and, on weekends, live music. The nearby public beach has restrooms, changing areas, a medical post, and plenty of free parking. On Sunday night, this place gets packed with locals strolling the boardwalk. If you're feeling adventurous, some kiosks sell baggies of fish meant for feeding the tarpons that surround the pier; just watch out for the greedy pelicans! ✉ *End of Rte. 14, La Guancha* ☎ *787/844–3995* 🎫 *Free.*

★ Museo Castillo Serrallés

HISTORIC HOME | FAMILY | This lovely Spanish-style villa—so massive that townspeople dubbed it a castle—was built in the 1930s for Ponce's wealthiest family, the makers of Don Q rum. Guided tours provide a glimpse into the lifestyle of a sugar baron, and a permanent exhibit explains the area's sugarcane and rum industries. Highlights include the dining room, with original hand-carved furnishings, and the extensive garden, with sculptured bushes and a shimmering reflection pool. A large cross looming over the house is an observatory; from

A Good Tour: Greater Ponce

The **Museo de Arte de Ponce** is on Avenida Las Américas, south of Plaza de las Delicias and not far from the Luis A. Ferré Expressway (Route 52). Anyone with a taste for art can happily while away many hours in its galleries. East of the museum you can pick up Route 14 south to the Caribbean and **La Guancha,** a boardwalk with food kiosks, a playground, and a child-friendly public beach. It's a good place to relax and let youngsters burn off energy. From here, if you retrace your path north past downtown, you'll be heading to Calle Bertoly and El Vigía (Vigía Hill), where the **Cruceta del Vigía** towers over the city and the **Castillo Serrallés,** a former sugar baron's villa, is a popular attraction.

Farther north on Route 503 is the **Centro Ceremonial Indígena de Tibes,** which displays native artifacts dating back more than 1,500 years. You'll have to backtrack to reach Route 10, then head north to **Hacienda Buena Vista,** a former coffee plantation that's been restored by the Conservation Trust of Puerto Rico. (Call ahead to arrange a tour; reservations are required.) You'll need a car or a cab to parade around the town, since roads are long and temperatures are too high to be walkable.

the top, you can see the Caribbean. ✉ *17 El Vigía, El Vigía* ☎ *787/259–1774* 🌐 *www.museocastilloserralles.com* 🎫 *From $12* 🕒 *Closed Mon. and Tues.*

★ Museo de Arte de Ponce
ART MUSEUM | Designed by Edward Durell Stone, who also designed the original Museum of Modern Art in New York City and the Kennedy Center in Washington, D.C., Ponce's art museum is easily identified by the hexagonal galleries on its second story. It has one of the best art collections in Puerto Rico, which is why residents of San Juan frequently make the trip. The 4,500-piece collection includes works by famous Puerto Rican artists such as Francisco Oller, represented by a lovely landscape called *Hacienda Aurora.* After a series or hurricanes and earthquakes, the museum has faced a long stretch or reconstruction. Only the second and third floors are currently open, and some prized pieces have been moved to other museums during this process. In the meantime, the museum also offers special exhibits, three sculpture gardens, and a café. ✉ *Museo de Ponce, 2325 Bul. Luis A. Ferré Aguayo (Hwy. 163), Sector Santa María* ☎ *787/840–1510* 🌐 *www.museoarteponce.org* 🎫 *$6* 🕒 *Closed Sun.–Wed.*

Beaches

Isla Caja de Muertos (*Coffin Island*)
ISLAND | **FAMILY** | Named for its shape, this island, which stretches for 3 km (2 miles) and is 8 km (5 miles) off the coast, has the best beaches near Ponce and some of the best snorkeling in southern Puerto Rico. Due to hawksbill turtle nesting (May–December), the island is protected by the Reserva Natural Caja de Muertos, but you can still swim, snorkel, and dive here. A 30-minute hike across the island leads to a small lighthouse dating from 1887. Scheduled boats aren't currently available, but some of the many boatmen at La Guancha will take you out for about $40 round-trip. You must pack what you need (food and drink) and remember to take your garbage with you! **Amenities:** toilets. **Best for:** snorkeling; swimming; walking. ✉ *La Guancha, end of Rte. 14, Ponce* 🎫 *$40 round-trip.*

The stately lobby of the Museo de Arte de Ponce

La Guancha

BEACH | FAMILY | Ponce's public beach is simple but lovely, with shallow water perfect for small children. You'll find bathrooms, a playground, and a few kiosks selling fried food. There's some shade under thatched umbrellas, but bring sunscreen. **Amenities**: food and drink; parking (no fee); toilets. **Best for**: swimming. ✉ *At the end of Rte. 14, Ponce* 🎫 *Free.*

Restaurants

El Negocio de Panchi

$$ | CARIBBEAN | This Caribbean restaurant updates Puerto Rican favorites with contemporary touches, and the menu features a rotating cast of daily specials, which include octopus with saffron butter, shrimp stir-fry with coconut rice, and pork satay in peanut sauce. **Known for:** fresh seafood; osso buco; guava cheesecake. [$] *Average main: $20* ✉ *Rte. 14, in front of El Monte Town Center, Ponce* ☎ *787/848–4788* ⏲ *Closed Sun. and Mon. No lunch.*

Santorini Ocean Lounge

$$$ | GREEK | The only Greek restaurant in Ponce, this open-air establishment has successfully captured the cuisine and atmosphere of its namesake island. Statues of goddesses line the pathway leading to a bi-level dining area, decorated with 1960s-era movie posters from Greece, and nearly every dish is bathed in olive oil and vinegar, including the salads and sandwiches. **Known for:** grilled lobster; churrasco; baklava. [$] *Average main: $25* ✉ *Rte. 2, Km 218, Sector Las Cucharas* ☎ *787/651–6110* ⏲ *Closed Mon. and Tues.*

Hotels

Hilton Ponce Golf & Casino Resort

$$$ | RESORT | FAMILY | The south coast's biggest resort sits on a black-sand beach about 6 km (4 miles) south of downtown Ponce. **Pros:** good golf; large casino; game room and pool for kids. **Cons:** isolated location; must drive to off-property restaurants and attractions; fees for both valet and self-parking. [$] *Rooms from:*

$260 ✉ *1150 Av. Caribe, La Guancha* ☎ *787/259–7676* 🌐 *www.hilton.com* 🍽 *No Meals.*

Holiday Inn Ponce & Tropical Casino
$$ | **HOTEL** | **FAMILY** | This five-story hotel has a 24-hour casino, a huge pool, and a restaurant and bar where live music can be heard on weekends. **Pros:** game room for kids; large pool area; all rooms have refrigerators. **Cons:** 15 minutes by car from the beach; lots of events are hosted here, so parking and crowds can be an issue; lots of foot traffic from casino and bar. $ *Rooms from: $151* ✉ *3315 Ponce Bypass, west of downtown, Ponce* ☎ *787/844–1200* 🌐 *www.holidayinn.com/ponce* 🛏 *116 rooms* 🍽 *No Meals.*

Nightlife

CASINOS

The casinos in Ponce are smaller than their San Juan counterparts, but still a good option for late-night entertainment outside of the town center.

Hilton Ponce Casino
GATHERING PLACES | Hilton Ponce Golf & Casino Resort has small casino that's open 24 hours a day, with a couple of slot-machines and bars in the same Hilton space. ✉ *1150 Av. Caribe, La Guancha* ☎ *787/259–7676* 🌐 *www.hilton.com.*

Holiday Inn Ponce Casino
GATHERING PLACES | This small casino has 346 slot machines and 10 tables. It's open 24/7. ✉ *3315 Ponce Bypass, Ponce* ☎ *787/844–1200* 🌐 *www.holidayinn.com/ponce.*

Shopping

Centro Del Sur Mall
MALL | **FAMILY** | Centro del Sur Mall has more than 60 stores and small vendors, and a small food court with local and chain options. Some large names include Marshall's, Burlington, and Baby Depot. This mall is known for hosting costume conventions with dozens of small vendors and hundreds of visitors from around the island. ✉ *Blvd. Miguel A Pou, Ponce* ☎ *787/622–9600* 🌐 *www.centrodelsurmall.com.*

Plaza del Caribe Mall
MALL | **FAMILY** | Located just outside town, this is Ponce's largest mall and has such stores as Chicos, Clarks, Foot Locker, and American Eagle Outfitters. An ample food court has both chain and local food options. The a/c makes it a great stop during hot summer days in Ponce. ✉ *Rte. 2, Km 224.9, Ponce* ☎ *787/259–8989* 🌐 *plazadelcaribe.com.*

Activities

GOLF

Costa Caribe Golf and Country Club
GOLF | Ponce's only golf course has 27 holes, a driving range, and pro shop adjoining the Ponce Hilton. To get here, take Route 12 to Avenida Caribe. ✉ *1300 Sancho's Ave., Ponce* ☎ *787/812–2695* 🌐 *www.costacaribe-resort.com* 🎫 *From $69* ⛳ *27 holes, 3397 yards, par 36.*

Juana Díaz

21 km (13 miles) northeast of Ponce, 27 km (17 miles) southwest of Coamo.

Juana Díaz doesn't figure prominently in the typical travel itinerary, but for the traveler who has a bit of extra time, a stop in this small town is worth the effort. Juana Díaz is the epicenter of a very important cultural tradition in Puerto Rico: the celebration of the Three Kings. Technically an extension of the municipality of Ponce, Juana Díaz was nicknamed "The Versailles of Ponce" by famed Puerto Rican poet Luis Lloréns Torres. While some of the glory that earned it that name may have faded, the massive Three Kings sculpture in the town's main square and its Three Kings Museum make for an interesting side trip on a drive between Ponce and Coamo.

Sights

Three Kings Museum

OTHER MUSEUM | FAMILY | No doubt, Christmas is an important holiday in Puerto Rico, but Three Kings Day, celebrated on January 6, is perhaps even more important, observed with a special parade and other festivities across the island. Every day is Three Kings Day at this small museum in Juana Díaz, where Puerto Rico's Three Kings tradition started in 1884 and where it continues today. Visitors can learn more about the holiday and see traditional costumes, sculptures, and other displays, as well as hear about local folklore from on-site guides. ✉ *Rte. 14 (Calle Comercio), Km 13.9, Juana Díaz* ☎ *787/260–0817* 🌐 *www.reyesdejuanadiaz.com* 🎫 *$3* ⏲ *Closed Mon. and Tues.*

Coamo

27 km (17 miles) northeast of Juana Díaz, 40 km (25 miles) northeast of Ponce, 20 km (13 miles) northwest of Salinas.

Founded by the Spanish in 1579, Coamo was the third city established in Puerto Rico. It dominated the south of the island until the mid-1880s, when political power shifted to Ponce. The town, however, remained an important outpost; several decisive battles were fought here during the Spanish–American War in 1898.

The thermal springs outside Coamo are believed by some to be the Fountain of Youth for which Ponce de León was searching. In the mid-1800s, a fashionable resort was built nearby, and people have been coming to soak in the waters ever since. Coamo is also famous for the San Blás Half-Marathon, which brings competitors and spectators from around the world. The race, held in early February, covers 18 km (13 miles) of the city's hilly streets.

GETTING HERE AND AROUND

Coamo sits fairly close to the Luis A. Ferré Expressway (Route 52), the toll road that connects San Juan and Ponce. To reach Coamo, you can take the turnoff onto Route 153, although there is also access from several points in the Cordillera.

Sights

★ Hot Spring Pools

HOT SPRING | In Coamo you can take a dip at the famous Piscinas Aguas Termales, the thermal springs said to have curative powers. There's a changing room at the end of a path. Note that parking is somewhat limited here, especially on weekends, when the attraction is visited by locals from all over the island. There's a gift shop with everything you need to enjoy the pools and bring memories home. ✉ *Rte. 546, Km 1.7, Coamo* ☎ *787/825–6668, 787/003–7000* 🎫 *$3.*

Iglesia Católica San Blás

CHURCH | On Coamo's main square, the Iglesia Católica San Blás has a gorgeous neoclassical facade. Dating from 1563, the whitewashed building is one of the oldest churches on the island. ✉ *Calle Mario Braschetti, Coamo* ☎ *787/825–7006 WhatsApp, 787/379–8711.*

Museo Histórico de Coamo

HISTORIC HOME | Off the main square, the Museo Histórico de Coamo is appropriately housed in the former residence of one of the city's illustrious citizens, Clotilde Santiago, a wealthy farmer and merchant born in 1826. The museum is on the second floor of this sprawling, tangerine-color building, which dates from 1863. Several rooms are decorated with colonial-style furnishings; photographs of the town and the Santiago family line the walls. ✉ *29 Calle José I. Quintón, Coamo* ☎ *787/825–1150* 🎫 *Free* ⏲ *Closed weekends.*

Southeastern Coast
Naranjito
Caribbean National Forest
El Toro
Lomas
SIERRA DE LUQUILLO
Aguas Buenas
Gurabo
Caguas
Juncos
Pueblito del Rio
Orocovia
Comerío
Jayuya
San Lorenzo
Las Piedras
Ruta Panorámica (Panoramic Drive)
Cerro Almirante
Cidra
Barranquitas
Divisoria
Aibonito
Humacao
CORDILLERA CENTRAL
Villalba
Cerro La Santa
Cayey
Bosque Estatal Carite
Coamo
Largo Carite
CUCHILLA DE PANDURA
Coto Laurel
Juana Díaz
Hot Spring Pools
Cerro Laurel
Yabucoa
Faro De Manaubo
Cerro La Pandura
Albergue Olímpico
Largo Patillas
Maunabo
Pta. Yeguas
Potala Pastillo
Patillas
Pta. Toro
Playa Punta Tuna
Pta. Tuna
Ponce see detail map
Salinas
Coquí
Guayama
Arroyo
Inches
La Guancha
Santa Isabel
Bahía de Rincón
B. de Jobos
Puerto Arroyo
Puerto Patillas
El Bajo de Patillas
Punta Petrona
Balneario Punta Guilarte
Cayo Alfeñique
Cayos Caribes
Punta Ola Grande
Cayo Berberia
Cayos de Barcas
Isla Caja de Muertos
Caja de Muertos
CARIBBEAN SEA
0
6 mi
0
6 km

Restaurants

El Platanar

$$ | PUERTO RICAN | FAMILY | As the name of the restaurant hints, the menu's protagonist is a Puerto Rican favorite; plantains. This is your chance to try island staples such as *arañitas*, mofongo, and more. **Known for:** mofongo with red snapper; tostones; plantain flan. *Average main: $20 Rte. 153, Km. 8, Santa Isabel 787/219–6507 Closed Mon. and Tues.*

La Ceiba

$$ | PUERTO RICAN | FAMILY | The highway leading to Coamo is lined by dozens of fast-food restaurants. Luckily, there are a few worthwhile family-owned eateries, one of the best of which is this open-air cantina. **Known for:** stuffed mofongo; cheesecake in various flavors; great margaritas. *Average main: $15 Rte. 153, Km 12.8, Coamo 787/825–2299.*

Salinas

25 km (15 miles) southeast of Coamo, 42 km (26 miles) east of Ponce.

Most visitors are familiar with Salinas only because they see its name on an exit sign along Route 52. Islanders, however, know that the road from the expressway exit to Salinas leads to some of Puerto Rico's best seafood restaurants. Most of them are along the seafront in the Playa de Salinas area, reached by heading south on Route 701.

GETTING HERE AND AROUND

You can take either the Luis A. Ferré Expressway (Route 52), the toll road that connects San Juan and Ponce, or the more scenic Route 1 along the coast east from Ponce to reach Salinas.

Sights

Albergue Olímpico

SPORTS VENUE | FAMILY | Puerto Rico's Olympic training center isn't just for world-class athletes; it's a massive multiuse sports complex that's open to the public and virtually unknown to anyone other than locals. Just off the main highway on the drive from San Juan to Ponce, the Albergue has 45 different training centers—from gyms and pools to shooting ranges—where visitors can watch athletes train. There's also an Olympic Museum, food and beverage concessions, two water parks, a climbing wall for young kids, and even an 18-hole mini-golf course. Although the center is technically open year-round, the outdoor recreational facilities and public spaces tend to be open only from April to September; at other times of the year, visitors will need to make an appointment if they wish to see the museum, for example. *Rte. 712, Km 0.3, Salinas 787/824–2200 www.albergueolimpico.com $16.99 (varies by season) Some facilities closed seasonally.*

Restaurants

El Balcón del Capitán

$$$ | SEAFOOD | FAMILY | This *mesón gastronómico,* hidden among a string of oceanfront restaurants south of the center in the Playa de Salinas area, is one of the most popular on Puerto Rico's southern coast. Sit in either the open-air patio or air-conditioned dining room and bar and sample specialties like mofongo *relleno de mariscos* (seafood-stuffed plantains) or the many preparations of mahimahi, red snapper, *arrayao* (mahogany snapper), octopus, lobster, or conch. **Known for:** seafood-stuffed mofongo; red snapper; seafood paella. *Average main: $25 Rte. 701, Playa de Salinas 787/824–6210.*

El Roble

$$$ | PUERTO RICAN | FAMILY | In operation since 1961, this restaurant is still considered one of the best in town. Don't be surprised to see flapping fish delivered straight off the boats and into the kitchen, where chefs prepare dishes like grouper fillet stuffed with seafood. **Known for:** fresh seafood, including delicious red snapper; good selection of wine; children's menu. *$ Average main: $22 ✉ Rte. 701, Playa de Salinas ☎ 787/824–2377.*

Hotels

Aloft Ponce

$$ | HOTEL | FAMILY | Located half an hour west of Salina is a recently built Aloft Hotel by Marriott, complete with an on-property Hard Rock Café and free parking for both guests and visitors. **Pros:** Hard Rock Cafe on property; new construction from known brand (Marriott); modern areas great for events. **Cons:** can be expensive for the location; bands can be too loud when playing; located too far from other Ponce attractions. *$ Rooms from: $190 ✉ Carr No. 2, Av. Santiago de los Caballeros, Ponce ☎ 787/861–7080 🌐 marriott.com 152 rooms No Meals.*

Guayama

29 km (18 miles) east of Salinas; 69 km (43 miles) east of Ponce.

Guayama was founded in 1736, but the city was destroyed by fire in the early 1800s. It quickly recovered when the sugarcane industry grew, and the wealth that the surrounding plantations brought to the town is evident in the number of striking neoclassical homes on the streets surrounding the main square. Some have been beautifully restored, while others are crumbling. One of the finest 19th-century homes, Casa Cautiño, is now a museum.

The nearby countryside is home to Paso Fino horses. Each March, at the Marcelino Blondet Stadium, you can watch these high-stepping show horses strut their stuff during the Feria Dulce Sueño, a fair named after one of the island's most famous thoroughbreds. Folk music and crafts are part of the festivities.

GETTING HERE AND AROUND

From the north or west, take either Route 53 or the coastal Route 3 to reach Guayama. On Sunday, Guayama has a free trolley that runs to many sights.

CONTACTS Guayama Trolley. *✉ Alcaldía de Guayama, Calle Vicente Pales, Guayama ☎ 787/864–7765.*

Sights

Casa Cautiño

HISTORIC HOME | Built for sugar, cattle, and coffee baron Genaro Cautiño Vázquez and his wife, Genoveva Insúa, Casa Cautiño is an elegant neoclassical home dating from 1887. The painstakingly restored exterior features a balcony with ornate grillwork. You'll be swept back in time walking through the rooms, which are filled with the original Victorian-era furnishings. Don't miss the modern-for-its-time bathroom, complete with a standing shower. The museum is on the main square. *✉ 1 Calle Palmer, at Calle Vicente Palé Matos, Guayama 🌐 www.visitaguayama.com Free Closed Sun. and Mon.*

Centro de Bellas Artes

HISTORIC HOME | FAMILY | Just a few blocks from the main square, the Centro de Bellas Artes is housed in a beautifully restored neoclassical building. Paintings by local artists fill its 11 rooms. *✉ Calle McArthur at Carretera 3, Guayama ☎ 787/864–7765 Free Closed Mon.*

Iglesia San Antonio de Padua

CHURCH | One of the prettiest churches on the southern coast, Iglesia San Antonio de Padua was begun in 1827, but not completed until 40 years later. Don't set

A Guide to Puerto Rico's Carved Saints

Hand-carved wooden santos (saints) are one of Puerto Rico's oldest traditional art forms, but to find authentic examples, you have to know where to look for the artisans—and their handiwork. Authentic santos will simply not be found in most souvenir shops.

History of the Santos

The history of these figures can be traced back to the arrival of Spanish missionaries in the late 15th and early 16th centuries. The missionaries spread God's word by telling stories animated and illustrated with carved santos. According to carver Miguel Díaz, missionaries left santos behind with prospective converts since churches were few and far between. Santos placed on home altars could help keep the spirit of God alive between their visits. Although missionaries are long gone, santos still enjoy a place of honor in many Puerto Ricans' homes and are highly prized by collectors on the island and abroad.

About the Saints

They are not unique to Puerto Rico; just as Spanish missionaries brought santos here, they also carried them to many other countries as well. In Puerto Rico, the most common figures are the Three Kings, St. Barbara, St. Francis, and *La Mano Poderosa* (The Powerful Hand, in which a member of the Holy Family tops each finger of a hand bearing the stigma). Typically carved in cedar, they are brushed with a coat of gesso and then painted. Some santos are ceramic, and some artisans even use innovative recycled materials to create one-of-a-kind pieces.

Where to Find Them

Artisans can often be found working wood and selling their santos during craft fairs held along Old San Juan's **Plaza Dársena**, between the cruise piers and Paseo de la Princesa. Friday and Saturday evenings are sure bets, as are Sunday afternoons.

MUSAN (Museo de los Santos y Arte Nacional) just opened its doors in San Juan, and is open on weekends. Their specialty is artisanal crafts of saints and other local art inspirations, with personal collections of over 400 pieces added to the museum's inauguration. *1637 Av. Ponce de León, Parada 22 Santurce* ☎ *787/455–4217*

Some prominent artisans, many with work displayed in MUSAN, include:

Miguel Díaz. He specializes in wooden carvings of the Three Kings, saints, and traditional Puerto Rican artscapes. His work is available for purchase in local fairs in Carolina, or through direct contact. ☎ *787/392–8857 tallertabonuco@gmail.com.*

Prices

Prices vary depending on the size and quality of the craftsmanship. Prices for santos begin at $40 but may go up to several hundred dollars for larger or more elaborate pieces. Most of the carvers don't bargain; the first stated price is likely the lowest he or she is willing to go.

your watch by the time on the clock; the hand-painted face is frozen at the time the church was "baptized." The bells in the tower were cast in gold and bronze in 1835. Mass is still held here, but visitors can come by any time. ✉ *5 Calle Palmer, Guayama* 🎫 *Free.*

Activities

GOLF

El Legado Golf Resort

GOLF | This resort, designed by golf legend and native son Chi Chi Rodríguez, is a 7,213-yard, 18-hole course with 12 lakes. The course is closed on Mondays. ✉ *Rte. 713, off Rte. 53, Guayama* ☎ *787/866–8894* 🌐 *www.ellegadopuertorico.com* 🎫 *From $60* ⛳ *18 holes, 7213 yards, par 72.*

Patillas

18 km (11 miles) east of Guayamo, 82 km (51 miles) east of Ponce.

Patillas, often known as the Emerald of the South, is a tranquil city of about 19,000 "Patillences," with a small plaza and steep, narrow streets. The best sightseeing is along the coast east of town, where Route 3 skirts the Caribbean Sea. This stretch passes rugged cliffs and beautiful beaches, many of which have not yet been discovered by visitors.

GETTING HERE AND AROUND

Patillas is a short drive east of Guayama on Route 53, but there is also access from the east along Route 3 and from the north in Guavate along Route 184.

Beaches

★ Playa Punta Tuna

BEACH | Punta Tuna Beach is on Puerto Rico's southeast coast. Strong currents make it unsafe to swim here, but this is a beautiful place to relax with a book or take a long walk on the beach. This is also home to the Punta Tuna Reserve, a nesting site for turtles from March to July. Climbing the rock formations at one of the end beach provides a beautiful view. You can also visit the Punta Tuna Lighthouse perched above the beach. **Amenities**: parking (no fee). **Best for**: solitude; walking. ✉ *PR 7760, Maunabo* ✥ *21 km (13 miles) east of Patillas, 31 km (19 miles) south of Humacao.*

Restaurants

El Mar de la Tranquilidad

$$ | **CARIBBEAN** | **FAMILY** | Here you can get a table on the terrace at the edge of the Caribbean. You'll find good Puerto Rican cuisine and lots of seafood, including lobster, red snapper, and mofongo. **Known for:** fried seafood; Puerto Rican cuisine; long list of daiquiris. [$] *Average main: $19* ✉ *Rte. 3, Km 120.8, 9 PR-3, Patillas* ☎ *787/839–6469* ⏲ *Closed Mon.– Wed.*

Guánica

38 km (24 miles) west of Ponce.

Juan Ponce de León first explored this area in 1508, when he was searching for the elusive Fountain of Youth. Nearly 400 years later, U.S. troops landed first at Guánica during the Spanish–American War in 1898. The event is commemorated with an engraved marker on the city's *malecón*, or jetty. Sugarcane dominated the landscape through much of the 1900s, and the ruins of the old Guánica Central sugar mill, closed in 1980, loom over the town's western area, known as Ensenada. Today Guánica's biggest draws are its beaches and forests.

GETTING HERE AND AROUND

From Ponce, Route 2 connects with Guánica via Route 116 and extends to San Germán and Mayagüez. The town hugs Guánica Bay and runs almost immediately into the neighboring village of Ensenada.

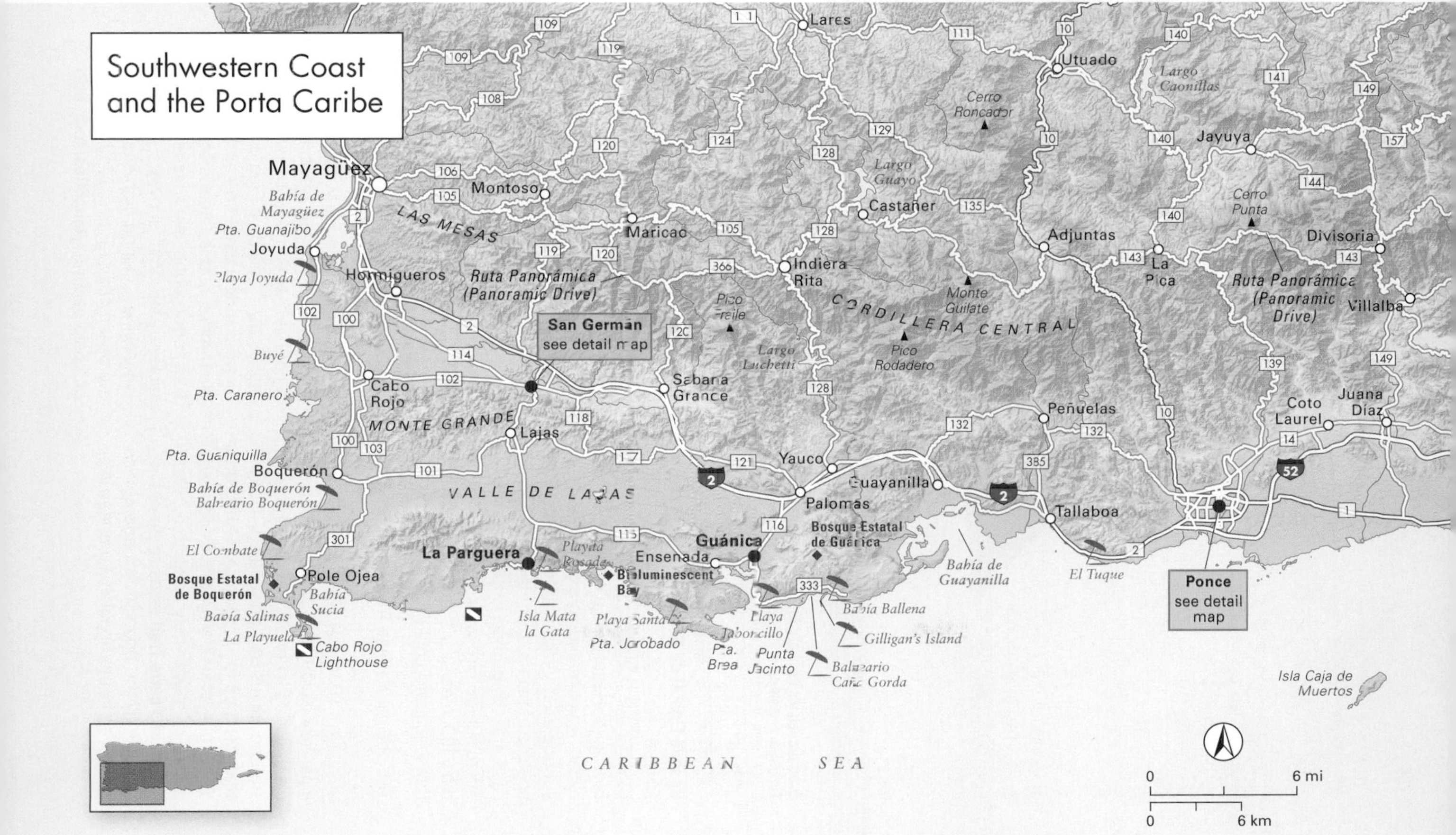
Southwestern Coast and the Porta Caribe
Mayagüez
Bahía de Mayagüez
Pta. Guanajibo
Joyuda
Playa Joyuda
Hormigueros
Buyé
Pta. Caranero
Cabo Rojo
Monte Grande
Lajas
Pta. Guaniquilla
Boquerón
Bahía de Boquerón
Balneario Boquerón
El Combate
Bosque Estatal de Boquerón
Pole Ojea
Bahía Sucia
Bahía Salinas
La Playuela
Cabo Rojo Lighthouse
Montoso
Las Mesas
Maricao
Ruta Panorámica (Panoramic Drive)
San Germán see detail map
Valle de Lajas
La Parguera
Playita Rosada
Isla Mata la Gata
Bioluminescent Bay
Playa Santa
Pta. Jorobado
Ensenada
Guánica
Sabana Grande
Pico Freile
Largo Luchetti
Indiera Rita
Lares
Utuado
Largo Guayo
Castañer
Cordillera Central
Monte Guilate
Pico Rodadero
Cerro Roncador
Yauco
Palomas
Guayanilla
Bosque Estatal de Guánica
Playa Jaboncillo
Pta. Brea
Punta Jacinto
Bahía Ballena
Gilligan's Island
Balneario Caña Gorda
Bahía de Guayanilla
Adjuntas
La Pica
Peñuelas
Tallaboa
El Tuque
Largo Caonillas
Jayuya
Cerro Punta
Divisoria
Villalba
Coto Laurel
Juana Díaz
Ponce see detail map
Isla Caja de Muertos
Caribbean Sea
0 6 mi
0 6 km

Even though it's not safe to swim here, the views of the lighthouse and rock formations make Playa Punta Tuna worth visiting.

Sights

Bosque Estatal de Guánica (*Guánica State Forest*)
FOREST | This 9,900-acre United Nations Biosphere Reserve is a great place for hiking. An outstanding example of a subtropical dry forest, it has some 700 species of plants, from the prickly-pear cactus to the gumbo limbo tree, and offers superb bird-watching; its more than 100 species include the pearly-eyed thrasher, lizard cuckoo, and nightjar.

The popular **Ballena Trail,** which begins at the ranger station on Route 334, is an easy 2-km (1¼-mile) walk that follows a partially paved road past a mahogany plantation to a dry plain covered with stunted cactus. A sign reading "Guayacán centenario" leads you to an extraordinary guayacán tree with a 6-foot-wide trunk. The moderately difficult, 5½-km (3½-mile) **Fuerte Trail** leads to an old fort built by the Spanish Armada. It was destroyed in the Spanish-American War in 1898, but you can see ruins of the old observatory tower.

In addition to using the main entrance on Route 334, you can enter on Route 333, which skirts the forest's southwestern quadrant. You may also wish to explore the less-trafficked area west of the town of Guánica, off Route 325. ✉ *Rte. 334, Guánica* ☎ *787/821–5706* *Free.*

Beaches

Balneario Caña Gorda
BEACH | **FAMILY** | The gentle waters at this beach on Route 333 wash onto a wide swath of sand fringed with palm trees. This is one of the few beaches in Puerto Rico that meets the high environmental standards of the Blue Flag program. There is a designated area roped off for swimmers, and lifeguards remain on duty most afternoons. You'll also find picnic tables, restrooms, showers, and changing facilities. During high season there are beach-chair rentals, food vendors, and paid parking. **Amenities:** food and

drink; lifeguards; parking (fee); toilets. **Best for:** snorkeling; swimming; walking. ✉ *Rte. 333, Km 5.9, west of Copamarina Beach Resort, Guánica* 🎫 *Free.*

Playa Jaboncillo

BEACH | FAMILY | Rugged cliffs make a dramatic backdrop for this little cove off Route 333, but the water can be rough. The road down to the beach is extremely steep and rocky and shouldn't be attempted without a four-wheel-drive vehicle. Locals tend to visit this spot for family cookouts and relaxation by the water's edge. **Amenities**: parking (no fee). **Best for**: solitude; sunset. ✉ *Rte. 333, west of Copamarina Beach Resort, Guánica* 🎫 *Free* ☞ *Hurricane/rainy season makes the path dangerous.*

Playa Santa

BEACH | FAMILY | You can rent canoes, kayaks, and pedal boats at this beach at the end of Route 325 in the Ensenada district. This beach is popular with local teenagers and can get congested, but the mile-long shoreline is kept clean. The light sand and clear water are great for smaller children and people who just want to relax by the ocean. **Amenities:** food and drink; parking (no fee); water sports. **Best for:** sunset; swimming; walking. ✉ *Rte. 325, west of town, Ensenada* 🎫 *Free.*

Restaurants

Restaurante Alexandra

$$$$ | CARIBBEAN | Puerto Ricans drive for miles to reach this restaurant in the Copamarina Beach Resort. The kitchen takes traditional Puerto Rican dishes and turns them into something extra special, and the elegant dining room looks out onto well-tended gardens. **Known for:** fresh seafood; great lobster; Sunday brunch. $ *Average main: $32* ✉ *Copamarina Beach Resort, Rte. 333, Km 6.5, Guánica* ☎ *787/821–0505* 🌐 *www.copamarina.com* 🕑 *Closed Mon.–Wed. No dinner Sun. No lunch.*

Hotels

★ **Copamarina Beach Resort and Spa**

$$ | RESORT | FAMILY | The most beautiful resort on the southern coast is set on 16 palm-shaded acres facing the Caribbean. **Pros:** plenty of activities; great dining options; good-size guest rooms. **Cons:** somewhat distant from other attractions; expensive 20% resort fee; beach just OK. $ *Rooms from: $220* ✉ *Copamarina Beach Resort and Spa, Rte. 333, Km 6.5, Guánica* ☎ *787/821–0505* 🌐 *www.copamarina.com.*

Parador Guanica 1929

$$ | HOTEL | FAMILY | This 1929, colonial-style building is very pretty, with lovely arches adding more character than you usually find along the southern coast, but sadly it's not on the beach. **Pros:** historic setting; pretty pool area; basketball and volleyball courts. **Cons:** no beach; slightly off the beaten path; rooms are small. $ *Rooms from: $150* ✉ *Rte. 3116, Km 2.5, Ensenada* ☎ *877/821–0099* 🌐 *www.guanica1929.com* 🍽 *All-Inclusive.*

Activities

DIVING AND SNORKELING

Dramatic walls created by the continental shelf provide great diving off the Guánica coast. Shallow gardens around Cayo de Caña Gorda (off Balneario Caña Gorda) also attract snorkelers and divers.

Dive Copamarina

SNORKELING | Dive Copamarina offers snorkeling trips and rents kayaks, paddleboards, and Hobie Cats. Snorkeling rates are $125 per person, including gear, with rate discounts for people staying at the Copamarina Hotel. Scuba diving starts at $200 per person, with boat charters going up to $1,100 per person for a maximum of six people. ✉ *Copamarina Beach Resort, Rte. 333, Km 6.5, Guánica* ☎ *787/821–0505* 🌐 *www.copamarina.com* 🎫 *From $125.*

La Parguera

13 km (8 miles) west of Guánica, 56 km (35 miles) west of Ponce.

La Parguera is best known for its bioluminescent bay. Although it is not as bright as the one in Vieques, it's still a beautiful sight on a moonless night. Both sightseeing and night swimming tours are available in the bay. During the day you can explore the nearby mangrove forest.

The town bursts at the seams with vacationers from other parts of the island on long holiday weekends and throughout the summer. The dock area is full of locals selling souvenirs, handmade jewelry, food, and drinks. Loud music comes from the always-full restaurants, competing with the sound of hundreds of visitors chattering away and enjoying the evening.

If you're driving through the area between February and April, keep your eyes open for roadside vendors selling the area's famous pineapples, called *piñas cabezonas*. In late June there's the colorful Fiesta de San Pedro, honoring the patron saint of fishermen.

GETTING HERE AND AROUND

You can reach La Parguera from Guánica via Route 116, which turns into Route 318 when it heads to San Germán. Cars are necessary to get there, but parking can be a bit tricky. Getting there early will be key to finding a spot closer to where the action is.

Sights

Bioluminescent Bay (*Phosphorescent Bay*)
BODY OF WATER | FAMILY | As soon as the sun sets, large and small boats line the dock to take visitors out to view the Bioluminescent Bay. Microscopic dinoflagellates glow when disturbed by movement, suffusing the waves with thousands of starlike points of light. The bay's glow has been diminished substantially by pollution—both light pollution from nearby communities and water pollution from toxic chemicals dumped into the bay and constant boat traffic. This bay isn't as bright as the one in Vieques, but it's the only swimmable bio bay on the island. While it's not necessary to make a reservation—plenty of operators try to rustle up customers on the docks around sunset—Paradise Scuba runs the most reputable excursions in the area. Visit their dive shop for more information. ✉ *Rte. 304, Km 3.5, La Parguera* ☎ *787/899–7611* 🌐 *www.paradisescubasnorkelingpr.com* 🎫 *$90* ✍ *Reservations in advance highly recommended.*

Bosque Estatal de Boquerón (*Boquerón State Forest*)
FOREST | FAMILY | The eastern section of the Bosque Estatal de Boquerón is made up of miles of mangrove forests that grow at the water's edge. Boats from the dock in La Parguera can take you on cruises through this important breeding ground for seabirds. You can also organize a kayak trip. ✉ *La Parguera marina, off Rte. 304, La Parguera* 🎫 *Free.*

Beaches

Isla Mata la Gata
BEACH | For about $5 per person, boats will ferry you to and from this small island just off the coast for a day of swimming and snorkeling. This island is unique for its fenced in ocean section, providing a safe area for families to swim surrounded by a pier. There are changing rooms and grilling areas. **Amenities**: showers; toilets. **Best for**: snorkeling; swimming. ✉ *La Parguera marina, off Rte. 304, La Parguera* 🎫 *Island is free, transportation from $5.*

Playita Rosada
BEACH | FAMILY | The small beach doesn't compare to some of the longer beaches on the southwestern coast, but it's a convenient place for a quick swim. There's also a square dock built like a picture

La Parguera is the perfect destination for all nature-related activities.

frame where locals gather to splash in the center of this natural swimming pool. ✉ *End of Calle 7, La Parguera* 🎫 *Free.*

Restaurants

★ El Piñatón

$ | PUERTO RICAN | FAMILY | Pina coladas may have been invented in San Juan, but nobody does them better than Lajas. This popular spot is literally shaped like a pineapple, Lajas's most important grown fruit, and serves piña coladas inside whole pineapples! **Known for:** mango frappés; virgin piña coladas for kids; piña colada inside a pineapple. 💲 *Average main: $10* ✉ *La Parguera* ☎ *787/717–0770* 🕓 *Closed Mon.*

Isla Cueva

$$ | BURGER | FAMILY | This restaurant along La Parguera's main street has the biggest variety of beer on tap in the entire area. Food is a great mix of Puerto Rican classics, along with a make-your-own burger menu that appeals to all visitors. **Known for:** St. Louis–style ribs with barbecue beer sauce; beer on tap; burgers. 💲 *Average main: $20* ✉ *Carr 304, Km 3.2, La Parguera* ☎ *787/920–4274* 🌐 *islacueva.com.*

Hotels

La Jamaca

$ | HOTEL | This boutique hotel oozes tranquility in the otherwise busy Parguera area. **Pros:** super-relaxed atmosphere; food and drinks on property; spa services offered. **Cons:** some rooms look dated; not an easy walk from the Parguera center; restaurant closes earlier that most nearby spots. 💲 *Rooms from: $125* ✉ *Carr 304 Reparto Laborde Colinas, La Parguera* ☎ *787/899–6162* 🌐 *lajamacapr.com* 🛏 *17 rooms* 🍽 *No Meals.*

Villa Parguera

$ | HOTEL | FAMILY | The rooms in this gingerbread-trimmed hotel are clustered around small courtyards filled with bright tropical flowers. **Pros:** family atmosphere; on-site entertainment options; walking distance to the marina. **Cons:** pool area gets crowded; can be crowded during formal events; noise from nearby bars. *Rooms from: $140* *Rte. 304, Km 3.3, La Parguera* *787/899–7777* *villaparguerapr.com* *74 rooms* *No Meals.*

Shopping

Outdoor stands near the docks sell all kinds of souvenirs, from T-shirts to beaded necklaces, many of them handmade. Keep an eye out for unique items like your name on a grain of rice, or jewelry with seashells right from La Parguera's waters.

Activities

BOATING

Alelí Tours

BOATING | FAMILY | One alternative to the ubiquitous party boats in La Parguera, Alelí Tours and its staff have a earned a reputation for their personal touch, knowledgeable commentary, and the good condition and safety of their watercraft. Snorkeling rates are $75 per person, and nature tours are $85 per person. *Rte. 304, Km 3.2, La Parguera* *787/390–6086* *aleliecotours.com* *From $75.*

Caribbean Chiliboats ()

BOATING | FAMILY | There's no better way to explore the ocean than on one of Caribbean Chiliboat's water bikes. They're incredibly steady, and smooth on the clear water where, if you're lucky, manatees and turtles can be spotted! Some physical condition is necessary, as the tour takes about two hours in total. Life vests are provided, as well as water bottles and a snack once you arrive at the island destinations. *La Parguera* *787/397–7453, 787/397–7452* *caribbeanchiliboats.com* *$65.*

DIVING AND SNORKELING

Endangered leatherback turtles, eels, and an occasional manatee can be seen from many of the sites that attract divers and snorkelers from all parts. There are more than 50 shore-dive sites off La Parguera, including the famous Black Wall that starts out at 60 feet and then suddenly drops 150 into a vast canyon.

Paradise Scuba

SCUBA DIVING | Paradise Scuba offers classes and trips, including night-snorkeling excursions in phosphorescent waters. Divers will enjoy the 150-foot vertical drop at the Black Wall, considered one of the most spectacular dive sites in Puerto Rico. Their most popular package is the sunset snorkel tour, which includes snacks, drinks, and a trip to the bioluminescent bay. Dives start at $100. *Rte. 304, Km 3.5, La Parguera* *787/899–7611* *www.paradisescubasnorkelingpr.com.*

FISHING

Parguera Fishing Charters

FISHING | You can spend a half or whole day fishing for blue marlin, tuna, or reef fish with Capt. Mickey Amador at Parguera Fishing Charters. Lunch is included in the price. Rates can vary based on time and amount of people, starting at $750 for four hours, $950 for six hours, and $1,150 for a full eight hours. A maximum of six people can board, with an additional cost of $35–$50. *Rte. 304, Km 3.8, La Parguera* *787/382–4698* *www.puertoricofishingcharters.com* *From $750.*

San Germán

10 km (6 miles) north of La Parguera, 56 km (35 miles) northwest of Ponce, 166 km (104 miles) southwest of San Juan.

During its early years, San Germán was a city on the move. Although the first settlement's exact founding date and location remains at issue, the town is believed to have been established in 1510 near Guánica. Plagued by mosquitoes, settlers moved north along the west coast, where they encountered French

Sights ▼

1 Antigua Casa Alcaldía C3
2 Capilla de Porta Coeli .. C3
3 Casa de Lola Rodríguez de Tió D3
4 Iglesia de San Germán de Auxerre B3
5 Museo de Arte y Casa de Estudio .. D4

Restaurants ▼

1 King's Cream C2
2 Pórticos 1606.......... C3

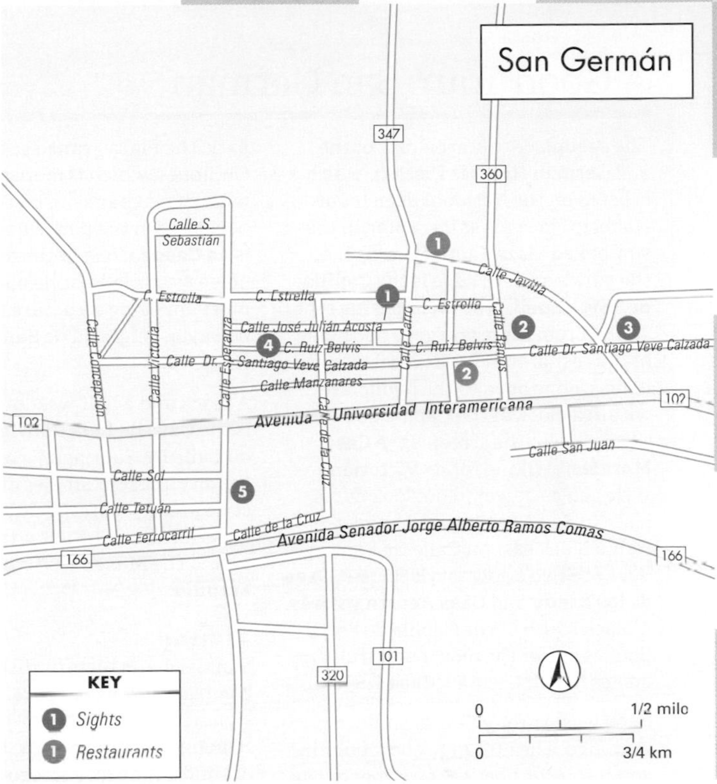

pirates and smugglers. In the 1570s, they fled inland to the current location, but they endured further harassment. Determined and creative, they dug tunnels and moved beneath the city (the tunnels are now part of the water system). Today San Germán has a population of 35,000, and its intellectual and political activity is anything but underground. This is very much a college town, and students and professors from the Inter-American University often fill the bars and cafés.

Around San Germán's two main squares—Plaza Santo Domingo and Plaza del Recreo—are buildings in every conceivable style of architecture found on the island, including mission, Victorian, criollo, and Spanish colonial. Most of the buildings are private homes; two of them—the Capilla de Porta Coeli and the Museo de Arte y Casa de Estudio—are museums. Both plazas are surrounded by locally owned stores and a huge variety of amazing restaurants.

GETTING HERE AND AROUND

San Germán sits just off Highway 2 between Ponce and Mayagüez on Route 122. A car is a must, since it's a long drive no matter which airport you arrive at. Once you're here, though, you can walk all of downtown, since most sights are within a few blocks of the main square.

Sights

Antigua Casa Alcaldía (*Old Municipal Building*)
GOVERNMENT BUILDING | At the eastern end of Plaza Francisco Mariano Quiñones, this Spanish colonial–style building served as the town's city hall from 1844

A Good Tour: San Germán

The best place to start a tour of the San Germán Historic District, which is listed on the National Register of Historic Places, is at its center, in the sun-baked Plaza Santo Domingo. At the park's eastern edge is the **Capilla de Porta Coeli,** atop an imposing set of stairs. From there you get a good view of the rest of the city. Several historic homes, none open to the public, are within a block of the Capilla de Porta Coeli. Across the street is the **Casa Morales,** striking for its Victorian-style gables. It would not look out of place in any New England hamlet. Half a block east on Calle Dr. Santiago Veve are two criollo-style houses, **Casa de los Kindy** and **Casa Acosta y Forés.** A block south of the Capilla de Porta Coeli is one of the most beautiful homes in San Germán, **Casa Perichi.**

Head west through Plaza Santo Domingo. The hulking yellow building you see at the northwest corner of the park is the rear of the **Antigua Casa Alcaldía.** It faces the town's other park, the Plaza Francisco Mariano Quiñones, which is more popular with locals thanks to tree-shaded benches. On the park's northern edge is **La Casona,** one of the town's best-preserved criollo-style buildings. The most imposing structure on the park, however, is **Iglesia de San Germán de Auxerre.**

A block and a half west of the church is the **Casa de Lola Rodríguez de Tió,** on Calle Dr. Santiago Veve. It's one of the city's best examples of criollo-style architecture. Backtrack to Calle Esperanza, and head two blocks south to find the **Museo de Arte y Casa de Estudio.**

Timing

San Germán's historic district is compact, so you can cover all the sights in about an hour. You'll want to budget a bit more time to stroll around the nearby streets. Be sure to wear comfortable shoes, as there will be a lot of walking uphill and down on cobbled streets.

to 1950. Once used as a prison, it is now houses the town's tourism office. ✉ *East end of Plaza Francisco Mariano Quiñones, San Germán.*

Capilla de Porta Coeli (*Heaven's Gate Chapel*)
CHURCH | One of the oldest religious buildings in the Americas, this mission-style chapel overlooks the long, rectangular Plazuela de Santo Domingo. It's not a grand building, but its position at the top of a stone stairway gives it a noble air. Queen Isabel Segunda decreed that the Dominicans should build a church and monastery in San Germán, so a rudimentary building was erected in 1609, replaced in 1692 by the structure seen today. (Sadly, most of the monastery was demolished in 1866, leaving only a vestige of its facade.) The chapel functions as a museum of religious art, displaying painted wooden statuary by Latin American and Spanish artists. ✉ *East end of Plazuela Santo Domingo, San Germán* *$5* *Closed Mon. and Tues.*

Casa de Lola Rodríguez de Tió
HISTORIC HOME | This criollo-style house bears the name of poet and activist Lola Rodríguez de Tió. Although a plaque claims she lived here, town officials believe it actually belonged to her sister. Rodríguez, whose mother was a descendant of Ponce de León, was deported several times by Spanish

authorities for her revolutionary ideas. She lived in Venezuela and then in Cuba, where she died in 1924. The museum, which houses Rodríguez's desk and papers, doesn't maintain regular hours; call ahead to schedule a tour with the local Interamerican University. ✉ *13 Calle Dr. Santiago Veve, San Germán* ☎ *787/892–5634* *Free.*

Iglesia de San Germán de Auxerre
CHURCH | Dating from 1739, this neoclassical church has seen many additions over the years. The impressive crystal chandelier, for example, was imported from Barcelona and added in 1866. Be sure to take a look at the carved-wood ceiling in the nave. This church is still in use, so the only time you can get a look inside is during services or through local tour guides. ✉ *West side of Plaza Francisco Mariano Quiñones, San Germán* ☎ *787/892–1027* *Free.*

Museo de Arte y Casa de Estudio
ART MUSEUM | **FAMILY** | This early-20th-century home—built in a criollo style with some obvious neoclassical influences—has been turned into a museum. Displays include colonial furnishings, religious art, and artifacts of indigenous peoples; there are also rotating exhibits by local artists. ✉ *7 Calle Esperanza, San Germán* *Free* *Closed Mon.–Wed.*

Restaurants

King's Cream
$ | **ICE CREAM** | **FAMILY** | This ice-cream shop is a town staple, run by the same family for generations in San Germán. Their unique ice cream textures come in cones, cups, and milkshakes; flavor varieties include classics like chocolate and vanilla, and tropical flavors like coconut and pineapple. **Known for:** ice cream milkshakes; coconut ice cream; corn ice cream with cinnamon. *Average main: $6* ✉ *47 C. Luz Celenia Tirado, San Germán* ☎ *787/892–7767* *Closed Sun.*

Pórticos 1606
$$$ | **CARIBBEAN** | **FAMILY** | This bright-blue historic building houses one of San Germán's best-kept culinary secrets. Pórticos 1606 has a great mix of classic Puerto Rican food and specialty dishes from other Caribbean countries. **Known for:** wah gwaan (beef meatballs in a Jamaican stew); El Porta Coeli (layered dish with root vegetables and plantain mash, seasoned pork, cheese, and garlic); Plaza Santo Domingo (Puerto Rico, República Dominicana, Cuba, and Jamaica all in one plate). *Average main: $30* ✉ *Calle Dr. Santiago Veve Esquina, C. Alonso X, San Germán* ☎ *787/978–3556.*

Index

Photo Credits

Front Cover: Michele Falzone / Alamy Stock Photo [**Description:** Caribbean, Puerto Rico, San Juan, Old Town, Paseo Del Morro and La Muralla]. **Back cover, from left to right:** Maridav/Shutterstock. Dennisvdw/iStockphoto. Dennis Van de Water/Shutterstock. **Spine:** Sepavo/Dreamstime. **Interior, from left to right:** Spirit/Shutterstock (1). IsaacRuiz/iStockphoto (2-3). Fldlcc/Shutterstock (5). **Chapter 1: Experience Puerto Rico:** Sean Pavone/Shutterstock (6-7). Chad Zuber/Shutterstock (8-9). Eric Rivera/Dreamstime (9). Sorin Colac/Dreamstime (9). Marina Movschowitz/Alamy (10). In collaboration with Discover Puerto Rico (10). Stevengaertner/Dreamstime (10). Chad Zuber/Dreamstime (10). In collaboration with Discover Puerto Rico (11). Sorin Colac/Dreamstime (11). Ioana Catalina E/Shutterstock (12). Hacienda Santa Ana, Bayamón, Puerto Rico. (12) Littleny/Dreamstime (12). Arena Creative/Shutterstock (12). Dennis van de Water/Shutterstock (13). Peter Kim/Shutterstock (14). Frank FF47 (CC BY-NC 2.0) / Flickr (14). Edgar Torres, (CC BY 3.0) / Wikimedia Commons (14). In collaboration with Discover Puerto Rico (14). Terri Butler Photography/Shutterstock (15). Oliver Gerhard/ Alamy (15). Gowithstock/Shutterstock (18). Focal point/Shutterstock (18). in collaboration with Discover Puerto Rico (18). Peredniankina/Shutterstock (18). Etorres/Shutterstock (19). in collaboration with Discover Puerto Rico (19). Arturoosorno/Dreamstime (19). Nehophoto/ Shutterstock (19). In collaboration with Discover Puerto Rico (20). Planetpix/Alamy (20). John DiRoma/Shutterstock (20). AVN Photo Lab/Shutterstock (20). Roberto Galan/Dreamstime (21). in collaboration with Discover Puerto Rico (21). Courtesy of Don Collins (21). Rog01/Wikimedia Commons (21). Dennis van de Water/Shutterstock (22). GP Images/Alamy (22). By Discovor Marco (22). Spirit/Shutterstock (23). Andre Nunez (23). **Chapter 3: San Juan:** Sea Pavone (51). Npgal77/Dreamstime (60-61). Demerzel21/Dreamstime (69). Sepavo/Dreamstime (70). Fldlcc/Shutterstock (73). Lawrence Roberg/ Shutterstock (73). Efrain Padro / Alamy Stock Photo (73). Oquendo/Flickr (74). TexPhoto/iStockphoto (74). Runneralan2004/Flickr (75). Gastonebaldo/ Dreamstime (75). Prknlot/Flickr (75). Runneralan2004/Flickr (75). Napa735/Dreamstime (76). Heaslet/Dreamstime (81). Eddtoro35/ Dreamstime (88-89). Dennisvdwater/Dreamstime (91). Hank Anderson/Flickr (99). Martinmark/Dreamstime (104). Spphotos/Dreamstime (109). Craig Lovell / Eagle Visions Photography / Alamy (110). Agefotostock/Alamy Stock Photo (111). Viviane Teles (111). Yannp/Dreamstime (111). Barselonadreams72/Dreamstime (111). Urbazon/iStockPhoto (112). Courtesy of Giovan Cordero Photographer (117). **Chapter 4: El Yunque and the Northeast:** Dennis van de Water/Shutterstock (119). Caroon Albanese/iStockphoto (122). WMarissen/iStockphoto (123). Lynghyvej/Dreamstime (123). Dennis Van De Water/Dreamstime (124). Jmjm/Dreamstime (125). SuperStock/Alamy (132). Discover Puerto Rico (136). Wirepec/Dreamstime (139). Dennisvdwater/Dreamstime (140-141). Vankok/Dreamstime (142). Lanaturegraphics/ Dreamstime (145). SVongpra/Shutterstock (146). Discover Puerto Rico (152-153). **Chapter 5: Vieques and Culebra:** Khecker/Dreamstime (155). Discover Puerto Rico (166-167). Flyingdolphin/Dreamstime (169). Discover Puerto Rico (173). Discover Puerto Rico (174). John MacIlwinen/Alamy Stock Photo (175). Division_CSIRO_.wikimedia commons (176). Claudia Salgado/Shutterstock (182-183). Iinapat B/Shutterstock (185). **Chapter 6: The North Coast and the Cordillera Central:** Javier Cruz Acosta/Shutterstock (187). Dorado Beach, a Ritz-Carlton Reserve (194). Vankok/Dreamstime (196). Jbermudez/English Wikipedia (199). Jason P Ross/Dreamstime (201). Gastonebaldo/Dreamstime (202). **Chapter 7: Rincón and the Porta del Sol:** Marlise Kast (205). Wirepec/Dreamstime (213). Wirepec/Dreamstime (214). Littleny/Dreamstime (217). Caribphoto/Dreamstime (218 219). Discover Marco/Shutterstock (224). LibniPhotos/Shutterstock (227). Samortiz/Dreamstime (230). Israel Pabon/Shutterstock (237). Mia2you/Shutterstock (238-239). **Chapter 8: Ponce and the Porta Caribe:** Jozoam/Dreamstime (241). Luis Fernandez/Dreamstime (244). Luis Fernandez/Dreamstime (245) Nicholas Gill/Vejigante masks (245). Stockphotofan1/Shutterstock (251). Felix Lipov/Shutterstock (252) SkylinePicture/Shutterstock (254-255). Albertoloyo/Dreamstime (259). Greg Vaughn/Alamy (261). Dennisvdw/ iStockphoto (270). Kristina_M/shutterstock (273). **About Our Writers:** All photos are courtesy of the writers.

*Every effort has been made to trace the copyright holders, and we apologize in advance for any accidental errors. We would be happy to apply the corrections in the following edition of this publication.

Notes

Notes

Notes

Fodor's PUERTO RICO

Publisher: Stephen Horowitz, *General Manager*

Editorial: Douglas Stallings, *Editorial Director*; Jill Fergus, Amanda Sadlowski, *Senior Editors*; Brian Eschrich, Alexis Kelly, *Editors;* Angelique Kennedy-Chavannes, *Assistant Editor;* Yoojin Shin, *Associate Editor*

Design: Tina Malaney, *Director of Design and Production*; Jessica Gonzalez, *Senior Designer*

Production: Jennifer DePrima, *Editorial Production Manager*; Elyse Rozelle, *Senior Production Editor;* Monica White, *Production Editor*

Maps: Rebecca Baer, *Senior Map Editor*; Henry Colomb and Mark Stroud (Moon Street Cartography), David Lindroth, *Cartographers*

Photography: Viviane Teles, *Senior Photo Editor;* Namrata Aggarwal, Neha Gupta, Payal Gupta, Ashok Kumar, *Photo Editors;* Eddie Aldrete, *Photo Production Intern;* Kadeem McPherson, *Photo Production Associate Intern*

Business and Operations: Chuck Hoover, *Chief Marketing Officer;* Robert Ames, *Group General Manager*

Public Relations and Marketing: Joe Ewaskiw, *Senior Director of Communications and Public Relations*

Fodors.com: Jeremy Tarr, *Editorial Director;* Rachael Levitt, *Managing Editor*

Technology: Jon Atkinson, *Director of Technology;* Rudresh Teotia, *Associate Director of Technology;* Alison Lieu, *Project Manager*

Writers: Paulina Salach Antonetti, Jennifer Ruiz, Adriana Mercado

Editor: Angelique Kennedy-Chavannes

Production Editor: Jennifer DePrima

11th Edition

ISBN 978-1-64097-612-2

ISSN 1531-0396

PRINTED IN CHINA

10 9 8 7 6 5 4 3 2 1

About Our Writers

Paulina Salach Antonetti is the co-founder and managing director of Spoon® a sustainable travel company focused on culinary and cultural experiences in Puerto Rico. Since the company's creation in 2012, Paulina has overseen all business operations and helped grow Spoon into the premier tourism company in Puerto Rico. She is also a culinary consultant, event producer, real estate investor, and freelance travel writer. She is currently working on expanding her businesses abroad.

Jennifer Ruiz is a lawyer turned full-time travel blogger and writer. She is a bestselling author, TEDx speaker, and award-winning travel journalist. She is the solo female traveler behind Jen on a Jet Plane.

Adriana Mercado is a freelance writer based in Puerto Rico. Her career spans NASA proposal, tourism blogs, and everything in-between. When she's not typing away on the latest piece, you can find her outside enjoying the Caribbean paradise she calls home. Follow her on Instagram @nanamacnana.